MASTER AND SERVANT LAW

For Sarah, Naomi and Martin

Master and Servant Law
Chartists, Trade Unions, Radical Lawyers and the Magistracy in England, 1840–1865

CHRISTOPHER FRANK
University of Manitoba, Canada

ASHGATE

Published by
Ashgate Publishing Limited
Wey Court East
Union Road
Farnham
Surrey, GU9 7PT
England

Ashgate Publishing Company
Suite 420
101 Cherry Street
Burlington
VT 05401-4405
USA

www.ashgate.com

British Library Cataloguing in Publication Data
Frank, Christopher.
    Master and servant law: Chartists, trade unions, radical lawyers and the magistracy in England, 1840–1865.
    1. Master and servant – England – History – 19th century. 2. Master and servant – Wales – History – 19th century. 3. Labor unions – England – Political activity – History – 19th century. 4. Labor unions – Wales – Political activity – History – 19th century.
    I. Title
    322.2'0942'09034–dc22

Library of Congress Cataloging-in-Publication Data
Frank, Christopher, 1971–
    Master and servant law: Chartists, trade unions, radical lawyers and the magistracy in England, 1840–1865 / Christopher Frank.
    p. cm.
    Includes bibliographical references and index.
    ISBN 978-0-7546-6830-5 (hardcover: alk. paper) 1. Master and servant – England – History. 2. Employee discipline – England – History. 3. Artisans – Legal status, laws, etc. – England – History. 4. Labor movement – England – History. I. Title.
    KD3146.F73 2010
    346.4202'4–dc22
    2009025134

ISBN 9780754668305 (hbk)
ISBN 9780754694809 (ebk)

Mixed Sources
Product group from well-managed forests and other controlled sources
www.fsc.org Cert no. SA-COC-1565
© 1996 Forest Stewardship Council
FSC

Printed and bound in Great Britain by
MPG Books Group, UK

Contents

Abbreviations

Archive Abbreviations

NA   National Archives of the United Kingdom

Reference Guides

ODNB   Oxford Dictionary of National Biography Online Edition

Newspapers and Periodicals

BJ	*The Birmingham Journal*
DA	*Durham Advertiser*
DC	*The Durham Chronicle*
GMBG	*The Glamorgan, Monmouth and Brecon Gazette Cardiff Advertiser and Merthyr Guardian*
JP	*The Justice of the Peace*
LO	*The Legal Observer*
MA	*The Miners' Advocate*
MC	*The Morning Chronicle*
MCLGA	*Manchester Courier and Lancashire General Advertiser*
ME	*The Manchester Examiner*
MG	*The Manchester Guardian*
MM	*Monmouthshire Merlin*
MSA	*The Manchester and Salford Advertiser and Chronicle*
MT	*The Manchester Times*
NC	*The Nonconformist*
NS	*The Northern Star*
PFP	*Pontypool Free Press*
PEWA	*The Potters' Examiner and Workman's Advocate*
SA	*The Staffordshire Advertiser*
SRI	*The Sheffield and Rotherham Independent*
ST	*The Sheffield Times*
WA	*The Walsall Advertiser*

Law Journals

A. & E.	*Adolphus and Ellis Reports*
B. & C.	*Barnenall and Cresswell Reports*
B. & S.	*Best and Smith's Reports*
C. B.	*Common Bench Reports*
C. B. N. S.	*Common Bench Reports, New Series*
D.	*Dunning's Reports*
E. & B.	*Ellis and Blackburn's Reports*
E. & E.	*Ellis and Ellis's Reports*
E. R.	*The English Reports*
Ex.	*The Exchequer Reports*
F. & F.	*Foster and Finlason's Reports*
H. & C.	*Hurlstone and Coltman's Reports*
H. & N.	*Hurlstone and Norman's Reports*
J. P.	*The Justice of the Peace Reports*
L. J.	*The Law Journals Magistrates' Cases*
L. J. C. P.	*The Law Journals Common Pleas Cases*
L. J. Exch.	*The Law Journals Exchequer Cases*
L. J. Q. B.	*The Law Journals Queen's Bench Cases*
L. R. C. P.	*Law Reports Common Pleas*
L. T.	*The Law Times Reports*
M. & W.	*Meeson and Welsby Reports*
Q. B.	*The Queen's Bench Reports*
W. R.	*The Weekly Law Reports*

Acknowledgments

At the completion of this book I find myself greatly indebted to many friends for their comments and assistance. This monograph was inspired by Douglas Hay and Paul Craven's 'Master and Servant Project' at York University. Years ago I traveled a considerable distance to study under Douglas Hay, a decision that ranks among the best I have ever made. His guidance, insights, suggestions and mentorship at every stage of this project improved the quality of the final product. James Muir and I entered the graduate program at York together, and our mutual interest in the social history of the law grew into one of my most valued friendships. James read every draft of this book, providing constructive criticism and useful ideas. I have also benefited from the expertise and input of Paul Craven, Nicholas Rogers, Craig Heron, Judy Fudge, Jeanette Neeson, Susan Houston, John Saywell, Bettina Bradbury, Stephen Brooke, Jim Phillips, Doug Harris, Karen Pearlman, Balfour Halevy, James Moran, Lisa Chilton, Dmitry Anastakis, Camille Soucie, Stephen Henderson, Steve Penfold, Magda Fahrni, Sheila McManus, Matthew Evenden, Robin Ganev, Jeet Heer and Gum Fa Ng.

My colleagues in the history department at the University of Manitoba have lived with this project for many years, reading drafts and providing feedback on presentations from the manuscript. I have enjoyed my collaboration with Greg Smith, a 'partner in crime' in the department, and I am grateful for his comments and efforts in the Law and Society Research Cluster. David Churchill, Jila Ghomeshi, Arlene Young and Natalie Johnson provided encouragement, support and an excellent intellectual environment in the Institute for the Humanities at the University of Manitoba. I am privileged to have the friendship of an exciting community of scholars in Winnipeg that includes Mary Kinnear, Mark Gabbert, Peter Bailey, Adele Perry, Barry Ferguson, Tina Chen, James Hanley, Rossin Cossar, Len Kuffert, Essylt Jones, Michael Kinnear, Julie Guard, Deborah Parkes and Jarvis Brownlie. Bruce Smith, Jamie Bronstein, Richard Soderlund, Richard Price, Marc Steinberg, Tom Green and Robert Steinfeld also provided helpful advice.

Some material in Chapters 1 and 2 was used in a previously published chapter, 'Defeat of the 1844 Master and Servants' Bill' in Hay and Craven (eds), *Masters, Servants and Magistrates in Britain and Empire, 1562–1955* (University of North Carolina Press, 2004), pp. 402–21. Some material in Chapter 4 was used in '"He might almost as well be without trial": Trade Unions and the 1823 Master and Servants Act – the Warrington Cases', *Historical Studies in Industrial Relations* 14 (Autumn 2002): 3–44. Some of the material in Chapter 7 appeared in '"Let but one of them come before me and I'll commit him": Trade Unions, Magistrates and the Law in Nineteenth Century Staffordshire', *Journal of British Studies* 44/1

(January 2005): 64–91. My thanks to the publishers of these works for granting permission to use this material. I would also like to thank Emily Yates, Anne Keirby, Lianne Sherlock and Gail Welsh at Ashgate for all of their assistance.

My deepest debts are those that are closest to the heart. I am grateful for the love and support of Marty and Janet Frank, Wayne and Naomi Elvins, and Julie and Nathan Elliott. I would like to thank my wife, Sarah Elvins, who was involved with this project since the beginning and steered me through the process of publishing a book. Having Sarah and our children, Naomi and Martin, in my life has made the completion of this project a wonderfully happy journey.

Introduction
'Constitutional Law versus Justices' Justice'

A Master and Servant Prosecution in Staffordshire

Late in the evening of 7 January 1845 constables in Longton, Staffordshire, set out to arrest John Williams, John Harding, John Sillitoe and John Pointon. The armed constables shocked the unsuspecting men by bursting into their homes and dragging them off into the night as their frightened families watched. The detainees were led in shackles to a dark, damp and cold lockup. Here they uncomfortably waited overnight for a hearing before two magistrates scheduled for the next morning. As bad as their situation was, the four had reason to fear that soon it would be considerably worse. One of the adjudicating magistrates was infamous throughout northern Staffordshire for his hostility toward anyone accused of the offence that had brought these men to the lockup. They were not wanted for murder, manslaughter or assault. These prisoners were not thieves, counterfeiters or receivers of stolen property. They were colliers accused of the crime of quitting work (to go on strike) without giving the fortnight notice their master insisted was required for leaving their employment.[1]

The next morning the four tired and nervous colliers were brought before magistrates Thomas Bailey Rose and Charles Harvey, the latter of whom was suffering from a severe attack of gout. Harvey's pain and Rose's renowned hostility toward Chartists and trade unionists did not bode well for the defendants. The men were charged under one of the Master and Servant Acts, but it is not clear which one because the magistrates did not think it necessary to specify to the defendants, or in the court documents, the precise statute under which they were acting.[2] The magistrates could have chosen from several Master and Servant Acts, all part of

---

[1]   The employer was butty collier Joseph Mitcheson of Millfield Gate Pit. National Archives (hereafter, NA): KB/ 1/131/42; 'Constitutional Law versus Justices' Justice', *The Northern Star* (hereafter, *NS*), 8 February 1845, pp. 4, 8. For a brief description of the lockup where prisoners awaited their hearings before magistrate Thomas Bailey Rose, see Charles Shaw, *When I Was a Child* (London, 1903), p. 41. For T. B. Rose's behavior toward those charged with master and servant offences, and his reputation with local workers, see Robert Fyson, 'The Crisis of 1842: Chartism, the Colliers' Strike, and the Outbreak in the Potteries', in Dorothy Thompson and James Epstein (eds), *The Chartist Experience: Studies in Working Class Radicalism and Culture, 1830–1860* (London, 1982), and Chapter 7, this volume.

[2]   The warrants of commitment in this case do not state the statute under which the prisoners were convicted and their incarceration was justified. NA: KB 1/131/42.

a very large and growing family tree of legislation that dated back centuries and had extended in a variety of forms to nearly all jurisdictions in the British Empire. Master and servant statutes granted magistrates the power to enforce summarily employment agreements in particular trades with penal sanctions. These acts were characterized by a double standard of penalties, which treated breach of contract by workers as a criminal offense, but offered only civil remedies when employers violated agreements.[3] For example, the 1823 Master and Servant Act (4 George IV, c.34) allowed magistrates to punish workers' breach of contract with imprisonment for up to three months at hard labor, abatement of part of their wages, or termination of their contract and the loss of all wages. Employees in many different trades could be charged under the 1823 Act with leaving work without proper notice or before the agreement had expired, refusing to begin contracted work, being absent without permission, performing work negligently or poorly, or committing some broadly-defined form of misbehavior. In cases where employers failed to fulfill their contractual obligations to workers by not paying wages owed, magistrates were permitted to award unpaid wages below £10 each or release them from their contracts (many other master and servant statutes set the limit below £5). The emphasis on the subordination of workers was underscored by the way in which employers and employees answered charges under these acts. A master accused of breach of contract was always summoned to appear before the magistrate, while workers in the same position were usually apprehended by constables under an arrest warrant and treated as criminals.[4] The midnight arrest of the Longton prisoners was not an anomaly, but rather an increasingly common practice in master and servant proceedings.[5] The provisions of the master and servant statutes were characterized by inequality, and the four Longton colliers were about to discover that their administration was as well.

The magistrates denied the colliers' request for an adjournment so that their union could find an attorney to defend them, as they believed was their right under Section 2 of the 1836 Prisoners' Counsel Act.[6] Although the miners expressed

---

³   Douglas Hay and Paul Craven, 'Introduction', in Hay and Craven (eds), *Masters, Servants, and Magistrates in Britain and the Empire, 1562–1955* (Chapel Hill, 2004), pp. 1–2.

⁴   Douglas Hay, 'Master and Servant in England: Using the Law in the Eighteenth and Nineteenth Centuries', in Willibald Steinmetz (ed.), *Private Law and Social Inequality in the Industrial Age: Comparing the Legal Cultures of Britain, France, Germany, and the United States* (London, 2000), pp. 227–9, 238; Hay, 'England 1562–1875: The Law and its Uses', in Hay and Craven, *Masters, Servants, and Magistrates*; Robert Steinfeld, *Coercion, Contract, and Free Labor in the Nineteenth Century* (Cambridge, 2001), pp. 47–51.

⁵   Raymond Challinor, *Radical Lawyer in Victorian England: W. P. Roberts and the Struggle for Workers' Rights* (London, 1990), pp. 142–3.

⁶   6 & 7 William IV, c.114, s.2 (1836), which states 'In all cases of summary conviction persons accused shall be admitted to make their full answer and defence, and to have all witnesses cross examined by an attorney'. While the defendants enjoyed the right to have

a desire to be tried separately, insisting that their cases were different from one another, the magistrates determined that it was more convenient to try them together in a single hearing. They then heard witnesses against the defendants testify that the men were employees of the prosecutor and had left work without giving the customary two weeks' notice for quitting. In master and servant cases, the 'custom of the trade' or 'custom of the country' was often considered to be an implicit part of the contract of employment. Usually the magistrate determined what was, and was not, recognized custom. Some employers stipulated in written contracts that they were to have the sole right of interpreting custom.[7] The testimony of these witnesses was not given under oath, as required by at least one master and servant statute, 4 George IV, c.34, s.1–2 (1823). It does not appear that these witnesses were cross-examined by the defendants, or that much of a defense, if any at all, was presented. It took only a few minutes for Rose and Harvey to hear the evidence, convict and sentence the four unfortunate colliers to two months' imprisonment. The magistrates, unsatisfied with this sentence, later amended the warrant of commitment to add 'with hard labour' to the prison term. A correspondent for the *Northern Star*, the prominent Chartist journal, called the hearing a 'mock trial'.[8] Before lunchtime, the colliers were on their way to Stafford Gaol.

If the case had ended here, it would not be remarkable to either legal or labor historians. No one familiar with the history of magistrates' summary jurisdiction would be surprised by the speed of the hearing or the relaxed approach toward paperwork and procedure.[9] Magistrates' summary rulings were unlikely to be

---

an attorney present their case, they were not necessarily entitled to an adjournment in the proceedings that would enable them time to find an attorney. Allyson May, *The Bar and the Old Bailey, 1750–1850* (Chapel Hill, 2003); David Cairns, *Advocacy and the Making of the Adversarial Trial, 1800–1865* (Oxford, 1998); John Beattie, 'The Scales of Justice: Defense Counsel and the English Criminal Trial in the Eighteenth and Nineteenth Centuries', *Law and History Review* 9/2 (1991): 221–67; John Langbein, 'The Prosecutorial Origins of Defense Counsel in the Eighteenth Century: The Appearance of the Solicitors', *Cambridge Law Journal* 58/2 (1999): 314–65.

[7]   Hay, 'England, 1562–1875', p. 69; Marc Steinberg, 'Capitalist Development, Labor Process and the Law', *American Journal of Sociology* 109/2 (2003): 445–95. While workers could not leave their employment prior to serving the customary notice period, by the 1840s the courts had given employers wide latitude to terminate contracts of servants immediately without recourse to a magistrate. See: *Spain v. Arnott* (1817), 117 E. R. 638; *Amor v. Fearson* (1839), 9 A. & E. 548; *Turner v. Mason* (1845), 153 E. R. 411; Brian Napier, 'The Contract of Service: The Concept and its Application' (D.Phil thesis, Cambridge University, 1975), p. 84; Steinfeld, *Coercion*, pp. 107–21; Hay, 'England 1562–1875', pp. 110–112.

[8]   'Constitutional Law versus Justices' Justice', *NS* (8 February 1845), p. 4.

[9]   For a definition of Summary Jurisdiction, see Appendix, this volume and Peter King, 'Summary Courts and Social Relations in Eighteenth Century England', *Past and Present* 183 (May 2004): 126; Bruce Smith, 'The Presumption of Guilt and the English Law of Theft, 1750–1850', *Law and History Review* 23/1 (Spring 2005): 146, 154; Norma Landau, *The Justice of the Peace* (Berkeley, 1984), p. 246.

questioned by judges of the higher courts or officials in the Home Office and there were considerable obstacles to punishing them for mistaken or malicious behavior. They enjoyed a flexibility and discretion in their application of the law that was considerable even by the standards of the English justice system. Indeed, this is part of what made summary justice attractive to many individuals. By the 1830s, however, in master and servant cases, workers were growing alarmed by the fact that this discretion was increasingly being exercised by magistrates who did not have the appearance of disinterested adjudicators.[10]

If this were the last appearance of the Longton colliers in the historical record, their story would not surprise those scholars exploring the history of master and servant statutes and their role in the governing employment relationships throughout the common-law world. Paul Craven and Douglas Hay have studied the enactment, judicial interpretation, local usage and dissemination of these acts to nearly every jurisdiction in the British Empire. By exploring the process and timing by which distinct provisions of these acts were adopted, adapted and applied in different jurisdictions, Hay and Craven demonstrate that these laws were central to creating and maintaining labor markets favorable to employers and regimes of workplace discipline throughout the world.[11]

Hay's work on the English context, focusing largely upon the period between 1700 and 1830, traces the evolution of the statute and case law relating to master and servant. He also uses archival materials, including justices' notebooks and house of correction calendars to examine the changing use of these laws in diverse

---

[10]   Hay and Craven, 'Introduction', pp. 2, 5, 56; Bruce Smith, 'Circumventing the Jury: Petty Crime and Summary Justice in London and New York City, 1790–1855' (PhD dissertation, Yale University, 1996); Thomas Sweeney, 'The Extension and Practice of Summary Jurisdiction in England, c. 1790–1860' (PhD dissertation, Cambridge University, 1985); Peter King, *Crime, Justice and Discretion in England, 1740–1820* (Oxford, 2000), pp. 83–6; Hay, 'England, 1562–1875,' pp. 105–9; Smith, 'Presumption of Guilt', pp. 135, 159–64.

[11]   Hay and Craven (eds), *Masters, Servants, and Magistrates in Britain and the Empire, 1562–1955* (Chapel Hill, 2004); R. McQueen, 'Master and Servant Legislation and Social Control: Rule of Law in Labour Relations on the Darling Downs, 1860–1870', *Law in Context* 10 (1992): 123–39; Christopher Tomlins, 'The Ties that Bind: Master and Servant in Massachusetts, 1800–1850', *Labor History* 30 (1989): 193–227; Robert Steinfeld, *The Invention of Free Labor: The Employment Relation in English and American Law and Culture, 1350–1870* (Chapel Hill, 1991); Steinfeld, *Coercion*; M. Linder, *The Employment Relationship in Anglo-American Law: A Historical Perspective* (New York, 1989); Otto Kahn-Freund, 'Blackstone's Neglected Child: The Contract of Employment', *The Law Quarterly Review* 93 (October 1977): 508–28; Napier, 'Contract of Service'; Simon Deakin, 'The Contract of Employment, A Study in Legal Evolution', *Historical Studies in Industrial Relations* 11 (Spring 2001): 1–36. Marc Steinberg, 'Unfree Labor, Apprenticeship and the Rise of the Victorian Hull Fishing Industry: An Example of the Importance of the Law and the Local State in British Economic Change', *International Review of Social History* 51/2 (2006): 243–76; Steinberg, 'Capitalist Development'.

regions of the country. Although master and servant statutes trace a genealogy back to the late Middle Ages, in the early industrial period they were by no means anachronistic holdovers from a bygone era. Throughout the eighteenth and nineteenth centuries, at the behest of employers, mine owners and manufacturers, Parliament regularly supplemented and updated these statutes with new legislation applying to additional categories of labor and containing increasingly harsh sanctions for workers who left or failed to complete work, performed it poorly, or committed acts of misbehavior. Once part of a more comprehensive regime of labor regulation, as the eighteenth century progressed the statute law and interpretations of the courts shed earlier characteristics of employment law, such as rules governing conditions of apprenticeship and local wage setting by justices of the peace.[12] By the second quarter of the nineteenth century the administration of these laws in many regions became more 'employer oriented', meaning that employers took advantage of the cheap and easy process they provided far more often than workers. Furthermore, magistrates, who in industrial regions were increasingly likely to be employers of labor themselves (sometimes in the same trade as the plaintiffs), began handing down harsher sentences.[13]

The importance of these laws in industrial relations, right up to the repeal of most penal sanctions for workers' breach of contract in Britain in 1875, would be difficult to exaggerate. National statistics for the prosecution of workers under Master and Servant Acts become available only after 1858, and they are of uncertain reliability. They demonstrate, however, that for the last two decades of the existence of penal sanctions for breach of contract in England, between at least 7,300 and 17,000 workers a year were prosecuted, and in years of low unemployment the figure was usually over 10,000.[14] This is to say nothing of the far more numerous instances in which the threat of prosecution and imprisonment was used to compel reluctant employees to return to work and complete unfavorable contracts.

In the nineteenth century master and servant law was combined in a number of industries with standardized annual contracts, which bound workers exclusively to a single employer, but allowed manufacturers to retain a wide freedom to control labor costs through payment by piece-rates, the power to fine and the sole right to determine custom and judge the quality of work. These contracts were enforced by local magistrates, who had strong political, social and economic ties to local

---

[12]　Hay, 'England, 1562–1875', pp. 66, 82–8.

[13]　Hay, 'England, 1562–1875', pp. 82–110; Steinberg, *Coercion*, p. 480; D. C. Woods, 'The Operation of the Master and Servant Acts', *Midlands History* 7 (1982): 102; Willibald Steinmetz, 'Was There a De-Jurification of Employment Relations in Britain?', in Steinmetz (ed.), *Private Law and Social Inequality in the Industrial Age: Comparing the Legal Cultures of Britain, France, Germany and the United States* (London, 2000), p. 102; King, 'Summary Courts', p. 142, 165–8.

[14]　Steinfeld, *Coercion*, p. 76.

employers.[15] The areas where master and servant law was most thoroughly used by employers were also the places that witnessed the largest transfusions of mine owners, ironmasters and textile manufacturers to the magisterial bench. Collective action in such trades was difficult because there were only limited periods when workers were not under contract and free to strike. Employees were not free to walk off the job in response to an employer's violation of the terms of contract, no matter how flagrant or fundamental, as only in the rarest instances were magistrates willing to accept an employer's prior offence against the agreement as an adequate defense for a worker's breach of contract.[16] In trades using highly skilled workers, employers used these laws in conjunction with much longer term agreements (in some cases up to 10 years for glass-blowing and file-making trades) to prevent bidding wars for valuable laborers. Staggered long-term agreements made collective action in these trades very difficult.

Legal historians confronted with this case study would also observe that there was nothing theoretically shocking in the use of imprisonment to compel the four colliers, who were 'free laborers', to complete their contract. There has been a growing recognition that discreet categories of 'free' and 'unfree' labor are not always useful as categories of historical analysis. Hay and Craven emphasize that 'coercion is a complex continuum of forms and practices', and they are hardly alone in this observation. Many legal historians have analyzed the impact of master and servant statutes upon the historical development of the contract of employment and argue that these acts were an integral part of what eighteenth- and nineteenth-century contemporaries understood as free labor. Free labor included the ability of masters to compel the specific performance of employment contracts, and to discipline reluctant workers with sanctions that included whipping and imprisonment.[17] The higher courts repeatedly supported the use of these laws to force workers to complete their agreements by ruling that imprisonment for breach of contract did not terminate the agreement, and if a worker refused to re-enter his or her service after a conviction and imprisonment under these acts, he or she could be prosecuted again. This was at odds with the prevailing understanding of most other types of contract.[18] The historical literature on master and servant law and the contract of employment focuses on the role of the statute law in shaping

---

[15]   Steinberg, 'Unfree Labor' and 'Capitalist Development'; Raymond Challinor and Brian Ripley, *The Miners' Association: A Trade Union in the Age of Chartists* (London, 1968), Chapter 6; Woods, 'Master and Servant', pp. 57, 71–8, 80–86, 95, 113–14.

[16]   Steinmetz, 'De-Juridification', pp. 275–6.

[17]   Quote from Hay and Craven, 'Introduction', 27; Steinfeld, *Free Labor*; Steinfeld, *Coercion*; Linder, *Employment Relationship*; Kahn-Freund, 'Blackstone's Neglected Child'; Napier, 'Contract of Service'; Deakin, 'The Contract of Employment'.

[18]   In Re: *William Baker* (1857), 2 H. & N. 219–41; Hay, 'England 1562–1875', pp. 59–60; Steinfeld, *Coercion*, pp. 50, 58–72; John Orth, 'Contract and the Common Law', in N. Scheiber (ed.), *State and the Freedom to Contract* (Stanford, 1998); Patrick Atiyah, *The Rise and Fall of Freedom of Contract* (Oxford, 1979).

the employment relationship, notions of free labor and labor markets, but there is very little discussion of worker resistance to the coercive elements of the law.

Labor historians also have surprisingly little to say about resistance to the use of these laws. Indeed, thus far the Staffordshire case appears consistent with the interpretation of the law offered by many historians of early trade unions, which is that nineteenth century workers were subject to unjust laws and a biased legal system that they learned to avoid. According to this view, labor's greatest victories of the nineteenth century came when 'mature' unions turned to direct political action beginning in the 1860s. If the story of the four Longton miners had ended with their transfer to Stafford Gaol, their tale might have simply added to what Willibald Steinmetz argues was the strong aversion to the courts that developed among trade unions and workers during the second half of the nineteenth century.[19]

Workers might not have been alone in this aversion. It was not always in the best interests of employers, especially in highly competitive environments, to resort to the coercive laws available to them. Employers needed to exercise caution in how they imposed their will on employees, lest the latter find other employment at the first legal opportunity or withhold the effort that the master required. In periods of economic expansion in competitive industries, an employer having skilled workers imprisoned might miss lucrative contracts due to a lack of available labor.[20] Furthermore, using the courts could occasionally backfire on employers, especially if employees obtained legal representation. An employer who attempted to use the law to coerce workers during a labor dispute, and failed due to a technical error, could escalate the conflict, strengthen the resolve of those on strike and blacken his or her name with workers.

Influenced by this insight, some historians of early industrial relations in England have suggested that the emphasis upon the coercive nature of labor statutes has deflected attention away from the rules, expectations and understandings of

---

[19]   Steinmetz, 'De-Juridification'; K. Brown, 'Trade Unions and the Law', in C. Wrigley (ed.), *History of British Industrial Relations, 1875–1914* (Amherst, 1982), pp. 116–34; K. Burgess, *The Origins of British Industrial Relations: The Nineteenth Century Experience* (London, 1975), pp. 100–101, 169–70, 177; G. D. H. Cole, *A Short History of the British Working Class Movement 1789–1947* (London, 1948), pp. 86–7, 142, 197–8, 208, 212; W. H. Fraser, *A History of British Trade Unionism, 1700–1998* (Hampshire, 1999); R. Martin, *TUC: The Growth of a Pressure Group* (Oxford, 1980), pp. 19–25; A. E. Musson, *British Trade Unionism 1800–1875* (London, 1972); H. Pelling, *Popular Politics in Late Victorian Britain* (London, 1968), pp. 62–81; R. Price, *Labour in British Society: An Interpretive History* (London, 1986), pp. 40–43; D. N. Pritt and R. Freeman, *The Law Versus the Trade Unions* (London, 1958); Gerald Abrahams, *Trade Unions and the Law* (London, 1968), Introduction and Chapter 4; R. Y. Hedges and A. Winterbottom, *The Legal History of Trade Unionism* (London, 1930); J. Saville, *The Consolidation of the Capitalist State* (London, 1994), pp. 21–3.

[20]   John Orth, *Combination and Conspiracy: A Legal History of Trade Unionism, 1721–1906* (Oxford, 1991).

workplace bargaining created by workers and employers that were 'beyond or beneath' the law. By examining the operation of industries with long traditions of informal collective bargaining, these historians suggest that the role of the legal system in employment negotiations has been over-simplified or misunderstood. Most scholars offering this interpretation still recognize that the law had far greater *potential* as a weapon for employers than for workers hoping to protect their rights.[21]

This book will demonstrate that the statute law, in fact, loomed very large for workers in many trades in leading sectors of the economy. Local systems of collective bargaining were always shaped by the possibilities of the criminal law, even in sectors of the job market where that law was not applied.[22] Many historians exploring regimes of labor recruitment and discipline have demonstrated that in a variety of regions and trades, the penal characteristics of nineteenth-century employment law, enforced locally by largely unsupervised magistrates, were absolutely central to employer strategies for retaining and controlling workers at low costs.[23] On the morning of 8 January 1845, John Williams and his three workmates had no doubt whatsoever that in nineteenth-century labor relations, the law mattered a great deal.

The case of the four Staffordshire miners was not an ordinary master and servant proceeding that ended with a hasty summary conviction, and therefore does not conform to historians' expectations. This case was part of an extraordinary and under-explored political and legal effort by trade unionists and Chartists which took place during the 1840s and 1850s. A central argument of this book is that in mid nineteenth-century England and Wales, the law and the courts were hotly contested terrain between employers and laborers at both the local and national level, and this struggle had far-reaching social, cultural, political and legal

---

[21]   James Jaffe, *Striking a Bargain: Work and Industrial Relations in England 1815–1865* (Manchester, 2000), p. 90; Michael Huberman, *Escape from the Market: Negotiating Work in Lancashire* (Cambridge, 1996); John Rule, *The Labouring Classes in Early Industrial England, 1750–1850* (London, 1986), pp. 260, 312; John Foster, *Class Struggle and the Industrial Revolution: Early Industrial Capitalism in Three English Towns* (London, 1975), pp. 48–52; J. H. Porter, 'Wage Bargaining Under Conciliation Agreements, 1860–1914', *Economic History Review* 23 (1970): 460–474.

[22]   Hay and Craven, 'Introduction', pp. 24–8, 32–3; Steinfeld, *Coercion*, Introduction.

[23]   Steinberg, 'Unfree Labor' and 'Capitalist Development'; Challinor and Ripley, *Miners' Association*; Richard Fynes, *The Miners of Northumberland and Durham: A History of Their Social and Political Progress* (Wakefield, 1873), Chapters 7–8; Robert Colls, *The Pitmen of the Northern Coalfield: Work, Culture and Protest, 1790–1850* (Manchester, 1987), pp. 64, 73, 293–4. Woods, 'Master and Servant'; William Warburton, *History of Trade Union Organization in the North Staffordshire Potteries* (London, 1931), pp. 44–6, 90–98, 105; J. H. Morris and L. J. Williams, *The South Wales Coal Industry, 1841–1875* (Cardiff, 1958) pp. 268–9; J. W. Turner, 'Newcastle Miners and the Master and Servant Act, 1830–1862', *Labour History* 30 (1969).

consequences. These coercive labor statutes and their biased enforcement did not make laborers turn away from the law, but rather encouraged them to formulate innovative strategies for resistance both inside and outside of the courtroom. Workers were not simply passive victims of laws that were intended to compel them to work under unfavorable conditions, but instead struggled to impede and de-legitimize their use by employers.

An essential part of this resistance was the funding of legal counsel. During the mid nineteenth century there is evidence that workers did not, in fact, fear the legal system in its entirety as a forum for resolving disputes. Trade unions fiercely defended and aggressively pursued their interests on a wide range of issues before the courts at both the local and the appellate level, ranging from master and servant law, to truck wages, to workplace injury.[24] The legal representatives engaged by labor during these years enjoyed a high level of success in contesting master and servant prosecutions. The case of the Longton colliers occurred during an unusual juncture, a short-lived historical moment in the middle of the century when trade unions and workers confidently looked to radical elements in the solicitors' profession and the high courts in Westminster Hall for industrial justice, and surprisingly, were not often disappointed. The attitudes of unionized workers toward the law and the legal system were more complex than the current literature acknowledges. Radical solicitors engaged by trade unions sought to shape the enforcement of labor laws by previously unsupervised magistrates and bring greater accountability to these proceedings. In doing so, they gave unionized workers and Chartists a legal language for expressing their grievances and contributed to the enactment of important reforms of the forms and procedures for magistrates' summary proceedings. Labor-funded litigation was not only central to the development of the early trade union movement, but to the law as well. This has not been fully appreciated from a perspective that takes into account both law and legal process *and* the full social contexts in which these conflicts occurred.

After the conviction, the miners' union contacted William P. Roberts, a Chartist solicitor who had achieved fame during the previous 15 months as 'The Miners' Attorney-General' for successfully defending pitmen in a number of well-publicized master and servant cases. Roberts had been hired in August of 1843 by the Miners of Northumberland and Durham to provide representation and legal advice, particularly in master and servant cases. By 1844, Roberts' practice had expanded to include the entire National Miners' Association and a large number of unionized trades. He spent the next 25 years representing workers in areas as diverse as master and servant, picketing offences, truck wages, worker injury and embezzlement by union officials. He assisted in the defense of nearly every major trade union common-law conspiracy case that occurred during his professional

---

[24]   Frank, 'Anti-Truck Prosecution Societies and the Law in Mid-Nineteenth Century Britain', American Society for Legal History, Annual Meeting, Radisson Plaza, Baltimore, Maryland, 16–18 November 2006; Jamie Bronstein, *Caught in the Machinery: Workplace Accidents and Injured Workers in Nineteenth Century Britain* (Stanford, 2008).

lifetime. He also defended Chartists and Fenians. Politically active right up to his death in 1871, Roberts was a vital contributor to trade-union campaigns against master and servant law in 1844 and the 1860s, and wrote a pamphlet critical of the 1871 Criminal Law Amendment Act.[25]

Upon arriving in Staffordshire, Roberts examined the convictions and warrants of commitment of the colliers, looking for legal errors that might provide grounds for their release from prison. After finding several, Roberts initiated writs of habeas corpus and certiorari on behalf of the prisoners, and paid for two barristers to bring their case before the Court of Queen's Bench at Westminster Hall.[26]

On 25 January 1845 barristers W. H. Bodkin and J. W. Huddleston stood before Mr Justice Wightman of the Court of Queen's Bench, insisting that the prisoners should be freed because of an omission in the warrant of commitment. They argued that the warrant of commitment failed to state explicitly that the prisoners were present when evidence under oath against them was heard, and therefore it did not demonstrate that the adjudication of the magistrates was sufficient to justify a conviction and imprisonment. Mr Justice Wightman, applying the strict legal formalism that the judges often adhered to when reviewing cases of summary conviction, ordered the prisoners' immediate discharge.[27] To some observers, it might have appeared that Roberts, Huddleston and Bodkin had seized upon *technical* errors to free their clients, mere clerical omissions on the warrant of commitment that had little to do with the actual 'merits' or 'truth' of the case. After all, it appears clear from the newspaper report that the prisoners were in fact present when the evidence against them was heard, even if this was not made explicit on the warrant of commitment. Defenders of the convictions would argue that during the 1840s the material that needed to be included on a valid warrant of commitment was continually evolving, making it difficult for even conscientious magistrates. In contrast, the families and co-workers of Williams, Harding, Sillitoe and Pointon, who had witnessed the rushed and informal hearing conducted by Rose and Harvey, saw justice in the discharge.

---

[25]   See Challinor, *Radical Lawyer*.

[26]   For definitions of solicitor, warrant of commitment, conviction, barrister, writ of certiorari and writ of habeas corpus, see Appendix.

[27]   'Ex Parte John Williams', *The Justice of the Peace* (hereafter, *JP*) 9/6 (8 February 1845), p. 84; 'Legal Intelligence', *NS* (8 February 1845), p. 8; Smith, 'Circumventing the Jury', p. 190; Napier, 'Contract of Service', p. 123; W. R. Cornish and G. de N. Clark, *Law and Society in England 1750–1950* (London, 1989), p. 35; Smith, 'Presumption of Guilt', p. 136. Smith argues that the English criminal justice system was 'two tiered' in the first half of the nineteenth century, as 'heightened procedural and evidentiary protections for defendants tried in the higher courts for felonies co-existed with a system of reduced protections for defendants tried summarily for misdemeanors'. While this is correct, it is important to note that between 1800 and 1850 on the rare occasions when the higher courts had the opportunity, they attempted to impose more stringent procedures on summary proceedings.

This is a common occurrence in the case studies explored in this book. Although many of the legal victories won by labor before the higher courts were criticized for being decided on 'technicalities' as opposed to 'the merits of the case', when the full social context of the conflicts are examined it is clear that such charges mask far deeper injustices in the workplace and the magistrates' proceedings, to say nothing of the fundamental unfairness of the master and servant statutes themselves. This is why this legal and political campaign, and the strategies its leaders pursued, can be fully understood only when a social history approach is combined with an understanding of nineteenth-century law.

A large crowd in Longton celebrated this legal victory by marching with the freed prisoners, and waving banners as a band played 'merry music'. The procession of miners and their families stopped in front of the bank owned by magistrate Charles Harvey, where the band struck up 'See the Conquering Hero Comes'. The celebrations culminated with a well-attended evening meeting where cheers of thanks were offered to the colliers, W. P. Roberts, and the Judges of Queen's Bench. The *Northern Star* observed that the legal victory boosted the spirits of those suffering and sacrificing during the strike, noting 'every man was proud to be a miner that day'.[28] These types of celebrations were typical of the popular response to Roberts' victories, as were town halls and courtrooms filled to capacity with workers to observe Roberts in action before uncomfortable magistrates. In Victorian England, even people from a humble social background followed the activities of the local and national courts with interest, and saw the potential for these contests to legitimate their hopes and aspirations.[29]

The reporting of the *Northern Star* spread the news of this case far beyond Longton. Its 8 February 1845 issue contained three articles on the subject, including one titled 'Constitutional Law versus Justices' Justice', which praised Roberts and the Judges of the Court of Queen's Bench while expressing contempt for the magistrates' legal ignorance and bias against labor. Regular readers of the *Northern Star* would have been familiar with these themes because nearly every one of Roberts' high court victories was accompanied by an article expressing reverence for the judges of the higher courts and accusations that employers and magistrates were colluding to deprive workers of their constitutional rights. In the previous year there had been no shortage of victories to report. In fact, in 'Constitutional Law versus Justices' Justice', the author worried that 'We have so often commented upon the frequent legal triumphs of Mr. Roberts' that they 'may

---

[28]   'Great Rejoicing of the Staffordshire Miners', *NS* (15 February 1845), p. 1. 'See the Conquering Hero Comes', was the song bands had often played to announce the arrival of famed radical Orator Hunt. It became Roberts' theme music as well. James Epstein, 'Understanding the Cap of Liberty: Symbolic Practice and Social Conflict in Nineteenth Century England', *Past and Present* 122 (1989): 96.

[29]   James Epstein, 'The Constitutional Idiom: Radical Reasoning, Rhetoric and Action in Early Nineteenth Century England', *Journal of Social History* 23/3 (1990): 553–74.

lose their novelty from repetition'.[30] The social, legal and political context and consequences of these frequent triumphs provide the subject matter of this book.

This monograph focuses upon one area of nineteenth-century union-funded litigation and its wider consequences for labor, popular politics and the development of the law and its legitimacy. It explores the tactics, arguments and rhetoric utilized during a legal and political campaign by trade unions, Chartists and a few radical solicitors during the mid nineteenth century in England and Wales. This campaign challenged employers' use of the penal sanctions in master and servant law (and to a lesser extent, the 1825 Combination Laws Repeal Amendment Act). Trade union representatives used every legal and political tool available to obstruct imprisonment for breach of contract. Many of the arguments practiced inside and outside of the courtroom during these years became central to subsequent lobbying efforts before Parliament that ultimately led to the repeal of these hated sanctions. While master and servant law was very much a part of the experience of Scottish workers, and their efforts in the 1860s were instrumental in the eventual repeal of penal sanctions for breach of contract, the Scottish experience will not be dealt with in this book. Scotland's separate legal system, rules, procedures, as well as its unique traditions with non-pecuniary compulsion to labor (especially in the mining industry) require it to be treated in a different volume.

While there is widespread agreement that the end of workers' imprisonment for breach of contract came about due to the prolonged and determined resistance by trade unions, that history is still incomplete. Daphne Simon's pioneering work incorrectly claims that the 'struggle for reform' began only in 1863, and she focuses largely on the political lobbying of the 'mature' new model unions and trades councils.[31] Early resistance by trade unions to the penal sanctions of master and servant law has not yet been fully explored.[32]

This book will demonstrate the importance of early organized resistance to master and servant law, both for the eventual repeal of penal sanctions for breach of contract in 1875 and for the development of the trade union movement more generally. It also had very important consequences for the development of the law that governed magistrates' summary hearings. Organized labor achieved considerable success before the courts during the 1840s, not because those who made and administered public policy were sympathetic to the trade union goals, but because radical solicitors skillfully framed issues to reflect the wider concerns and ideologies held by many judges and members of Parliament. The strategy of legally, politically and rhetorically attacking abuses of power by magistrates furthered the trade union cause in the short term when the expansion of summary

---

[30]   'Constitutional Law versus Justice's Justice', *NS* (8 February 1845), p. 4.

[31]   Daphne Simon, 'Master and Servant', in John Saville (ed.), *Democracy and the Labour Movement: Essays in Honour of Donna Torr* (London, 1954), pp. 160–200; Mark Curthoys, *Governments, Labour and the Law in Mid-Victorian Britain: The Trade Union Legislation of the 1870s* (Oxford, 2004).

[32]   For a legal history perspective, see Steinberg, *Coercion*, Chapter 4.

justice was frequently being debated in Parliament. This strategy also, however, contributed to the pressure on Parliament for wide-ranging reform of the magistracy that paradoxically hindered trade union legal efforts in the 1850s. These reforms paved the way for the further expansion of magistrates' summary jurisdiction in the nineteenth century. Labor's role in these reforms has not been adequately acknowledged by legal historians. Finally, this project will explore how union-funded litigation affected understandings of the law and informed popular protest. An examination of this legal and political campaign can illuminate the ways in which the law mediated social relations in mid-Victorian Britain. This book will take a different view of summary justice in the nineteenth century than Peter King in his examination of eighteenth-century summary hearings in Essex. King sees summary courts as a source of accessible justice used by the poor, characterized by mediation and compromise between social classes. King acknowledges that this situation was changing by the nineteenth century, in part because of the changing social composition of the magistracy. This book will argue that in industrial regions, when adjudicating labor cases, the nineteenth-century magistracy was more likely to divide and embitter than heal and reconcile.[33]

Trade Union Resistance, the Magistracy and Law Reform

A new phase in trade union legal resistance to the use of master and servant laws by employers began in August 1843, when the miners of Northumberland and Durham hired W. P. Roberts to provide them with legal representation.[34] Although Roberts was not the only solicitor whose practice included a high proportion of unionized workers, more than any other individual he was primarily responsible for the success that trade unions enjoyed before the courts during the 1840s. Roberts attended Petty Sessions to defend workers charged under the Master and Servant Acts, and gave them a skilled and spirited defense in what had previously been open-and-shut cases.[35] Prosecutions that had once taken mere minutes to be 'rubber-stamped' by partial adjudicators now dragged on for hours and hours, and exposed employers and magistrates to considerable inconvenience, cost and embarrassment.[36] Mine owners, who suddenly needed to pay attorneys to conduct their prosecutions, described these systematic legal challenges as an outright 'rebellion' by 'their miners' which undermined the longstanding system of labor

---

[33]   King, 'Summary Courts', pp. 128, 142, 147, 164–8.

[34]   Challinor and Ripley, *Miners' Association*, pp. 9–10.

[35]   For a definition of Petty Sessions and Quarter Sessions, see Appendix.

[36]   Challinor, *Radical Lawyer*, pp. 92–101. John G. H. Owen of South Wales and William Broomhead Sr. and William Broomhead Jr. in Sheffield were all solicitors who during the 1840s and 1850s devoted a very large part of their practice to promoting and protecting the interests of unionized workers.

discipline.[37] When unsuccessful at the local level, Roberts used writs of habeas corpus and certiorari to bring cases before Queen's Bench.

Some labor leaders disagreed with this strategy, expressing doubts as to whether this campaign was the wisest use of scarce union funds. Others blamed Roberts' confrontational tactics, inflammatory language and Chartist politics for hardening the position of employers and the state.[38] It is highly doubtful, however, that many of these prosecutions would have been contested in the absence of union funding, as few workers could afford the costs.

In his defense of workers both inside and outside of the courtroom Roberts developed two strong arguments against master and servant law, which informed the subsequent three decades of trade union protest. The first was that employment agreements should be treated as all other contracts, according to classical contract doctrine. The focus of this struggle was originally over the amount of consideration required to make contracts of employment valid, and whether these agreements conferred obligations that were *mutually binding*. Roberts often defended workers in these cases by demonstrating that the agreement was so one-sided as to be invalid, or that the employer had so regularly broken the contract before the employee absconded that it had long ceased to govern the employment relationship.[39] Eventually opponents of master and servant law argued that imprisonment for breach of an employment agreement and the compulsion of specific performance was completely at odds with the prevailing understanding of contract. The second, and more commonly used argument during the 1840s, was that the enforcement of coercive labor law by lay magistrates drawn increasingly from the class of industrial employers, who were often indifferent to legal formalities, represented a serious threat to the liberty of the subject.

Between 1843 and the early 1850s, Roberts won dozens of very well-publicized actions before Queen's Bench based upon errors of law or omissions in the warrants of commitment written by magistrates. These victories created obstacles to master and servant prosecutions by tightening rules that magistrates had to follow when handling these cases if they wanted to be safe from embarrassing civil proceedings for false imprisonment. This provoked persistent complaints from magistrates, who demanded a simplification of legal forms, clarification of statutes, and greater

---

[37]   NA: HO 45/644, 'Lord Londonderry to Sir James Graham', 27 May 1844; 'To the Editor of the Times', *The Times* (17 July 1844), p. 6; 'Aristocratic Insolence – The Durham Autocrat', *NS* (13 July 1844), p. 4; 'The Coal Miners', *NS* (22 March 1845), p. 6.

[38]   Working Class Movement Library, Manchester: 'To the Miners of Northumberland and Durham', 2 February 1844, F62, Box 10. For other attacks on Roberts in 1845, see: 'Nobody's Child', *NS* (6 June 1845), p. 4; 'Mr. Roberts', *NS* (8 November 1845), p. 4; 'Charges Against Mr. Roberts and the Miners' Association', *NS* (15 November 1845), p. 6. In the mid-1860s, Alexander Macdonald and his supporters in the union leadership struggled with local branches to drive Roberts out of the organization as a legal advisor. See Challinor, *Radical Lawyer*, Chapter 14, and Conclusion, this volume.

[39]   Steinfeld, *Coercion*, pp. 107–21.

protection for 'honest errors' made in their hearings. In addition to this litigation, trade unions also directed large-scale protests and parliamentary petitions against the abusive conduct of individual magistrates, and agitated against the expansion of summary jurisdiction generally. It is clear that these protests were informed by the legal work of Roberts, which had severely damaged workers' faith in the ability or desire of magistrates to administer the law fairly and correctly. In contrast, these cases greatly enhanced the popular legitimacy of the Judges of Queen's Bench, who acquired support during the 1840s that might have surprised them.[40]

Another notable 'poor man's attorney', who was active during the 1840s and 1850s was John G. H. Owen of Monmouthshire. Though less confrontational than Roberts, Owen was equally controversial with local elites. Owen regularly provided legal representation to miners and ironworkers in labor-related cases. In fact, these groups appear to have made up a large portion of his practice. Owen aggressively defended workers in master and servant cases, and he dragged out the proceedings by raising every argument he could to prevent a conviction, making the use of these statutes less convenient for employers. Owen sometimes represented miners in their negotiations with employers. He also conducted a significant number of prosecutions under the 1831 Truck Act in order to fight the pervasive practice in South Wales of paying miners' and ironworkers' wages in goods, rather than currency, at company stores. Owen's work, along with the rise of Anti-Truck prosecution societies in Staffordshire, was instrumental in drawing greater government attention to the issue of truck during the 1850s. He gave detailed testimony before the 1854 Select Committee on the Payment of Wages about the failure of the 1831 Truck Act to prevent the payment of wages in kind in the South Wales mining and iron industries. Owen was highly disruptive to the cozy relationship between mine and ironmasters and magistrates.[41]

---

[40] J. Fellague Ariouat, 'Rethinking Partisanship in the Conduct of Chartist Trials, 1839–1848', *Albion* 29/4 (Winter, 1998): 596–621. Ariouat describes how the political trials of the 1840s were conducted in a cautious way that won the presiding judges praise even in radical circles. This is born out by two flattering obituaries printed in the *Northern Star*. That journal wrote upon the death of Peel's Attorney-General, Sir William Follett, that he 'will go down to posterity as one of England's greatest and best' legal figures, and 'his character was without blemish'. When Lord Chief Justice of Common Pleas Sir Nicholas Tindall died the *Northern Star* recounted his fairness in the political trials he presided with the following story: 'A person connected with Chartism forwarded a message to the bench, stating that he was refused admission to the court because he was a Chartist, although he was employed by the solicitor for the defense. The learned Judge instantly rejoined "Let the man be admitted, we know nothing of politics here; indeed, for my part, I don't know what a Chartist is"'. See: 'Death of an Attorney-General', *NS* (5 July 1845), p. 6; 'Death of the Right Honourable Lord Chief Justice Tindall', *NS* (11 July 1846), p. 3.

[41] See 'Awfully Sudden Death of J. G. H. Owen, Esq. Solicitor', *Pontypool Free Press* (hereafter *PFP*) (25 April 1863), p. 1; 'The Late Mr. Owen', *PFP* (2 May 1863), p. 1; 'Report of the Select Committee on the Payment of Wages Bill', *Parliamentary Papers*, Vol. 16 (283), p. 1, Q. 4724–5028; Morris and Williams, *The South Wales Coal Industry*,

The rise in trade union litigation and protest against the behavior of magistrates frequently coincided with debates in Parliament about the merits of expanding the types of cases that could be determined summarily, eliminating jury trials for certain small-scale offences. Roberts often used this controversy to his advantage on behalf of labor. The growth of magistrates' summary jurisdiction at the expense of the jury trial was an on-again, off-again, political struggle from the late seventeenth century through to the first half of the nineteenth century. Dissertations by Thomas Sweeney and Bruce Smith analyze the attempts made by merchants, landowners, clerics, industrialists and magistrates to change workplace thefts, juvenile crime and certain moral offences from jury trials to cases determined summarily by magistrates. Both Sweeney and Smith also describe the stubborn rearguard resistance to the considerable expansion of the 'bloodless code', both inside and outside of Parliament.[42]

In the 1790s Patrick Colquhoun, Jeremy Bentham and others advocated the expansion of magistrates' powers to hear cases of petty theft, particularly workplace and juvenile misappropriation. These proponents argued that trial by jury was expensive, time-consuming and maddeningly uncertain for the prosecutor. They claimed that juries were not sure to convict, judges 'overprotected' defendants and lawyers exploited technicalities that freed the guilty. This led to what Bentham called 'the immunity of the criminal'.[43] The explicit objective of proponents of expanding magistrates' summary powers was to encourage prosecutors, discourage criminals and secure the highest possible rate of convictions by 'circumventing the jury trial'. The certainty of a conviction would better protect property from workplace theft. Sweeney finds that Bentham's attraction to summary procedure was precisely that it had fewer safeguards for the accused.[44]

Resistance among some respected and influential members of Parliament, the high courts and the general public slowed attempts at legislating an expansion of magistrates' summary jurisdiction. Reverence for the Englishman's traditional right of trial by jury, as well as the perception of poor conduct and a lack of legal knowledge among magistrates, were the most frequently articulated arguments against summary jurisdiction. The writings of William Blackstone, who described the jury trial as the 'Palladium of British Liberty', which needed to be protected

---

pp. 268–9; E. W. Evans, *The Miners of South Wales* (Cardiff: Wales University Press, 1961), pp. 65, 70–71.

[42]   Sweeney, 'Summary Jurisdiction', pp. 14, 105–14; Smith, 'Circumventing the Jury', pp. 41, 114; Smith, 'Presumption of Guilt', pp. 154, 158–9. Magistrates appropriated even wider summary judicial powers by taking advantage of clauses of the Vagrancy Act, 5 George IV, c.83, s.4 (1824), and other acts that gave magistrates summary powers to detain 'reputed thieves'. *The Times* frequently protested against this 'abuse' of these powers.

[43]   Sweeney, 'Summary Jurisdiction', pp. 94–102; Smith, 'Circumventing the Jury', pp. 30–34; Smith, 'Presumption of Guilt', pp. 137–48.

[44]   Sweeney, 'Summary Jurisdiction', pp. 86, 95, 98–9, 141; Smith, 'Circumventing the Jury', pp. 79, 102–16; Smith, 'Presumption of Guilt', pp. 149–64.

from 'new and arbitrary methods of trial, by justices of the peace, commissioners of the revenue, and courts of conscience', proved highly influential among people of diverse social backgrounds.[45] Even if the jury trial was not always the safeguard of liberty its proponents said it was, celebration of trial by jury was a very common feature of radical rhetoric in the eighteenth and nineteenth centuries. Chartists held banquets celebrating the anniversary of the acquittal by jury of Thomas Hardy and John Horne Tooke, where radical speakers asserted 'Trial by jury was, in fact, the best specimen of the English living spirit'. At another commemoration of the acquittal of these famous members of the London Corresponding Society, a speaker toasted 'the purity of trial by jury' and noted that 'when tyrannous objects sought to be effected through the forms of law they were defeated by the virtue of a jury'. Radicals perceived the jury trial as a fundamental right of the 'freeborn Englishman'.[46]

The unprofessional magistracy, on the other hand, had long provided an easy target for reformers seeking more representative and qualified local governance and justice. Popular images of 'trading justices', reports of fox-hunting magistrates enforcing the game laws and the association of magistrates with unpopular forms of taxation and political repression undermined their legitimacy among radicals. Such was the power of these arguments that although the issue was raised repeatedly in Parliament, particularly in the second quarter of the nineteenth century, it was not until 1847, after years of advocacy by supporters, that legislators were able to secure the right of magistrates to summarily try juveniles accused of larceny under 5s, and then only with the consent of the defendant.[47]

The legal community, also influenced by Blackstone, had a tradition of distrusting lay magistrates.[48] Roberts was not the first lawyer to expose the legal ignorance of magistrates by challenging their rulings with writs of certiorari and habeas corpus. During the eighteenth century, on the rare occasions when they had the opportunity to scrutinize summary rulings, the higher courts often strictly

---

[45]   Sweeney, 'Summary Jurisdiction', pp. 86, 96, 98–9, 111, 118, 132, 141, 156; Smith, 'Circumventing the Jury', pp. 75–6, 84, 118–26, 189–97, 416–19, 424, 430, 433, 440.

[46]   'Trial by Jury', *NS* (8 November 1851), p. 1; 'Trial by Jury', *Silurian* (17 November 1838), p. 2; Epstein, 'Understanding the Cap of Liberty', p. 84.

[47]   10 & 11 Victoria, c.82 (1847); Smith, 'Presumption of Guilt', p. 164; Sweeney, 'Summary Jurisdiction', pp. 10–13, 91–3, 96, 101, 106–8, 111, 113–14, 116–20, 129–33, 139, 145–6, 148–53, 156–9; Smith, 'Circumventing the Jury', p. 405; Cornish and Clark, *Law and Society in England*, 618; David Philips, *Crime and Authority in Victorian England: The Black Country, 1835–1860* (London, 1978), pp. 132–4; King notes that magistrates' enforcement of the game laws has been exaggerated by historians, but it was still a useful line of attack for radicals. King, 'Summary Courts', p. 154.

[48]   Most magistrates and justices of peace in the 1840s were unpaid volunteers appointed by the Lord Chancellor with the recommendation of the Lord Lieutenant of the county. Very few had formal legal training. By mid-century, there was an increase in the number of stipendiary magistrates, who were trained barristers or solicitors and were paid salaries by the government.

construed the statutes that gave magistrates their judicial authority. They were also prepared to quash magistrates' rulings if their convictions or warrants of commitment contained legal errors or failed to establish fully their jurisdiction. It was thought that the application of such strict legal formalism provided protection for the accused in instances where the supervision of a jury was absent.[49]

Trade union legal actions and the rhetoric of popular protests initiated against master and servant prosecutions during the 1840s took advantage of the existing critique of the magistracy, but also supplemented it in important ways. One difference was simply one of scale. During the eighteenth century, an active magistrate might rarely have a ruling quashed by the Court of Queen's Bench.[50] The more aggressive role of trade unions in funding challenges to magistrates' rulings, and their remarkable rate of success, represented a new phenomenon.[51] Roberts insisted that his intention was to contest, and if necessary, appeal, every attempt by mine owners to use master and servant law to discipline workers or enforce non-reciprocal contracts of employment.[52] Between December 1843 and January 1846, Roberts initiated motions to the Court of Queen's Bench that resulted in the release of *at least* 37 miners who had been convicted before magistrates under the Master and Servant Acts, to say nothing of his clients in other trades.[53] Roberts brought the rulings of a single magistrate, T. B. Rose of Staffordshire, before that court as many as nine times.[54] Each of these cases was publicized in the *Northern Star*, labor journals such as the *Potters' Examiner* and *Miners' Advocate*, and law journals like the *Justice of the Peace*. Local newspapers also gave coverage to these proceedings. Chartist lecturers integrated the injustices that these cases revealed into their public arguments for universal male suffrage. This reporting and publicity influenced popular understandings of the English legal system and carried the critique of unprofessional summary justice to a wider audience than ever before. Collectively, such cases reduced the legitimacy of the magistracy and provided ammunition for those opposed to an expansion of their summary judicial powers. Roberts drew organized labor into law reform debates, and brilliantly, if temporarily, merged the concerns of trade unions with a shrinking

---

[49]   Smith, 'Circumventing the Jury', pp. 25, 36, 75–7, 84, 118–26, 186, 197–8; Sir Thomas Skyrme, *History of the Justice of the Peace* (3 vols., Chichester, 1991), Vol. 2, pp. 75, 79, 123–32, 137, 165–9; Cornish and Clark, *Law and Society in England*, p. 35.

[50]   Hay, 'Master and Servant in England', pp. 245–6.

[51]   Steinfeld, *Coercion*, pp. 123, 159.

[52]   Challinor, *Radical Lawyer*, pp. 88, 105; Steinfeld, *Coercion*, p.110.

[53]   'More Extraordinary Proceedings of the Lancashire Magistrates Under the Master and Servants Act, and the Singular Triumph of the Miners' Attorney General, W. P. Roberts, Esq.', *NS* (14 February 1846), p. 1.

[54]   *R. v. Williams and Three Others* (1845) 9 J. P. 84; *R v. Rose* (1850) NA: KB 1/190/22, KB 1/191/60; *R v. Austin* (1850) NA: KB 1/190/29; *R. v. Askew* (1851) NA: KB 1/199/47; *R. v. Gesswood* (1853) 23 L. J. 35; *R. v. Baker* (1857) 2 H. & N. 219. See Chapter 7, this volume.

number of influential judges and members of Parliament who were distrustful of the expansion of magistrates' administration of summary proceedings.

Roberts was only the most public part of a new challenge for magistrates. Solicitors became a more common presence at Petty Sessions by the mid nineteenth century. This presence added to the pressure on magistrates, who had little more than a justice's handbook and sometimes a clerk (often a solicitor) to guide them, to conduct their hearings with greater attention to the proper procedure and forms. There is evidence of an increase in tension between the solicitors' profession and the magistracy during the 1840s.[55] Law journalists, and magistrates themselves, frequently described solicitors as 'sharp practitioners', or desperate professionals seeking to cause delay and drive up fees by seizing upon the smallest technical flaws in summary rulings and suing 'honest' magistrates, without any consideration for the 'merits' of the case.

In the 1840s, labor mobilized against a vastly different magistracy than their radical forebears confronted. The magistrates who found themselves the targets of increasing litigation and public criticism were less likely to be landed gentlemen or Anglican clergy, but rather, industrialists and large employers of labor.[56] In practical terms this meant that workers sometimes had to defend themselves in

---

[55]   Most trials at Quarter and Petty Sessions continued to be conducted without legal counsel on either side. However, during the 1840s the law journal *The Justice of the Peace* repeatedly received queries from magistrates asking about the attorney's right of attendance at Petty and Quarter Sessions, or how to handle inappropriate or disrespectful behavior toward the bench by advocates. There were also a number of questions about whether they were required to allow solicitors access to court documents, such as the information, warrant, conviction and warrant of commitment for scrutiny. For a sample, see 'Debighshire Quarter Sessions – Audience of Attorneys', *The Justice of the Peace* (hereafter, *JP*) 10/5 (31 January 1846), pp. 66–8. Also see 'Practical Points' from the following issues of the *JP*: 7/6 (11 February 1843), p. 54; 8/34 (24 August 1844), p. 573; 8/35 (31 August 1844), p. 591; 9/21 (24 May 1845), p. 332; 9/22 (31 May 1845), p. 351; 9/25 (21 June 1845), p. 394; 10/16 (18 April 1846), p. 249; 10/24 (13 June 1846), p. 377; 10/28 (11 July 1846), p. 446; 11/11 (13 March 1847), p. 206. May, *The Bar and the Old Bailey*, pp. 200–201.

[56]   David Foster, 'The Social and Political Composition of the Lancashire Magistracy, 1821–1851' (PhD dissertation, University of Lancaster, 1972); Foster, 'Class and County Government in Early Nineteenth Century Lancashire', *Northern History* 9 (1974): 48–61; B. Godfrey, 'Judicial Impartiality and the Use of the Criminal Law Against Labour', *Crime, History, and Societies* 3/2 (1999): 57–72; J. Knipe, 'The Justice of the Peace in Yorkshire, 1820–1914: A Social Study' (PhD dissertation, University of Southern California, 1970); David Philips, 'The Black Country Magistracy, 1835–1860: A Changing Elite and the Exercise of its Power', *Midlands History* 3 (1976): 161–90; R. Swift, 'The English Urban Magistracy and the Administration of Justice During the Early Nineteenth Century: Wolverhampton 1815–1860', *Midlands History* 17 (1992): 75–92; D. C. Woods, 'The Borough Magistracy and the Authority Structure of Black Country Towns, 1860–1900', *West Midlands Studies* 12 (1979): 93–115; Woods, 'Master and Servant'; C. Zangrel, 'The Social Composition of the Country Magistracy in England and Wales', *The Journal of British Studies* 11 (1971): 113–25.

master and servant prosecutions before magistrates who happened to be employers in the same trade.[57] Worse still was when magistrates imprisoned workers in cases where they had a direct interest in the outcome, sometimes without permitting the prisoners to speak in their defense.[58] These conflicts of interest when determining labor disputes between employers and employees assumed a much larger place in trade union criticism of the magistrates' summary proceedings during the 1840s.[59] Radical journals frequently accused magistrates of colluding or conspiring with fellow employers to subvert the 'real law' and the rights of workers. In December of 1844 Roberts explained to a meeting of 3,000 Lancashire miners that it was only by bringing cases before the Court of Queen's Bench that they could 'bring the laws of England to bear upon the rights of labour'. This new context gave the old radical critique of the magistracy new meaning and much more clearly defined class component characteristic of much Chartist rhetoric of the age. These articles usually argued that the only remedy short of universal male suffrage and the appointment of stipendiary magistrates was the use of union-funded legal counsel.[60]

Defenders of the magistracy argued that these officials were usually correct on the practical facts, or 'merits' of the case, and were only frustrated by 'technical' errors and the unreformed state of the law. They argued that the industrial background of an increasing number of magistrates made them better judges in labor cases because of their familiarity with trade customs and practices. Neither of these arguments survives a close examination of the local context of the cases challenged by Roberts, which reveal the procedural unfairness and gross bias against labor that characterized many magistrates' hearings. It also masks the impunity with which employers often disregarded their contractual obligations to workers.[61]

---

[57]   Philips, 'Black Country Magistracy', p. 169. For specific examples see: *R. v. Lewis* (1844), *R. v. Tordoft* (1844), *R. v. Sheldon* (1844) and *R. v. Leigh* (1848).

[58]   Challinor, *Radical Lawyer*, pp. 103–4; J. E. Williams, *The Derbyshire Miners, A Study in Industrial and Social History* (London, 1962), p. 97; Hay, 'Master and Servant in England', pp. 245–6.

[59]   Magistrates themselves were often unsure about what constituted a conflict of interest, as demonstrated by a number of articles on this subject in *The Justice of the Peace*. For a sample, see 'On the Inability of Justices to Decide Upon Matters in Which They are Legally Interested', *JP* 7/13 (1 April 1843), p. 158; 'Practice at Sessions – Interest in Parties in a Decision', *JP* 9/4 (25 January 1845), pp. 49–50; 'Practical Points', *JP* 9/12 (22 March 1845), p. 186; 'Practical Points', *JP* 9/25 (21 June 1845), p. 399; 'Case of an Attorney Acting as Clerk to Justices and as Legal Advisor to a Party Before Them', *JP* 10/24 (13 June 1846), pp. 369–70.

[60]   'Tremendous Explosion of a Coal Pit Conspiracy', *NS* (24 March 1844), p. 4; 'Turn Out of the Lancashire and Cheshire Coal Miners', *Manchester and Salford Advertiser and Chronicle* (hereafter, *MSA*) (7 December 1844), p. 4; Epstein, 'Understanding the Cap of Liberty'; Epstein, 'The Populist Turn', *Journal of British Studies* 32/3 (1993): 181.

[61]   See Chapter 3, this volume. This book will challenge the suggestion by James Jaffe that magistrates were honest brokers and trusted arbiters in early collective bargaining.

The trade union strategy of taking advantage of the controversy over magistrates' expanding judicial powers to challenge master and servant rulings in the courts and in public also had very important consequences for the development of the law. These consequences ultimately worked against trade unions. Between 1842 and 1848 frustrated magistrates and their supporters complained in the pages of the *Justice of the Peace* about the quashing of master and servant rulings and civil suits for false imprisonment. Editorials and angry letters made it clear that magistrates perceived themselves to be the victims of crafty attorneys, opaque statutes and hostile judges in a manner that was entirely new. Justices and journalists demanded greater guidance, support and protection from the high courts and Parliament. The frustration and anger expressed by the targets of labour's legal campaign forced members of Parliament to recognize that the expansion of summary jurisdiction had to be preceded by wider- ranging reform of the magistracy.

The diminished legitimacy of summary proceedings that was fostered by trade unions was a concern commonly expressed by magistrates, employers and members of Parliament between 1842 and 1848. In 1848, Parliament responded to these frequent complaints by passing the Jervis Acts. The four Jervis Acts of 1848–1849 were intended to protect, and enhance the legitimacy of, magistrates when handling both indictable offences and summary hearings. An 'Act to Facilitate the Performance of Duties of Justices of the Peace Out of Session in England and Wales, with Respect to Summary Convictions and Orders', consolidated and clearly established the proper forms and procedures that magistrates were required to follow in summary hearings.[62] It also protected magistrates by providing short template forms for summons, informations, warrants, convictions, warrants of commitment and orders. This made it less likely magistrates or their clerks would make errors in form. These new forms made it more difficult to challenge summary rulings through certiorari because the template forms in the act for convictions and commitments provided far less detail about the case than previously had been required by the high courts, taking away ammunition for attorneys and barristers. 'Faceless' convictions and warrants of commitment made certiorari a nearly useless remedy for those attempting to challenge magistrates' rulings.[63] 'An Act to Protect Justices of the Peace from Vexatious Actions for Acts done in Execution of their Office', provided magistrates with far greater immunity against civil actions for non-malicious errors committed in their official capacity.

The Jervis Acts, along with the appointment of more legally trained stipendiary magistrates, silenced many critics of summary proceedings by creating the

---

Jaffe, *Striking a Bargain*, pp. 115–21.

[62]   Because summary jurisdiction is for the most part a statutory creation the rules and forms for summary proceedings before 1848 were spread across a large number of statutes and high court rulings. This made it potentially very confusing for magistrates to properly conduct hearings. Smith, 'Circumventing the Jury', pp. 81, 119, 444–5.

[63]   Smith, 'Circumventing the Jury', pp. 450–453; W. R. Cornish and G. de N. Clark, *Law and Society in England*, p. 35.

perception that magistrates were conducting more uniform hearings. Given the new difficulties with using certiorari, there was now less frequent public evidence to the contrary. This opened the door for Parliament to pass acts of 1847, 1850 and 1855 which considerably expanded the range of cases magistrates could decide summarily.[64] By the mid-1850s, the higher courts became far more reluctant to overturn magistrates' rulings due to errors in form, though this did not stop labor and its representatives from trying. Historians of the magistracy and summary proceedings have failed to provide a compelling explanation for the timing of these acts. Litigation and protest by trade unions against the magistracy during the 1840s represent an explanation which will be explored in this book.[65]

Chapter Outline

The chapters that follow explore the social, political and legal context and consequences of the early trade union struggle against the penal sanctions of employment law. Chapter 1 describes how in the second quarter of the nineteenth century Queen's Bench gave a strict reading to the jurisdiction conferred by Master and Servant Acts, limiting the type of workers to which they applied. The distinctions drawn by that court confused and frustrated magistrates while inconveniencing employers. These difficulties were brought to a boiling point by the publicity given to the legal efforts of Roberts on behalf of miners in late 1843 and 1844. Magistrates and employers lobbied Parliament to simplify the scope of master and servant law by expanding it to include nearly all types of workers with the exception of domestic servants. A bill that embodied their hopes was introduced into Parliament in February of 1844 and appeared to have considerable support.

Chapter 2 examines the strategies and tactics used by Roberts, the Miners' Association and Chartists to defeat this bill. A massive campaign of petitioning and public meetings carried out by trade unions, short time committees and Chartist clubs pressed Parliament to abandon this bill by May 1844. By merging the protest against a more comprehensive Master and Servant Bill with the demands of Chartism, the ten hours movement and trade unions, labor made the abandonment of this bill an easy concession for the government to grant relative to tough factory

---

64   Smith, 'Circumventing the Jury', pp. 463–6. Steinfeld, *Coercion*, Chapter 4.

65   Esther Moir, *The Justice of the Peace* (London, 1969); Sweeney, 'Summary Jurisdiction'; D. Freestone and J. C. Richardson, 'The Making of the English Criminal Law: Sir John Jervis and His Acts', *The Criminal Law Review* (1980): 5–16; Bertram Osborne, *The Justice of the Peace, 1361–1848: A History of the Justices of the Peace for the Counties of England* (Dorset 1960), pp. 223–8; Skyrme, *History of the Justice of the Peace*, Vol. 2, pp. 176–8; Steinfeld, *Coercion*, pp. 159–61; Wes Pue, 'The Criminal Twilight Zone: Pre-Trial Procedure in the 1840s', *The Alberta Law Review* 21/2 (1983): 335–63; Smith, 'Circumventing the Jury', pp. 89, 118–26, 211–12, 197–313, 405, 414, 416–30, 447–53, 463.

regulation and universal suffrage. Historians of Chartism often argue that such timely concessions were an important factor in the maintenance of order in England in an era when it was dissolving throughout the rest of Europe.[66] Roberts and other union representatives skillfully positioned themselves by repeatedly raising the issue of magistrates' summary enforcement of master and servant law. The protest rhetoric about the Englishman's traditional right to the jury trial was strategically intended to win favor with members of Parliament who were concerned about the expansion of magistrates' judicial powers. It became clear to supporters of the magistracy that they would have to take a less direct legislative route to undermine the courtroom strategies pursued by labor.

The success of Roberts before the Court of Queen's Bench between 1843 and 1848 is the subject of Chapter 3. Roberts and the barristers he engaged demonstrated great skill in manipulating the legal ignorance of magistrates, the strict reading by the Judges of Queen's Bench to the statutes conferring summary powers and the rules of precedent, to labor's advantage.[67] Roberts did more than simply seize upon legal errors. This chapter explores the social contexts of these cases, and demonstrates that Roberts' victories due to legal flaws in magistrates' warrants of commitment and convictions actually mask the tremendous injustices that regularly occurred in these hearings.

The pressure on Parliament for wide-ranging reform of the magistracy was not only the result of labor's courtroom victories, but also of trade-union protests and petitions to Parliament directed against the conduct of specific magistrates. These protests were informed by the reporting of master and servant cases in the labor press, which emphasized the bias and legal ignorance of the magistracy. Chapters 4 and 5 look at two well-timed protests and petitions to the Home Office directed by trade unions against magistrates from Warrington and Sheffield in 1847.

In the Warrington case magistrates convicted four file forgers to three months' imprisonment at hard labor for absconding from their work despite strong arguments made in their defense by Roberts. He petitioned Parliament for an inquiry into the case and a pardon for the prisoners, using it to illuminate several common and widespread abuses in magistrates' summary hearings in Lancashire. This case is also an example of the use of master and servant law and long-term contracts by employers of highly skilled workers to control the labor market.

---

[66]   Dorothy Thompson, *The Chartists: Popular Politics and the Industrial Revolution* (New York, 1984); Thompson, *The Outsiders: Class, Gender, and Nation* (London, 1993), Chapter 1; G. Stedman Jones, *The Languages of Class: Studies in Working Class History, 1832–1982* (London, 1983); F. C. Mather, 'The Government and the Chartists', in A. Briggs (ed.), *Chartist Studies* (London, 1959), pp. 380, 384–5, 399; R. G. Hall, *Voices of the People: Democracy and Chartist Political Identity, 1830–1870* (London, 2007), p. 158; Malcolm Chase, *Chartism: A New History* (Manchester: Manchester University Press, 2007).

[67]   J. Evans, 'Change in the Doctrine of Precedent During the Nineteenth Century', in Lawrence Goldstein (ed.), *Precedent in Law* (Oxford, 1987), pp. 35–72.

In Sheffield, artisans petitioned Parliament for an inquiry into the conduct of magistrate Dr Wilson Overend between 1842 and 1847. No friend of labor, Overend often convicted workers under the 1825 Combination Laws Repeal Amendment Act for 'obstructing, molesting, or intimidating' their employers or replacement workers on flimsy evidence in informal hearings. Of the 18 workers Overend convicted of such offences, all were set free upon appeal to Quarter Sessions. He made harsh speeches against unions, which brought his impartiality into question. The cases Overend adjudicated showed conflicts between three types of law: the law enforced at the local level by magistrates; the law as defined by Parliament and the higher courts; and a customary and traditional law of the local artisan community in Sheffield. Employers and employees each appealed to different levels of law to legitimate their ambitions and practices. The conflict over Overend's stated determination to use the administration and interpretation of the law to transform industrial relations in Sheffield anticipates the more famous conflicts over the 'outrages' of the 1860s.

Both protests also had national implications. These protests occurred during a period when the administration of justice by magistrates was being debated in Westminster, as Parliament was considering legislation to permit magistrates to summarily determine cases of petty larceny under 5s committed by juveniles. The arguments articulated by labor's representatives in these petitions were often quite similar to those made against the further expansion of magistrates' summary powers in Parliament. These petitions, along with several others protesting against individual magistrates' behavior that were sent to Parliament in 1847 (many from labor cases), also influenced the passage of the Jervis Acts. Both of these case studies provide insight into the use of the law at the local level, popular understandings of the law and its legitimacy and the tactics and arguments used by radical solicitors to undermine the use of biased labor laws to shape labor markets and discipline their clients.

The publicity given to these cases not only mobilized trade unionists to protest against magistrates' abuses of power; it also compelled the magistracy to demand greater guidance and protection from Parliament. In publications such as the *Justice of the Peace*, magistrates and their supporters editorialized upon the need for the courts to distinguish between technical errors and malicious errors made in the conduct of their duties. Chapter 6 demonstrates how these arguments ultimately contributed to the final form of the Jervis Acts (1848–9). It also shows how the legitimacy conferred by these acts led the high courts to follow the will of Parliament by the mid-1850s, less frequently overturning magistrates' hearings due to errors of form.

Chapter 7 returns to where this book began, in Staffordshire with magistrate T. B. Rose. If the Jervis Acts enhanced the legitimacy of magistrates' summary hearings among the elites, they failed to do so with laborers. After 1848, the biased enforcement of the law by magistrates remained an important concern of trade unionists and, indeed, these arguments continued to be articulated for decades to come. By the 1850s, Queen's Bench was prepared to accept a lower standard of conduct from magistrates than it had previously. This chapter uses the magisterial career of T. B. Rose, and his frequent clashes with W. P. Roberts, to explore the resourcefulness of trade union legal representatives in finding new ways, and reviving old ones, to make biased or ignorant magistrates fully accountable for their behavior. In 1850 Roberts sought the infrequently utilized remedy of the criminal information against Rose, and met with mixed success. This book concludes by examining the changes in the approach taken by the high courts to magistrates' hearings in the 1860s, and the implications of this monograph for our understanding of labor, popular politics and the role of law in Victorian society.

Chapter 1

The Introduction of the 1844 Master and Servant Bill: 'The statutes relating to master and servant are nearly useless'

Introduction

During the spring of 1844, a large campaign of petitioning and public meetings by Chartists, trade unionists, and short-time committees throughout England and Wales forced Parliament to abandon a bill that would have greatly expanded the power of magistrates to determine disputes under master and servant law. This bill was actively promoted by the Home Secretary and had the enthusiastic support of the magistracy.[1] Less than 40 days before the bill was abandoned it had its first two readings in the House of Commons without any sign of opposition. When Thomas Duncombe, W. P. Roberts and the *Northern Star* informed the miners' and potters' unions of the bill's full implications, however, the response of labor was both rapid and intense.[2] According to the *Journal of the House of Commons*, within a month 213 petitions opposing the bill originating from public meetings were presented

---

[1] Though the measure was promoted by Home Secretary Sir James Graham, it was not a government bill. *Hansard Parliamentary Debates: Third Series: Commencing with the Accession of William IV* (London, 1844), Vol. 73, cols. 1306–8; Vol. 74, col. 526; 'Masters and Servants', *JP* 8/9 (2 March 1844), pp. 154–5; 'Master and Servants Bill', *The Legal Observer* (hereafter, *LO*) 27 (16 March 1844), p. 426; 'Parliamentary Intelligence', *The Times* (3 May 1844), p. 4.

[2] Thomas Slingsby Duncombe (1796–1861) was one of the nineteenth-century's great political champions of labor and popular politics. He entered Parliament in 1826 for Hertford, but is primarily associated with the borough of Finsbury, which he represented for nearly 30 years. During that time Duncombe presented several Chartist petitions to the House of Commons, and also agitated for the more humane treatment of political prisoners, greater freedom for trade unions, stricter mine and safety regulations, reform of the 1834 Poor Law, and freeing Jews from civil disabilities. He also frequently brought bad behavior by magistrates to the attention of the House and served as president of the National Association of United Trades for the Protection of Labour, which figures prominently in Chapters 4 and 5. See 'Death of T. Slingsby Ducombe, M.P.', *Liverpool Daily Post* (16 November 1861), p. 7; 'Death of T.S. Duncombe', *Manchester Daily Examiner* (15 November 1861), p. 5; P.W. Kingsford, 'Radical Dandy: Thomas Slingsby Duncombe, 1796–1861', *History Today* 14/6 (1964): 399–407; J. Bronstein, 'Thomas Duncombe: "Radical Dandy" or "Member for All England"?', Western Conference of British Studies, Albuquerque, New Mexico,

to the Lower House. Dozens more arrived too late for consideration. Duncombe declared in Parliament that these petitions represented over two million signatures, twice the number that signed the first Chartist petition. Faced with this sudden and unexpected opposition, the bill's supporters watched helplessly as Duncombe carried a proposal to postpone consideration of the bill for six months, a de facto death sentence.[3] Its defeat was an important episode in the long campaign by workers against the penal characteristics of employment law.

This chapter examines the factors that made an expansion of master and servant law desirable to the bill's supporters. Chapter 2 describes the movement of the bill through Parliament, as well as the strategies and language that labor used to mobilize opposition and secure its defeat. Together these chapters reveal the importance of labor's tactics and arguments in politically and legally fighting master and servant law, which shaped popular understandings of the law and its legitimacy and contributed to the longstanding debate over summary jurisdiction and reform of the magistracy.[4]

The controversial bill, officially called, 'A Bill for Enlarging the Powers of Justices in Determining Complaints between Masters, Servants, Artificers, and for the More Effectual Recovery of Wages Before Justices', was introduced into the House of Commons in February 1844 by three career Tory backbenchers. Their stated purpose was to clarify what types of workers and employment relationships fell within the statutes by simply extending master and servant law to cover all employment relationships with the exception of domestic service.[5]

2–3 November 2007; Matthew Lee, 'Duncombe, Thomas Slingsby (1796–1861)', *ODNB* (Oxford 2004, Online edn 2005).

[3]   *Hansard Debates*, Vol. 74, col. 522; *The Journals of the House of Commons*, Vol. 99 (1844), pp. 184, 212, 217, 224, 229, 232, 243, 252–4, 258, 269, 282; M. Haynes, 'Employers and Trade Unions, 1824–1850', in J. Rule (ed.), *British Trade Unionism, 1750–1850: The Formative Years* (London, 1988), p. 248; Sidney and Beatrice Webb, *The History of Trade Unionism* (London, 1902), p. 167; Raymond Challinor, *Radical Lawyer in Victorian England: W. P. Roberts and the Struggle for Workers' Rights* (London, 1990), pp. 144–5; Robert Steinfeld, *Coercion, Contract and Free Labour in the Nineteenth Century* (Cambridge, 2001), pp. 136–41; The final vote was 97:54 to postpone.

[4]   Bruce P. Smith, 'Circumventing the Jury: Petty Crime and Summary Justice in London and New York City, 1790–1855' (PhD dissertation, Yale University, 1996), pp. 2, 4, 36 8, 75 8, 81, 84, 118–22, 124, 126, 197 8, 213–14, 417 9, 424–5, 430, 437, 440; Thomas Sweeney, 'The Extension and Practice of Summary Jurisdiction in England, c.1790–1860' (PhD dissertation, Cambridge University, 1985), pp. 91–3, 96, 101, 111–21, 131–52, 158.

[5]   'A Bill For Enlarging the Powers of Justices in Determining Complaints Between Masters, Servants and Artificers, and for the More Effectual Recovery of Wages Before Justices' (24 February 1844), *Parliamentary Papers*, Vol. III (58), p. 223. The three sponsors were William Miles, Robert Palmer and Sir Henry Gally Knight. Friedrich Engels later described them as 'quite obscure members of Parliament'. Friedrich Engels, *The Condition of the Working Class in England* (London, 1845), p. 319; *Journals of the House of Commons*, Vol. 99 (22 February 1844), p. 52; *Hansard Debates*, Vol. 74, cols. 523, 529–

Magistrates, who usually lacked formal legal training, often had to administer statutes that were imprecisely written and defined by a complex and evolving body of case law. During the 1820s and 1830s the Court of King's Bench made the deliberations of magistrates more difficult by ruling that individuals in trades not specifically enumerated in master and servant statutes, as well as those hired by the job or piece (not for a specific period of time), were outside the scope of these coercive laws.[6] Many magistrates and employers felt that these rulings limited the usefulness of master and servant law, undermining both the legitimacy of magistrates and the authority of masters. During the 1840s, this problem was discussed in diverse publications by trade unionists, employers, justices of the peace and lawyers. Each articulated grievances with the law's current operation, but proposed different solutions to the problem.

The rulings of King's Bench had not always represented such an inconvenience for employers and magistrates because in the eighteenth and early nineteenth centuries workers rarely had legal representation in master and servant cases, and almost never challenged convictions. Knowing that their decisions were unlikely to come under scrutiny, magistrates, who were increasingly likely to be industrial employers themselves, often interpreted their jurisdiction to whatever fitted the needs of the moment.[7] By 1843, W. P. Roberts and other solicitors at Petty Sessions gave workers charged under master and servant statutes a more rigorous defense, pressing magistrates into greater conformity with the rulings of the higher courts.[8]

30; Brian Napier, 'Contract of Service: The Concept and Its Application' (D.Phil thesis, Cambridge University, 1975), pp. 106–12.

[6] *Hardy v. Ryle* (1829), 9 B. & C. 603–12; *Lancaster v. Greaves* (1829), 9 B. & C. 627–32; *Kitchen v. Shaw* (1837), 6 A. & E. 729–35; *Bramwell v. Penneck* (1827), 7 B. & C. 536–42; 'Recent Decisions Under the Master and Servant Act (4 George IV, c.34, s.3)', *JP* 8/9 (2 March 1844), pp.131 –2; 'The Liability of Justices of the Peace to Actions in the Exercise of Summary Jurisdiction', *JP* 9/5 (1 February 1845), pp. 65–6; Napier, 'Contract of Service', pp. 85–7, 106–12. Robert Steinfeld notes that though these rulings excluded piece workers under the 'general' Master and Servant Acts (Acts of 1747, 1766, 1823, see below), piece workers in a small number of specific trades were still covered by the statutes 17 George III, c.56 (1777) and 6 & 7 Victoria, c.40 (1843). He concedes, however, that it was widely perceived by masters, magistrates, and workers that piece and job workers were outside the provisions of master and servant law. Steinfeld, *Coercion*, pp. 129–32, 134–41.

[7] Challinor, *Radical Lawyer*, pp. 71–3; Douglas Hay, 'England 1562–1875: The Law and its Uses', in Douglas Hay and Paul Craven (eds), *Masters, Servants, and Magistrates in Britain and the Empire, 1562–1955* (Chapel Hill, 2004), p. 91.

[8] Smith, 'Circumventing the Jury', pp. 221–6; R. Trainor, *Black Country Elites: The Exercise of Authority in an Industrialized Area, 1830–1900* (Oxford, 1993), p. 231; Douglas Hay, 'Master and Servant in England: Using the Law in the Eighteenth and Nineteenth Centuries', in Willibald Steinmetz (ed.), *Private Law and Social Inequality in the Industrial Age: Comparing the Legal Cultures of Britain, France, Germany, and the United States* (London, 2000), pp. 240–241; Hay, 'Dread of the Crown Office: The Magistracy and King's

In many important industrial regions of the country, these efforts temporarily made master and servant law a less convenient method of labor discipline. The reporting of these cases raised questions among workers (particularly miners and potters) about the reciprocity of their contracts with their employers, and whether one-sided agreements were, in fact, enforceable.[9] In the 1840s it was not uncommon for employment agreements to bind an employee to work exclusively for an employer, but not necessarily oblige that employer to provide sufficient work and wages. The enforceability of such non-reciprocal agreements was a legal battle fought by Roberts with mixed results before Queen's Bench. His efforts caused workers to loudly question validity of such contracts in journals such as the *Potters' Examiner* and the *Northern Star*. Roberts' ambitious work before Queen's Bench between 1843 and 1848 helped to define and enforce the procedures, forms and limits of summary jurisdiction. It also had a lasting impact on the legitimacy of the magistrates' judicial role among workers, making it easier to mobilize labor against the 1844 bill.[10]

Magistrates frequently petitioned Parliament for greater protection from the costs, damages and embarrassment that reversals of their rulings brought. Mine owners complained to the Inspector of the Mines about harassment from crafty attorneys and a loss of control over their enterprises. It is against this backdrop that the 1844 bill was introduced.

Bench 1740–1800', *Law, Crime and English Society, 1660–1840* (Cambridge, 2002), p. 9; Raymond Challinor and Brian Ripley, *The Miners' Association: A Trade Union in the Age of Chartists* (London, 1968), pp. 96–116.

[9]   Steinfeld, *Coercion*, pp. 92, 104–5, 106–23; *Sykes v. Dixon* (1839) 8 L. J. 102; *Williamson v. Taylor* (1843) 5 Q. B. 173; The Working Class Movement Library, Salford: *Report of the Colliery Case Williamson v. Taylor and Others Tried at the Northumberland Assizes, 4 August 1843 Before Mr. Justice Wightman; Involving the Question Whether the Legal Construction of the Agreement Commonly Called the Pit Bond, Entered into between the Owners and W. Holywell Colliery Near Earsdon and Their Workmen, Enables the Men to Claim Reasonable Wages When The Pit is Laid Off Work* (Newcastle, 1843); 'The Contract Between Master and Servant Necessary for Giving Justices Jurisdiction in Differences Between Them', *JP* 6/33 (20 August 1842); Josiah Wedgwood, *The Staffordshire Pottery and its History* (London, 1913), pp. 170–171.

[10]   Challinor, *Radical Lawyer*, pp. 88–90; *Pilkington v. Pemberton*, NA: KB 1/140/17 and KB 1/143/2; C. B. Barker, *The Pilkington Brothers and the Glass Industry* (London, 1960), Chapter 7. Also see: *Lonsdale and Harrison v. Gameside Pit*, 'Cases Before the Magistrates', *NS* (16 September 1843), p. 4; *Thomas Lamb v. Jarrow Colliery*, 'More Cases Before the Magistrates', *NS* (30 September 1843), p. 5; *Walker v. Gardmonsway Moor Colliery, Durham Chronicle* (hereafter *DC*) (16 September 1843), p. 3; *Moodie v. John and George Carr*, 'North Shields Court', *NS* (2 September 1843), p. 5; 'More of Labour's Triumphs: Manchester and Wigan', *NS* (30 November 1844), p. 1; In Re: *Lord* (1848) NA: KB 1/152/25; 17 L. J. 181; Steinfeld, *Coercion*, p. 117.

Interpreting Master and Servant Law in the Court of King's Bench, 1747–1837

The 1844 proposal was intended to remedy two potential sources of confusion about the extent of magistrates' jurisdiction under master and servant law. This jurisdiction, as settled by the higher courts, depended upon the existence of a relationship of service between the parties and employment in a trade specifically listed in one of the master and servant statutes. The precise definition of a relationship of service, however, was not self-evident to employers, workers or magistrates.[11] Did an agreement to perform a specific task for an employer create a relationship of service? Were out-workers servants in the eyes of the law, even though they might accept work from a number of different masters? In the second quarter of the nineteenth century the Court of King's Bench ruled that for a relationship of service to exist, a master had to be able to claim the exclusive service of his or her employee. This definition excluded many forms of piece, job or subcontracting work.[12]

The second source of confusion was the precise trades that were covered by these statutes. This question arose from confusing language in the clauses that defined their scope, as can be seen from three examples of 'general' master and servant acts.[13] 'An Act for the Better Adjusting and More Easy Recovery of the Wages of Certain Servants; and for the Better Regulation of Such Servants', passed in 1747, contained a mixture of both precise and more open-ended language in the clause that defined its reach. The act gave magistrates the power to imprison a servant for up to one month, abate wages or issue a discharge when the servant neglected work, was absent without permission, absconded or committed any 'misdemeanor, miscarriage, or ill-behavior in such his or her service'. It also allowed servants to apply to magistrates for the collection of unpaid wages below £5 or £10, depending upon their trade, and to be released from their agreement. Its provisions were said to apply to any servant in husbandry, 'artificer, handicraftsman, miner, collier, keelman, pitman, glassman, potter, and *other labourer, employed for any certain time, or in any other manner*'. Did the italicized phrase mean that the act applied merely to 'other labourers' in the previously mentioned trades, or to any other

---

[11]　Hay, 'Master and Servant in England', p. 230; Napier, 'Contract of Service', p. 107.

[12]　*Hardy v. Ryle* (1829), 9 B. & C. 603–12; *Lancaster v. Greaves* (1829), 9 B. & C. 627–32; Napier, 'Contract of Service', pp. 108–10, 120; John Orth, *Combination and Conspiracy: A Legal History of Trade Unionism, 1721–1906* (Oxford, 1991, pp. 107–9; Orth, 'Contract and the Common Law', in N. Scheiber (ed.), *State and the Freedom to Contract* (Stanford, 1998), p. 53; T. Tholfsen, *Working Class Radicalism in Mid-Victorian England* (London, 1976), pp. 181–3; B. W. Haines, 'English Labour Law and the Separation from Contract', *The Journal of Legal History* 1/3 (December 1980): 268–9; Steinfeld, *Coercion*, p. 47; Hay, 'Master and Servant in England', pp. 240–245.

[13]　20 George II, c.19 (1747); 6 George III, c.25 (1766); 4 George IV, c.34 (1823).

laborer in any trade? The higher courts offered conflicting answers to the question between 1796 and 1837.[14]

The 1766 statute, 'An Act for the Better Regulating of Apprentices, and Persons Working Under Contract', applied to the same trades as the 1747 Act, with the addition of calico printers.[15] At the end of the listing of the trades covered by the statute, however, where the 1747 Act used the phrase 'and other labourers', the 1766 statute placed the words 'labourers, and others'.[16] This separation could have been interpreted by reasonable magistrates as inviting an even broader scope than the 1747 Act.

In 1801 a parliamentary committee acknowledged that magistrates were often confused about their jurisdiction to hear master and servant disputes, and employers would benefit from an interpretation of these laws which enlarged their reach. They concluded that the existing jurisdiction under these laws was deficient because of the strict reading the statutes were sometimes given by the higher courts. The committee recommended that Parliament explicitly grant magistrates the authority to hear cases involving job and piece workers as well as trades not mentioned in the statutes, particularly domestic servants and menial workers.[17] Parliament took no action on the committee's recommendations.

In 1823, as part of an effort by Joseph Hume to ease politically the repeal of the Combination Acts, another general Master and Servant Bill was enacted that consolidated a number of earlier statutes. This act probably provided the basis for most of the master and servant prosecutions in the nineteenth century. The statute borrowed the language of the 1766 Act to define the jurisdiction it conferred. In the third clause, after listing the trades the act covered, the drafters added the still broader phrase 'or other labourer, or other person, [who], shall contract with any person or persons whomsoever, to serve him, her, or them, for any time or times whatsoever, or in any other manner'.[18] The framers of this statute seem to have

---

[14]   Italics added. 20 George II, c.19 (1747); Napier, 'Contract of Service', pp. 86–7, 105.

[15]   The 1766 Act was harsh even by the standards of master and servant law. It contained no provisions for the collection of unpaid wages or protection for cruelly treated apprentices and lengthened the period of imprisonment for offending workers to a minimum of one month and a maximum of three. Steinfeld, *Coercion*, pp. 44–5; Hay, 'Master and Servant in England', pp. 240–45.

[16]   6 George III, c.25 (1766).

[17]   'The Report on the Laws Between Masters and Servants' (1801) *Parliamentary Papers*, Vol. III (62), p. 135; Napier, 'Contract of Service', pp. 81–8.

[18]   4 George IV, c.34 (1823). The penal sanctions for workers remained at a maximum of three months imprisonment, and the amount of unpaid wages collectable £10. None of the statutes consolidated by this act were repealed. Napier, 'Contract of Service', p. 103; Daphne Simon, 'Master and Servant', in J. Saville (ed.), *Democracy and the Labour Movement: Essays in Honour of Donna Torr* (London, 1954), pp. 171–3; Hay, 'Master and Servant in England', pp. 251–2, 255; D. George, 'The Combination Laws', *Economic*

intended a very wide jurisdiction even though they retained the listing of specific trades.[19]

Because the two broad questions of the precise definition of the relationship of service, and the trades to which master and servant acts applied remained ambiguous in the legislation, an opening existed for the higher courts to participate in the law-making process.[20] One important case on this subject was Lowther v. the Earl of Radnor (1806). In 1804, Mr Lowther of Wiltshire promised to pay two menial laborers to dig a well. When the men completed their job, Lowther refused to pay them. The disgruntled men sued Lowther in order to collect their unpaid wages under the 1747 Act. When Lowther failed to answer the summons, the two sitting magistrates awarded the plaintiffs £4 13s 6d in back wages. Lowther appealed this ruling to the Quarter Sessions, where a panel of magistrates upheld the order, and charged him an extra £2 in costs. When he refused to satisfy the judgment, the magistrates ordered a distress upon his goods.

This provoked Lowther to bring suit against the magistrates for trespass, claiming that they had no jurisdiction to determine the case or remove his possessions to satisfy their judgment. The case was appealed to King's Bench, where the issue was 'whether or not the apparently compendious phrase "other labourers" (used in the 1747 Act to determine its scope) should be interpreted to cover a person employed to dig wells'.[21]

Chief Justice Ellenborough and the Court ruled the magistrates had jurisdiction to determine the case, because 'unless these words "other labourers" mean to comprehend a different description of persons from those before particularly mentioned, it is difficult to account for their insertion at all'. He declared that 'the words of the act extended to servants in husbandry, to workmen in different branches of trade, and to other labourers employed for any certain time, or in any other manner', including the ones that Lowther had refused to pay.[22] In ruling for the magistrates, Ellenborough had greatly, though temporarily, expanded their jurisdiction to hear master and servant cases.

By the second quarter of the nineteenth century this situation had changed considerably. When presented with writs of habeas corpus and certiorari, judges closely scrutinized magistrates' forms for legal errors, and adopted a much narrower reading of the Master and Servant Acts. One legal journalist of the time observed that 'summary convictions are proceedings by no means in favour with our courts

---

History Review 6/2 (April 1936): 172–8; D. C. Coleman, 'Combinations of Capital and Labour in the Paper Industry, 1790–1825', *Economica* 21/1 (February 1954): 32–54.

[19]   Steinfeld, *Coercion*, p. 48.

[20]   Hay, 'Master and Servant in England', p. 230.

[21]   20 George II, c.19 (1747); quote from: Steinfeld, *Coercion*, p. 126; *Lowther v. the Earl of Radnor* (1806), 8 East 113–24; Napier, 'Contract of Service', p. 107.

[22]   Alternatively, Ellenborough might have asked why the legislature bothered to insert a list of so many specific trades in the statutes if it had intended the act to apply generally. *Lowther v. Earl of Radnor* (1806), 8 East 124–5; Steinfeld, *Coercion*, p. 126.

... [and] there is no denying that they are still watched with considerable jealousy by the judges of the superior courts'.[23] Four of these cases before the Court of King's Bench had direct relevance to the 1844 bill, as they were frequently cited by barristers and legal journalists when debating the reach of master and servant law.

In 1828, Thomas Hardy of Macclesfield agreed to weave some silk in his home for Thomas Hall, but neglected to complete his work. Hall brought Hardy before magistrate John Ryle under the 1823 Act, where Hardy was found guilty and sentenced to imprisonment for one month. Upon his release, Hardy brought a civil suit against Ryle for trespass and false imprisonment, arguing that Ryle had exceeded his jurisdiction.

The issue at stake was whether a relationship of master and servant existed between Hardy and Hall. The barristers for Hardy argued that the 1823 Act, 'clearly applies only to contracts of service; and a person cannot be said to become the servant of another, unless he enters into his service exclusively'.[24] Hardy had agreed only to perform the specific task of weaving particular pieces of silk, and could have taken in additional work from other masters. Justices Bayley and Littledale agreed, ruling that 4 George IV, c.34 (1823) clearly stipulated that for a magistrate to have jurisdiction there must be a contract to serve between the parties. Bayley emphasized that in a relationship of service the employer had to be able to claim the exclusive service of the employee at all reasonable hours.[25]

The case of *Lancaster v. Greaves* (1829) was decided on similar grounds. Lancaster made an agreement to build a carriage road, but stopped his work before it was completed. His employer summoned him before a magistrate under 4 George IV, c.34 (1823), and had him convicted to one month's imprisonment. Like Hardy, Lancaster sued the convicting magistrate for trespass and false imprisonment on the grounds that independent contracting was not a relationship of service, 'but a contract between parties who remained equal'.[26] When the case reached King's Bench, Littledale and Bayley agreed, employing a similar definition of service to that used in *Hardy v. Ryle*. Because these two cases turned on the definition of the relationship of service, rather than the meaning of the phrase 'other labourers' in the statutes, they could both be reconciled with Ellenborough's ruling in *Lowther*. Master and servant law could still be applied to all trades ('other labourers'), as long as a contract of service existed.

---

[23]   Quote from 'Claim of Right as a Defense to Summary Convictions', *JP* 11/45 (6 November 1848), pp. 785–6; W. R. Cornish and G. de N. Clark, *Law and Society in England 1750–1950* (London, 1989), pp. 34–6; Steinfeld, *Coercion*, p. 127; Smith, 'Circumventing the Jury', pp. 197–230.

[24]   4 George IV, c.34 (1823); *Hardy v. Ryle* (1829), 9 B. & C. 611; Steinfeld, *Coercion*, pp. 129–30.

[25]   *Hardy v. Ryle* (1829), 9 B. & C. 611–12; Napier, 'Contract of Service', pp. 117–19.

[26]   *Lancaster v. Greaves* (1829), 9 B. & C. 628–32; Napier, 'Contract of Service', pp. 86, 107, 111–12; Steinfeld, *Coercion*, pp. 127–8.

These cases were of considerable importance, because by emphasizing the exclusivity necessary for a master and servant relationship, King's Bench had in effect excluded nearly all work that was done by the job, task or piece from the jurisdiction of magistrates under 'general' master and servant acts. In many regions of England, work by the job or piece was the most common type of employment. After 1829, a servant in husbandry who had contracted to work for a year could collect unpaid wages using 4 George IV, c.34 (1823), while an agricultural laborer who agreed to hoe a field could not, *even though the two might work side by side.*

The case of *Bramwell v. Penneck* (1827) was really about preventing the expansion of magistrates' jurisdiction in master and servant cases to unacceptable categories of workers. Bramwell, a Cornwall attorney, hired Mr Richards, a clerk, to keep possession some items. Their agreement 'appears to have been informal and excessively vague in its terms', and Bramwell refused to pay Richards.[27] Richards summoned Bramwell before a magistrate to recover his wages under 20 George II, c.19 (1747), arguing that he was a laborer. The plaintiff was probably stretching the meaning of the phrase 'other labourers' further than Ellenborough had envisioned. When the magistrate ordered Bramwell to pay Richards wages and costs, he refused, resulting in a distress on his goods. Bramwell sued the magistrate for trespass and break and enter, arguing that the statute granted no jurisdiction to hear this case because the phrase 'other labourers' did not include the type of work that Richards performed. Mr Justice Bayley agreed, ruling that 'it seems to me that Richards was not that sort of labourer, nor the service rendered by him that sort of labour, which is mentioned and intended in 20 George II, c.19'.[28] This case was still largely reconcilable with *Lowther v. Earl of Radnor*, because one could still interpret the phrase 'other labourers' fairly broadly, even if King's Bench had put certain types of non-manual work outside its meaning.

Ten years later the case of *Kitchen v. Shaw* (1837) reversed Lowther, and greatly restricted the jurisdiction of magistrates in master and servant cases. Kitchen was a 14-year-old domestic servant employed by Mr Hobson. After a conflict over her wages, she left his house, prompting him to charge her with unlawful absence under 6 George III, c.25 (1766). Magistrate Shaw found her guilty and committed her to prison for one month. After her release, she brought a suit against Shaw for false imprisonment. As with the previous cases, it reached Queen's Bench on appeal.

Kitchen's barristers argued that 6 George III, c.25 (1766) did not give Shaw the power to hear disputes involving domestic servants because such employment was not explicitly named in that statute. The court was once again asked to define that confusing phrase 'labourers, or other persons'. Lord Chief Justice Denman reversed Lowther, ruling 'we find ourselves compelled to say that "other persons" are not all persons whatever who enter into engagements to serve for stated periods, but

[27] Napier, 'Contract of Service', p. 111.

[28] *Bramwell v. Penneck* (1827), 7 B. & C. 536–42, quote from 539; Steinfeld, *Coercion*, p. 127.

persons of the same description of those before enumerated'.[29] By ruling that Shaw had acted without jurisdiction, Denman excluded from magistrates' jurisdiction all types of labor not explicitly listed in the applicable master and servant statute.

Employers and magistrates found these four decisions inconvenient, and hoped to reverse them with the 1844 Master and Servant Bill. Robert Palmer was one of the bill's three sponsors and had served as a justice of the peace in Berkshire and Wiltshire before beginning his 30-year career in Parliament. He understood that the narrow interpretation of these acts that prevailed in the superior courts failed to meet the demands of employers for maintaining labor discipline while creating headaches for magistrates. In May of 1844 he pleaded to the Lower House that 'An alteration in the law had become advisable in consequence of some recent decisions of the Court of Queen's Bench' which made administering master and servant law more confusing for magistrates and less convenient for employers.[30]

Interpreting Master and Servant Law in Petty Sessions, 1842–8

To what extent did these high court rulings affect the manner in which magistrates conducted master and servant hearings? There is evidence that magistrates found these high court rulings confusing and difficult to reconcile with the needs of local employers at the exact moment when the more frequent presence of solicitors at Petty Sessions sometimes made it dangerous to apply their own interpretation.[31] They complained regularly about this situation, often in the pages of the *Justice of the Peace*.

Keeping up to date with the rulings of the courts in Westminster could present a challenge for magistrates. These officers sometimes relied upon legally trained clerks and manuals or handbooks (for example Burns' *Justice of the Peace*) for assistance in accurately interpreting and understanding the law.[32] Additionally, they could turn to the *Justice of the Peace*, an authoritative weekly law journal that contained articles, commentary on high court decisions and editorials related to the duties of magistrates. It also provided a weekly question and answer section, called 'Practical Points', in which magistrates (or interested parties) wrote asking for advice on cases before them. Between 1842 and 1848, questions and answers in 'Practical Points' relating to the jurisdiction of magistrates in master and servant cases were common. There were also articles and editorials complaining about the difficulty and dangers magistrates faced when enforcing master and servant

---

[29]   *Kitchen v. Shaw* (1837), 6 A. & E. 729–35. Quote from p. 734. Her counsel also raised the fact that she was a minor, but the court did not rule on this ground.

[30]   *Hansard Debates*, Vol. 79, col. 530.

[31]   Steinfeld, *Coercion*, p. 133; Smith, 'Circumventing the Jury', p. 226.

[32]   Sir Thomas Skyrme, *History of the Justice of the Peace* (3 vols., Chichester, 1991), Vol. 2, pp. 48–9, 67–8; D. Bentley, *English Criminal Justice in the Nineteenth Century* (London, 1998), pp. 22–3, 25–6; Hay, 'England 1562–1875', pp. 71–7.

law, including: (1) confusion over the extent of their jurisdiction; (2) questions about the technical requirements for making valid convictions and warrants of commitment in summary hearings; and (3) queries about the criteria necessary to form a binding contract. Robert Steinfeld has identified these three broad categories of query by magistrates as the three major fronts in the 'struggle over the rules' of master and servant law waged by Parliament, the high courts, employers and labor during the second quarter of the nineteenth century. The first category provided much of the stimulus for 1844 bill, and the other two areas of confusion will be addressed in detail in Chapter 3.[33]

Many magistrates were confused about the definition of 'servant', settled by *Hardy v. Ryle* and *Lancaster v. Greaves*. One correspondent asked if job and piece workers were covered under the master and servant statutes, adding that recent articles had 'occasioned considerable doubts in the bench with which I act, as to the class of persons for whom orders may safely be made'.[34] Others appeared oblivious to such developments, convicting under the statutes in cases where they lacked jurisdiction. 'A Magistrate', wrote that he was stunned to discover that master and servant statutes were applicable only in cases where a contract to serve existed. In his region, 'magistrates have very generally acted where there is strictly no contract to serve, but only to do a piece of work, supposing they had the authority to do so under ... Lowther v. the Earl of Radnor'.[35]

Many justices of the peace, using the example of the laborers digging wells found in *Lowther v. the Earl of Radnor*, wondered if their jurisdiction extended to cover individuals hired for specific short-term projects. They asked if they could hear cases involving men hired specifically to produce well pipes, build dams, dig wells, construct mill-ponds or transport items on a canal. In every case, the legal experts of the *Justice of the Peace* responded that magistrates should refrain from hearing these types of disputes, because they involved agreements to do jobs or tasks, not contracts to serve.[36] One 'Original Subscriber' complained that 'The judges seem to wish to construe the statute as strictly as possible'.[37]

---

[33] D. Daintree, 'The Legal Periodical: A Study in the Communication of Information' (PhD dissertation, University of Sheffield, 1975), pp. 187–90; Steinfeld, *Coercion*, pp. 104–6.

[34] 'Practical Points', *JP* 8/26 (29 June 1844), p. 446.

[35] 'Practical Points', *JP* 7/32 (12 August 1843), p. 484. For other examples see, 'Practical Points', *JP* 6/9 (26 February 1842), p. 110; 'Town Hall', *PEWA* 1/9 (27 January 1844), p. 72.

[36] See 'Practical Points' in *JP* from the following issues: 6/12 (26 March 1842), p.178; 6/21 (21 May 1842), p. 304; 6/48 (3 December 1842), p. 751; 7/38 (23 September 1843), p. 569; 7/44 (4 November 1843), p. 663; 8/50 (14 December 1844), p. 830; 10/19 (9 May 1846), p. 302; 'Claims for Wages', *Manchester and Salford Advertiser* (hereafter, *MSA*) (31 May 1845), p. 5.

[37] Quote from: 'Practical Points', *JP* 6/26 (2 July 1842), p. 399. For similar queries, see: 'Practical Points', *JP* 6/15 (16 April 1842), p. 222; 'Practical Points', *JP* 6/26 (2 July

These letters reveal that the difference between a contract to serve and an agreement to do a job was often quite subtle. On three different occasions the *Justice of the Peace* informed questioners from the building trades that a contract to provide 18,000 bricks was a contract to do a task (and beyond magistrates' jurisdiction), but an agreement to make bricks generally for a period of time was a contract to serve.[38] Similarly, miners who contracted to produce specific quantities of limestone, copper or coal created considerable doubt among readers of this journal. In many mining areas, including parts of South Wales and South Staffordshire, mine owners contracted with subcontractors called 'butties' to mine coal at a fixed rate per ton. The butty would then hire the workers and provide the small supplies. Under this arrangement it appeared that the butty could not use master and servant statutes to collect unpaid wages from the employer.[39] Magistrates in agricultural regions also learned from 'Practical Points' the distinction between a worker hired for the harvest (a contract to serve) and one hired to harvest 122 acres of corn (a contract to do a job).[40]

Letters written to 'Practical Points' often expressed a concern that master and servant law, as it was currently interpreted, no longer applied to the reality of employment relationships in many regions of the country. One magistrate pleaded that in his district 'the practice of employing husbandry labourers by the job is becoming every year more prevalent, and advantage is frequently taken of it to commit gross injustice, under the notion that the magistrates have no jurisdiction' when disputes arose.[41] Another justice from a mining region complained that 'as nine men out of ten in this district work by the piece or contract, the authority of magistrates can hardly in any case be appealed to'. Another letter noted that because 'it has long been the custom here among agriculturalists to put out their work, as it is here called "by the great" or "by the piece" ... the bench has invariably declined in making any order' in master and servant disputes.[42] Cottage manufacture remained common for most of the nineteenth century, and letters reveal that magistrates could scarcely believe that these employment relationships were outside their jurisdiction. A writer for the *Justice of the Peace* acknowledged that 'the statutes

---

1842), p. 399.

[38]   'Practical Points', *JP* 6/13 (2 April 1842), pp. 190–191; 'Practical Points', *JP* 10/26 (27 June 1842), p. 413; 'Practical Points', *JP* 11/29 (17 July 1847), p. 525.

[39]   See 'Practical Points', from the following issues of the *JP*: 6/37 (17 September 1842), p. 574; 8/10 (15 March 1844), p. 189; 9/47 (22 November 1845), pp. 766–7; 10/44 (31 October 1846), p. 702; 11/20 (15 May 1847), pp. 363–4; 11/31 (31 July 1847), p. 559.

[40]   'Practical Points', *JP* 7/34 (26 August 1843), pp. 500–501; 'Practical Points', *JP* 8/33 (17 August 1844), p. 558; 'Practical Points', *JP* 8/39 (28 September 1844), p. 651.

[41]   'Practical Points', *JP* 12/15 (8 April 1848), p. 236.

[42]   'Practical Points', *JP* 6/3 (22 January 1842), p. 32; 'Practical Points', *JP* 6/6 (12 February 1842), p. 81.

relating to master and servant are nearly useless' in many parts of the country.[43] Another essayist complained that this narrow interpretation of the statutes' scope had 'nearly nullified the statutes, they cannot be safely executed'.[44]

Between July and October of every year, 'Practical Points' filled with queries relating to the extent of magistrates' jurisdiction over agricultural laborers, particularly those hired by the job. Since the late eighteenth century, the practice of the yearly hiring in agriculture was becoming less common. One magistrate argued in favor of hiring by the job because it was 'injurious to the farmer to hire his harvestmen monthly, as advantage would be taken by delay, and his crops much injured'.[45] Several magistrates wrote to ask if master and servant law applied to the numerous cases in which farmers hired laborers to perform tasks in specific quantities, such as mowing, plowing, threshing, reaping, spreading peat, grubbing, cleansing or picking a field. The *Justice of the Peace* always advised against acting in such cases.[46]

It is clear that magistrates often felt pressure to hear and determine cases under these acts where there was not a master and servant relationship. There are several examples of magistrates convicting workers unlawfully under these acts. Convicting a worker in a case where he lacked jurisdiction could expose a magistrate to expense, embarrassment and damages.[47]

Another set of questions to 'Practical Points' dealt with the meaning of the phrase 'other labourers' that was defined expansively in Lowther, and then narrowed in *Kitchen v. Shaw*. Correspondents wrote to ask if the phrase 'other labourers' gave them the authority to hear cases involving nursery governesses,

---

[43]   Quote from 'Practical Points', *JP* 7/48 (3 December 1843), p. 751. For queries on cottage manufacture, see: 'Practical Points', *JP* 6/11 (12 March 1842), p. 141; 'Practical Points', *JP* 7/28 (15 July 1843), p. 409. The *Justice of the Peace* never suggested using the 1777 or 1843 Acts referenced by Steinfeld.

[44]   'Practical Points', *JP* 8/38 (21 September 1844), p. 636.

[45]   Quote from 'Practical Points', *JP* 6/29 (23 June 1842), p. 449. On the yearly hiring, see: A. Kussmaul, *Servants in Husbandry in Early Modern England* (Cambridge, 1981); K. D. M. Snell, *Annals of the Labouring Poor: Social Change and Agrarian England, 1660–1900* (Cambridge, 1985).

[46]   From 'Practical Points' in the following issues of *JP*: 6/16 (16 April 1842), p. 220; 6/25 (25 June 1842), p. 380; 6/29 (23 July 1842), p. 449; 6/36 (10 September 1842), p. 555; 7/13 (1 April 1843), p. 170; 7/29 (22 July 1843), p. 426; 7/32 (12 August 1843), p. 470; 7/34 (26 August 1843), pp. 501–3; 7/43 (28 October 1843), p. 649; 8/27 (6 July 1844), p. 459; 8/33 (17 August 1844), p. 558; 8/35 (31 August 1844), p. 591; 8/39 (28 September 1844), p. 651; 9/21 (7 June 1845), p. 349; 9/23 (21 June 1845), p. 394; 9/39 (20 September 1845), p. 602; 9/39 (27 September 1845), p. 624; 10/26 (27 June 1846), p. 412; 10/44 (31 October 1846), p. 698; 11/42 (16 October 1847), p. 748; 12/12 (18 March 1848), p. 185.

[47]   For three examples of suits for false imprisonment, see: NA: HO 43/67, 171–2 (13 July 1844), 314–15 (24 August 1844); J. H. Morris and L. J. Williams, *The South Wales Coal Industry, 1841–1875* (Cardiff, 1958), pp. 267–8; *Lindsay v. Leigh* (1848), described in Chapter 3, this volume.

masters and matrons of workhouses, butchers, coal meters, millers, stewards, blacksmiths and dozens of other trades. There were also queries about bricklayers, masons, plasterers, tray makers, shopmen, plumbers, glaziers, dressmakers, cinder burners, inn keepers, trammers, twig basket makers, maltsters, blazers and many others. The *Justice of the Peace* always responded by citing *Kitchen v. Shaw.*[48] The considerable expansion of railways in the 1830s and 1840s produced numerous queries regarding magistrates' jurisdiction over railway laborers.[49] Many magistrates clung tightly to *Lowther v. Earl of Radnor*. In December of 1844, a Lancashire magistrate insisted over the objections of Roberts that the 1823 Master and Servant statute comprehended all descriptions of servants, wrongfully convicting an engineer who raised and lowered tubs into a coal pit to a month's imprisonment with hard labor.[50]

So frequent were questions relating to 'other labourers' and *Kitchen v. Shaw* that in 1846 the journal devoted a two-page article to the subject, apologizing that 'if our readers are not yet tired of this subject, we know who else is'. It went on to recommend that magistrates, 'unless they have a magnanimous disregard for actions and damages', they should refrain from interpreting the phrase '"other labourers" … as one of any significance in its place in these statutes'.[51] An essay from the year before warned that although 'the wisdom of these decisions may be questionable', magistrates had to follow the interpretation of 'other labourers' endorsed by the higher courts.[52] Complaining about the outcome of a recent case litigated by Roberts, an author warned that 'according to the construction put

---

[48]   'Practical Points' in the following issues of *JP*: 6/4 (29 January 1842), p. 45; 6/14 (26 March 1842), p. 178; 6/39 (1 October 1842), p. 465; 6/52 (31 December 1842), p. 819; 7/9 (4 March 1843), p. 98; 7/38 (23 September 1843), p. 570; 7/44 (4 November 1843), pp. 665–6; 8/15 (13 April 1844), p. 252; 8/41 (12 October 1844), p. 682; 9/13 (30 March 1845), p. 203; 9/34 (23 August 1845), p. 541; 9/40 (4 October 1845), p. 653; 9/43 (25 October 1845), p. 702; 9/48 (29 November 1845), p. 781; 9/49 (6 December 1845), p. 795; 10/2 (10 January 1846), p. 31; 10/30 (25 July 1846), p. 473; 10/51 (19 December 1846), p. 827; 11/1 (2 January 1847), p. 14; 11/5 (30 January 1847), p. 79; 11/17 (24 April 1847), p. 302; 12/26 (24 June 1848), p. 415. Also see: NA: KB 1/125/38. 'Ex Parte Cresswell', *JP* 8/46 (16 November 1844), p. 758.

[49]   'Servants – Form of Commitment – Railway Labourers, Whether Within the Act', *JP* 9/49 (6 December 1845), pp. 785–6; 'To the Editor of the Justice of the Peace' and 'To the Editor of the Justice of the Peace', *JP* 9/49 (6 December 1845), p. 799. Also see 'Practical Points' from the following issues of the *JP*: 7/47 (25 November 1843), p. 711; 6/30 (30 July 1842), p. 465; 7/51 (23 December 1843), p. 773; 7/43 (21 October 1843), p. 634; 8/38 (21 September 1844), p. 636; 9/25 (22 June 1845), p. 411; 11/14 (3 April 1847), p. 252; 11/31 (31 July 1847), p. 559.

[50]   *MSA* (4 January 1845), p. 5.

[51]   'Servants; Meaning of the Word "Labourer," in 6 George III, c.23, s.4, and 4 George IV, c.34, ss.3, 4. In Re: James Lord', *JP* 10/47 (21 November 1846), pp. 753–4.

[52]   'Servants – Form of Commitment – Railway Labourers, Whether Within the Acts', *JP* 9/49 (6 December 1845), pp. 785–6.

on these words, by our course of law ... they have little or no meaning, and no justice of the peace can safely act upon them'.[53] William Miles, one of the three co-sponsors of the 1844 bill, declared 'one of the main reasons for the bill was to define the term "other persons" which had been registered in the respective courts to persons *ejusdem generis*'. Another of the co-sponsors, Gally Knight, used the perceived absurdity of 'other persons' to argue for the bill's passage:

> If an agricultural labourer comes to me, as a magistrate, and represents that he has been reaping, or hedging, and cannot get the money which is due to him, I am obliged to say, 'I am very sorry for you; if you had been making pots I could have assisted you, because a potter is named in the act, but as you have only been reaping, I can do nothing for you'.[54]

The extent of magisterial annoyance regarding *Kitchen v. Shaw* is revealed by the number of questions regarding jurisdiction over domestic servants, which was explicitly settled by that case. 'A Magistrate's Clerk' wrote to complain that in his 'practical experience' the law of master and servant had become 'very inconvenient and unsatisfactory' in its scope. He argued that 'with reference to domestic servants ... there seems no good reason why that numerous class of servants should be without the justices' jurisdiction'.[55] Another law journal, the *Legal Observer*, agreed that 'the magistrates are not, however, enabled to interfere regarding domestic servants, the reason for which we do not perceive. We believe that there is a general wish that such powers be given'.[56] Curiously, domestic servants were the only class of laborers specifically exempted from the jurisdiction of magistrates in the 1844 bill, in spite of Mr Barclay's attempts to amend it to include them. The lack of enthusiasm among members of Parliament for including domestic servants in master and servant law was probably due to the large supply

---

[53]   'Recent Decisions Upon the Master and Servants Act', *JP* 8/9 (2 March 1844), pp. 131–2.

[54]   *Hansard Debates*, Vol. 74, cols. 523, 529–30. Concerns over the meaning of 'other person' continued for decades. See the testimony of Sheriff Barclay before the Select Committee on the Laws of Master and Servant. 'Report From the Select Committee on Master and Servant: Together With the Proceedings of the Committee and the Minutes of Evidence, Appendix, and Index', *Parliamentary Papers* (July 1865), Vol. VIII (370), p. 1.

[55]   Quote from 'To the Editors of the Justice of the Peace', *JP* 12/45 (4 November 1848), p. 735. For queries related to domestic servants, see: 'To the Editors of the Justice of the Peace', *JP* 8/12 (23 March 1844), p. 207; 'Recent Decisions under the Master and Servants Act', *JP* 8/9 (2 March 1844), pp. 131–2 and 'Practical Points' from the following issues of the *JP*: 6/52 (31 December 1842), p. 823; 7/12 (25 March 1843), p. 154; 8/15 (13 April 1844), p. 253; 8/41 (12 October 1844), p. 687; 9/33 (6 August 1845), p. 523; 10/30 (25 July 1846), p. 474.

[56]   'The Masters and Servants Bill', *LO* 27 (27 March 1844), p. 406.

of these inexpensive workers and their heavy dependence on employers' references for obtaining future work, making non-pecuniary compulsion unnecessary.[57]

The letters to 'Practical Points' reveal that even magistrates who were well-informed had to struggle with semantic anomalies. Was a domestic servant who also milks cows and feeds chickens a servant in husbandry, and thus within the statutes? What about grooms who helped with farm work? The *Justice of the Peace* warned that 'Indeed the statutes will take a very limited range if all indoor farm servants are held not in the scope of them'.[58] Were men who metered coal onto ships keelmen? A market gardener argued before a magistrate that the women he employed to sell fruit were servants in husbandry and subject to 4 George IV, c.34 (1823). Both employers and servants sometimes played semantic games with job descriptions in order to stretch or evade the reach of master and servant statutes.[59]

Many cases were so anomalous, that even the judges of Queen's Bench could not reach agreement. In September of 1842, calico printer John Hargreaves and his partners engaged Eli Ormond to an exclusive five-year contract to design patterns. In December 1843, Hargreaves charged Ormond with 'misconduct' under 4 George IV, c.34 (1823) for embezzling certain patterns. Immediately after Ormond was convicted and sentenced to three months' imprisonment he moved to quash the conviction on the grounds that he was outside the jurisdiction of the magistrates, because he was not a calico printer. Ormond claimed he was 'an artist' hired 'to form designs and plans and ideas for the production of patterns to be afterwards engraved upon copper rollers'. Ormond insisted that 'he did not at any time do any other business connected with calico printing'.[60]

The majority of Queen's Bench ruled that Ormond was engaged in the business of calico printing, and thus within the jurisdiction of the magistrates. Mr Justice Wightman, however, dissented, arguing 'the magistrates had no jurisdiction in this case'. The occupation of the defendant was not such as to bring him within

---

[57] Hay, 'England, 1562–1955', pp. 88–90; *Hansard Debates*, Vol. 73, col. 1306.

[58] 'Recent Discharges Under the Master and Servants Act', *JP* 8/9 (2 March 1844), pp. 131–2. Another particularly obnoxious case involved a Welsh dairymaid imprisoned for six weeks under 4 George IV, c.34, who actually served longer than her sentence before being discharged. In Re: *Ellen Griffith*. NA: KB 1/120/57; 'Triumph of Labour', *NS* (11 May 1844), p. 4; 'In Re: Ellen Griffith', *JP* 8/20 (18 May 1844), p. 326; 'R v. Ellen Griffith', *JP* 8/22 (1 June 1844), p. 358; 'In Re: Ellen Griffith', *JP* 8/23 (8 June 1844), p. 373; 'R v. Ellen Griffith', *JP* 9/2 (11 January 1845), pp. 23–4; NA: KB 1/225/42. For more queries, see 'Practical Points' in the following issues of the *JP*: 7/25 (24 June 1843), p. 362; 7/29 (22 July 1843); 8/27 (6 July 1844), p. 459; 8/38 (21 September 1844), p. 633; 9/1 (4 January 1845), p. 12.

[59] For examples, see 'Practical Points' from the following issues of the *JP*: 6/36 (10 September 1842), p. 563; 7/44 (4 November 1843), pp. 665–6; 10/27 (4 July 1846), p. 430; 10/33 (15 August 1846), p. 527; 11/5 (30 January 1847), p. 79; 11/16 (17 April 1847), p. 285; 12/23 (3 June 1848), p. 363.

[60] NA: KB 1/117/39; Steinfeld, *Coercion*, pp. 54–6.

the act because 'a designer cannot be considered a labourer. His duties are of a higher character'. Wightman compared the majority's ruling to calling an architect a building laborer.[61] If the judges of Queen's Bench could not agree on the trades covered, perhaps it was too much to expect consistency from magistrates.

As reports of successful actions against magistrates' rulings increased, the *Justice of the Peace* took up the cause of demanding that Parliament and Queen's Bench provide greater support and protection for magistrates when enforcing these 'troublesome acts'.[62] One writer editorialized that 'There are few if any subjects within the cognizance of justices which occasion them more difficulty than these ... ill-omened acts' because 'they have been construed with a strictness which is not surpassed by the decisions on any branch of the law, and which is equaled in but a few'.[63] A similar article on high court rulings related to master and servant law suggested that 'the judges have departed very widely from the original intention of the legislature'. The author recommended that 'except in cases of absolute certainty justices should decline to act under statutes which serve only to entrap them, and involve them in costs and damages'.[64] A year later, the *Justice of the Peace* lamented that because of 'the annoyances and expenses of an action for false imprisonment ... summary jurisdiction has become, in short, a trap to catch unwary justices'.[65] In 1845, the *Justice of the Peace* warned 'for the one hundredth time, that as a construction so vague has been laid upon these acts, the safest way is to keep ... to the very letter of them'.[66] In 1843, the journal's lead article was devoted to desirable legislation that Parliament could pass in the coming session. Of its priorities, 'foremost is an act to explain and amend the acts relating to servants and justices' jurisdiction over them', because as they were currently interpreted they were of 'very limited utility'.[67] Five years later, 'magistrates ... need[ed] no reminding of the truth' that master and servant law remained 'in a most anomalous and unsatisfactory state'. Expanding magistrates' jurisdiction

---

[61]   'Ex Parte Ormond', *JP* 8/31 (3 August 1844), pp. 521–2.

[62]   'The Contract Between Master and Servant Necessary for Giving Justices Jurisdiction in Differences Between Them', *JP* 6/33 (20 August 1842); 'Form of Adjudication under the 20 George II, c.19 & 4 George IV, c.34', *JP* 8/30 (27 July 1844), p. 498; 'Practical Points', *JP* 8/23 (8 June 1844), pp. 381–2; 'Liability of Justices of the Peace in the Exercise of Summary Jurisdiction', *JP* 9/5 (1 February 1845), pp. 65–6.

[63]   'Proceedings in Matters Relating to Servants', *JP* 12/41 (7 October 1848), pp. 657–8.

[64]   'The Recent Discharges on Writs of Habeas Corpus, of Persons Committed Under the Statutes Relating to Servants, Artificers, etc', *JP* 8/20 (18 May 1844), pp. 323–4.

[65]   'Actions Against Justices For Technical Errors', *JP* 9/12 (22 March 1845), pp. 177–8.

[66]   'Servants – Form of Commitment – Railway Labourers – Whether Within the Acts', *JP* 9/49 (6 December 1845), pp. 785–6.

[67]   'Bills in Parliament Proposed or Required Respecting Summary Jurisdiction', *JP* 7/7 (18 February 1843), pp. 61–2.

in master and servant cases was considered desirable to 'afford protection and encouragement to its administrators' who were caused 'so much trouble and anxiety' by the current state of the law.[68] By widening magistrates' jurisdiction, the 1844 bill would have removed several grounds upon which their decisions could be challenged. It is hardly surprising that they were among the bill's most vocal supporters, and the most disappointed when the measure was dropped.[69]

Labor's Campaign Against Master and Servant Law, 1843–1844

The demands of employers and magistrates for a more comprehensive act were the direct result of organized labor's more determined resistance to employers' use of master and servant law. Between 1843 and 1848, in many parts of the country trade unions challenged the perceived partnership between employers and the magistracy in enforcing these laws through the use of speeches, pamphlets, newspaper editorials, direct protest against specific magistrates and, most importantly, the use of legal counsel. Toward this end, on 11 August 1843, the miners of Northumberland and Durham hired W. P. Roberts to provide their membership with legal representation for a reported salary of £1,000 during the first year, and £500 per year thereafter.[70]

Master and servant litigation was central to the strategy of the National Miners' Association, which sought to improve conditions for its members in the north by undermining their employers' use of these laws to enforce an unfavorable interpretation of their bond. The bond was an unequal contract of employment that miners in the northeast were required to sign. In Northumberland and Durham, the terms of this eleven-and-a-half-month contract were set by an employers' combination known as 'the vend', which carefully timed the binding day to fall during a period when demand for coal was low and miners' desperation for work was high.[71] In 1843, Benjamin Embleton, a miner, described how mine owners

---

[68] 'On the Present State of the Law of Master and Servant', *JP* 12/44 (28 October 1848), pp. 705–6.

[69] 'Masters and Servants', *JP* 8/9 (2 March 1844), pp. 154–5; 'Masters and Servants; Extent and Effect of the Lost Bill', *JP* 8/18 (4 May 1844), p. 290; 'To the Editors of the Justice of the Peace', *JP* 8/20 (18 May 1844), p. 335.

[70] 'From the Newcastle Journal', *Durham Advertiser* (hereafter, *DA*) (1 September 1843), p. 3; 'From the Morning Herald', *DA* (29 December 1843), p. 3; Challinor and Ripley, *Miners Association*, p. 9; Welbourne, *The Miners' Unions of Northumberland and Durham* (Cambridge, 1923), pp. 66–7; Richard Fynes, *The Miners of Northumberland and Durham: A History of their Social and Political Progress* (Wakefield, 1873), Chapter 8; Challinor, *Radical Lawyer*, p. 21.

[71] Challinor and Ripley, *Miners' Association*, Chapter 6. James Jaffe argues that while in most years after 1826 the main clauses of the bond were standard and not subject to negotiation, the variety of conditions between pits necessitated some flexibility in the terms,

exploited the pitmen's desperate need for work to force them into accepting a highly unfavorable contract every April:

> The coal owners ... have a standing union with regular meetings for combined action. At these meetings they ascertain how many unbound men each of them have in his employ, and five or six weeks before the binding, the unbound men are discharged. Of course they soon have empty pockets and hungry bellies. The consequence was ... that when binding morning came, the unbound men were such as to be close to 'clagged' up against the office door to accept whatever terms were offered ... It was thus out of the power of the pitmen to have a voice in the terms of the bond. When binding morning come, and the viewer ... saw the hungry unbound men coming up the road and clustered around the office door ... he ... began his speech by saying 'We're not going to bind so many this year as last.' Then the poor hewers pressed still nearer to the door, and cared little what was in the bond when they heard it read.[72]

Any violations of this agreement by miners were punishable by three months imprisonment at hard labor.

The regional contract was highly advantageous to employers, for it left only one time per year when miners could legally strike. It bound pitmen to work exclusively for their employer, but provided owners with a wide range of tools for controlling the actual amount of wages paid. These included the discretion to fine workers, to 'set aside' corves of coal deemed to contain too much 'foul' rock, and to keep men idle for up to five days per week without paying them.[73]

---

allowing for some 'colliery-level bargaining'. Jaffe, *Striking a Bargain: Work and Industrial Relations in England 1815–1865* (Manchester, 2000), pp. 128–9, 162–76; Jaffe, 'Industrial Arbitration, Equity, and Authority in England, 1800–50', *Law and History Review* 18/3 (Fall 2000): 543–9. For divergent views, see: 'Report of the Select Committee on Master and Servant' (1866), pp. 24–33, 40–47, 55–9, 63–81, 93–106; Robert Colls, *The Pitmen of the Northern Coalfield: Work, Culture, and Protest, 1790–1850* (Manchester, 1987), pp. 67, 70, 293–4; Challinor, *Radical Lawyer*, p. 85; Tholfsen, *Working Class Radicalism*, p. 186; S. Webb, *Story of the Durham Miners (1622–1921)* (London, 1921), pp. 8–10, 12–15.

[72]   Challinor, *Radical Lawyer*, pp. 85–6.

[73]   Mitchell, *What do the Pitmen Want?*, in *Repeal of the Combination Acts* (London, 1972), pp. 6, 11–12, 14–16, 18; 'West Holywell Colliery', *Miners' Advocate* (hereafter *MA*) 1/2 (16 December 1843), p. 10; 'Case of the Thornley Men', *MA* 1/3 (30 December 1843), p. 20; 'The Collier's Bond', *NS* (6 January 1844), p. 3; 'The Collier's Movement', *NS* (6 April 1844), p. 7; 'Brethren in Bondage', *NS* (27 April 1844), p. 8; 'The Colliers' Strike', *NS* (4 May 1844), p. 4; 'The Miners' Magazine – May', *NS* (25 May 1844), p. 2; 'The State of the Colliery Districts in the North', *The Times* (18 April 1844), p. 6; 'The Colliers' Strike', *The Times* (4 April 1844), p. 7; 'The Pitmen's Strike', *The Morning Chronicle* (hereafter, *MC*) (11 April 1844), p. 3; Challinor, *Radical Lawyer*, pp. 57, 85–6, 95, 113–14, 129–30; Welbourne, *The Miners' Unions of Northumberland and Durham*, pp. 16–17, 68–9 72–3; Colls, *The Pitmen of the Northern Coalfield*, pp. 64, 73, 293–4; A. J. Taylor,

One miner complained that he 'had not the power to claim one farthing if they chose to construe the bond in its most rigid sense'. He further noted that 'should resistance be made to this detestable tyranny, a magistrate is applied to', who would always rule for the employer.[74] The *Northern Star* charged that this unequal bond combined with master and servant law gave masters complete control over the discipline and costs of their labor:

> the invariable practice being firstly to have the slaves bound no matter how unjust the conditions; and second, to rely upon the summary justice of the district bench as a means of enforcing the most repressive terms, not always putting these conditions into full force, but reserving the power of doing so with the assistance of magistrates as a sure means of compelling their hands to submit.[75]

Roberts was hired to change the manner in which magistrates interpreted and enforced these agreements, as well as to assist miners in writing a new bond that would be the basis of their negotiations with employers in the spring of 1844.[76]

A similar system of labor discipline was exercised in the North Staffordshire pottery trade. The first Parliamentary returns of convictions, beginning in 1858, show that significantly more Staffordshire workers were prosecuted under the Master and Servant Acts than workers from any other county, and a high proportion of these were miners and potters from the northern part of the county.[77] It appears that potters in 1844 suspected as much:

'Entrepreneurial Paternalism: The Third Lord Londonderry and the Coal Trade', *Durham University Journal* 33 (1973–4): 253; Jaffe, *Striking a Bargain*, p. 163.

[74]   W. Mitchell, 'The Question Answered: What do the Pitmen Want?' (Newcastle, 1844), published in *Labour Disputes in the Mines: Eight Pamphlets, 1831–1844* (New York, 1972); J. W. Turner, 'Newcastle Miners and the Master and Servant Act, 1830–1862', *Labour History* 30 (1969).

[75]   'The Colliery Bond', *NS* (6 January 1844), p. 4.

[76]   In 1844, the owners refused to consider any of the men's proposals in the bond written by Roberts, or acknowledge the union or its representatives. The 1844 strike is hardly mentioned in Jaffe's descriptions of collective bargaining in the north. See Jaffe, *Striking a Bargain*, Chapters 3–4; 'The Bond Proposed by the Men versus the Bond Proposed by the Owners', *NS* (1 June 1844), p. 3; 'The Miners' Union', *NS* (8 June 1844), p. 1; Colls, *Pitmen of the Northern Coalfield*, 73; Steinfeld, *Coercion*, pp. 109–12.

[77]   Marc Steinberg, 'Capitalist Development, Labour Process and the Law', *American Journal of Sociology* 109/2 (2003), pp. 445–95; 'To The Editor of the Potters' Examiner', *PEWA* 1/8 (20 January 1844), p. 54; 'A Catechism: For the Use of the Swinish Multitude, Necessary to be Had in All Sties', *PEWA* 1/2 (9 December 1843), p. 16; David Philips, 'The Black Country Magistracy, 1835–1860: A Changing Elite and the Exercise of its Power', *Midlands History* 3 (1976), pp. 176–81; Woods, 'Master and Servant'; Wedgwood, *The Staffordshire Pottery*, p. 170; Jaffe, *Striking a Bargain*, p. 127–8; W. H. Warburton, *The History of Trade Union Organization in the North Staffordshire Potteries* (London, 1931), pp. 44–6, 90–98, 105; Steinfeld, *Coercion*, pp. 79–80; also see Chapter 7, this volume.

The most trifling complaint … made … is considered a breach of insubordination, and the poor potter punished accordingly. Magistrate at hand, no sooner said than done – away goes [the potter] … to prison. It is also a notorious fact, that, according to the prison books, there are more committed for trifling or supposed offences from the pottery district than all other parts of the county of Stafford put together.[78]

It was hoped that the more aggressive use of legal counsel might act as a break on this rapid and simple process by which masters could imprison workmen or press them back to work on their terms.

During 1843 and 1844, Roberts defended scores of miners against such prosecutions, and used the same statutes to recover back-wages and assist in the enforcement of the few clauses in the bond favorable to pitmen. Other branches of the National Miners' Association often used Roberts' services, as did unions in other trades. Roberts used a variety of arguments to defend workers against master and servant prosecutions. He sometimes disputed whether the defendant was a servant within the meaning of the act, or was engaged in one of the trades it covered. In other cases he argued that the contract of employment was invalid because it lacked sufficient consideration, or if it was valid, that the master had broken it first by failing to adhere to its terms. Another strategy was to prove that the employer had voided the agreement through illegal activity, such as paying wages in truck or at a public house. He also sometimes claimed that mine-owners voided their contracts by using uninspected, unstamped or inaccurate weighing machines for determining the men's wages. Roberts often used 'variance' (or discrepancies) between the evidence found in the information (the formal charge) and the summons, warrant or testimony of the prosecutor to force magistrates to drop the charge.[79]

John G. H. Owen of Monmouthshire utilized similar strategies when defending pitmen or ironworkers in master and servant prosecutions at local Petty Sessions. Like Roberts, Owen often used every imaginable argument to free his clients and make the hearing a public forum for raising employee grievances. For example, on 18 March 1843, Owen was engaged to defend 10 miners in Newport charged with leaving work to go on strike without serving the proper notice. Owen began his defense of the miners by objecting to the form of the information. An information was the statement under oath by the prosecutor before the magistrate that informed him of an offence within his jurisdiction that required a warrant or a summons. An

---

[78]   'To the Editor of the Potters' Examiner', *PEWA* 1/5 (9 March 1844), p. 116.

[79]   Smith, 'Circumventing the Jury', pp. 189–90; 'Oldham', *ME* (21 March 1846), p. 7; 'The Colliers Strike', *The Times* (4 April 1844), p. 7; 'The Colliers' Strike', *NS* (4 May 1844), p. 4; 'The Colliers' Movement', 'Public Meetings' and 'Colliers Strike', *NS* (18 May 1844), pp. 4, 6; 'Miners' Union', *NS* (8 June 1844), p. 4; 'Practical Points: Coals-Weight – Defective Machine', *JP* 9/2 (11 January 1845), p. 28; Fynes, *Miners of Northumberland and Durham*, pp. 53–4.

information was explicitly required under 4 George IV, c.34 (1823), and the case had to be determined by the same magistrate who first took the information. Owen argued that the information did not contain the name of the magistrate who heard the plaintiff's oath. His objection was overruled.

After the underground agent testified to the terms of the verbal agreement and the men's breach of it, Owen subjected him to a 'severe cross-examination', in which the witness showed considerable 'prevarication' in his answers. Owen demonstrated that the witness was not the actual person who had made the verbal agreement with the defendants, meaning there was no direct evidence of a contract or its specific terms and therefore the men should be released. The magistrates did not accept this argument. Owen then asked the witness about the gaseous state of the pit and its system of ventilation, arguing that if the mine was in a state of imminent danger, the magistrate could not legally compel his clients to continue working there. The witness insisted, unconvincingly, that although an explosion had occurred last December, the mine was perfectly safe. Owen then grilled the witness about a variety of new tasks that the employer had recently introduced which did not add to the miners' wages, and were not part of their agreement or the local custom of the trade. Owen argued that the employer had breached the contract by demanding the extra labor of the men, and had unilaterally increased the size of a ton of coal, the unit by which they were paid. Owen told the bench that he had 'distinctly proved that the employer was the first violator of the contract, for the alleged breaking of which he now seeks to send these poor men to prison. When contracts are entered into should not the masters be obliged to observe conditions as well as the men?'. The magistrates were reluctant to imprison the defendants in the face of Owen's many arguments, and asked the prosecutor how much wages in hand he currently owed to the defendants. The prosecutor said that the employer currently had unpaid wages for one week owing to each of the defendants, so the magistrates abated those wages from each of the defendants, an outcome which the union interpreted as a victory. Owen later addressed a crowd of 4,000 miners that voted to thank him for 'defending our rights and protecting us from injustice', and to have Owen represent them in negotiating a settlement with their employers, which he did shortly after the meeting.[80]

When arguments like the above were insufficient, and Roberts lost at Petty Sessions, he initiated writs of habeas corpus and certiorari to Queen's Bench by seizing upon omissions on the convictions or warrants of commitment, which were required to establish fully the jurisdiction of the magistrate. When the barristers he engaged won these cases, Roberts used them as precedents in future ones, shaping much of the pre-1848 rules of summary procedure.

---

[80]   'Colliers' Strike' and 'Colliers' Meeting', *The Glamorgan, Monmouth and Brecon Gazette Cardiff Advertiser and Merthyr Guardian* (hereafter *GMBG*) (18 March 1843), p. 3; 'Division of Newport', *Monmouthshire Merlin* (hereafter *MM*) (18 March 1843), p. 3; 'Important Meeting between the Coal Proprietors and the Working Colliers', *GMBG* (1 April 1843), p. 4; 'The Colliers Strike', *The Welshman* (24 March 1843), p. 3.

At one point in 1843, Roberts had 18 actions against the rulings of Durham magistrates pending before Queen's Bench. These magistrates begged the Home Secretary, Sir James Graham, for new master and servant legislation and financial help with their legal costs. In August of 1844, a group of Durham magistrates settled with Roberts, paying his clients £200 and all legal costs in return for dropping civil proceedings against them. Graham declined to have the Government reimburse them for this settlement, leaving the magistrates out-of-pocket.[81] Within months of being hired, Roberts had used Queen's Bench to overturn master and servant convictions of miners in seven counties.[82] Engels wrote that 'the miners' attorney general ... seemed to be everywhere at once, striking terror into the hearts of coal owners'.[83]

By challenging as many cases as possible, Roberts robbed master and servant law of the speed and convenience that made it so attractive to employers. Raymond Challinor, in his biography of Roberts, used an 1843 master and servant prosecution at Thornley Colliery in Durham as an example of this point. The miners there had refused to work in protest of the heavy fines that were reducing their earnings. Under normal circumstances, such a case could have been resolved successfully for the owners in a matter of minutes, but Roberts dragged the proceedings out for six very expensive days before the defendants were convicted. He used the courtroom as a platform for informing the public of the miners' grievances. He then initiated a habeas corpus and a certiorari to the Court of Queen's Bench, where a discharge was ordered due to improperly written warrants of commitment. Fear of a similar experience caused employers in St Helens, Preston and Manchester to drop master and servant prosecutions against workers when they heard that Roberts was engaged for the defense.[84]

Roberts' victories were well reported in the *Northern Star*, *Miners' Advocate* and *Miners' Monthly Magazine*, making him a celebrity among the pitmen. Advertisements for the *Northern Star* promised to give a portrait of Roberts

---

[81] NA: HO 43/67, pp. 171–2 (12 July 1844), pp. 314–15 (24 August 1844); 'Report of the Commissioner Appointed Under the Provisions of the Act 5 & 6 Victoria, c.99 to the Operation of That Act, and Into the State of the Population of the Mining Districts' (London, 1846), p. 10; *Parliamentary Papers*, Vol. 24 (737), p. 383.

[82] NA: KB 1/123/39, KB 1/119/31, KB 1/119/30, KB 1/119/29; 'Liberation of the Staffordshire Colliers: Triumph of the Law and Trade Unions', *NS* (20 January 1844), p. 3; 'Liberation of the Knutsford Collier Victims', *NS* (24 February 1844), p. 4; 'Steam Gaol Delivery: Another Glorious Triumph of Constitutional Law Over Magisterial Ignorance', *NS* (10 February 1844), p. 5; 'Another Triumph for the Miners', *NS* (2 March 1844), p. 4; 'Strike at Thornley Colliery', *DC* (15 December 1843), pp. 2–3; Challinor, *Radical Lawyer*, Chapter 7.

[83] Engels, *The Condition of the Working Class in England*, p. 289.

[84] 'Mr. Roberts – To Prevent Any Mistake', *NS* (20 April 1844), p. 4; Challinor, *Radical Lawyer*, pp. 88, 92–101, 103, 105; Engels, *The Condition of the Working Class in England*, pp. 288–9; Webb, *Story of the Durham Miners*, p. 41.

with every new three-month subscription. On the 24 February 1844, that journal carried a very flattering biographical article on 'the miners' attorney-general'.[85] On many occasions when entering towns to represent miners, Roberts was met and escorted by processions of workers carrying banners with bands playing 'See the Conquering Hero Comes'.[86] Miners, Chartists and other union workers regularly traveled significant distances to listen to his speeches. Miners and their families wrote a number of folk songs and ballads expressing gratitude and admiration for the 'miners' attorney-general'.[87]

The fame achieved by Roberts made him one of the 'gentlemanly leaders' that were characteristic of radicalism and popular politics throughout the nineteenth century. Some historians suggest that the presence of these gentlemanly leaders help to explain the ease with which radicalism and Chartism evolved into popular liberalism under the leadership of Gladstone and Bright. John Belcham, James Epstein and Paul Pickering all challenge this claim by demonstrating that radical leaders and Chartists were fundamentally different from later liberal leaders in their context, sites of discourse, and culture styles and practices of agitation. Although on the surface, Roberts' bourgeois values, deep religious conviction and faith in the law and moral force might suggest similarities with popular liberal heroes, he was much closer in style to his friend Feargus O'Connor. Roberts was comfortable on the rowdy mass platform as well as the more respectable courtroom. Roberts' style turned the courtroom into a site of very confrontational, class-based discourse, and he was not at all a 'bridging figure' to popular liberalism. Although Roberts never donned a fustian jacket, he could demonstrate his loyalty to workers through his imprisonment for supporting the Chartist cause and the fact that in his work he only represented workers, never employers. This was uncommon among the profession in this period. This contributed to making Roberts something of a 'displaced gentleman' because despite his strict moral values, the manner in

[85]   The advertisements are in: *NS* (2 September 1843); *NS* (16 September 1843). For the biography: 'W.P. Roberts', *NS* (24 February 1844), p. 2. For Roberts' celebrity among pitmen, see: Fynes, *Miners of Northumberland and Durham*, p. 241.

[86]   'Procession in Honour of W.P. Roberts', *NS* (26 April 1845), p. 1; 'Justice Room Hemsworth', *The Sheffield and Rotherham Independent* (hereafter, *SRI*) (15 June 1844), pp. 5, 8; 'Paying Colliers in Stuff', *SRI* (15 June 1844), p. 8; 'Town Hall', *SRI* (15 June 1844), p. 8; 'Adjourned Colliers Cases', *SRI* (29 June 1844), p. 5; 'Oxclose Colliery', *SRI* (29 June 1844), p. 5; 'Renshaw Colliery', *SRI* (29 June 1844), p. 5; *MSA* (12 April 1844), p. 5; 'Great Rejoicing of the Staffordshire Miners', *NS* (15 February 1845), p. 1; 'Grand Procession of the Miners at Wigan in Honour of W.P. Roberts, Esq.', *NS* (4 October 1845), p. 1; F. Machin, *The Yorkshire Miners: A History* (Huddersfield, 1958), pp. 51–2.

[87]   During the 1840s, the pages of the *Northern Star, Manchester Examiner, Manchester and Salford Advertiser, Miners' Advocate, and Manchester Times* report scores of speeches delivered by Roberts. For the folk songs, see: Challinor, *Radical Lawyer*, pp. 106–7.

which he practiced law made him 'disreputable', a 'sharp practitioner'. He was passionate and uncompromising in his support of workers.[88]

Chartists constructed Roberts' victories as proof of a conspiracy by magistrates and coal masters to bend the law to thwart union activity and deprive workers of their rights. At a commemoration of Thomas Paine's birthday, one of the toasts was 'To W. P. Roberts, the people's attorney-general, may the working classes cheer him in his onslaught against tyrant magistrates and bloated capitalists'.[89] When the National Miners' Association held a conference at Glasgow, one of the proposals was 'That there be a law fund established throughout the United Kingdom, as we consider it would be a terror to both masters and magistrates'.[90] The *Northern Star* claimed that Roberts' legal victories in the Court of Queen's Bench 'now proved' a conspiracy of 'injustice, and illegality of the "Coal Kings" and those magistrates who have been found ready instruments in their hands'. The article made the accusation that 'the magistrates had no jurisdiction in any single case brought by the masters against their men. In fact, both the magistrates and the masters have not only acted illegally, but have acted without any, the slightest colourable power'.[91]

For workers there was a stark contrast between the legitimacy of the higher courts at Westminster Hall and the summary powers of magistrates. Following the quashing of a magistrate's ruling in December of 1843, the Chartist journal wrote:

> So that while our readers are stuck with the horrible picture we have drawn of 'club law,' they will rejoice to find that in the Real Law there is yet protection for the poor. To get the law is the thing, and Mr. Roberts appears to have discovered the magical process by which this desideratum is to be achieved.[92]

This rhetoric was commonplace, as when Roberts promised a Wigan crowd that he would drag local magistrates 'to the rail of the Court of Queen's Bench, where justice, not magistrates' law, could be readily obtained'.[93] At another public meeting, Roberts expressed confidence in the 'real law', stating 'that there is law

---

[88]   J. Belcham and J. Epstein, 'The Nineteenth Century Gentleman Leader Revisited', *Social History* 22/2 (1997), pp. 174–93; P. Pickering, *Chartism and Chartists in Manchester and Salford* (Basingstoke, 1995).

[89]   J. Epstein, 'Some Organizational and Cultural Aspects of the Chartist Movement in Nottingham', in D. Thompson and J. Epstein (eds), *The Chartist Experience: Studies in Working Class Radicalism and Culture, 1830–1860* (London, 1982), p. 244.

[90]   'The Colliers' Strike', *The Manchester Guardian* (hereafter, *MG*) (20 March 1844), p. 4.

[91]   'Tremendous Explosion of a Coal Pit Conspiracy', *NS* (24 February 1844), p. 4.

[92]   'Constitutional Law versus Coal King Law: Good News for the Miners', *NS* (23 December 1843), p. 4.

[93]   'Meeting of Colliers in Worsley', *NS* (22 June 1844), p. 5.

for the poor man as well as the rich man, and through it they were ... to defend their rights'.[94] Feargus O' Connor told miners that 'the law of the land will protect you against the injustice of tyrants; and to deprive you of the law's protection is now the aim and object of your foes'.[95] Other Chartists went so far as to suggest 'the law will always protect the labourer in a fair contest with the employer'.[96]

This construction of Roberts' appellate victories had the effect of seriously damaging the legitimacy of magistrates, while at the same time curiously reinforcing faith in the institutions of high justice in England. Headlines in labor journals like 'Constitutional Law versus Coal King Law', 'Constitutional Law versus Justices' Justice', 'Liberation of the Staffordshire Colliers: The Triumph of the Law and Trade Unions', 'Steam Gaol Delivery: Another Glorious Triumph of Constitutional Law Over Magisterial Ignorance', 'Another Glorious Triumph Achieved by Means of the Law' and 'More of Labour's Triumphs: The Value of the Law When Honestly Administered' fostered the notion that magistrates were perverting the English legal process.[97]

The authors of these articles portrayed the Queen's Bench Judges as possessing superior knowledge and integrity, which they contrasted sharply with those administering law at the 'inferior level'. After a successful action initiated by Roberts, the *Northern Star* observed 'Thus a second English Judge has awarded a triumph to the law and affixed the stamp of ignorance upon the "great unpaid" of a second county'.[98] In March of 1844, the journal reported the discharge of more miners by the Court of Queen's Bench, suggesting

> Three cases have been now tried; and all before different judges: Mr. Justice Patteson, Mr. Justice Williams, and Mr. Justice Wightman; all of whom have rescued the unjustly punished victims from the illegal grasp of their persecutors. Could *condemnation* be stronger?[99]

---

[94] 'Meeting of Colliers', *MA* 2/25 (8 February 1845), p. 229.

[95] 'Tremendous Explosion of a Coal Pit Conspiracy', *NS* (24 February 1844), p. 4.

[96] 'Liberation of the Staffordshire Colliers: Triumph of the Law and Trade Unions', *NS* (20 January 1844), p. 4.

[97] 'Constitutional Law versus Coal King Law', *NS* (23 December 1843), p. 8; 'Liberation of the Staffordshire Colliers: The Triumph of the Law and Trades' Unions', *NS* (20 January 1844), p. 4; 'Steam Gaol Delivery: Another Glorious Triumph of Constitutional Law over Magisterial Ignorance', *NS* (10 February 1844), p. 4; 'More of Labour's Triumphs: The Value of the Law When Honestly Administered', *NS* (11 May 1844), p. 4; 'Another Glorious Triumph for the Miners' Association', *MA* 1/5 (27 January 1844), p. 37; 'More Glorious Triumphs for the Miners' Association', *MA* 1/9 (29 March 1844), pp. 68–9. 'Constitutional Law versus Justices' Justice', *NS* (8 February 1845), p. 4; 'Another Glorious Triumph Achieved By Means of the Law', *NS* (5 July 1845), p. 8.

[98] 'Liberation of the Staffordshire Colliers', *NS* (20 January 1844), p. 4.

[99] 'Steam Gaol Delivery: Another Glorious Triumph of Constitutional Law Over Magisterial Ignorance', *NS* (10 February 1844), p. 4.

A month later, the court quashed the conviction a group of Knutsford colliers under the 1823 Act, prompting the *Northern Star* to report 'They were liberated by a constitutional judge', meaning Mr Justice Coleridge, 'who proclaimed the triumph of constitutional law over magisterial ignorance'.[100] In another case, they thanked the Queen's Bench for 'vindicating the law by discharging the victims of its perversion'.[101]

The United Branch of Operative Potters, whose members were sometimes represented by Roberts in master and servant cases, also adopted the interpretation of a 'foiled conspiracy' between magistrates and masters. The *Potters' Examiner* warned stipendiary magistrate Thomas Bailey Rose,

> that the cases which have been brought before you, for what is termed breach of agreement, and for which you have sent individuals to the house of correction for one, two and three months to hard labour are such as would not come under the interference of the law. *Barristers* of *long standing* and men of much *progress* in judicial pursuits have given their decided opinion that from the agreement between master potters and their men, containing no stamp and no reciprocity of interest, *is not valid in law*. The want of reciprocity alone, it is stated, is enough to make it illegal.[102]

The author praised Roberts' victories as 'sunny spots on the black pages of magisterial misrule', which proved that their one-sided agreements were illegal and only enforced due to collusion between employers and magistrates. It called the Potters' bonds:

> A vile burlesque on the laws of our country, and would not exist for a single day but for the connivance of unprincipled magistrates. It to is to the latter that the hiring system in the potteries owes its existence. If it had to depend on legal validity for its support, it would have long ago sunk into obscurity.[103]

The article concluded by lauding the high court judges, or 'patriarchs of the law, who by their example teach partial and vindictive magistrates the folly and wickedness of their ways'.[104] The following week, the *Potters' Examiner* again

---

[100] 'Another Triumph for the Miners', *NS* (2 March 1844), p. 7.

[101] 'More of Labour's Triumphs: The Value of the Law When Honestly Administered', *NS* (11 May 1844), p. 4.

[102] Italics in original. 'The Hiring System, To the United Branches of Operative Potters', *PEWA* 1/19 (6 April 1844), p. 145; 'To T.B. Rose, Stipendiary Magistrate for the Borough of Stoke-Upon-Trent', *PEWA* 1/18 (30 March 1844), pp. 137–9; Steinberg, 'Capitalist Development'.

[103] Ibid.

[104] Ibid.

reported the role of the common law judges in suppressing the magistrate–master conspiracy:

> It is a fact experienced by colliers, and well known to the nation that many working men have been unjustly imprisoned … and have afterwards been released by the more dispassionate and enlightened decision of our national judges … How far do these men surpass our village dogberries in their professional career! … Do those good men shine above the eager, passionate, and localized creatures who exercise judicial authority on the magisterial benches of our provincial courts.[105]

Roberts' work before Queen's Bench shaped the law of summary jurisdiction, inconvenienced employers, exposed magistrates to costs and had a significant impact on how union members perceived different levels of the law.

Were these judges ruling in favor of organized labor? It might be more accurate to suggest that the Queen's Bench was reluctantly ruling against magistrates. While the courts and legislators were anxious to encourage magistrates to be active and not impede their important work, by the 1840s there was some concern about the lack of procedural protections for the accused in summary hearings. The extent of magistrates' summary judicial powers was a source of regular debate between 1790 and 1855, a controversy to which labor made a significant contribution. The jury trial, Blackstone's 'Palladium of English Liberty', was widely perceived as an important constitutional safeguard with great symbolic significance.[106] In addition to fears about the arbitrary exercise of judicial authority, critics of magistrates' summary powers were also concerned about the lay status of most magistrates, which was at odds with increasing professionalization of the English legal system. In the Victorian era there was pressure to tailor notions of legal professionalism to science, by constructing the law as a scientific system with an approach that provided a single correct answer to every legal question. The relatively unsupervised administration of an ever-growing proportion of the law by lay magistrates conflicted with this ideal.[107] It is not surprising that common-law judges sought methods of asserting their authority, methodology and hierarchy

---

[105]   Ibid. The term 'Dogberries' is probably a reference to William Shakespeare's *Much Ado About Nothing*.

[106]   J. S. Cockburn and Tom Green (eds.), *Twelve Good Men and True: the Criminal Jury Trial in England, 1200–1800* (Princeton, 1988); Peter King, 'Decision Makers and Decision Making in the English Criminal Law, 1750–1800', *Historical Journal* 27 (1984): 25–8; J. M. Beattie, *Crime and the Courts in England, 1660–1800* (Princeton, 1986), pp. 378–88, 406–29.

[107]   Jim Evans, 'Change in the Doctrine of Precedent During the Nineteenth Century', in Lawrence Goldstein (ed.), *Precedent in Law* (Oxford, 1987); A. R. Blackshield, 'The Legitimacy and Authority of Judges', *University of New South Wales Law Journal* 10 (1987): 164–7.

over these local hearings. Harry Arthurs has found that between 1830 and 1870 the legal profession and the common-law judges were also asserting their authority over a wide range of specialized courts and private tribunals that administered distinctive local systems of law. For centuries common-law judges had felt that summary jurisdiction 'existed in derogation of the common law' and used the opportunity presented by Roberts' writs of habeas corpus and certiorari to quash summary rulings in order to force uniform practice on magistrates.[108]

This was particularly important for the Court of Queen's Bench when handling convictions brought under the 1823 Master and Servant Act. Many acts conferring summary jurisdiction to magistrates compensated for the absence of the jury trial by permitting parties who felt aggrieved by the magistrates' judgment to appeal to Quarter Sessions, where all evidence could be reheard. Other acts, like the 1831 Truck Act, stipulated that the adjudicating magistrates could not be in the same trade as either the prosecutor or defendant.[109] The 1823 Act permitted no appeal to quarter sections and imposed no restrictions upon the number or types of magistrates permitted to determine cases. The only method available to a defendant for overturning a conviction under this act was a writ of certiorari or habeas corpus to one of the higher courts. These writs did not permit the judges to re-interpret the evidence of the case, but only to quash convictions or warrants of commitment on the basis of errors in law that appeared on their face. As this was one of the very few means of redress in cases of erroneous summary rulings, higher court judges gave these documents a very careful reading.

As a result, judges in the Court of Queen's Bench adopted a strict legal formalism with these documents as a safeguard for defendants prosecuted summarily, and to force magistrates to conduct their hearings and write their forms in a 'legalistic' manner.[110] In all of the cases Roberts brought before Queen's Bench, there were considerable procedural unfairness and injustices that occurred in the magistrates' hearings. Strict formalism by the high courts provided a 'safety valve' for summary convictions, by freeing the victims of egregious injustice. These 'technicalities' were hardly trivial considering that magistrates were entrusted with power of imprisonment. It was perfectly reasonable for judges to insist that informations, convictions and warrants of commitment clearly demonstrated that the defendant's freedom was taken away as the result of an offence over which the magistrate had been given jurisdiction by Parliament, and that his deliberations followed the due process of law.

If Roberts' legal victories were 'triumphs of law' for Chartists and trade unionists, they were serious miscarriages of justice to employers who wanted

---

[108]   H. W. Arthurs, *Without the Law: Administrative Justice and Legal Pluralism in Nineteenth Century England* (Toronto, 1985); Smith, 'Circumventing the Jury', pp. 118–20.

[109]   Section 12 of the Combination Laws Repeal Amendment Act, 6 George IV, c.129 (1825), is one example of a statute conferring summary jurisdiction permitting an appeal to Quarter Sessions.

[110]   Smith, 'Circumventing the Jury', pp. 122, 190–233.

to enforce employment agreements. Employers perceived that it was extremely important to be able to control labor costs and avoid work stoppages through the use of long-term contracts. If a union engaged Roberts, it could make enforcing these covenants expensive, time-consuming, embarrassing and generally counter-productive.[111]

These victories could also cause workers to question the legality of their contracts with their employers.[112] In a letter to the Commissioner of Mines, pit owner John Taylor complained that 'the pitmen's legal advisor, Mr. Roberts, commenced action after action on points arising out of a bond which was ... drawn up in good faith, and well understood by the parties concerned'. 'The vexatious legal proceedings' initiated by Roberts impaired their ability to enforce the bond using master and servant law, making 'the agreement for twelve months binding upon them [the owners] and not upon the workmen'.[113] In an 1844 letter to the Home Office, the Committee of the Coal Trade of Northumberland pleaded that due to Roberts' legal work, 'last year ... control of the collieries no longer remained with the viewers or owners'.[114] Out of frustration, one mine owner claimed that Roberts had been hired 'specifically for the purpose of annoying them'.[115]

Writers at the *Justice of the Peace* suspected that Roberts' motives had more to do with profit:

> The industry of the profession, sharpened perhaps, in common with all, by the necessity of the times, has of late years fastened upon summary proceedings, with a view to turn them to profitable account; with what success every term furnishes melancholy proof; strewed as it is with wrecks of orders and convictions and warrants; and this evil is likely to increase as ... the numbers and activity of the profession increases.[116]

---

[111]   For one example, see: 'Law Intelligence – Labour's Triumph: Manchester and York', *MA* 1/23 (14 December 1844), p. 200. This strategy continued to be used. See the 1866 testimony of mine owner William Mathews observed describing legal obstruction by trade unions in case of workers convicted under the Master and Servant Act who used the 1857 Summary Jurisdiction Act to have a case stated before the Court of Queen's Bench. 'Report From the Select Committee of Master and Servant', p. 118, Question 2423; Steinfeld, *Coercion*, p. 43.

[112]   See the case of *Pilkington v. Pemberton* (1845–1846), Chapter 3; NA: KB 1/140/17, KB 1/143/2; Barker, *Pilkington Brothers*, pp. 101–7; Challinor, *Radical Lawyer*, 105.

[113]   'Report of the Commissioner ... Into the State of the Population of the Mining Districts ... (1846)', p. 10.

[114]   NA: HO 45, Box 644 (8 June 1844).

[115]   Ibid.

[116]   'Liability of Justices of the Peace to Actions in the Exercise of The Summary Jurisdiction', *JP* 9/5 (1 February 1845), pp. 65–6.

Both magistrates and employers frequently used what Andrew Rowley has defined as the stereotype of 'the sharp practitioner' to discredit Roberts. A sharp practitioner was a fee-grubbing, mercenary attorney, concerned only with costs, technicalities and delay, but never the actual merits of a given case. The perception that the solicitors' profession was full of sharp practitioners was one of the most serious barriers to improving its low social standing relative to other professions.[117]

The non-labor press frequently portrayed Roberts as a shady operator who profited from creating discord between masters and men. Lord Londonderry accused Roberts, 'the insidious advisor', of making it his 'trade ... to feast upon the simplicity' of poor and ignorant miners. Others charged that 'Roberts seemed determined to practice once more on the well-proven gullibility of his "clients"'. The *Durham Chronicle* alleged that 'the pitmen starve that Mr. Roberts may live the life of a gentlemen'. The *Leicester Journal* wrote that while Roberts' 'professional alchemy could extract the gold from the miners' bodily toils', he did not share the poverty that the pitmen faced when his work cost them their jobs and savings. The *Morning Chronicle* warned the pitmen they should be more careful in selecting their leaders to avoid 'the selfishness of well-paid ... law agents'. Some accused Roberts of using the miners to pursue his subversive political agenda, falsely reporting that he had been transported for radical activity in the 1830s (he was, in fact, jailed), or that he was the cousin of the transported radical John Frost. Though not related, Roberts was, in fact, a close friend of John Frost.[118] Many miners rejected attempts to portray them as the dupes of Roberts, including Richard Fynes. Years later he defiantly reflected on Roberts' work, writing 'the fact was that the miners never did, nor never could, pay him one tithe of what they were indebted to him for the many valuable services he rendered them'.[119]

John Owen was also frequently attacked for his representation of miners and ironworkers in Wales. Editorials and letters in local newspapers frequently accused Owen of exploiting miners and attempting to earn costs by stirring up discontent

---

[117] A. S. Rowley, 'Professions, Class and Society: Solicitors in Nineteenth Century Birmingham' (PhD dissertation, University of Aston in Birmingham, 1988), p. 100; 'To the Editor of the Times', *The Times* (16 July 1844), p. 6; 'Aristocratic Insolence – The Durham Autocrat', *NS* (13 July 1844), p. 4.

[118] Wigan Public Library: D/DZ/A31/35, D/DZ/A31/98, The Pitmen's Strike Collection; NA: HO 45 Box 644, 'Lord Londonderry to Sir James Graham', 27 May 1844; 'State of the Colliery District in the North', *The Times* (18 April 1844), p. 6; 'Colliers Strike', *The Times* (29 April 1844), p. 4; 'The Colliery Strike in the North', *The Times* (16 May 1844), p. 8; 'To the Editor of the Times', *The Times* (17 July 1844), p. 6; 'The Pitmen's Strike', *MC* (31 May 1844), p. 7; 'The Pitmen', *MC* (1 June 1844), p. 7; 'The Strike of the Pitmen', *MC* (10 June 1844), p. 4; 'The Marquis of Londonderry', *MC* (28 June 1844), p. 5; 'Pitmen's Strike in the County of Durham', *The Times* (17 August 1844), p. 6; 'State of the Colliery Districts in the North', *MT* (20 April 1844), p. 3; Challinor, *Radical Lawyer*, pp. 123–6; D. Williams, *John Frost: A Study in Chartism* (New York, 1969), pp. 161, 172, 283, 320.

[119] Fynes, *Miners of Northumberland and Durham*, p. 241.

and bad feeling among workers who would otherwise be perfectly happy to be
paid in truck and compelled to work against the threat of imprisonment. In August
of 1843, while Owen was prosecuting an ironmaster for paying his workers in
truck, one of the managers of the works, James Brown, accused Owen in open
court of having no concern for his clients, only costs. When Owen sued Brown
for slander, the defense counsel accused 'instead of making up the quarrels of
neighbours, and mitigating their animosities, [Owen] busies himself with creating'
them. He added, 'The object of Mr. Owen is to obtain costs – which he loves more
than his own character', and for that reason he encouraged the jury to return a
verdict for the defendant. The jury returned a verdict for Owen, but awarded him
only a farthing in damages. The judge refused to certify the proceedings, so Owen
could not obtain the costs that he allegedly loved so much.[120]

Distrust of attorneys was, however, shared by many of the miners that Roberts
represented. The *Miners' Advocate* in 1844 wrote 'what are lawyers? Men of little
or no principle, who live upon the distress of mankind, and who scruple not to
use the most vile and base means to fill their pockets'![121] At a conference of the
National Miners' Association in April of 1844, delegates distributed a sharply-
worded anonymous handbill that questioned the merits of the law fund and
Roberts' ever-growing role in the union. It noted that Roberts had 'received in less
than six months £1,000 from men who can scarcely get bread for their families'.
It challenged the wisdom of the 'glaring sums' of hundreds of pounds spent in the
Thornley and Wingate Grange cases. The handbill and its authors were strongly
rebuked in a resolution by the conference, calling it 'unworthy of consideration',
but Roberts faced some tough questioning from delegate Cloughan, who wanted
to know if Roberts won cases on their merits or by mere technicalities. It was not
the last time that Roberts would be attacked from within the union.[122]

Roberts' victories in Petty Sessions and the Court of Queen's Bench strongly
contributed to the desire for an expansion of master and servant law. For employers
in many trades, the Master and Servant Acts were the critical to labor discipline.

---

[120]   'Action for Slander', *MM* (5 August 1843), p. 4; 'Owen v. Brown', *GMBG* (5
August 1843), p. 4.
[121]   'Veritas – Law', *MA* 1/14 (1 June 1844), p. 111.
[122]   Working Class Movement Library, Salford: F62, Box 10, F63, Box 1; Wigan
Public Library: D/DZ/A31/23, Pitmen's Strike Collection; 'Miners' Association of Great
Britain and Ireland National Conference At Glasgow', *MA* 1/10 (6 April 1844), pp. 76–7,
80; Challinor and Ripley, *Miners' Association*, pp. 21–2, 83–4, 89–92; 'Nobody's Child',
NS (6 June 1845), p. 4; 'Mr. Roberts', *NS* (8 November 1845); 'Charges Against Mr. Roberts
and the Miners Association', *NS* (15 November 1845), p. 6. The handbill complained in
scathing terms about Roberts' salary, and the £335 that it cost to free six Thornley Colliery
miners from a master and servant conviction. It also complained of his growing role in
union decision-making. Within six months Roberts had recovered much of the costs in the
Thornley Colliery Case with an out-of-court settlement with Durham magistrates in a false
imprisonment case. NA: HO 43/67, 17 July 1844, 3 September 1844.

Magistrates wanted to be able to enforce these laws without the risk of expensive and time-consuming legal actions. Both groups found that their authority was severely undermined by Roberts' work. The *Northern Star* had no doubts as to who was responsible for the introduction of the 1844 bill:

> It would appear that these frequent triumphs of the law, affording, as they do, a sort of protection of labour, though a costly one, have raised the alarm of the capitalists. A bill has been very snugly and quietly introduced into the House of Commons, ostensibly for the purpose of giving increased powers to 'Servants and Artificers for the More Effectual Recovery of Wages Before Justices'; yet for the real purpose of conferring additional powers upon masters and their justices. The bill has been prepared and brought by Mr. William Miles, Mr. Robert Palmer, and Mr. Gally Knight … Can anyone tell us, whether these three honourable gentlemen, or any of them, are connected with, or have any interest in mines or collieries?[123]

Chapter 2 will explore the direct connections between members of Parliament and external interests, but it is clear the legal campaign initiated by the miners of Northumberland and Durham, and executed by Roberts, provoked the introduction of the 1844 bill. Both magistrates and mine owners pleaded loudly for Parliament to reverse the uncertainty inflicted upon them by scheming lawyers and quibbling judges. Trade unions' engagement with the law had created this chaos, and their direct action would soon prevent a legislative remedy.

---

[123]   'Liberation of the Knutsford Colliery Victims', *NS* (2 March 1844), p. 4.

Chapter 2

The Defeat of the 1844 Master and Servant Bill: 'Triumph for Labour! ... The Damnable Bill Crushed!'

Introduction

On 4 May 1844, a long headline in the *Northern Star* proclaimed 'Triumph for Labour! Government Defeated! The Damnable Bill Crushed! Hurrah for Duncombe! Hurrah for Ourselves!' Feargus O'Connor and his Chartist colleagues were celebrating the success of a remarkable 35-day campaign that defeated the 1844 master and servant proposal, or 'the labour degradation bill'.[1] This was the first organized and large-scale national working-class expression of discontent with master and servant law, beginning the tradition of trade union opposition that ultimately led to the repeal of penal sanctions for breach of contract in 1875. This chapter describes how largely disenfranchised groups were able to use their limited representation in Parliament to maximum advantage. It is an example of how unions' courtroom efforts informed their members' perception of the law. To defeat this bill labor strategically used rhetoric that placed them at the center of debates about magistrates' expanding judicial powers, the perceived social problem of female labor, working-class demands for representation, the regulation of trade unions and the meaning of free labor. Labor representatives skillfully framed the issue of the Master and Servant Bill in such a way that support for its passage melted.

This chapter examines the political struggle over this proposal and the language used by participants in the debate. The promoters of the bill sought to secure its passage by emphasizing that their measure provided job and piece workers with an easy process for collecting unpaid wages, ignoring the fact that by the early nineteenth century master and servant statutes were more commonly used by employers to prosecute workers or compel them to return to work under unfavorable conditions.[2] Home Secretary Sir James Graham amended the bill to consolidate

---

[1]   'Triumph For Labour! Government Defeated! The Damnable Bill Crushed! Hurrah for Duncombe! Hurrah for Ourselves!', *NS* (4 May 1844), p. 4; 'To the Working Classes', *NS* (11 May 1844), p. 1.

[2]   Douglas Hay, 'Master and Servant in England: Using the Law in the Eighteenth and Nineteenth Centuries', in Willibald Steinmetz (ed.), *Private Law and Social Inequality in the Industrial Age: Comparing the Legal Cultures of Britain, France, Germany, and the United*

and clarify master and servant law, unintentionally placing more emphasis upon the bill's criminal sanctions against workers. This added considerable fuel to the developing protest. Duncombe, Roberts, the National Miners' Association, the United Branch of Operative Potters, and the *Northern Star* mobilized labor, short-time advocates and Chartists against the 1844 bill. These groups used rhetoric linking its potential dangers to their own agendas.

Workers also frequently expressed a lack of confidence in the impartiality of magistrates' summary rulings. These doubts and suspicions were fostered by Chartist and trade journals, which reported instances of magistrates determining cases where their own interests were at stake, as well as the quashing of their rulings by the higher courts. Organized labor's representatives contributed to broader political debates about the merits and deficiencies of summary justice by persistently critiquing the conduct of magistrates. The flood of petitions against the bill that flowed into Parliament during April of 1844 clearly took the government by surprise.

The Early Debate Over the 1844 bill

On 22 February 1844, William Miles, Robert Palmer, and Gally Knight presented, 'A Bill for Enlarging the Powers of Justices in Determining Complaints Between Masters, Servants, and Artificers, and for the More Effectual Recovery of Wages Before Justices', which passed its first reading the following day.[3] As the title suggests, the bill's supporters promoted the measure as extending an easy process for workers to recover unpaid wages from their employers. It did, in fact, expedite the recovery of unpaid wages in cases where employers were absentee, allowing workers to instead summon 'stewards, bailiffs, foremen, or managers' before magistrates to answer their complaint. It raised the limit of recoverable wages to a maximum of £10 for all workers. Some previous master and servant statutes had limited judgments to £5.[4]

States (London, 2000), pp. 231–7, 250, 255–8; Hay, 'Patronage, Paternalism, and Welfare: Masters, Workers, and Magistrates in Eighteenth Century England', *International Labor and Working Class History* 53 (Spring 1998): 36–9; Daphne Simon, 'Master and Servant', in J. Saville (ed.) *Democracy and the Labour Movement: Essays in Honour of Donna Torr* (London, 1954), pp. 161–5; D. C. Woods, 'The Operation of the Master and Servants Act in the Black Country, 1858–1875', *Midlands History* 7 (1982): 102; R. Steinfeld, *Coercion, Contract and Free Labour in the Nineteenth Century* (Cambridge, 2001), pp. 136–7.

   [3]   *The Journal of the House of Commons*, Vol. 99, pp. 52, 57.

   [4]   'A Bill for Enlarging the Powers of Justices in Determining Complaints Between Masters, Servants, and Artificers, and for the More Effectual Recovery of Wages Before Justices' (24 February 1844), s. 4, p. 3, lines 1–34. *Parliamentary Papers* (1844), Vol. III (58), p. 223.

The bill's preamble stated that confusion existed about the scope of four current Master and Servant Acts, particularly with respect to the precise meaning of phrases like 'labourers' and 'other persons', and whether they applied when a relationship of service did not exist. The bill's fifth section proposed to remove these doubts by having 'all and every powers, authorities, clauses, and matters therein contained' in the four Master and Servant Acts extend 'to all labourers and other persons, although not employed in any of the trades enumerated in the said several recited acts, and although the relation of master and servant may not actually subsist'.[5] The form of this bill was clever, because its only new clauses related to the recovery of unpaid wages by servants. The criminal sanctions for absence without leave, neglect of work, or misbehavior by workers did not appear in this bill, but were contained in the four acts that it proposed to extend, making it easier to emphasize the wage recovery provisions.

The *Northern Star* was not fooled by this sleight of hand, and in early March warned its readers that the bill proposed extend imprisonment for breach of contract 'to every order of labour in the land'. The author argued that the bill was a direct response by mine owners and magistrates to Roberts' successful actions against master and servant convictions. The writer feared that the bill might end the courtroom victories of labor, noting 'how soon capital can protect itself, because it has the power of law-making in its hands'.[6] One week later, the *Northern Star* printed the bill's text, along with another warning about its content. A speaker in Merthyr also believed that the measure had been brought to meet the legal work of Roberts, and argued that the 'law, if administered properly, would protect them. But it was too weak in the opinion of despots to answer their purpose, and as they had the power of making the laws, brought forward this measure'.[7]

The *Justice of the Peace* also noticed the bill in its early stages. The 2 March issue of that journal included two articles supportive of the bill, but urged Parliament to go even further. The author of the first article complained that 'the proposed enactment seems hardly explicit enough'. He suggested some additional language for extending the provisions of the four 'general acts' in the bill (the *Justice of the Peace*'s recommended additions are italicized):

> to all labourers, *journeymen*, and other persons, *employed in any trade, occupation, or employment whatsoever, and to those employed in any of the trades, occupations, or employments enumerated in the said several recited*

---

[5]   'A Bill for Enlarging the Powers of Justices' (24 Feburary 1844), s. 5, p. 4, lines 21–6. The Four Statutes the bill would have extended were: 20 George II, c.19 (1747), 31 George II, c.11 (1758), 6 George III, c.25 (1766) and 4 George IV, c.34 (1823).

[6]   'Liberation of the Knutsford Colliery Victims', *NS* (2 March 1844), p. 4.

[7]   'Masters and Servants', *NS* (9 March 1844), p. 4; 'Great Public Meeting in Merthyr', *MM* (20 April 1844), p. 3.

acts; and although the relation of master and servant may not actually subsist
between such labourers, *journeymen,* or other persons, and their employers.[8]

The overly thorough nature of these proposed additions was testimony to how
concerned magistrates were by their recent treatment in Queen's Bench.

The second article blamed the actions, costs and damages magistrates
experienced when enforcing 4 George IV, c.34 (1823) on the poor drafting of
laws in Parliament. It pleaded with the legislature to be precise when framing a
new Master and Servant Act, because 'generalities invariably lead to difficulties in
construction and in very many cases expose innocent parties to whom is confided
the administration of the law to liabilities of a very serious nature. To no act of
Parliament are these observations more applicable' than 4 George IV, c.34 (1823).
The writer complained in 1844 that 'it is much to be regretted that the legislature
in framing acts of Parliament should be so prone to use general terms; tautology
is infinitely preferable to obscurity'.[9] It is likely that these suggestions influenced
Home Secretary Sir James Graham's decision to amend the 1844 bill.

On 6 March the bill passed through its second reading without division or
debate, and on the thirteenth it was committed. Graham re-wrote the bill in
committee, saying that 'he agreed with the object of the bill, but thought that the
means that were taken for attaining that object were inexpedient'. He decided that
rather than add yet another statute to an already large and complex body of law,
he would repeal six existing Master and Servant Acts, and then enact in a single
statute 'all the portion that was really valuable in those acts'. This single statute
would apply to all forms of labor with the exception of domestic service. Miles,
Palmer and Knight agreed that Graham's bill was 'more clear and precise', and it
was printed in its new form.[10]

Graham was primarily responsible for the bill's final form. Although he refused
to take responsibility for the measure by making it a government bill, there can
be no doubt that by mid-March he was the driving force pushing for its passage.
The Home Office papers show that during the spring of 1844, Graham was in
regular contact with northern coal owners like Lord Londonderry and the Duke of
Newcastle. He also corresponded with the Bishop of Durham and a committee of
northern magistrates about the miners of Northumberland and Durham, who were
about to commence one of the longest strikes of the decade.[11] Durham magistrates

---

[8]   'Masters and Servants', *JP* 8/9 (2 March 1844), pp. 154–5.

[9]   'Recent Decisions under the Master and Servants Act (4 George IV, c.34, s.3)', *JP*
8/2 (2 March 1844), pp. 131–2.

[10]   *Journals of the House of Commons*, Vol. 99, p. 90; *Hansard Debates*, Vol. 73, col.
980. The six statutes the amended 1844 bill proposed to replace were 5 Elizabeth I, c.4
(1563), 20 George II, c.19 (1747), 27 George II, c.6 (1754), 31 George II, c.11 (1758), 6
George III, c.25 (1766) and 4 George IV, c.34 (1823).

[11]   NA: HO 45, Boxes 644 and 646; Raymond Challinor and Brian Ripley, *The Miners'
Association: A Trade Union in the Age of Chartists* (London, 1968, Chapter 8.

informed Graham of Roberts' work in frustrating prosecutions under master and servant law, as well as the resulting actions he brought against them. These unpaid officers were responsible for maintenance of law and order in the north, so their concerns were always important to the Home Secretary.[12] Another source of worry for Graham was that Roberts' employer was the National Miners' Association, a union widely, though incorrectly, believed to have over 100,000 members, and an annual income of £50,000 (also an exaggeration).[13] Graham ordered the Home Office to watch this union, and Roberts, very closely. In addition to reports from mine owners and magistrates, Graham received information from plain-clothes policemen about the union that employed Roberts.[14] This could explain why Graham actively participated in the drafting and promotion of the 1844 bill, while leaving it in the hands of three backbenchers.

This approach was not shrewd. Graham, whose 'personal unpopularity was extreme' in 1843–1844, was roundly criticized both inside and outside the House of Commons for refusing to make the proposal a government bill.[15] One MP argued that if this measure was in the best interest of the nation, it 'ought to have been begotten by the government, reared by the government, and nursed by the legal authorities of the government, not left to the accidental assistance of any independent member'.[16] An editorial in *The Times* accused Graham of 'foul dealing' for using Miles, Knight and Palmer as lightning rods. It argued that if Graham made backbenchers of low stature responsible for controversial bills, the effectiveness and accountability of the government would be lost. It charged that 'should the bill be successful, then of course it will not be forgotten that he was its strongest advocate. Should it lead to ... the general impression that laws were made for the rich and the strong, then to the broad backs of Mr. Miles and the other gentlemen ... will be transferred the odium'.[17]

Although Graham's bill would have achieved the same ends as the original bill, extending master and servant law to all types of labor, Duncombe complained that it 'had been altered without one word, from the first line of the preamble down to

---

[12]   NA: HO 43/67, pp. 171–2 (13 July 1844), pp. 314–15 (24 August 1844).

[13]   Challinor and Ripley, *Miners' Association*, pp. 7–8, 82; 'Report of the Commissioner ... Into the State of the Mining Districts' (1846), p. 13. *Parliamentary Papers* (1846), Vol. XXIV (737), p. 383.

[14]   Challinor and Ripley, *Miners' Association*, pp. 21–2.

[15]   *MC* (13 April 1844), p. 2; 'London: Thursday, May 2nd', *The Times* (3 May 1844), p. 4; T. M. Torrens, *The Life and Times of the Rt. Hon. Sir James Graham, Bart., G.C.B., M.P.*, Vol. 2 (London, 1958), pp. 272–3, 232–40; N. Gash, *Sir Robert Peel: The Life of Sir Robert Peel After 1830* (New York, 1972), pp. 438–44; T. L. Crosby, *Sir Robert Peel's Administration, 1841–1846* (London, 1976), pp. 63–70; *Hansard Debates*, Vol. 73, col. 1590.

[16]   *Hansard Debates*, Vol. 74, col. 527; 'London: Thursday, May 2nd', *The Times* (3 May 1844), p. 4.

[17]   Ibid.

the end, of the original bill remaining in it'.[18] Graham's bill repealed six Master and Servant Acts, and then re-enacted their common characteristics, including the penal clauses. These were contained in the fourth clause of the bill, which stated that any worker who was absent without permission, left work unfinished, or was guilty of any misbehavior could be sentenced by a magistrate to two months' imprisonment with hard labor. Imprisonment for breach of contract was no innovation, but its bold wording altered the emphasis of the bill for labor. This form made it more difficult for supporters to promote the bill as merely an effort to ease the collection of unpaid wages. In fact, opponents of the bill often suggested that in committee a benevolent bill that had passed two readings had been exchanged for a harsh one that needed only a single reading to become law.[19]

This became apparent when the amended bill was discussed in Parliament on 20 March. Duncombe and Benjamin Hawes each spoke against the fourth clause of the new bill, arguing that 'it gave the magistracy some extremely harsh powers'. Both Graham and Miles argued in vain that under existing law, magistrates could imprison some workers guilty of the same offenses for *three* months, rather than the two proposed in the fourth clause. They stressed that the bill created no new law, but merely extended and clarified the law that already existed.[20] Graham and Miles clearly failed to anticipate the depth of labor's hostility to the existing master and servant law.

The Mobilization of Labor against the 1844 bill

After this debate, Duncombe wrote to Roberts 'concerning a bill that would strike a serious blow at the miners of this country'. Roberts was en route to a delegate conference of the National Miners' Association convening in Glasgow.[21] This union, which represented approximately 50,000 miners, consisted of a network of local branches held together by traveling lecturers and regional delegates, making it an ideal apparatus for spreading information about the bill and organizing a protest. The *Northern Star* urged the pitmen's union to 'adopt a means for ensuring the opposition of all members over whom they can exercise any countrol [sic]'.[22]

---

[18]   Ibid.

[19]   'A Bill [As Amended by Committee] For Enlarging the Powers of Justices in Determining Complaints Between Masters, Servants, and Artificers, and for the More Effectual Recovery of Wages Before Justices' (13 March 1844), clause 4, lines 1–3, 34–43; *Parliamentary Papers* (1844) Vol. III (111), p. 229; Steinfeld, *Coercion*, pp. 136–7; 'Freedom of Labour at Stake: The Damnable Bill', *NS* (6 April 1844), p. 4; 'Masters and Servants', *NS* (30 March 1844), p. 5; *Hansard Debates*, Vol. 74, col. 518–23.

[20]   *Hansard Debates*, Vol. 73, col. 1306–8.

[21]   'The Colliers' Conference', *NS* (30 March 1844), p. 8.

[22]   'The Colliers' Conference and Chartist Convention', *NS* (23 March 1844), p. 4; Challinor and Ripley, *The Miners' Association*, pp. 74–83, 93; J. Epstein, 'Feargus O'

The size and structure of the miners' and potters' unions, the circulation of the *Northern Star* and the existence of active short time committees and the National Charter Association in the spring of 1844 combined to produce a large number of public meetings and petitions with astonishing speed.

On 25 March Roberts addressed the miners' conference about the bill which 'struck at the liberties of the working classes'. Roberts distributed copies of the bill to the delegates and explained each of its 11 clauses. Roberts stressed to the assembled miners that 'all that was necessary by this bill to secure the imprisonment of a man' was the 'oath of any underlooker, viewer, foreman, or deputy' that the defendant 'contracted with the master to sink a certain number of yards, or drive a shaft a certain length'. If this low standard of proof was met, a magistrate could 'drag a man from his family and send him to the dungeon'. At the end of his speech, the conference resolved that Roberts should prepare a petition to Parliament protesting the bill for delegates to sign and circulate.[23]

Roberts addressed the conference the following morning.[24] In his petition, he focused upon dangers to civil liberties in the summary process that the bill proposed. His strategy was to exploit the pre-existing controversy over magistrates' judicial powers by objecting to the bill's want of protections for defendants. Roberts calculated that these procedural and constitutional concerns were more likely to sway members of Parliament, just as they had the judges at Queen's Bench.

Appealing to their constitutional rights as 'freeborn Englishmen', the petition stated that the summary procedure outlined in the bill lacked 'the most necessary safeguards against a harsh, hasty, or capricious exercise of judicial authority'. The bill gave greater powers to 'the unchecked jurisdiction of a single magistrate', than were usually exercised by common law judges acting alone, which was 'more despotic … than is consistent with the liberty which your petitioners are taught to regard as their birthright'. Roberts pleaded 'that so large an abrogation of the right of TRIAL BY JURY … is calculated to impair public faith in the stability of the British Constitution'.[25]

In the petition Roberts argued that because the bill did not require magistrates to summon an accused worker, but only issue a warrant, a defendant 'may receive no notice of his [or her] immediate trial but the warrant by which he is apprehended'. Once seized by constables, the case could be heard by 'any magistrate', even one who lived 'one hundred miles off'. The bill did not require the magistrate to hear

---

Connor and the Northern Star', *International Review of Social History* 21 (1976): 97; Cris Yelland, 'Speech and Writing in the *Northern Star*', *Labour History Review* 65/1 (2000): 22–40.

[23] 'Coal Miners' Conference', *NS* (30 March 1844), p. 8; 'National Miners' Association of Great Britain and Ireland Conference at Glasgow', *MA* 1/10 (6 April 1844), pp. 76–7, 80.

[24] 'Coal Miners' Conference', *NS* (30 March 1844), p. 8.

[25] Capitals in original. Wigan Public Library: D/DZ/A31/23, Pitman's Strike Collection; 'Freedom of Labour at Stake: The Damnable Bill', *NS* (6 April 1844), p. 4.

the case in public, which Roberts argued 'was entirely subversive to freedom'.[26] These objections could have been leveled against almost any of the master and servant statutes, so it is clear that Roberts was also using this opportunity to raise questions about the current state of the law. Roberts was frequently hired to initiate actions in cases where workers were whisked away in the middle of the night by constables, tried under informal proceedings in magistrates' private dwellings, and then sent to a house of correction before their friends could find an attorney. The petition objected that the bill required only one witness to establish the existence of a written or verbal agreement, or prove the offence of 'misbehaviour', a very low standard for a prosecuting employer.[27] For these reasons, the petitioners prayed that Parliament not pass the bill.

Roberts explained to the conference that this bill would make defending workers charged with breaking their contracts much more difficult. Unless the conference took action he believed the bill 'had every chance of passing into law'.[28] The conference adopted the petition, and asked every delegate to sign it and pass copies to their constituents. The *Northern Star* and *Miners' Monthly Magazine* reprinted the petition, encouraging readers to have it adopted and signed at every public meeting, union gathering or short time protest during the next fortnight. The *Northern Star* gave its readers instructions for mailing the petitions to Duncombe in Parliament and also printed a pamphlet written by Roberts.[29]

In his pamphlet, Roberts reminded miners that if the bill passed, they, their wives and their children would labor under the threat of imprisonment, no matter how casual their employment. He painted an image of entire families walking the treadmill together. This image of domestic harmony shattered by the law was a strategic appeal to middle-class sensibilities. Roberts was adopting a rhetorical strategy that had become common among Chartists and short-time advocates, using the language of domesticity, masculine citizenship and the family wage.

---

[26]   It was not until the passage of the Summary Jurisdiction Act of 1848 that magistrates' hearings were required by statute to be 'open' and 'public'. See 11 & 12 Victoria, c.43, s.12 (1848). Bertram Osborne, *The Justice of the Peace, 1361–1848: A History of the Justices of the Peace for the Counties of England* (Dorset, 1960), pp. 226–8; Wigan Public Library: D/DZ/A31/38, Pitmen's Strike Collection; David Philips, 'The Black Country Magistracy, 1835–1860: A Changing Elite and the Exercise of its Power', *Midlands History* 3 (1976): 169; Raymond Challinor, *Radical Lawyer in Victorian England: W. P. Roberts and the Struggle for Workers' Rights* (London, 1990), p. 89; D. C. Woods, 'The Borough Magistracy and the Authority Structure of Black Country Towns, 1860–1900', *West Midlands Studies* 12 (1979), p. 24.

[27]   The concerns related to the low standard of proof needed for securing a prosecution could have applied to a large number of statutes giving magistrates summary jurisdiction. See Bruce P. Smith, 'The Presumption of Guilt and the English Law of Theft, 1750–1850', *Law and History Review* 23/1 (Spring 2003): 133–71 .

[28]   Wigan Public Library: D/DZ/A31/23, Pitmen's Strike Collection.

[29]   'The Colliers' Conference', *NS* (30 March 1844), p. 8; 'Freedom of Labour at Stake: The Damnable Bill', *NS* (6 April 1844), p. 4.

Anna Clark suggests that because some male Chartists argued that their property in a skill qualified them for political rights, and blamed increased female labor for deskilling, they believed that the removal of women from the workforce was a necessary pre-condition for men getting the vote. Tory paternalists, evangelicals and working-class radicals linked women working outside the home to a wide range of social ills. For working-class men the answer was to pay them a wage sufficient to fully support their wives in the protected domestic sphere. While this was never practical because of the heavy dependence of the working-class family on the paid and unpaid labor of women and children, it was a powerful rhetorical weapon. This masculine notion of citizenship promised female Chartists greater protection by more responsible husbands, and the privileges of middle-class women. It also allowed male Chartists to claim respectability, answer charges that they lacked the moral standards necessary for participation in the political process and promise elites more harmonious social relations. Adopting domesticity language divided and greatly undermined nineteenth-century Chartism because it required the exclusion of women from political space and made radicalism more subservient. By emphasizing the disruption the 1844 bill would cause to the stability of the working-class family, Roberts drew attention to the ways in which it could work against efforts to encourage middle-class moral values.[30]

Roberts also commented on the absurdity of thinking it was 'expedient' to 'alleviate doubts' about the scope of an unjust body of laws by extending them so everyone would suffer under their weight rather than repealing them entirely. Neither Roberts nor the judges of Queen's Bench had any doubts about the jurisdiction of magistrates, even if that jurisdiction was inconvenient for mine owners. He observed that Parliament had never shown any inclination to alleviate doubts about the meaning of 'misbehaviour' in the statute, which the Queen's Bench had defined quite broadly. He urged readers to 'Petition! Petition! Petition!!' because 'if they do not stir, and quickly too, their hands will be bound down beyond the point of stirring!!'.[31]

---

[30] Anna Clark, *The Struggle for the Breeches: Gender and the Making of the English Working Class* (Berkeley, 1995), pp. 215, 220–222, 234, 237–8; Robert Shoemaker, *Gender in English Society, 1650–1850: The Emergence of Separate Spheres?* (London, 1998), pp. 198–206; R. Gray, 'Languages of Factory Reform in Britain, c. 1830–1860', in P. Joyce (ed.), *The Historical Meanings of Work* (London, 1987), pp. 150–152; Gray, *The Factory Question and Industrial England, 1830–1860* (Cambridge, 1996); D. Thompson, *Outsiders: Class, Gender and Nation* (London, 1993); S. Alexander, 'Women's Work in Nineteenth Century London: A Study of the Years 1820–1850,' in J. Mitchell and A. Oakley (eds.), *The Rights and Wrongs of Women* (London, 1976), pp. 60–63; Malcolm Chase, *Chartism: A New History* (Manchester, 2007), p. 43; James Epstein, 'The Constitutional Idiom: Radical Reasoning, Rhetoric and Action in Early-Nineteenth Century England', *Journal of Social History* 23/3 (1990): 565–6.

[31] 'Freedom of Labour at Stake: The Damnable Bill', *NS* (6 April 1844), p. 4; *Spain v. Arnott* (1817), 171 E. R. 638; *Amor v. Fearson* (1839), 9 A. & E. 548–54.

The *Potters' Examiner* also used its circulation to rally workers in Staffordshire. The fourth clause of the proposal was reprinted in its 30 March 1844 issue, and the editors informed their readers that the bill's purpose was intended 'to meet the conduct of provincial magistrates in their late attempt to destroy the liberty of working men, by acting from their own vindictive minds, and not from the letter of the law'. It warned that if the bill passed, 'trade unions will become a non-entity, as strikes cannot, by any possibility, take place, except in defiance of the dungeon'. For this reason 'it is the duty of every operative to affix his signature to those petitions, and to use all the exertions in his power to get them numerously signed'.[32]

Were it not for the efforts of Duncombe at Westminster, the protest would not have had time to begin. On two occasions opponents were able to delay the bill's third reading. The day after Roberts' petition was adopted by the National Miners' Association, the bill stood as the seventh item on the orders of the day in Parliament. Duncombe objected that the amended bill should be withdrawn and re-introduced because it was so different in form. He also argued that because the measure was of such importance to workers, they should have the opportunity to be heard. Graham and Sir Robert Peel refused to withdraw the bill, but because sponsor William Miles was inexplicably absent, debate on the measure was postponed. On 18 April, as scores of petitions opposing the bill were arriving daily, Duncombe was again able to postpone debate on the legislation until May first, by which time the momentum for its passage had been entirely reversed.[33]

The Protest against the 1844 bill

The four April issues of the *Northern Star* contain coverage of 66 meetings that passed resolutions and presented petitions opposing the 'damnable bill'. These reports are useful in demonstrating the language and strategies that speakers drew upon to motivate their audiences and influence those in Parliament. The focus of these speeches and resolutions was as much on the injustices of existing master and servant law as on the changes proposed in the 1844 bill. On this point, my interpretation of the protest against the 1844 bill diverges from that of Robert Steinfeld. He argues that the aims of this protest were entirely limited to preventing the expansion of penal sanctions to job and piece workers. He suggests that in the second quarter of the nineteenth century, 'total repeal of criminal sanctions

---

[32]   'To T. B. Rose Esq. Stipendiary Magistrate for the Borough of Stoke-Upon Trent', *PEWA* 1/18 (30 March 1844), p. 138; 'The Hiring System: To the United Branch of Operative Potters', and 'The Potters' Examiner and Workman's Advocate', *PEWA* 1/19 (6 April 1844), pp. 146, 158.

[33]   *Hansard Debates*, Vol. 73, col. 1588–90; 'Masters and Servants Bill', *NS* (30 March 1844), p. 5; *Journals of the House of Commons*, Vol. 99, p. 214; 'Master and Servants Bill', *Manchester Times* (hereafter, *MT*) (30 March 1844), p. 3.

was not an imaginable possibility even for those closest to working people in the Parliamentary community'. He argues that in the discussion of the 1844 bill 'no one was heard to say that the entire apparatus of penal sanctions should be dismantled'. Steinfeld's examination of the protest is limited to Engels and the reported Parliamentary debates, and he does not acknowledge that Duncombe articulated opposition to imprisonment for breach of contract, just as Francis Place had 21 years earlier.[34] A closer examination of the debate beyond Parliament demonstrates profound dissatisfaction with the existing law. Evidence of this can be found in the focus on Section 4 of the bill, which contained the penal sanctions, as well as the prominent role that the miners' and potters' unions played in the protest.[35] Many existing master and servant statues had applied to workers in these trades for centuries, so the bill represented little change for them, yet they were the most active in bringing about the bill's defeat. These groups feared the consequences of a more universal and deeply entrenched master and servant law, and welcomed the opportunity to raise awareness. One might dismiss workers' use of rhetoric comparing a waged labor regime under master and servant law to slavery or serfdom as simply part of a long tradition in radical language. In this context, however, it appears to demonstrate that workers could indeed imagine a world in which there were no criminal sanctions for breach of contract. One should not mistake the language of members of Parliament as evidence of widespread acceptance of the existing state of the law.

In addition to the Miners' and Potters' Associations, dozens of other unions rallied to protest against the 1844 bill.[36] Master and servant law was the most effective legal weapon an employer had against trade union activity. Breach of contract was easy to prove, so employers were often able to use these statutes

---

[34] Steinfeld, *Coercion*, pp. 97, 135–42; *Hansard Debates*, Vol. 74, col. 518–23; Willibald Steinmetz, 'Was There a De-Juridification of Employment Relations in Britain?', in Willibald Steinmetz (ed.), *Private Law and Social Inequality in the Industrial Age: Comparing the Legal Cultures of in Britain, France, Germany, and the United States* (London, 2000), p. 266.

[35] Steinfeld, *Coercion*, p. 141.

[36] 'Great Meeting of the Seamen of Sunderland', 'Meeting of the Fustian Cutters of Manchester', 'Hyde', 'Bristol – Trades Movement Against the Masters and Servants Bill', 'Sheffield – Great Meeting of the Colliers', 'Newcastle – Glorious Demonstration of the Coal, Lead, and Ironstone Miners', *NS* (13 April 1844), p. 8; 'Tailors Conference – Public Meeting – Concert and Ball', 'Benthal Green – Meeting of the Broad Silk Hand Loom Weavers', 'Meeting of the Dyers of Glasgow', 'Painters of Manchester', 'Leeds', 'Manchester', 'Great Meeting of the Western Division of the Journeymen Boot and Shoemakers to Petition Against the Masters and Servants Bill', 'Newcastle Upon Tyne – Meeting of the Cordwainers', *NS* (20 April 1844), pp. 6–8; 'London Boot and Shoe Makers', 'London Engineers and Machinists', 'Huddersfield', 'Bristol', *NS* (27 April 1844), pp. 6, 8.

to defeat strikes before they began.[37] Roberts expressed fear that if the 1844 bill passed, vague offences like 'misbehaviour' might be interpreted as 'belonging to the union'. In its report of a meeting against the bill held by the seamen of Sunderland, the *Northern Star* warned readers, 'there is not a trade society ... in the kingdom, but ought to have its petition against the bill aimed at its very existence'.[38]

Many unionists agreed that 'let this bill become law and every trades union in the Kingdom will be crushed – annihilated!'.[39] Thomas Leeming, a shoemaker, warned 'the object of this bill was to annihilate all unions of working men'. Mr Crawford saw 'the death-blow of trades' societies in the bill'.[40] William Fleming, the secretary for the dyers of Glasgow, told an audience that the bill 'struck at the root of trade unions, and was intended to prevent the working classes from meeting to protect themselves against the avarice and duplicity of tyrannical employers'.[41] Sheffield collier George Moore was certain that the 'bill was brought forward solely to put down the Colliers' Movement'.[42] London shoemaker William Clark thought that the bill 'was undoubtedly an onslaught on trades unions'. He feared the bill's consequences for his own union, because 'sometimes they had to stand out for wages; but let this bill become law, and who would dare come out for them? Where would they get men to take upon themselves the awful responsibility of being their officers?'.[43] Trade unions technically had enjoyed legal status for only 20 years, and still had a dubious standing before the law. Given the wide range of legal weapons employers could use against them, the fear that unions could be 'annihilated' before the courts was more than hyperbole.[44]

If the focus of the bill's supporters was the recovery of unpaid wages, for unionists it was the dreaded fourth clause, which contained the penal sanctions. Even though imprisonment for breach of contract had been a part of the meaning of free labor for some time, speakers still expressed great shock at the contents of that clause. Mr Steward read the fourth clause to the crowd and demanded to know why there was no imprisonment for employers who violated verbal contracts? Mr

---

[37]   Challinor, *Radical Lawyer*, pp. 72–3, 84–5; Hay, 'Master and Servant in England', pp. 251–5.

[38]   'Labour's Struggle', *NS* (13 April 1844), p. 4; 'Freedom of Labour at Stake: The Damnable Bill', *NS* (6 April 1844), p. 4; 'Newcastle Upon Tyne – Meeting of the Cordwainers', 'Barnsley Cordwainers', *NS* (20 April 1844), pp. 7, 8; 'Bristol', 'Huddersfield', *NS* (27 April 1844), p. 8.

[39]   'Freedom of Labour at Stake: The Damnable Bill', *NS* (6 April 1844), p. 4.

[40]   'Newcastle-Upon-Tyne – Meeting of Cordwainers', *NS* (20 April 1844), p. 6.

[41]   'Meeting of the Dyers of Glasgow', *NS* (20 April 1844), p. 7.

[42]   'Sheffield – Great Meeting of Colliers', *NS* (13 April 1844), p. 5.

[43]   'Great Meeting of the Western Division of Journeymen Boot and Shoe Makers, to Petition Against the Masters and Servants Bill', *NS* (13 April 1844), p. 8.

[44]   John Orth, *Combination and Conspiracy: A Legal History of Trade Unionism, 1721–1906* (Oxford: Clarendon Press, 1991.

Burroughs told an audience of handloom weavers that the 'truly detestable and diabolical clause' was 'utterly destructive to every principle of liberty'. In Bath, as Mr Bolwell described the penal sanctions in the fourth clause, it 'created a considerable sensation, and called forth repeated bursts of disapprobation' from the audience. For many unions, the bill was a direct threat because their trades were either neglected in previous Master and Servant Acts, or were dominated by job and piece work. Other unions, however, had labored under the oppressive weight of these laws for three centuries, and used the opportunity to articulate longstanding grievances.[45]

During April of 1844, short-time committees throughout Britain, particularly in Lancashire and Yorkshire, held large public meetings to rally support for Lord Ashley's ten-hours amendment. At many of these meetings a second petition opposing the Master and Servant Bill was also adopted and circulated. These two campaigns were informed by the same gender politics. Speakers at these meetings often opposed the Master and Servant Bill and advocated the ten-hours bill with the same language that emphasized masculine citizenship and the necessity of 'protecting our women and children'.[46] Roberts set this tone early in his pamphlet against the 1844 bill, writing:

> The woman who refused to work eleven hours may, in the opinion of a long-chimneyman be 'guilty of misbehaviour,' – The child who shrieks as the Billy-Roller bruises his young flesh, may be guilty of 'misbehaviour' … WOMEN AND CHILDREN! English blood boils at the thought.[47]

---

[45] 'Tailors' Conference – Public Meeting – Concert', 'Benthal Green – Public Meeting of the Broad Silk Hand Loom Weavers', and 'Bath', *NS* (20 April 1844), pp. 5, 7, 8; 'Great Meeting of the Western Division of the Journeymen Boot and Showmakers To Petition Against the Masters and Servants Bill', *NS* (27 April 1844), p. 6; 'Duncombe: Triumph of Labour. "The Labourer is Worthy of his Hire"', *NS* (11 May 1844), p. 4.

[46] 'Mr. Thomas Gisborne's Vote on the Factory Bill – Meeting at Nottingham', 'Wigan – Meeting in Support of the Ten Hours Bill', 'Factory Bill', 'Ten Hours Meeting at Bradford', 'Huddersfield', 'Halifax', 'Great Meeting of the Seamen of Sunderland', *NS* (13 April 1844), p. 8; 'Benthal Green – Public Meeting of the Broad Silk Hand Loom Weavers', 'Meeting in Bermondery', 'Meeting at Dundee', 'Manchester Ten Hours Meeting', 'Great Meeting at Bolton', 'Barnsley', 'Silden, Near Bradford', 'Public Meeting at Burnley', 'Meeting at Preston', 'Leeds', 'Meeting at Warrington', 'Meeting at Knightley', 'Manchester, Sunday Night', 'Meeting at Marylebone', *NS* (20 April 1844), pp. 7–8; 'Bolton', 'Brighton', 'Public Meeting in Carlisle', 'Glasgow: Triumphant Refutation of the Assertion by the Manufacturers that Operatives are not in Favor of A Reduction in the Hours of Labour', 'Littletown', 'Lynn', *NS* (27 April 1844), pp. 4, 7, 8; 'Ten Hours Factory Bill', *MT* (20 April 1844), p. 3; 'Chartism', *MT* (20 April 1844), p. 8.

[47] Capitals in original. 'Freedom of Labour at Stake: The Damnable Bill', *NS* (6 April 1844), p. 4.

It is clear that Roberts was speaking to male workers. To emphasize their dependent state, he lumped women workers in with the abused 'shrieking child', the ultimate defenseless victim.[48] Roberts encouraged male workers with an appeal to their English manhood, which should 'boil at the thought' of their families walking the treadmill. He was also making an obvious appeal to short-time committees by emphasizing the bill's threat to the 'woman who refused to work eleven hours'.

The rhetoric of men protecting women from excessive factory hours and harmful master and servant legislation was calculated to impose 'maleness' upon the public world of work, politics and the law.[49] As stated earlier, adopting the rhetoric of domesticity allowed working-class men to address the tensions caused by increasing competition from female and child labor in a number of trades, and the resulting loss of status and wages. Ten-hours advocates argued that women's work 'was destructive to their health, morals, and religion', and made them less fit for marriage and motherhood, harming the stability of the working-class family.[50] Factory reform advocates accused mill owners of undermining working-class family life by pulling women away from their domestic duties in the private sphere and exploiting them in factories. The Rev. J. R. Stephens told a public meeting that factory owners had usurped husbands' natural patriarchal authority over their wives.[51] Opponents of the 1844 bill argued that its provisions would add to the tyrannical powers that mill owners had over the protesters' wives, and further undermine the working-class family.

Many of the male speakers protesting against the Master and Servant Bill implied that it would extend imprisonment for breach of contract to women for the first time. In reality, master and servant statutes made no explicit distinctions between genders, and women were often prosecuted under existing acts. In many trades women also sometimes used these statutes to recover unpaid wages from employers.[52] Roberts certainly knew this because he had defended women charged

---

[48]   Clark finds that chartist men 'were determined to define themselves as protectors of passive female factory girls, who could not act for themselves, despite evidence to the contrary'. Clark, *Struggle for the Breeches*, pp. 232, 234, 242; J. Schwarzkopf, *Women in the Chartist Movement* (New York, 1991), p. 228.

[49]   S. Rose, *Limited Livelihoods: Gender and Class in Nineteenth Century England* (Los Angeles, 1992); Clark, *Struggle for the Breeches*; Shoemaker, *Gender in English Society*, pp. 205–7; Gray, *Factory Question*.

[50]   'Tailors Conference – Public Meeting – Concert', *NS* (20 April 1844), p. 5; 'Brighton', *NS* (27 April 1844), p. 7; Clark, *Struggle for the Breeches*; Alexander, 'Women's Work', pp. 58–64.

[51]   Clark, *Struggle for the Breeches*, pp. 222, 226; Alexander, 'Women's Work', pp. 61–2; C. Morgan, *Women Workers and Gender Identities, 1835–1913: The Cotton and Metal Industries in England* (London, 2001), pp. 29, 33–56.

[52]   Douglas Hay, 'England 1562–1875: The Law and its Uses', in Douglas Hay and Paul Craven (eds), *Masters, Servants, and Magistrates in Britain and the Empire, 1562–1955* (Chapel Hill, 2004), pp. 67, 96. For just a few examples from 1843–5, see: 'Leaving Work Without Notice', *MSA* (6 July 1844), p. 3; 'Summons for Wages', *MSA*

under master and servant law.[53] By suggesting that the 1844 bill presented new dangers to women, speakers were expressing the common Chartist assumption that skilled labor was a 'masculine monopoly', while casual, irregular and poor paying work was 'female'. Though it is true that women were frequently engaged in casual job and piece work, so were substantial numbers of men. Women also worked in a number of trades covered by these statutes. In 1843 Factory Inspector Leonard Horner, informed by the same assumptions about the supplemental nature of women's work, argued that it was possible for the state to interfere with women's employment contracts by limiting their hours of their work because they were 'much less free agents' than men. Working-class men thought that this distinction advanced their claims of full citizenship.[54] By suggesting that the 1844 bill would have a disproportionate impact upon female workers (a proposition that was possibly true), Chartists and short-time advocates were appealing to middle-class ideas about women's right to contract. The 1844 bill was unjust because it enforced contracts made by 'less than free agents' with penal sanctions.

Male workers' insistence that they were petitioning to protect their wives and families assumed that the latter could not protect themselves, reasserting a masculine image of citizenship.[55] For example, a meeting at Bermondery resolved

---

(24 August 1844), p. 3; 'Enfield Turnout', *MSA* (2 November 1844), p. 8; 'Turn Out in Mr. Wm. Morris' Mill', *MSA* (23 November 1844), p. 8; 'Rochdale', *MSA* (21 June 1845), p. 8; 'Silk Weavers' Wages', *MSA* (16 August 1845), p. 3; 'Ashton: Leaving Work', *MSA* (13 September 1845), p. 3; 'Leaving Work', *MT* (4 May 1844), p. 3; 'Bolton: Leaving Without Notice', and 'Wages', *MT* (22 June 1844), p. 8; 'Rochdale', *MT* (14 June 1845), p. 8; 'Stockport', *MT* (19 July 1845), p. 8; 'Summons for Wages', *MG* (29 March 1843), p. 3; 'Leaving Employment Without Notice', *MG* (17 May 1843), p. 3; 'Leaving Work Without Notice', *MG* (4 November 1843), p. 3; 'Leaving Without Notice', *MG* (10 January 1844), p. 3; 'Leaving Work Without Notice', *MG* (17 February 1844), p. 3; 'Leaving Work Without Notice', *MG* (21 February 1844), p. 3. Also see 'Case of Mary Dawson', *Hansard Debates*, Vol. 93 (1847), cols. 120, 947–53; 'Petition of William Scott', *Hansard Debates*, Vol. 85 (1846), cols. 470–479. For a sample at the appellate level, see NA: KB 1/120/57, KB 1/225/42, KB 1/264/26, KB 1/263/35, 37.

[53]   'Turn Out at Mr. Wm. Morris' Mill', *MSA* (23 November 1844), p. 8; Challinor, *Radical Lawyer*, pp. 215–17, 220–222. Roberts also frequently defended women on charges of intimidation under 6 George IV, c.129 (1825): 'Bury and Heywood', *MSA* (12 April 1845), p. 5; 'Strike of Spool Winders: Intimidation of Workpeople', *ME* (14 January 1852), p. 5; K. Sayer, 'Field-Faring Women: The Resistance of Women Who Worked in the Fields of Nineteenth Century England', *Women's History Review* 2/2 (1993): 185–98; women were also heavily coerced under the 1777 Worsted Act, see: Richard Soderlund, '"Intended as a Terror to the Idle and Profligate": Embezzlement and the Origins of Policing in the Yorkshire Worsted Industry, c.1750–1777', *Journal of Social History* 31/3 (1998): 647–70.

[54]   Alexander, 'Women's Work', pp. 73, 80–93, 97–103; Clark, *Struggle for the Breeches*, pp. 220–221, 233; Rose, *Limited Livelihoods*, p. 57; Gray, *Factory Question*.

[55]   Morgan, *Women Workers and Gender Identities*, p. 28; Clark, *Struggle for the Breeches*, pp. 236–44.

that 'feeling as we do the responsibility we are under to protect our wives and families, as well as the country at large, do hereby pledge ourselves to resist that most infamous measure to the fullest possible extremity'.[56] At Marylebone, workers gathered to protect 'weak women and little children' and 'domestic duty and domestic comfort' from the threat of the 1844 bill.[57] Other meetings opposed the bill to protect 'helpless children and suffering females'.[58] Despite the alleged dangers the 1844 bill posed to women, in the nearly 70 recorded meetings, there was not a single female speaker, and very little acknowledgment by the press of women in attendance. Dorothy Thompson and Anna Clark have argued that while women's involvement in the Chartist movement was extensive in the early period of the movement, by the mid-1840s their participation is much less in evidence. They blame this partially on the changes in the organizational structure that marginalized women, as well as the power of domesticity rhetoric. The use of family wage language by male Chartists to claim a respectable masculinity divided and greatly weakened the Chartist movement.[59] The protest against the 1844 bill is not inconsistent with these findings.

The leaders of Chartism, such as Feargus O'Connor, Patrick O' Higgins, Bronterre O' Brien, R. G. Gammage and Joshua Hobson all addressed Chartist meetings on the dangers of the 1844 bill.[60] The language of Chartism was ideally suited to address the injustice of master and servant law. Statutes that made breach of contract by workers a criminal offence, but treated employers' failure to fulfill agreements as civil matters were especially obnoxious examples of class legislation. Chartists argued that these laws were unjustly written and enforced because workers played no role in either process. Gareth Stedman Jones argues that

---

56   'Meeting at Bermondery', *NS* (20 April 1844), p. 7.

57   'Marylebone', *NS* (20 April 1844), p. 4.

58   'Labour's Struggle', *NS* (13 April 1844), p. 4; 'Great Meeting of the Western Division of Journeymen Boot and Shoe Makers to Petition Against the Master and Servants Bill', *NS* (27 April 1844), p. 6; 'Constitutional Law Versus Coal King Law', *NS* (23 December 1843), p. 5; 'The Masters and Servants Bill: Labour's Grateful Testimonial to T.S. Duncombe, Esq. M.P.', *NS* (11 May 1844), p. 1.

59   D. Thompson, 'Women and Nineteenth Century Radical Politics', in J. Mitchell and A. Oakley (eds), *The Rights and Wrongs of Women* (London, 1976), pp. 134–7; D. Thompson, *The Chartists: Popular Politics and the Industrial Revolution* (New York, 1993), Chapter 7; Morgan, *Women Workers*, p. 28; Clark, *Struggle for the Breeches*, Chapter 13; Chase, *Chartism*, p. 359; James Epstein, 'Understanding the Cap of Liberty: Symbolic Practice and Social Conflict in Early Nineteenth Century England', *Past and Present* 122 (1989): 100–107.

60   'Halifax', *NS* (13 April 1844), p. 8; 'Bermondery', 'Marylebone', *NS* (20 April 1844), p. 7; 'Grand Demonstration in Stevenson's Square to Petition Against the Irish Registration Bill, the Irish State Church, and The Master and Servants Bill', *NS* (27 April 1844), p. 8; 'Sheffield', 'Wigan', 'Public Meeting', 'Salford', 'Hall', 'Northampton', 'Great Meeting in Opposition to the Master and Servants Bill', *NS* (13 April 1844), pp. 1, 7; 'Emmett Brigade', 'Stockport', 'Carlisle', *NS* (20 April 1844), p. 1.

the language of Chartism was first and foremost political, directed at the political and legal capacity of the propertied, a continuity of eighteenth-century radicalism that identified one group's monopoly over law-making and law-enforcing power as the central cause of working-class woes.[61] Context matters, however, and the protest against laws enforced by magistrates likely to be industrial employers, that shaped labor markets and set boundaries on bargaining that greatly favored other industrial employers implied a clearly defined notion of class. Chartists accused mine owners, employers of industrial labor and magistrates as being the advocates of this proposed legislation.

Many speakers tied the bill to the cause of universal male suffrage. Thomas Clark of Stockport called the bill an example of how 'the House of Commons treated the people with contempt; but when two and a half million ... have the People's Charter, no power on earth would dare treat them with contempt'.[62] Mr Cuffy of Marylebone asserted that the bill 'was attributable to class or party legislation, and we have no hope of any permanent remedy save and except in the People's Charter'.[63] Mr Goulding of Manchester told the crowd that they had to 'show the House of Commons, even as it is presently constituted, that the working classes would not tamely submit to be trampled upon'. Bath Alderman Mr Crisp told an assembled crowd that the 1844 bill did not surprise him because 'the corruption of the House and their wholesale plunder of the people had long since induced him to expect nothing beneficial from them'. He argued that the solution to this problem was 'getting rid of them altogether and placing in their room men who would really be representative of their interests'.[64] These sentiments were often repeated.[65] Bronterre O' Brien used Miles', Palmer's and Knight's assertions that their intention was to assist the working class as evidence of the untrustworthiness of an unreformed Parliament.[66] Jones argues that a flaw in Chartist language was that its central argument could be undermined by limited concessions from the state, such as a ten-hours bill and moderation of the new poor law. Combined with a general improvement in the economy, these concessions made it more difficult to utilize the same rhetoric used by opponents of the 1844 bill.[67] Giving up on the 1844 bill was one of several instances in the 1840s when the state made

---

[61]   Gareth Stedman Jones, *The Languages of Class: Studies in Working Class History, 1832–1982* (London, 1983), pp. 102–6, 109.

[62]   'Great Meeting in Opposition to the Master and Servants' Bill', *NS* (13 April 1844), p. 7.

[63]   'Marylebone', *NS* (20 April 1844), p. 7.

[64]   'Bath – Public Meeting Against the Master and Servants Bill', 'Exeter', 'Bermondery', *NS* (20 April 1844), pp. 7–8.

[65]   'Public Meeting of the Associated Mercantile Trades of Manchester', *NS* (20 April 1844), p. 7; 'Meeting at Exeter', *NS* (20 April 1844), p. 8; 'Bristol', *NS* (27 April 1844), p. 6.

[66]   'Bermondery', *NS* (20 April 1844), p. 7.

[67]   Jones, *Languages of Class*, p. 166; Thompson, *Chartists*, pp. 330–339.

concessions that undermined the main argument of Chartism by demonstrating that improvements could be won for working-class people without the vote.

In the public meetings, language expressing the fear that passage of the 1844 bill would reduce workers into slaves or serfs was pervasive.[68] Sailor Thomas Robson likened the measure to 'the degradation of slavery or vassalage'. Mr Rogers of Bristol thought if 'the bill be passed into law it will render the working class the veritable slaves of the masters'. After reading the fourth clause to an audience of London tailors, Mr Parott exclaimed that it would place workers 'in a worse condition than the negroes' in America, and 'destroy their freedom altogether'.[69] Abolitionist rhetoric had been used in a wide range of radical movements since the eighteenth century, including the parliamentary reform, factory reform, anti-poor law, opposition to the introduction of machinery and the loss of skill, trade unionism and Chartism. Seymour Drescher has argued against historians who suggest that widespread working-class involvement in the abolitionist movement distracted them from domestic woes by pointing out that their involvement actually revitalized and informed working-class radicalism. This rhetoric was powerful, because 'freedom' was an important aspect of many Britons' feeling of superiority and was often defined in contrast to slave-holding Americans. Radicals and Americans often tried to puncture this self-image by comparing chattel slavery to wage slavery.[70] Opponents of the 1844 bill frequently used the metaphor of slavery to argue that its passage would undermine the freedom of labor responsible for British progress and superiority. Mr Jeffery argued that 'this country boasted of its liberty, but let this bill become law, and it would be reduced to lowest depth of slavery and universal barbarism'. Mr Bonner warned that the bill was 'calculated to take us back to the days of baron and serf'.[71]

Many organizations active in the spring of 1844 were able to link the dangers inherent in the 1844 bill with their own agendas and ambitions. Speakers couched

---

[68]   'Great Meeting of the Seamen of Sunderland', 'Meeting at Exeter', 'Newcastle upon Tyne – Meeting of the Cordwainers', 'Public Meeting of the Associated Mercantile Trades of Manchester', 'Great Meeting of the Western Division of Journeymen Boot and Shoe Makers', 'Merthyr Tydvil', 'Marylebone', *NS* (20 April 1844), pp. 6–8; 'Mossley', 'Bristol', 'Carlisle', 'Brighton', 'Tavistock', 'Devon', *NS* (27 April 1844), pp. 6, 8.

[69]   'Meeting of the Seamen of Sunderland', 'Bristol – Trades Movement against the Master and Servants Bill', *NS* (13 April 1844), p. 8; 'Tailors' Conference-Public Meeting-Concert', *NS* (20 April 1844), p. 5.

[70]   S. Drescher, *Capitalism and Anti-Slavery: British Mobilization in Comparative Perspective* (Oxford, 1986), pp. 145–66; M. Cunliffe, *Chattel Slavery and Wage Slavery: The Anglo-American Context, 1830–1860* (Athens, 1979), pp. 42–4; Steinfeld, *Coercion*, 13. Steinfeld suggests that workers did not perceive the use of penal sanctions to enforce contracts per se as making labor unfree. Steinfeld, *The Invention of Free Labour: The Employment Relationship in English and American Law and Culture, 1350–1870* (Chapel Hill, 1991), Introduction.

[71]   'Great Meeting of the Western Division of Journeymen Boot and Shoe Makers To Petition Against the Masters and Servants Bill', *NS* (27 April 1844), p. 6.

their arguments in rhetoric designed to intersect with concerns of the law-making class, such as the language of domesticity, anti-slavery and preserving the legitimacy of the unreformed Parliament. Radicals also exploited feelings about the expanding judicial powers of magistrates to reach a broader audience.

The Attack upon the Magistracy

Many opponents of the 1844 bill spoke out against the administration of master and servant law by magistrates, contrasting it with 'our ancient rights of trial by jury'.[72] This remained one of labor's most commonly articulated objections to master and servant law for the next three decades. Roberts and the *Northern Star* provided workers with numerous reports of egregious errors and misconduct by magistrates when enforcing these statutes. Yet there must be a larger explanation for this critique, because master and servant law treated workers and employers unequally in its provisions, no matter who enforced it. Even if master and servant cases were determined by trial juries, a worker would still be liable to imprisonment for breach of a civil contract. Those eligible to be jurors were not much closer to being the 'peers' of workers than magistrates.[73]

There was a strategic aspect to this focus on summary procedure. By criticizing the magistracy and opposing the extension of their powers to hear master and servant cases, representatives of labor were participating in a longstanding debate in Parliament over the expansion in the number of criminal offenses that magistrates could determine summarily. This debate had great urgency for unions because magistrates enforced a large proportion of labor law, and the type of men appointed to the bench changed during the nineteenth century. Protesters against the 1844 bill repeated the three most common complaints leveled against magistrates in the mid nineteenth century. They criticized magistrates' lack of legal knowledge, their conflicts of interest and that their growing judicial powers undermined the traditional procedural safeguards of the jury trial.

There was no formal requirement for magistrates to be legally trained. In fact, for much of the nineteenth century, there was considerable opposition to the appointment of solicitors or legally-educated stipendiary magistrates. Defenders of the lay magistracy feared that a professional and Government-paid magistracy would lack independence.[74] Raymond Challinor argues that before the growing presence of solicitors at Petty Sessions, a 'soothing balm of ignorance' had allowed magistrates to convict workers where they lacked jurisdiction. Only at

---

[72]   'Bermondery', *NS* (20 April 1844), p. 7.

[73]   J. S. Cockburn and Thomas Green (eds), *Twelve Good Men and True: The Criminal Jury Trial in England, 1200–1800* (Princeton, 1988).

[74]   David Foster, 'The Social and Political Composition of the Lancashire Magistracy, 1821–1851' (PhD dissertation, University of Lancaster, 1972), p. 2; Sir Thomas Skyrme, *History of the Justice of the Peace* (3 vols., Chichester, 1991), Vol. 2, pp. 146–7.

mid-century, as part of an effort to improve the legitimacy of summary hearings, did London and other large provincial cities begin to see the appointment of more legally-trained police magistrates.[75]

Chartists fostered the notion of an ignorant magistracy. Chapters 1 and 3 describe how the legitimacy of magistrates' judicial role was severely undermined by Roberts' speeches and legal work. Roberts and other Chartists assured workers that the law they experienced before magistrates was not 'real law' but a perversion of the legal system by ignorant and partial political appointees. Roberts told the National Miners' Association conference in March of 1844 that through his legal work 'he taught magistrates the law and how to make legal warrants'.[76] A year later, Roberts doubted his pupils were learning, because 'in Lancashire, magistrates, generally, are ignorant of the law, and look only to their own interests'.[77] The *Northern Star* appealed for Parliamentary protection for workers against 'the illegal, blundering, and ignorant manner in which they [magistrates] have recently discharged their judicial functions'.[78] It warned the miners that, without Roberts, the masters' will would always 'be backed by ignorant and interested justices'.[79] That journal showed a remarkable disrespect for magistrates, putting justice in quotation marks when referring to justices of the peace, or calling them 'just-asses', 'injustices of the peace' or 'dogberries'.[80] The *Nonconformist* told its readers to oppose the 1844 bill because

> All of the world is aware of the manner in which the laws are administered by the 'great unpaid' under the powers which they at present possess. 'Justices' Justice' has become a term of opprobrium throughout the United Kingdom.[81]

This criticism of the magistracy had remarkable staying power beyond 1844. Before the select committee investigating the operation of master and servant law in 1866, the most common objection by witnesses, after the double standard of sanctions, was the enforcement of the law by magistrates. Alexander MacDonald argued that

---

[75]   Challinor, *Radical Lawyer*, 73–4; Bruce P. Smith, 'Circumventing the Jury: Petty Crime and Summary Justice in London and New York City, 1790–1855' (PhD dissertation, Yale University, 1996), p. 405.

[76]   'The Miners' Association of Great Britain and Ireland National Conference at Glasgow', *MA* (6 April 1844), p. 80.

[77]   'Rochdale and Middleton', *MSA* (15 November 1845), p. 3.

[78]   'Trial and Conviction of the Coal-Owners for Conspiring Against the Pitmen and the Public', *NS* (8 June 1844), p. 4.

[79]   'Colliers' Conference', *NS* (16 March 1844), p. 4.

[80]   'Another Triumph For Labour', *NS* (25 May 1844), p. 8; 'More of Labour's Triumphs', *NS* (11 May 1844), p. 4; 'Constitutional Law versus Coal King Law', *NS* (23 December 1843), p. 4; 'Steam Gaol Delivery', *NS* (10 February 1844), p. 4; 'The Warrington Just-Asses', *NS* (20 March 1847) p. 1.

[81]   'Master and Servants Bill', *The Nonconformist* (hereafter, *NC*) (1 May 1844), p. 293.

'No question of master and servant should be brought before the justices due to their incompetence'.[82] Potter George Newton testified that 'as a rule, the justices of the peace are not sufficiently versed in law to administer it in these cases with the requisite precision'.[83] Even the secretary and law agent for a group of mine owners was forced to admit to the committee that magistrates demonstrated 'a frequent want of knowledge of the law'.[84]

The second most common complaint against magistrates was that due to their increasing social and economic ties with employers, they enforced the law in a biased or corrupt manner. Mr Crisp of Bath told his audience to fear the Master and Servant Bill because of 'the manner in which magistrates dealt at present with cases before them, he concluded that with this bill as law, the labourers' chance of obtaining justice would be small indeed'.[85] Another speaker warned a large London assembly that the 1844 bill would allow 'most probably, the master to be at one and the same time, master, accuser and judge'.[86] The *Northern Star* reminded Chartists that 'if the Master and Servant Bill had been the law of the land in 1842, employers, being justices as well, would have had the power to commit several operatives' during the strikes.[87] The *Potters' Examiner* cautioned its readers that if the bill became law 'the powers of the manufacturers would become almost omnipotent, as the magisterial benches are nearly wholly FILLED BY THEMSELVES!'.[88] Years later, Chartists argued that this problem was a direct result of an unreformed Parliament:

> One of our most bitter complaints is, that, under the present system, those in power have the appointment of the magistrate, the most important officer in the state, while the people – NEVER IN POWER – are either subject to justices' ignorance or whim, or to the farce of complaining of their injustice to those from whom they derive authority, and to whom, in return, they give their support. Neither character or fitness are now-a-days considered requisites in magistrates; partisanship, and hatred of the poor, are the necessary qualifications.[89]

In Merthyr, a local grocer warned a large audience that the bill would allow a miner to be imprisoned by a magistrate who 'would very frequently be the proprietor of

---

[82] 'Report From Select Committee on Master and Servant (1866)', p. 28, Questions 538, 539. *Parliamentary Papers* (1866), Vol. XIII (449), p. 1.

[83] Ibid., p. 9, Questions 149, 152, 153.

[84] Ibid., p. 108, Question 2300.

[85] 'Bath', *NS* (20 April 1844), p. 8.

[86] 'Great Meeting of the Western Division of Journeymen Boot and Shoe Makers, To Petition Against the Master and Servants Bill', *NS* (20 April 1844), p. 6.

[87] 'Duncombe: Triumph of Labour: The Labourer is Worthy of His Hire', *NS* (11 May 1844), p. 1.

[88] Capitals in original. 'The Hiring System', *PEWA* 1/19 (6 April 1844), p. 146.

[89] Capitals in original. 'The Warrington Shallows Again', *NS* (6 April 1847), p. 4.

the works'.[90] The background of magistrates in many regions made workers doubt their impartiality.

During the second quarter of the nineteenth century there was a significant shift in the social composition of the magisterial bench. Manufacturers and coal masters surpassed landed gentlemen and clergy as the dominant social groups on the bench in most boroughs in England and Wales, as well as the West Riding of Yorkshire, Lancashire and the Black Country. Landed gentlemen and clergy were simply too scarce in the areas where magistrates' judicial and administrative work was the most needed.[91] As a result, in many regions, magistrates were inevitably called upon to adjudicate labor disputes where it at least appeared that they had an interest in the outcome. David Philips observes 'on the test of the legal maxim that no man should be judge in his own cause, or one in which he had an interest, the Black Country magistrates would fail badly'.[92] In Northumberland and Durham, this transformation was less noticeable only because landed gentlemen and the church had been substantial coal-owners for some time. There was scarcely a magistrate in either of those counties unconnected to coal or iron.[93]

---

[90]   'Great Public Meeting at Merthyr', *MM* (20 April 1844), p. 3.

[91]   A shift in the political climate that accompanied the 1832 Reform Bill also contributed to this transformation. Carl Zangrel, 'The Social Composition of the County Magistracy in England and Wales' *The Journal of British Studies* 11 (1971): 113–25; Woods, 'Borough Magistracy', pp. 22–6; Woods, 'Master and Servants Act', pp. 93–115; Roger Swift, 'The English Urban Magistracy and the Administration of Justice During the Early Nineteenth Century: Wolverhampton, 1815–1860', *Midlands History* 17 (1992): 75–92; John Knipe, 'The Justice of the Peace in Yorkshire, 1820–1914: A Social Study' (PhD dissertation, University of Southern California, 1970); Foster, 'Lancashire County Magistracy'; David Foster, 'Class and County Government in Early Nineteenth Century Lancashire', *Northern History* 9 (1974): 48–61. For an exception to this phenomenon, see W. C. Lubenow, 'Social Recruitment and Social Attitudes: The Buckinghamshire Magistrates, 1868–1888', *The Huntington Library Quarterly* 40/3 (1977), pp. 247–68.

[92]   Philips, 'Black Country Magistracy', pp. 169, 181; A. Edgar, 'On the Jurisdiction of Justices of the Peace in Disputes Between Employers and Employed Arising from Breach of Contract', in George W. Hastings (ed.), *Transactions of the National Association for the Promotion of Social Science, 1859* (London, 1860), p. 687. For some examples of conflicts of interests among magistrates in labor cases, see: 'Meeting of the Colliers at Worsley', *NS* (22 June 1844), p. 5; 'The Colliers: Cases Before the Magistrates', *NS* (16 September 1843), p. 4; 'The Coal Kings and the Law', *NS* (23 September 1843), p. 4; 'Cases Before the Magistrates', *NS* (30 September 1843), p. 4; 'Cumberland Quarter Sessions', and 'Coal Kings and Their Law Breakings', *NS* (28 October 1843), pp. 4–5; 'The Colliers: A Most Foul and Damnable Case', *NS* (16 December 1843), p. 4; 'Constitutional Law versus Coal King Law', *NS* (30 December 1843), p. 4; 'More Tyranny of the Coal Kings: Magistrates in Derbyshire', *NS* (24 February 1844), p. 4; Challinor, *Radical Lawyer*, pp. 71, 89. Also see pp. 000–000, Chapter 3, this volume.

[93]   T. J. Nossiter, *Influence, Opinion and Political Idioms in Reformed England: Case Studies from the Northeast, 1832–1874* (London, 1975), pp. 9–10, 30–31, 147; Robert Colls,

This transformation might also have contributed to the changing use of master and servant law. Douglas Hay and Peter King suggest that in the eighteenth century the ratio of wage recovery cases to employee discipline cases was nearly equal, or even favorable to workers in some jurisdictions. Yet, by the 1860s employers were responsible for two-thirds of the master and servant cases in many regions. D. C. Woods examined 670 master and servant cases reported in the *Walsall Free Press* between 1858 and 1875, and found that only 13.4 percent of the cases were workers seeking redress against employers. Although this source is likely to under-report wage recovery cases, it is consistent with the general findings of other historians. Changes in the social composition of the magistracy in Wolverhampton and the Black Country resulted in a significant alteration in the enforcement of master and servant law, workplace theft and the payment of truck wages.[94]

The growing number of magistrates who were also employers in mining or manufacturing undermined the legitimacy of Petty Sessions for many workers. The *Northern Star* often referred to magistrates in Lancashire, Durham or Northumberland as either 'Cotton Lord Justices' or 'Coal King Justices'. The magistrates often played into this construction, as when Mr Wheildon, a magistrate and coal master, convicted three of his own employees to a month in prison without permitting them to speak in their defense.[95] In September of 1843, Roberts defended a group of miners against a master and servant charge before a magistrate who was the father of the prosecuting mine owner.[96] The *Potters' Examiner* argued that magistrates enforced employment contracts with much greater vigor against potters than their employers, and claimed that magistrates were dismissive of workers attempts to collect unpaid wages or those paid in truck. This was because magistrates believed that employers 'are very nice men, and it is really a pity that such honourable, kind, benevolent gentlemen should be annoyed by "a idle set of vagabonds". Thus saith the law'.[97] Between December of 1843 and May of 1844, the *Potters' Examiner* ran several editorials complaining about the biased administration of the law by magistrates.[98] Roberts wrote in *Miners'*

The Pitmen of the Northern Coalfield: Work, Culture, and Protest, 1790–1850 (Manchester: Manchester University Press, 1987), pp. 251–2.

[94] Hay, 'Patronage, Paternalism, and Welfare', pp. 36–9; Peter King, 'Summary Courts and Social Relations in Eighteenth Century England', *Past and Present* 183 (May 2004): 142; Philips, 'Black Country Magistracy', p. 176. Hay, 'Master and Servant in England', pp. 231–7, 250, 255–8; Woods, 'Master and Servants', p. 102; Simon, 'Master and Servant', pp. 160–71; Roger Swift, 'The English Urban Magistracy and the Administration of Justice During the Early Nineteenth Century: Wolverhampton, 1815–1860', *Midlands History* 17 (1992), pp. 76–92.

[95] 'Warwickshire', *MA* 1/15 (15 June 1844), p. 120; *NS* (23 December 1843).

[96] 'The Colliers: Cases Before the Magistrates', *NS* (23 September 1843), p. 5.

[97] 'To The Editor of the Potters' Examiner', *PEWA* 1/5 (30 December 1843), p. 34.

[98] 'The Potters' Examiner and Workman's Advocate', *PEWA* 1/2 (16 December 1843), p. 20; 'The Potters' Examiner and Workman's Advocate', *PEWA* 1/3 (23 December 1843),

Magazine that in previous cases where miners used master and servant law to recover unpaid wages from their bond, 'The case is dismissed – the men pay the costs – and master and magistrate dine together – the viewer having a jug of ale to his own self in the kitchen'.[99] In 1843, a Cumberland coal owner prosecuted some striking miners at Quarter Sessions for rioting. A miners' journal summed up the case as follows: 'Evidence was procured. A little goes a great way! The coal owners are the magistrates!'.[100] The *Northern Star* observed that a magistrate had to find it difficult to rule against 'a man with whom [he] dined but yesterday – to whom perhaps [his] estate is deeply mortgaged, or by whose permission, perhaps [he] was enabled to "qualify for a Justice"'.[101] In an article in the *Flint Glass Makers Magazine*, Roberts argued defending workers before magistrates was 'at best an uphill game' because 'all their tendencies and circumstances are against you', including 'hundreds of considerations … meetings, political counsels, intermarriages, hopes from wills'. In addition to these obvious conflicts of interest, Roberts suggested that magistrates and employers shared an ideology that made it hard for them to hear and understand the arguments of workers.[102]

This problem of magistrates' legitimacy was especially acute in Northumberland and Durham where 'most of the active magistrates were men with interest in the coal trade'. As early as 1832, General Sir Henry Bouverie recommended to the Home Office that Stipendiary Magistrates be appointed in Northumberland and Durham because 'the majority of magistrates in this district being themselves owners or interested in collieries – their decisions and proceedings were often liable to misrepresentation'.[103] Nine years later General Charles Napier was less diplomatic on the subject, calling the magistrates of those counties 'violent, irritable, uncompromising … sneaking and base'.[104] In April of 1844, the Bishop of Durham explained to Sir James Graham:

---

p. 29; 'To The Editor of the Potters' Examiner', *PEWA* 1/5 (30 December 1843), p. 34; 'The Potters' Examiner and Workman's Advocate', *PEWA* 1/6 (6 January 1844), p. 44; 'To Mr. Mason's Turnouts', *PEWA* 1/12 (17 February 1844), pp. 89–90; 'To the Editor of the Potters' Examiner', *PEWA* 1/15 (9 March 1844), p. 116; 'To T.B. Rose, Esq. Stipendiary Magistrates for the Borough of Stoke Upon Trent', *PEWA* 1/18 (30 March 1844), pp. 137–9; 'The Hiring System', *PEWA* 1/19 (6 April 1844), pp. 145–7.

[99]   Wigan Public Library: D/D2/A31/39, Pitmen's Strike Collection.

[100]   Wigan Public Library: D/D2 A31/121, Pitmen's Strike Collection.

[101]   'Mr. Roberts – Helper – Messrs. Halsam: "To Prevent Any Mistake"', *NS* (20 April 1844), p. 4.

[102]   Challinor and Ripley, *Miners' Association*, pp. 98–9.

[103]   Colls, *Pitmen of the Northern Coalfield*, pp. 251–2. This was echoed by the *Northern Star* in December of 1843. 'Durham Damnable Again', *NS* (23 December 1843), p. 4.

[104]   Challinor, *Radical Lawyer*, 78.

Property in coal mines is so widely diffused in the county of Durham that probably there are few magistrates who are not, somehow or another, connected with it ... The pitmen cannot divest themselves of the apprehension that they are before a partial tribunal, when disputes arise between them and their masters. And these jealousies are furthered by the arts of a man, named Roberts, who has unfortunately gained the confidence of the pitmen.[105]

The frequency with which Roberts defended cases involving pitmen before mine-owning magistrates, put the latter in a difficult position. If they ruled for the master, the *Northern Star* and Roberts could construct it as further evidence of their bias. If they ruled for the worker, the Chartist journal would report their hand was reluctantly forced by Roberts' legal acumen.[106] For example, after Roberts had successfully defended a group of miners before a bench of magistrates with strong political ties to the prosecutors, the *Northern Star* suggested:

It was universally believed that the decision was not in consequence of the illegality alone of the agreement as stated by them; but that they well knew that the objections taken by Mr. Roberts ... were perfectly tenable. They have lately had enough, it is to be hoped of Queen's Bench law, through 'doing as they liked' by overruling law and everything else ... and being completely upset by the decision of that court, and saddled with the whole expense to risk the trial of another ... they therefore had to swallow the bitter pill of deciding against themselves.[107]

The third most common complaint against magistrates was that their judicial powers encroached upon trial by jury, a sacred right in radicals' understanding of the constitution. Mr Flaxman warned his audience that the bill would 'deprive the British subject of his only safeguard – the trial by jury'.[108] Six days later in Carlisle, Mr Hanson worried that the bill was 'subversive to the best interests and true liberties of the people. It abrogates, in great measure, that best of all safeguards to English liberty – Trial by jury'.[109] A meeting of shoemakers resolved to fight a bill that was 'unjust in principle, tyrannical in practice, and a direct

---

[105]   NA: HO 45 Box 644, 'Bishop of Durham to Sir James Graham' (15 April 1844).

[106]   'Meeting of the Colliers at Worsley', *NS* (22 June 1844), p. 5; 'The Colliers: Cases Before the Magistrates', *NS* (16 September 1843), p. 4; 'The Colliers: More Cases Before the Magistrates', *NS* (23 September 1843), p. 4; 'Cases Before the Magistrates', *NS* (30 September 1843), p. 4; 'Cumberland Quarter Sessions', *NS* (28 October 1843), p. 5; 'The Colliers', *NS* (16 December 1843), p. 1; 'The Tyrant Coal Kings', *NS* (30 December 1843), p. 4; 'Tremendous Explosion of a Coal Pit Conspiracy', *NS* (24 February 1844), p. 4.

[107]   'Another Triumph for Labour: Important Colliers' Case-Mr. Roberts in Wigan', *NS* (21 May 1844), p. 8.

[108]   'Brighton', *NS* (27 April 1844), p. 6; Epstein, 'Cap of Liberty', p. 84.

[109]   'Public Meeting in Carlisle', *NS* (27 April 1844), p. 8.

violation of Britons' boast – trial by jury'.[110] *The Nonconformist* quoted Blackstone in opposing the bill's threat to 'the palladium of British Liberty – Trial by Jury'.[111] Many other speakers made reference to the jury trial as an essential right under the constitution.[112] When Roberts ran for Parliament in Blackburn in 1847, he pledged to fight 'the continual increase in the powers of magistrates, abrogating the principle of trial by jury'.[113]

The continuing struggle over the expansion of magistrates' summary powers was described in the introduction. At different times between 1792 and 1833, Charles Fox, Edmund Burke, William Cobbett, Lord Brougham and even Sir Robert Peel expressed the dangers of losing 'that most cherished principle of English law' to continually expanding summary jurisdiction. As Home Secretary, Peel had opposed allowing magistrates to try petty assaults by summary process, because 'great caution' should be observed in expanding their powers. In 1839, when Benjamin Hawes proposed expanding magistrates' summary jurisdiction to include larcenies in London, *The Times* warned that 'the friends of liberty and order' opposed any encroachment on trial by jury. The *Morning Herald* called trial by jury 'the boast of Englishmen' and 'a bulwark against tyranny'. Even the City Council of London resolved that it was opposed to any subversion of trial by jury.[114]

Opponents of giving more judicial powers to magistrates also mocked their knowledge and partiality. Lord Brougham delivered a scathing attack on magistrates' conduct in a speech before Parliament in 1828. In the same year Charles Bird compared summary hearings to Star Chambers, and complained of their conflicts of interest when administering the law. Cobbett mocked the partiality of magistrates in *Rural Rides* (1830). In 1840, Mr Wakely protested against expanding summary jurisdiction to include juvenile thefts because magistrates were 'characterized by ill-temper, faction, and the most besotted ignorance'.[115] Although there is a lot of continuity in the criticism of the magistracy, the changing social background of these officers profoundly changed the context of this familiar rhetoric.

The language used by labor in opposing the 1844 bill, and in nearly every subsequent protest against master and servant law, needs to be seen in the wider context of debates about the English legal system. Labor both made contributions to, and also took advantage of, the controversy over magistrates' expanding summary powers. Chapters 4 and 5 show that some of the trade unions' loudest

---

[110]   'Great Meeting of the Western Division of Journeymen boot and Show Makers, To Petition Against the Masters and Servants' Bill', *NS* (27 April 1844), p. 6.

[111]   'The Master and Servants Bill', *NC* (1 May 1844), pp. 292–3.

[112]   'Wigan', 'Bristol', *NS* (13 April 1844), pp. 7–8.

[113]   Challinor and Ripley, *Miners' Association*, p. 224.

[114]   Sweeney, 'Summary Jurisdiction', pp. 91, 120, 131–2, 145–9; Challinor, *Radical Lawyer*, p. 78.

[115]   Sweeney, 'Summary Jurisdiction', pp. 118–19, 132, 145–9, 156; Epstein, 'Cap of Liberty'; James Epstein, 'The Populist Turn', *Journal of British Studies* 32/2 (1993): 177–89.

protests against the actions of specific magistrates coincided with attempts in Parliament to expand magistrates' summary jurisdiction. The need to expand the judicial authority of magistrates as the business of the legal system swelled, combined with the publicity resulting from the legal conflict between labor and justices of the peace, forced Parliament to enact legislation that settled the forms and procedures of the summary process.[116]

Protesters against the 1844 bill strategically positioned themselves with members of Parliament by adopting familiar arguments against the expansion of summary procedure to oppose master and servant law. While this rhetoric was strategic, it also reflected the very real grievances of those who experienced first-hand how interested magistrates sometimes enforced these laws. This language was not only useful in defeating the 1844 bill, but when combined with their courtroom efforts, had a profound impact on developments in the English legal system as a whole.

The Defeat of the 1844 Master and Servant Bill

On 1 May, Thomas Duncombe presented to Parliament the last of the 213 petitions opposing the Master and Servant Bill. He began debate on the bill's third reading with a scathing attack on its sponsors, calling their proposal 'one of the most insidious, arbitrary, iniquitous, and tyrannical attempts to oppress the working class that had ever been made'. Undaunted by the laughter his hyperbole provoked, Duncombe drew attention to the petitions against the bill, observing that no petitions had been presented in favor of the bill. He further questioned the justice and wisdom of imprisonment for breach of a civil contract, asking 'were the treadmill and the policeman's stave the only ties the Rt. Hon. Baronet could think of to unite the labouring classes with their employers?' Before returning to his seat, Duncombe moved that consideration on the bill be postponed for six months. Joseph Hume, author of the 1823 Master and Servant Act, seconded the motion, suggesting a select committee thoroughly study the subject before proposing further legislation.[117]

The supporters of the bill expressed surprise at the reaction to their proposal, arguing that the petitioners had been misled. Gally Knight asserted that their only intention had been to assist workers in the collection of unpaid wages. Graham reminded the house that the penal sanctions in the fourth clause of the bill were 'already the law of the land' for many workers. Not only did it not create a new law, it made the old law more benevolent. The sponsors of the bill argued that it made it easier to collect unpaid wages, raised the amount collectable, allowed magistrates

---

[116]   David Bentley, *English Criminal Justice in the Nineteenth Century* (London, 1998), pp. 19–20; W. R. Cornish and G. de N. Clark, *Law and Society in England 1750–1950* (London, 1989), pp. 34–5.

[117]   *Hansard Debates*, Vol. 74, cols. 518–23.

the choice of summoning workers rather than issuing a warrant, and lowered the maximum prison sentence for breach of contract. Mr Granger responded by observing 'that if the working classes were asked whether they would, for the sake of ... the advantages this bill purported to give them, submit to be imprisoned ... for the non-performance of any specific contract, the answer ... would be a decided negative'.[118]

Other speakers either dismissed the bill as unnecessary, recommended further study of the issue by a committee or condemned the fourth clause as 'unreasonable'. However, as the debate lurched toward dinner time, members' interest in the discussion began to evaporate. Much of Robert Palmer's speech in defense of his bill was drown out by loud cries of 'Division! Division!'. When the division on the motion to postpone was finally held, the tellers for the ayes emerged with a nearly two-to-one victory.[119] The bill had been soundly defeated.

Responses to the bill's defeat were varied. The *Justice of the Peace* claimed that 'never was so harmless a production so unjustly vilified'. Its editorial argued that because of labor's successful campaign 'certain persons are to continue to be subjected to a bad law, and magistrates called on to execute an almost unintelligible one, simply because some object to being governed by any law at all'.[120] *The Times* and the *Nonconformist* attacked the government for 'foul dealing' because of the Home Secretary's involvement with a private member's bill. *The Times* stopped short of calling for a repeal of master and servant law, but did suggest that among job and piece workers at least, economic interest was sufficient to bind them to their employers, making legal compulsion unnecessary.[121]

The *Northern Star* proclaimed the 'Triumph of Labour' over 'the government attempt to make him a very slave of his employer'. For the next week it reported dozens of public testimonials to Thomas Duncombe, speculating on what could be achieved in Parliament if workers elected 20, 40 or 60 'Duncombes'. The trades of London created a 'Duncombe Testimonial Committee' to raise a penny subscription among its members to present Duncombe with a gift.[122]

In conclusion, Chapters 1 and 2 demonstrate the difficulties that unions created for employers and magistrates through their engagement of legal counsel. Magistrates and mine owners petitioned Parliament for legislation that would diminish the effects of unions' legal campaign against master and servant law. The

---

[118]   Ibid., cols. 524–30.

[119]   Ibid., cols. 523, 526, 527–8, 530; 'The Master and Servants Bill', *MC* (2 May 1844), pp. 2–4; 'Wednesday', *MT* (4 May 1844), p. 2.

[120]   'Masters and Servants; Extent and Effect of the Lost Bill', *JP* 8/18 (4 May 1844), p. 290.

[121]   'London: Thursday, May 2nd', *The Times* (4 May 1844), p. 4; 'The Master and Servants Bill', *NC* (1 May 1844), pp. 292–3.

[122]   'The Master and Servants Bill: Labour's Grateful Testimonial to T.S. Duncombe, Esq., M.P., "Vox Populi, Vox Dei!"' *NS* (11 May 1844), p. 1; 'Thanks to T.S. Duncombe', *SRI* (11 May 1844), p. 7.

massive mobilization of labor demonstrates that Roberts' legal work had an impact upon how workers felt about the law, and those who conducted its administration. Labor used a strategic language when protesting the provisions of the 1844 bill, which placed them at the center of a number of debates about the structure of the legal system, and the role of the state in Victorian society. The consequences of this involvement stretch far beyond 1844.

Chapter 3

Trade Union Legal Challenges to Master and Servant Prosecutions: 'The Value of the Law When Honestly Administered'

Introduction

The rhetoric used by trade unions against the 1844 Master and Servant Bill and in the variety of public protests against the behavior and actions of individual magistrates was informed by the labor-funded litigation of Roberts and other solicitors. Roberts was often paid to initiate writs of habeas corpus or certiorari to bring cases before Queen's Bench in instances where legal arguments at Petty Sessions were unsuccessful. In these cases unions fought the use of penal sanctions for breach of contract by taking advantage of the close scrutiny that high court judges gave magistrates' warrants of commitment and convictions when brought up by these writs. These high court justices were willing to overturn magistrates' rulings based upon the slightest legal error partly due to concern over the lack of procedural safeguards in summary hearings. They hoped to use the opportunity to assert their authority over, and impose more uniform forms upon, an expanding and largely unprofessional branch of the judicial system.[1] An examination of the full local context of the master and servant hearings that produced the cases brought before Queen's Bench suggests that the Judges' suspicion of magistrates' adjudications was well-placed.

These events coincided with frequent debates inside and outside of Parliament over the merits of expanding the summary powers of magistrates, discussions to which Roberts and organized labor made important contributions during the 1840s. Their efforts, and the resulting complaints of magistrates, added to longstanding pressure on Parliament to reform and consolidate the rules and forms of summary hearings. This litigation and its reporting had important consequences for the development of the law and legal reform, and also encouraged workers to view different levels of the legal system with different levels of trust.

The *Northern Star* and trade union journals gave heavy publicity to Roberts' victories because they legitimated many of the beliefs and aspirations of trade

---

[1] Bruce P. Smith, 'Circumventing the Jury: Petty Crime and Summary Justice in London and New York City, 1790–1855' (PhD dissertation, Yale University, 1996), pp. 186–99, 204–12; Jim Evans, 'Change in the Doctrine of Precedent During the Nineteenth Century', in Lawrence Goldstein (ed.), *Precedent in Law* (Oxford, 1987), pp. 35–72.

unionists and Chartists. Despite the fact that in most of Roberts' cases the higher courts ruled on errors in form on court documents, many trade unionists interpreted these rulings as the higher courts rejecting regimes of labor discipline that relied upon one-sided contracts enforced with penal sanctions by local magistrates with strong political and social ties to employers. In master and servant cases arising out of strikes, workers often interpreted the victory by Roberts as not merely a legal outcome, but as a validation of the justice of the cause for which they were striking. For Chartists, these outcomes in the higher courts meant that in the true constitution and the 'real law', the poor were protected as much as the wealthy, and, as with Parliament, the key was to win the access that was their right as 'freeborn Englishmen'. Chartists argued that a narrowly self-interested and corrupt class excluded working men from the Parliamentary franchise that was rightfully theirs. Worse still, this class was using its position to pass laws that were unfavorable to the poor, and take over the administration of law at the local level as magistrates, blocking the working man's rightful access to 'real law' under the constitution.

This chapter explores a selection of the master and servant litigation before Queen's Bench that was funded by trade unions during the 1840s, exploring the origins of these cases, as well as the reactions of radicals and organized labor to their outcome.[2] When one studies these actions from the case reports alone, it appears that organized labor was merely taking advantage of magistrates' 'technical' errors on the face of the warrants of committal. When one moves beyond the case report to explore the full context, however, it becomes clear that organized labor only contested master and servant convictions in Queen's Bench when there was injustice at the summary level. Labor's representatives had to make use of the only methods the law provided, however imperfect, for challenging magistrates' rulings in these cases.

Chapter 6 describes the difficulties that these efforts created for even the most honest and fair-minded magistrates. They complained about the increasing number of challenges to their rulings, and demanded greater protection from Parliament and the high courts. This undoubtedly added to the chorus of dissatisfaction with the rules of magistrates' summary proceedings and, almost certainly, the urgency for reform and clarification, which took the form of the Jervis Acts of 1848–1849.

---

[2]   Many actions before the Court of Queen's Bench that were initiated by Roberts have not been included here. Roberts' extensive work in Northumberland and Durham between August and December 1843, in which he attempted to make the miners' bond more reciprocally binding, is well covered in other secondary literature. See Raymond Challinor, *Radical Lawyer in Victorian England: W. P. Roberts and the Struggle for Workers' Rights* (London, 1990), pp. 89–101, 113–14; Robert Steinfeld, *Coercion, Contract and Free Labour in the Nineteenth Century* (Cambridge, 2001), pp. 107–11.

Master and Servant Prosecutions before Queen's Bench, 1843–1848

During the mid nineteenth century, local courts played an important role in determining the outcome of industrial conflicts. Employers used locally administered laws, such as the Master and Servant Acts and the poor law, to force striking employees to return to work. They also turned to magistrates for enforcement of the 1825 Combination Laws Repeal Amendment Act to prevent effective picketing and ease the recruitment of replacement workers. The magistracy figured prominently in dealing with the various assaults, scuffles, vagrancy offenses, evictions and riots that frequently accompanied industrial strife, all of which were vigorously prosecuted by employers. Not to be outdone, Roberts often brought actions against masters for withholding wages earned during the strikers' notice period, or paying wages in truck. The law set the boundaries within which these strikes occurred, and had the potential to provide tremendous advantages.

This can be seen clearly in nineteenth-century mining. The National Miners' Association of Great Britain and Ireland, formed in August of 1842, expanded to nearly 50,000 members during 1843–1844. Mine owners and subcontractors, anxious to prevent this organization from obtaining a foothold in their pits, were prepared to use every legal (and extra-legal) weapon at their disposal to check its growth, including master and servant statutes. The expansion of the union was followed by a wave of small turnouts at pits in six different counties, culminating in a large strike across Northumberland and Durham between April and August of 1844. This great strike was followed by an explosion of small rolling strikes in Lancashire that resulted in significant numbers of master and servant prosecutions.[3]

Roberts defended workers in these cases and sometimes sought writs of habeas corpus and/or certiorari to bring the case before Queen's Bench. He had great success with these writs because the warrant of commitment under the 1823 Master and Servant Act was tricky for magistrates and their clerks to write correctly. This act gave magistrates the authority to 'commit' (rather than 'convict') workers to the house of correction upon an information (the formal complaint) made under oath by an employer or his agent. The wording of the Act was ambiguous as to whether a written conviction was required by the statute to justify an imprisonment, or if it demanded only a warrant of commitment. Magistrates and their clerks were

---

[3]   Raymond Challinor and Brian Ripley, *The Miners' Association: A Trade Union in the Age of Chartists* (London, 1968), Chapters 6 and 7. The local institutions of justice were busy during the 1844 strike in Northumberland and Durham. In July of 1844, after the strike had been underway for three months, the *Nonconformist* reported that over 70 pitmen were convicted at the local Quarter Sessions for strike-related offences, observing that 'the county gaol is extremely crowded, there being about one hundred and fifty more prisoners in it now than at the corresponding period last year'. 'The Strike', *NC* (17 July 1844), p. 519; Rule, 'The Formative Years of British Trade Unionism', in Rule (ed.), *British Trade Unionism, 1750–1850: The Formative Years* (London, 1988), pp. 18–21.

frequently unsure what facts needed to be recited in a warrant of commitment if it was unaccompanied by a valid conviction form. Did it need to contain all the necessary facts and evidence to establish that the magistrate had acted within his jurisdiction, or could it appear in the less rigorous form of an order to the Keeper of the House of Correction? Magistrates and their clerks often assumed the latter, but during the 1840s, the justices of Queen's Bench consistently ruled that if the warrant of commitment was the only instrument justifying the imprisonment, then it needed to contain information found in a valid conviction form.[4] Roberts made use of this confusion with writs of habeas corpus and certiorari many times between 1843 and 1848.

Master and servant statutes were frequently used to attack union 'ringleaders'.[5] In South Staffordshire, one such conflict arose between the union and butty colliers James and Samuel Dabbs, who worked a pit owned by Philip Williams. The Dabbs encouraged non-union men to provoke fights with the employees organizing for the union, causing four miners to leave work early on 27 December 1843. The Dabbs later denied that the men left work due to a scuffle, but insisted that their absence was an unlawful protest against the continued employment of non-union workers. The next day the four miners returned to work, and were about to descend into the pit, when two of them were pulled out of the tub and hauled before a Bilston magistrate for absenting themselves from their work. The magistrate was an 'extensive Iron and Coal master, who had been sending circulars to the men advising them not to join the union'. The prisoners, Fairley and Jones, were convicted and sentenced to two months at hard labor under 4 George IV, c.34 (1823) without being allowed to speak or call witnesses in their defense.

The Dabbs then swore out another information, and the magistrate issued a warrant for a miner named Thomas Lewis, who had also left his work early on that Wednesday. Later that evening, the same magistrate convicted Lewis to two months imprisonment at hard labor without permitting him to speak in his defense, saying 'hush, you have been as bad as the others, now you must suffer the same'. The next day, the union hired an attorney named Mr James from Walsall, who demanded to have the cases reheard. When this request was denied, he asked to see the warrant of commitment, and again was refused.[6]

A Staffordshire delegate to the National Miners' Association contacted Roberts and asked him to investigate the case. While Roberts was in South Staffordshire, he was informed of another controversial conviction involving the same Bilston magistrate. At a pit worked by butty collier James Bailey, eight miners refused to continue working because of the dangerous state of the roof. Bailey summoned

---

[4]   Steinfeld, *Coercion*, pp. 153–8.

[5]   Daphne Simon, 'Master and Servant', in J. Saville (ed.) *Democracy and the Labour Movement: Essays in Honour of Donna Torr* (London, 1954), p. 172.

[6]   'The Tyrant Coal Kings', *NS* (30 December 1843), p. 4; 'Liberation of the Staffordshire Colliers: Triumph of the Law and Trade Unions', *NS* (20 January 1844), p. 4.

the men before magistrates for neglecting their work under an unspecified master and servant statute. As a matter of established law, workers had the right to refuse to work under clearly unsafe conditions, though in practice this right was often denied because it was not easy to prove the danger to a magistrate.[7] They were each fined 9s, which two of the miners could not (or would not) pay, and in default were committed to the House of Correction. As the magistrates were delivering their ruling, the roof at the pit collapsed. Roberts' Staffordshire assistant, William Peplow, observed that the magistrates had made eight men pay 9s each *for saving their own lives*.[8]

While the pit was idle after the cave-in, one of the convicted miners, James Spencer, brought an action against Bailey for the guaranteed wages in his contract, and won 4s. Bailey responded by obtaining a copy of the warrant of commitment that had been written out for Spencer's imprisonment in the event that he defaulted on his fine, and conveyed it to a police constable, who arrested Spencer and took him to the Stafford Gaol. At this point an attorney (not Roberts) intervened, and after some correspondence with the Keeper of the Stafford Gaol, Spencer was released.[9]

The possibility of being prosecuted under master and servant law for failing to perform contracted work made many workers hesitant to exercise their right to refuse to labor in unsafe conditions. Roberts often found himself involved in these type of cases. In 1843, at Wingate Grange Colliery, John Barkhouse was convicted under the 1823 Act for refusing to work because a wire rope used to lower men into the pit was in a state of disrepair. Roberts eventually negotiated the replacement of the damaged rope, but was unsuccessful in getting compensation for the time that Barkhouse and others were unable to work. In a similar case from November 1844, an engineer at a colliery in Pemberton was discharged for joining the miners' union, and was replaced by a man who was unqualified for the job. The miners working in the pit refused to work, citing the danger posed by having an inexperienced engineer raise and lower the tubs that men rode down into the pit. The owner charged them under the 1823 Act. After hearing testimony that the new engineer had allowed an empty tub to get pulled up into the gearings, which likely would have resulted in fatalities or serious injuries had there been men

---

[7]   *Priestly v. Fowler* (1837). In part of this famous ruling, Lord Abinger clearly stated that a servant could lawfully refuse an order from his master that he reasonably anticipated would endanger him. See A. W. B. Simpson, *Leading Cases in the Common Law* (Oxford, 1995), p. 108; J. Bronstein, *Caught in the Machinery: Workplace Accidents and Injury in Nineteenth Century Britain* (Stanford, 2008); Bartrip and Burman, *The Wounded Soldiers of Industry: Industrial Compensation Policy, 1833–1897* (Oxford, 1983).

[8]   Newspaper reports of master and servant cases often confused the abatement of wages, or the assignment of costs, with fines. In practice the two former sanctions acted as fines, but they are legally distinct. 'Tyranny of the Coal Kings in South Staffordshire', *NS* (13 January 1844), p. 4; Challinor and Ripley, *Miners' Association*, p. 106.

[9]   'Tyranny of the Coal Kings in South Staffordshire', *NS* (13 January 1844), p. 4.

inside, the magistrates ordered the employer to pay costs, find a proper engineer and permit his men to serve their notice. The owner refused. The union hired Roberts to summon the master for the wages that the men would have earned had they been allowed to serve their notice. After a hearing that lasted almost six hours, the employer was ordered to pay each miner £2 and costs.[10] Had the miners in any of these cases continued working and been killed or injured, their families would have been unlikely to collect damages in court from the employers for providing unsafe workplaces or hiring incompetent workmen. This was due to the employers' defenses of 'voluntary assumption of risk', 'contributory negligence' and 'doctrine of common employment'. The higher courts expanded these defenses in ways that made it nearly impossible to hold employers legally liable for creating unsafe working conditions.[11]

In the case of Lewis, Fairley and Jones, Roberts applied to Queen's Bench for writs of habeas corpus and certiorari. On 13 January, barrister W. H. Bodkin delivered arguments for Roberts before Mr Justice Williams. He asserted that the committals against Jones and Fairley were insufficient because they omitted the prisoners' occupation, which was necessary for establishing the magistrates' jurisdiction under the 1823 statute. Opposing counsel conceded this point, and Jones and Fairley were freed. Bodkin then argued that the commitment in the case of Lewis was invalid because it failed to state that the conviction had been founded upon evidence given under oath, as Section 2 of the 1823 Act required. Williams agreed and discharged Lewis. Williams ruled that 'It is essential to the jurisdiction of justices, that the hearing, as well as the information, should have been upon oath, and as there is no statement to that effect here, the warrant is bad, and the prisoner must be discharged'.[12] This ruling not only freed Lewis, but its precedent was used to free other workers in the future.

The case report leaves one with the impression that Lewis' barrister had freed his client by cleverly seizing upon a technical flaw in the form of the commitment that bore no relation to the actual case. Yet, in all likelihood, the evidence actually *was not* heard under oath, and perhaps that was one of the lesser injustices of the hearing. The case report did not mention that the magistrate in this case, a prominent union-busting mine owner himself, had not permitted the miners to speak, let alone present a defense. If during the 1840s the judges of the higher

---

[10]   'Wingate Grange Colliery', *NS* (2 September 1843), p. 7; 'Wingate Grange Colliery', *NS* (16 September 1843), p. 7; 'The Wingate Wire Rope Case', *NS* (3 August 1844), p. 4; Challinor, *Radical Lawyer*, pp. 89–90; 'More of Labour's Triumphs: Manchester and Wigan', *NS* (30 November 1844), p. 1.

[11]   Despite the hostility of the courts, over 60 civil suits against employers for workplace injuries were appealed to the common law courts during the 1850s and 1860s, many of them funded by trade unions. Bartrip and Burman, *The Wounded Soldiers*, pp. 119, 121–2; Bronstein, *Caught in the Machinery*.

[12]   'Reg v. Jones and others', *JP* 8/3 (20 January 1844), p. 56; *The Queen v. Lewis*, (1844) 13 L. J. 46; Steinfeld, *Coercion*, p. 154; Napier, 'Contract of Service', p. 123.

courts strictly construed statutes that gave magistrates summary powers, and carefully scrutinized their forms, perhaps they did so with some justification.[13]

The *Miners' Advocate* and the *Northern Star* pressed this argument, the latter in an article titled 'Liberation of the Staffordshire Colliers: Triumph of the Law and Trades' Unions'. The author praised the wisdom of Mr Justice Williams, and condemned the magistrate, who had three miners 'committed to prison, and retained there, with all the forms of law trodden under foot, merely to serve the convenience of the masters'. The writer lamented the great cost of obtaining 'real law', which the men could not have afforded without the help of the union. The article warned that an individual was no match for the alliance of employers and magistrates, who used locally administered law for their advantage. Therefore, the miners needed to unite and create a legal fund to protect their rights through the higher courts, where 'constitutional law' was found. The journal provided an address for W. H. Bodkin, who could provide a legal opinion on the validity of magistrates' rulings for £2 4s 6d. The freed miners were welcomed home with popular celebrations, and the week after Roberts' victory was reported, Staffordshire saw a substantial rise in membership of the National Miners' Association.[14]

One of the strategies of the Miners' Association for improving conditions for their membership was the policy of restriction of output. Beginning in May 1843, the miners decided to use their autonomy in the pit to limit the supply of coal. The stated goal was to correct overproduction by mine owners, raise the price of coal and spread employment to surplus labor. Some mine owners responded to this threat to their control of the workplace by using the clause in some employment contracts that stipulated that employees 'should do a sufficient day's work' to justify prosecution under the Master and Servant Acts.[15]

---

[13]   Steinfeld, *Coercion*, p. 153.

[14]   'The Liberation of the Staffordshire Colliers: Triumph of the Law and Trades' Unions', *NS* (20 January 1844), p. 4; 'Another Glorious Triumph For the Miners' Association', *MA* (27 January 1844), p. 37; 'South Staffordshire', *NS* (20 January 1844), p. 1. The frequency with which unionized workers held celebrations with music and processions to commemorate the release of workers convicted under the Master and Servant Acts speaks to the lack of legitimacy of these laws. For example, on 9 February 1844, the Potters' Union held a dinner at the Crown's Inn with over 100 guests to celebrate the release of Elijah Hume, who had completed a one-month sentence in the House of Correction for leaving the employment of C. J. Mason without notice. The occasion was marked by music, drinking and 'good cheer'. There was also the resolution that 'there was no moral stain upon his character from the punishment he [Hume] had undergone'. See 'Progress of Trade Reform: Fenton', *PEWA* 1/12 (17 February 1844), p. 93.

[15]   A. J. Taylor, 'The National Miners' Association of Great Britain and Ireland, 1842–48: A Study in the Problem of Integration', *Economica* 22/85 (1955): 52; Challinor and Ripley, *Miners Association*, pp. 69, 111–15, 138; Richard Fynes, *The Miners of Northumberland and Durham: A History of their Social and Political Progress* (Wakefield, 1873), pp. 50, 62, 67; Taylor, *Report of the Commissioner Appointed Under the Provisions*

Another benefit of restriction was that it prevented mine owners from accumulating large stockpiles of coal that they could use to their advantage during strikes.[16] In one instance, 120 Lancashire miners working for Lancaster and Co. gave their one month's notice to leave work and then proceeded to restrict labor to the point where they were each earning less than 6d per day. On 19 January 1844, the company prosecuted seven of these miners before a magistrate under 4 George IV, c.34 (1823) for neglecting their work. The magistrate informed the men that what they had done during their notice could not be considered working, 'but was the mere pretence of working'. He ordered them to return to work, and upon their refusal, he remanded them for a day so they could have 'further time for reflection'. Magistrates offering reluctant employees the choice between returning to work or prison were common outcomes of master and servant prosecutions.[17] The next day they again refused to return to work, and were committed to two months' imprisonment each. The Union immediately sent for Roberts, who applied for a writ of habeas corpus and, on 7 February, the miners were freed.[18]

Two weeks later Roberts had two other miners brought to Westminster on a writ of habeas corpus. These miners had been employed at Lord Vernon's Point and Worth collieries, and were convicted under the 1823 Act for leaving their employment. Huddleston argued the case before Mr Justice Coleridge, who quashed the conviction. Unfortunately, these cases do not appear in the law reports, and nothing in the Queen's Bench records indicates the precise grounds upon which the convictions were overturned. It is likely that they were ruled invalid because they failed to state that the magistrate was acting within the county where he had jurisdiction.[19]

These victories were reported in *Northern Star* articles titled 'Steam Gaol Delivery: Another Glorious Triumph of Constitutional Law Over Magisterial Ignorance', 'Liberation of the Knutsford Colliery Victims', 'Another Triumph For the Miners', 'Tremendous Explosion of a Coal Pit Conspiracy' and a lengthy

---

of the Act 5 & 6 Victoria, c. 99 to the Operation of That Act and Into the State of the Mining Districts (London, 1846), pp. 7, 10–13.

[16] 'More Coal-King Tyranny', *NS* (13 April 1844), p. 5; 'The Miners' Union', *NS* (8 June 1844), p. 1; 'Committal of Coal Miners for Neglect of Work', *MG* (24 January 1844), p. 7; Challinor, *Radical Lawyer*, pp. 121, 130, 167–8.

[17] For the use of master and servant law to compel specific performance of the contract of employment, see Steinfeld, *Coercion*, pp. 58–65.

[18] 'Committal of Coal Miners for Neglect of Work', *MG* (24 January 1844), p. 4; 'Steam Gaol Delivery: Another Glorious Triumph of Constitutional Law Over Magisterial Ignorance', *NS* (10 February 1844), p. 4; Challinor and Ripley, *Miners' Association*, p. 106; Challinor, *Radical Lawyer*, pp. 167–8. Four years later, Roberts returned to this colliery to represent the families of victims killed in a mine accident at the inquest, NA: HO/45/1873.

[19] 'Liberation of the Knutsford Colliery Victims', and 'Another Triumph for the Miners: Judges' Chambers, London, Feb. 24', *NS* (2 March 1844), pp. 4, 7; 'Commitments – Form', *JP* 8/20 (18 May 1844), p. 333.

biography of 'W. P. Roberts'. The articles followed the familiar pattern of heaping praise upon the judges at Westminster Hall, while accusing magistrates of corruptly conspiring with employers when enforcing master and servant law. After reporting the Knutsford victory, the author assured readers that Roberts would pursue actions for false imprisonment against all the magistrates involved in these cases.[20]

'The Tremendous Explosion of a Coal Pit Conspiracy', addressed the criticism that Roberts' victories had nothing to do with the 'merits' of the cases. The author argued that

> It may serve the purposes of magistrates and masters to assert that their proceedings have been set aside by three Justices of the Queen's Bench upon mere technical grounds; but we tell them that it is only because the judges of the land confined themselves strictly to the matters brought before them.

He went on to confess that he, too, 'fell into the common error, of ascribing Mr. Roberts' legal victories to mere omissions of technical forms in the necessary documents'. As the victories multiplied, however, he gave 'closer scrutiny of the whole question' by looking at the circumstances of these cases. He came to the conclusion that employers and magistrates were openly disregarding the law, acting where they lacked jurisdiction and not considering the defense of the prisoners in order to defeat the Miners' Union. The author argued that the 1844 Master and Servant Bill had been introduced to assist mine owners and magistrates in wrongfully using 'the terror of the law' against union members.[21]

In fact, *R. v. Lewis et al.* was by no means the only occasion on which magistrates sentenced miners to imprisonment at hard labor without bothering to hear their defense. On 25 March 1844, magistrate William Wooten Abney similarly treated a group of Derbyshire miners for absenting themselves from work. Two weeks later, the same magistrate sentenced four Leicestershire miners to three months' hard labor for breaking their contracts, again without allowing the prisoners to speak in their defense.[22]

Roberts was sent for to bring both cases before Queen's Bench, as well as the committal of five Yorkshire miners that occurred on 6 March. Issac Tordoft,

---

[20]   'Steam Gaol Delivery: Another Triumph of Constitutional Law Over Magisterial Ignorance', *NS* (10 February 1844), p. 4; 'W.P. Roberts', and 'Tremendous Explosion of a Coal Pit Conspiracy', *NS* (24 February 1844), p. 4; 'Liberation of the Knutsford Colliery Victims', and 'Another Triumph for the Miners', *NS* (2 March 1844), pp. 4, 7.

[21]   'Tremendous Explosion of a Coal Pit Conspiracy', *NS* (24 March 1844), p. 4.

[22]   Between January and March 1844, Derbyshire membership in the National Miners Association grew from 169 to 3,265. Alarmed mine-owners in this county responded by refusing to employ union members, leading to a number of strikes, including the one that led to the prosecution of Copestick. NA: KB 1/119/31, KB 21/64/ 18 April 1844, KB 1/119/30; J. E. Williams, *The Derbyshire Miners: A Study in Industrial and Social History* (London, 1962), pp. 90, 95–7; Challinor and Ripley, *Miners' Association*, pp. 107, 158–9.

John Hirbert, Marlin Fisher, Charles Green and John Priestley, who worked at Stainborough Colliery, were convicted under the 1823 Master and Servant Act for neglecting their work to attend a delegate meeting of their union. The first three months of 1844 were tense ones on the Yorkshire coalfield, as union lecturers were successfully organizing. Employers attempted to counter these efforts with summary dismissals, evictions from company housing, loyalty oaths, 'the document', heavy recruitment of replacement workers, and even violence. A March issue of the *Northern Star* contained complaints from miners at Stainborough Colliery, where Tordoft and the others worked. These miners alleged that stewards refused to raise men out of the pit until they had done sufficient work, and that 'daymen' with steel-capped sticks physically attacked union leaders who questioned this policy. The magistrates who convicted the five miners from Stainborough were also local mine owners heavily engaged in fighting unionization. On 18 April 1844, Roberts had Edwin Copestick of Derbyshire, the four miners from Leicestershire, and the five Yorkshire pitmen brought to Westminster on writs of habeas corpus.[23]

The case of *R. v. Walker, Bird, Richards and Bird of Leicestershire* was heard on 29 April 1844. The warrants of commitment which justified their imprisonment were defective because they failed to state that the convictions had been founded upon evidence given under oath, just as in the case of *R. v. Lewis*. On 15 April, however, after hearing that a habeas corpus was imminent, Abney sent four new warrants of commitment to the House of Correction in which this omission was corrected.[24]

It is possible that Abney got the idea of amending his committals from the 17 February 1844 issue of the *Justice of the Peace*, which contained an article responding to Roberts' three highly publicized victories at Queen's Bench in master and servant cases. The article, 'The Proper Course to Be Adopted by Justices (For Their Protection) Where a Prisoner Who Has Been Committed By Them On an Informal Conviction Applies for a Habeas Corpus', addressed the question of whether the warrant of commitment needed to recite the information contained in the written conviction. The article described the dilemma magistrates faced with the question: 'Will the court assume that the warrant is founded upon a good conviction? It will not. If anything, it will be that the committal correctly recites the conviction; and if one is bad, the other is bad also'. In other words, if

---

[23]   NA: KB 1/119/28, 29, 30, 31, KB 21/64/ 18 April 1844; Frank Machin, *The Yorkshire Miners: A History* (Huddersfield, 1958), pp. 47–53; Challinor and Ripley, *Miners' Association*, pp. 106–7; Challinor, *Radical Lawyer*, p. 104. The practice of refusing to raise men out of the pit until a sufficient quantity of coal was produced was also adopted in parts of Lancashire, 'Miners' Beware: More Coal King Tyranny', *NS* (4 January 1845), p. 7. In the 1850s and 1860s Roberts fought several cases that won the right of miners to come out of the pit when they believed that their work was completed.

[24]   These new warrants stated that the prisoners were 'convicted before me ... upon evidence on the oath of Mr. Benjamin Walker', who was their employer. In the matter of Richards, Bird, and Others, 13 L. J. 147; NA: KB 1/119/31, KB 21/64/ 18 April 1844.

a prisoner used a writ of habeas corpus to bring a warrant of commitment before Queen's Bench that did not recite the information necessary to make a valid conviction, or it was not accompanied by a correctly written conviction form, the prisoner would be released. The article warned that Queen's Bench had 'shown the necessity of great care ... in making convictions, since, through ... habeas corpus, a conviction may in effect be quashed entirely behind their backs, and they may be exposed to all the fearful consequences of an action at law'. The author then assured magistrates that there was a way around this problem:

> magistrates are not bound by the conviction first drawn up, but they are at liberty
> ... to draw up and return a more formal conviction, correcting any errors which
> may have existed ... provided the later one be according to the truth of the
> facts.[25]

There are reasons to doubt whether Abney's second warrants of commitment were in accordance with 'the truth of the facts' of his hearing, but his re-writing them was a clever legal move.

Bodkin and Huddleston handled the brief for Roberts. They argued that the second set of committals sent up by the magistrate were 'intended to substitute formal warrants for informal ones; but in order to do this effectively, the first warrants should have been altogether withdrawn'. They argued that because the first set had not been officially withdrawn, the instruments justifying the imprisonment were still bad. Lord Denman disagreed, ruling 'If the latter warrants are good, the court will not look at the former documents'. The prisoners were remanded to serve the remainder of their sentence.[26]

On the same day, Bodkin, Fry and Huddleston presented their arguments to free Edwin Copestick of Derbyshire. They argued that the warrant of commitment was bad because it failed to state his occupation, that the evidence against him had been presented under oath, and that the contract of employment had been either in writing or entered into by him (as required by Section 3 of the 1823 Act). No counsel appeared to support this warrant, so Copestick was discharged.[27]

---

[25]   'The Proper Course to be Adopted by Justices (For Their Protection), Where A Prisoner Who Has Been Committed By them on An Informal Conviction Applies for a Habeas Corpus', *JP* 8/7 (17 February 1844), pp. 100–101.

[26]   In the Matter of Richards, Bird, and Others, 13 L. J. 147–150; 'The Queen v. Walker and Others', *JP* 8/32 (10 August 1844), pp. 534–5.

[27]   Section 3 of the 1823 Act stated that a servant was liable to prosecution if he/she 'shall not enter into or commence his or her service according to his or her contract (such contract being in writing, and signed by the contracting parties), or having entered into such service shall absent himself or herself from his or her service before the term of his or her contract, whether such contract shall be in writing or not in writing'. 4 George IV, c.34, s.3 (1823); 'The Queen v. Copestick', *JP* 8/18 (4 May 1844), p. 297; Steinfeld, *Coercion*, p. 154.

The same three barristers also argued the case of the Yorkshire miners.[28] They argued that the warrants of commitment were bad because they failed to state that the charge was heard, and the evidence taken, in the presence of the prisoners. Opposing counsel argued that 'No case has gone the length of deciding that a commitment must contain every particular connected with the hearing. It is never stated that the party was present at each step in the case'. They further argued that the form used in this case was the same one found in several textbooks and justices' manuals. The court, however, ruled that the warrant of commitment was bad, asserting that if there was no conviction brought up to support the warrant of commitment, then it needed to contain 'all the necessary words to constitute a conviction'. Tordoft and the four others were discharged, and their case became a useful precedent that would later help to free the four Longton colliers mentioned in the introduction to this book.[29]

While the necessity of actually recording that the prisoner was present when the case against him/her was heard might appear like a 'technicality', in practice it was not something that could be safely assumed. Two weeks after these miners were convicted, a Welsh magistrate sent dairymaid Ellen Griffith to prison under 4 George IV, c.34 (1823) for two months without bothering to have her present at the hearing. Magistrates wrote to the *Justice of the Peace* to ask whether they were allowed to convict workers under the 1823 Master and Servant Act in their absence. The journal always insisted that it was very unwise to do so, but the doubts on this point suggest that workers were sometimes convicted of these offences in their absence.[30]

The Yorkshire miners were welcomed home by a well-attended parade, with workers waving green banners and other Chartist symbols, and playing music.[31] In 'More of Labour's Triumphs: The Value of the Law When Honestly Administered', and 'More Liberations of Miners', the *Northern Star* again praised the Judges of Queen's Bench. These men, unlike magistrates, were interested in 'ascertaining what the law of the case really was, and not … what the value of their judgment was to the masters'. The articles thanked them for 'vindicating the law by discharging the victims of its perversion' in two of the cases Roberts had brought before them. Denman's court ignored 'their interest, and the convenience of that class of society

---

[28]   Referred to in the Law Journals as 'In the Matter of Isaac Tordoft' (sometimes (Tordolf or Tordoff).

[29]   In the Matter of Isaac Tordoff, 13 L. J.145–7; 'The Queen v. Tordoff and Others', *JP* 8/19 (11 May 1844), p. 312; 'The Colliers' Strike in the North – Ex Parte Tordolf and others – Habeas Corpus – The Judgment', *MA* (4 May 1844), p. 54; Steinfeld, *Coercion*, p. 154; 'The Recent Discharges on Writs of Habeas Corpus, of Persons Committed Under the Statutes Relating to Sevants, Artificers, Etc.', *JP* 8/20 (18 May 1844), p. 323. The manuals were *Chitty's Burn's Justice of the Peace* and *D'Oyly & Williams Justice of the Peace*.

[30]   NA: KB 1/120/57; 'Master and Servant – Ex Parte Proceedings', *JP* 9/27 (5 July 1845), p. 411; 'Practical Points', *JP* 9/1 (4 January 1845), p. 11.

[31]   Machin, *The Yorkshire Miners*, pp. 51–2.

to which they belong ... [and] acting upon the pure principle of justice', which 'has gone far in every instance ... to negative the assertion that there is one law for the rich and another for the poor'. It noted that the judges must have been aware how valuable a ruling against the miners would have been to the owners in checking the progress of the union, but they resisted this temptation. The articles expressed hope that 'Lord Deman ... and his brothers of the Queen's Bench, will bring the Dogberries [magistrates] to their senses at last'![32] This constitutionalism and reverence for the common law are familiar radical idioms, but given the context of mine owner magistrates using and bending the law on behalf of other mine owners to defeat unions, this traditional language carried a much more focused class meaning.[33]

In April and May of 1844, miners in many parts of Yorkshire gave notice to go on strike, including 36 pitmen working at a mine owned by George Chambers and his brother's widow. Chambers' miners gave their one-month notice on 16 April 1844, after he rejected their demand for a 6d per ton increase of wages. Chambers claimed, however, that on 20 April he offered the men a 3d increase per ton, and threatened to stop the wages of six miners if they persisted in leaving in order to recover money he had advanced as a loan to them.[34] He asserted that these miners then withdrew their notice and entered into a new verbal contract with him. The six miners in question swore in an affidavit that they neither withdrew their notice, nor entered into a new agreement.

The miners stopped work on the evening of 14 May 1844. The next day two constables visited each of the six miners, instructing them to attend the office of John Otly of Rotherham at 2 p.m., but did not explain why, or show them a summons or warrant. When the miners arrived, magistrate Henry Walker, who was a part-owner of a lead mine, informed them that they were charged under 6 George III, c.25 (1766) with unlawfully leaving their work. One of the prisoners, William Sheldon, called the hearing that followed a 'pretended trial', because they were not permitted to contact an attorney, call witnesses to rebut the charges, or present a defense. A large crowd, made up of miners and the prisoners' families, was physically prevented by constables from approaching the office where the hearing was taking place. After refusing the employer's offer to drop the charges in return

---

[32] 'More Liberations of Miners', *NS* (4 May 1844), p. 4; 'More of Labour's Triumphs: The Value of the Law When Honestly Administered', and 'The Colliers – Ex Parte Copestick', and 'The Colliers Strike in the North – Ex Parte Tordoff and Others – Habeas Corpus', *NS* (11 May 1844), pp. 4–5.

[33] James Epstein, 'The Constitutional Idiom: Radical Reasoning, Rhetoric and Action in Early-Nineteenth Century England', *Journal of Social History* 23/3 (1990): 553–74.

[34] The six were William Sheldon, Thomas Straw, John Straw, Henry Brook, Charles Dickson and Joseph Herbert. Machin, *The Yorkshire Miners*, pp. 57–63.

for continuing work, the miners were sentenced to two months' imprisonment at hard labor within 20 minutes of their arrival at the office.[35]

Such rapid and closed hearings in labor cases were not uncommon. They were one of several strategies employers and magistrates used to reduce the value of the defendants' recently obtained right to legal counsel. Magistrates often refused to adjourn hearings so defendants could obtain counsel or collect witnesses. On occasions when Roberts was present, he sometimes had to argue forcefully with magistrates in order to gain access to his clients before the hearings began.[36] This was such an important issue for northeastern miners that it was included among their bargaining demands in 1844:

> 13. Trials before the magistrates. A man under the old bond has been taken up after breakfast, and sent to gaol for three months before dinner time, without having the opportunity of obtaining any witnesses or professional assistance whatsoever. The men require that before being tried and sent to gaol, they receive a week's notice of the charges, and the names of the witnesses to be brought against them.[37]

One of the innovations in the 1848 Summary Proceedings Act was the provision in Section 12, which stated that the room where magistrates conducted their hearings 'shall be deemed an open and public Court, to which the public generally may have access'.[38] Bertram Osborne has suggested that the 1848 Act would have been a great achievement 'if [it] had contained nothing more than the thirty-one words in Section 12'. In a bit of hyperbole, he compared this section to the Magna Carta in protecting liberty by 'declaring that its fulfillment was not secure behind the closed doors of a justice's parlour'.[39] Roberts' legal work contributed to securing this basic right for defendants in magistrates' summary hearings.

Roberts was sent for immediately, and by 25 May he and solicitor Thomas Pollit had begun preparing the action. On 5 June 1844, a barrister argued before Mr Justice Wightman in the Queen's Bench that the miners should be brought to Westminster on a writ of habeas corpus. He argued that the warrant of commitment was insufficient because it omitted to state that the person who actually made the complaint before the magistrate was the employer or agent with whom the

---

[35]   NA: KB 1/123/39; 'Sheffield', *NS* (25 May 1844), p. 8; 'Rotherham', *SRI* (25 May 1844), p. 2; 'The Colliery Cases', *SRI* (25 May 1844), p. 2.

[36]   Wigan Archives: D/DZ/A/ 39/ 94, Pitmen's Strike Collection; Challinor, *Radical Lawyer*, 142; 'Charge of Intimidation', and 'Charge of Intimidation', *MSA* (8 June 1844), pp. 3, 8, In Re: *Bailey* and In Re: *Collier*, see Chapter 6, this volume.

[37]   'The Miners' Magazine, May', *NS* (25 May 1844), p. 3.

[38]   11 & 12 Victoria, c.43, s.12 (1848).

[39]   Bertram Osborne, *The Justice of the Peace, 1361–1848: A History of the Justices of the Peace for the Counties of England* (Dorset, 1960), pp. 226–8.

defendants had contracted.[40] He did not raise the odd construction of the warrant of commitments, which stated that 'William Sheldon … hath not proved that he is not guilty of the said complaint'.[41] Wightman agreed and granted the writ. Oddly, the men were released from the Wakefield House of Correction without knowing that the Home Office had already freed them a day earlier. On the evening of 4 June 1844, Home Secretary Sir James Graham pardoned the miners at the request of Magistrate Henry Walker, who was perhaps responding to threats of an impending false imprisonment suit made by the Union's local secretary, Joseph Taylor.[42]

Roberts opened an office in Manchester in the autumn of 1844, and spent much of the next two years in Lancashire representing workers in a wide range of trades. He also attended a number of coroner's inquests in mine accidents, attempting to force mine owners to accept greater responsibility for the safety of their pits. His work on behalf of miners brought him into conflict with magistrate Col. James Lindsay, who was the son of the Earl of Balcarres. Balcarres was one of the most extensive mine-owners in Lancashire, and had spent much of 1844 fighting his striking employees.[43] Within eight months, Roberts had three of Lindsay's convictions quashed before Queen's Bench, and successfully sued him for false imprisonment.

William Leigh had worked at Ince Colliery in Mackersfield since April 1844 under an agreement that could be determined with a fortnight's notice on either side. According to the underlooker at the mine, Leigh was attracted by the wage increases won by miners at other pits, and on 9 August 1844 left his work. He returned the next day to give his notice, which he failed to complete. Leigh claimed that his contract with his employers required him to be available to work whenever they chose, but did not require that they provide him with a reasonable amount of work, and therefore lacked mutuality. He argued that his employers had failed to give him sufficient work, so he went elsewhere. On 23 August 1844, he was arrested and tried before Lindsay. Despite Leigh's request for an adjournment so he could procure legal counsel, Lindsay determined the case and within minutes sentenced Leigh and another miner to two months' imprisonment at hard labor.

---

[40]   Unlike 4 George IV, c.34 (1823), 6 George III, c.25 (1766) did not provide for the masters' agent to bring or defend charges in the employers' name. Charges under the 1766 Act had to be brought by the master.

[41]   See Bruce P. Smith, 'The Presumption of Guilt and the English Law of Theft, 1750–1850', *Law and History Review* 23/1 (Spring 2003): 133–71.

[42]   NA: HO 18/136/2, KB 1/123/39; 'Sheffield', *NS* (25 May 1844), p. 8; 'The Colliers', *SRI* (8 June 1844), p. 8; 'Ex Parte Sheldon', *JP* 8/30 (27 June 1844), p. 500.

[43]   In 1847, Lindsay won a tightly contested race for a seat in Parliament from Wigan against a leader of the Miners' Association, William Dixon. During this contest, Lindsay's profound unpopularity with local workers was much in evidence. His infamy with organized labor was added to in 1859, when he ordered troops to fire upon workers on strike at one of his saw-mills, wounding two. Challinor and Ripley, *Miners' Association*, pp. 117, 168, 219–22, 235; Challinor, *Radical Lawyer*, p. 201.

Roberts was engaged to apply to the Court of Queen's Bench for a writ of habeas corpus for Leigh and a miner named Morris. Roberts argued that the warrants of commitment failed to state that the men had either already entered into the service of their employer or were under a written contract, as required by Section 3 of the 1823 Act. On 17 September 1844, after the two miners had spent 25 days at hard labor, Judge Wightman ordered their discharge. On 23 September 1844, the released miners were welcomed home by a well-attended open-air meeting at Ringley. Roberts promised the assembled that although Col. Lindsay 'and his father had been taught that laws were made to wield against those who were below them, the miners would teach them that there was a law which could punish the oppressor and protect the oppressed!'.[44] A week later Roberts, riding in an open carriage, was escorted into Wigan by a procession of miners waving banners and a band playing 'See the Conquering Hero Comes'. Roberts spent nearly £15 in traveling expenses for himself and Leigh, expenses which he expected to recover from Lindsay's pocket. On 14 December 1844, Roberts gave Lindsay notice of William Leigh's intention to sue him for false imprisonment at the next Liverpool Assizes.

On 11 October 1844, Lindsay sentenced miners John Gray and Hugh Blaney to three months' imprisonment for leaving their work without giving adequate notice. Roberts initiated another writ of habeas corpus to bring the prisoners to Westminster, and on 12 and 13 November their cases were argued before Mr Justice Patteson. Bodkin and Huddleston argued the brief, pointing out that both warrants of commitment failed to state that the evidence in the hearing had been given under oath and in the presence of the prisoners. They added that the commitment of Gray failed to state that his contract was either in writing or entered into by the defendant. Opposing counsel, Mr Cowling argued the warrant of commitment required by the 1823 Act was an order, and as such did not require 'the same strict formalities ... and intendment will be made in favour of it'. Patteson replied 'I do not at all go along with you in your argument' and reminded the court that the statute permitted magistrates to hear and determine complaints without a jury, and inflict very serious punishments. He argued 'You may call this commitment what you like, but it is in fact a conviction, and a conviction under a highly penal statute'. He ruled that 'I consider the law to be, that, in convictions under this act of Parliament, where there is a conviction and commitment in one document, it is necessary it should appear that the examination took place in the presence of the party; and that examination was upon oath'. Gray and Blaney were discharged. Three days after the release of these miners, John Howard was discharged under

---

44   NA: KB 1/135/59; 'Meeting of Coal Miners at Ringley', *NS* (28 September 1844), p. 1; 'The Lord's Son and the Collier', and 'Northern Circuit: Action Against a Magistrate For Illegal Imprisonment', *NS* (12 April 1845), pp. 4, 8; *Lindsay v. Leigh*, 17 L. J. 50–57, 116 E. R. 547–50; Steinfeld, *Coercion*, pp. 156–7; 'Grand Procession of Miners at Wigan, In Honour of W. P. Roberts, Esq.', *NS* (4 October 1845), p. 1.

a writ of habeas corpus on the same grounds from the sentence he was serving at New Bailey in Salford.[45]

The pitmen were met with the usual popular celebrations and public rallies, and the *Northern Star* reported the case in an article titled 'Labour's Attorney General versus Labour's Persecutors'. The article praised Patteson for being a 'high-minded functionary', who released the 'victims of low-minded officials' like Lindsay who enforced 'justice-made law' for the convenience of employers. It further encouraged Roberts to pursue Lindsay for false imprisonment to 'make him pay dearly for his first lesson in English law'.[46]

This lesson came on 5 April 1845, when Roberts' barristers conducted an action against Lindsay for false imprisonment before Judge Coltman at the Liverpool Assizes. The prosecution opened by stressing the gulf in social position between the plaintiff and the defendant. They told the jury a story of how the wealthy and powerful son of the Earl of Balcarras had made a young, poor and humble miner, who was working to support his aged parents, spend 25 days at hard labor on the treadmill. They emphasized the considerable expense to which he had been put to obtain his freedom. In their prosecution, they stressed the three critiques of the magistracy that had become common in recent years: the importance of trial by jury as a safeguard, the conflicts of interest among magistrates, and the legal ignorance of these officers. They reminded the jury that the Master and Servant Act gave magistrates extraordinary powers:

> A single magistrate sitting alone was empowered to act as judge and jury. His decision was absolutely binding; he might, upon the single oath of the party complaining, *the other party not being heard at all*, direct the person complained against to be sent to gaol and kept to hard labour for three months; and therefore the power given by the Act was of the very strongest nature, and one which ought to be cautiously exercised, not only in regard to the individual upon whom it was exercised, but in order to satisfy the public that justice was done.

Baines argued that because Lindsay's father was among the most extensive mine-owners in Lancashire, 'he would have exercised a wise discretion if he had declined to act'. While it was not illegal for Lindsay to have acted, Baines pointed out that several more recent acts of Parliament conferring summary jurisdiction forbade interested parties from determining cases as justices in the peace. He then turned to the warrant of commitment and declared that it 'was so perfectly illegal in itself … wanting in almost every requisite that a warrant should have'. He asked the jury to be liberal in damages, as 'these tribunals, in which the accused was deprived of

---

[45]   Re: John Gray and Hugh Blaney, 14 L. J. 26–9; 'R v. John Gray', *JP* 8/49 (7 December 1844), p. 804; Steinfeld, *Coercion*, pp. 155–6; 'Ex Parte John Howard', *JP* 8/47 (23 November 1844), p. 774; 'In Re: John Howard', *JP* 8/4 (7 December 1844), p. 805.

[46]   'Labour's Attorney General Versus Labour's Persecutors', and 'A Public Meeting', *NS* (23 November 1844), pp. 4, 8.

the protection of a jury, where single magistrates were clothed in such extensive powers, should be most strictly watched'.

The prosecution called Roberts to testify to the expenses he had paid in procuring the habeas corpus for Leigh. On cross-examination, the defense attempted to utilize the stereotype of the 'sharp practitioner' who loved fees more than justice to discredit Roberts. To reduce the potential damages, they argued that all of Leigh's expenses were paid by the union, that Roberts was exceedingly well paid by the same union, and that Roberts' presence at Westminster had been unnecessary for obtaining Leigh's release. An unflappable Roberts replied that he had not yet been reimbursed for his expenses out of the union's general fund, his salary was commensurate with his important work and his assistance and consultations with Bodkin had been essential for securing Leigh's freedom.

After Leigh's release the previous September, Lindsay had sought to protect himself by writing a new conviction form for Leigh, which contained none of the errors found in the original warrant of commitment. This was the same strategy pursued by the magistrate in *R. v. Richards* (1844). His counsel presented this amended conviction to the court, and argued that it demonstrated that Lindsay had acted within his jurisdiction, which was protection against this action. Judge Coltman instructed the jury that this document afforded no such protection to the magistrate, and that they should find for the plaintiff. They did, awarding Leigh £30 and all costs, including all of Roberts' expenses for traveling to London. Lindsay's counsel took a bill of exceptions to Coltman's instruction to the jury, and the case eventually moved to the Exchequer Chamber where it took years to run its course.[47]

The *Northern Star* celebrated Roberts' victory in 'The Lord's Son and the Collier', a title that emphasized the equality of both before 'Constitutional Law'. The article reported that Lindsay's conduct had been so reprehensible that it was condemned by 'a jury of his own neighbours'. The author commented on the cross-examination of Roberts, suggesting 'it is no answer that Mr. Roberts is well remunerated for his services … inasmuch as the success of those services would render him, if purchasable, of … greater value to the grinding capitalists'. He observed that through union, men 'could procure that justice which, as individuals, none would be able ever to look for'. Anticipating the appeal to the Exchequer Chamber, the author proclaimed '*what a glorious spectacle!* A humble collier dragged from the bowels of the earth before the highest legal tribunal in the country, with a Lord's son as his opponent!'.[48] Nearly 1,000 Lancashire miners, weavers and mechanics celebrated the victory by marching with Roberts in yet another procession with banners and a band playing 'See the Conquering Hero

---

[47]   All italics in original. NA: KB 1/135/59; 'Northern Circuit: Action against a Magistrate for Illegal Imprisonment' and 'The Lord's Son and the Collier', *NS* (12 April 1845), pp. 4, 8.

[48]   Ibid.

Comes'.[49] It would be several years, in fact, before this ultimately very important case ran its full course and Leigh received his damages. While this case was before the courts, Roberts remained busy in Lancashire and Staffordshire.

The case of John Cresswell (1845) is important because it was an example of how employers could use master and servant law to compel the specific performance of highly dubious agreements. It also demonstrates how magistrates could thwart the use of certiorari and habeas corpus by simply giving shorter sentences. Cresswell was a tray-maker from Bilston, in the employ for J. P. Whitehead. On 13 January 1844, Cresswell was called into the manager's office and offered a £3 loan in return for placing his mark upon a one-year contract renewal written in the owner's memo book. The entire contract was as follows: 'I hereby promise to serve Mr. John Pulton Whitehead from the 13th day of January 1844 to the 13th day of January 1845'. Cresswell's mark was the only signature on the contract, his employer's was nowhere to be found. Clearly, this was not a mutually binding document, as there was no promise made by the employer to do anything in return for Cresswell's service. The tray-maker verbally agreed that the employer could deduct 5s from his pay every fortnight toward the debt. By the end of July 1844, Cresswell demanded a raise to bring his wages up to the level of competitors in the industry. Whitehead refused and Cresswell left work. Whitehead prosecuted Cresswell before magistrates John Foster and William Baldwin under 4 George IV, c.34 (1823) for unlawful absence, and they sentenced him to imprisonment for one month.

At the end of August, Cresswell was released and went to work for a competitor of Mr Whitehead's. On 5 November 1844, however, Cresswell was summoned again before Foster and Baldwin, who convicted him under 4 George IV, c.34 (1823) for refusing to complete his service to Whitehead. Cresswell insisted that Whitehead had not requested him to return to work before summoning him before the magistrates, which the employer conceded was true. The magistrates gave Cresswell a choice of serving out his term to his original master or going to prison. Cresswell refused the offer and was sentenced to two weeks' imprisonment.[50]

Attorney Thomas Harding of Birmingham took up Cresswell's cause and, on 9 November, a barrister requested that Mr Justice Patteson have the prisoner, warrant of commitment and conviction brought to Westminster under writs of habeas corpus and certiorari. He claimed that the magistrate had lacked jurisdiction to hear Cresswell's case and insisted that the contract was invalid because it lacked mutuality. It was signed by only one party, and had no specific provisions for the payment of wages. In fact, it obliged the master to do exactly nothing in return for Cresswell's service. So deeply entrenched was the use of master and servant law to compel specific performance that the fact that Cresswell was being convicted a second time for what was the same breach of contract was not even raised as

---

49   'Procession in Honour of W. P. Roberts, Esq.', *NS* (26 April 1845), p. 1.

50   NA: KB 1/125/38; 'Ex Parte Cresswell', *JP* 8/46 (16 November 1844), p. 758; 'Ex Parte Cresswell', *JP* 8/49 (7 December 1844), p. 805.

an issue before the court. Patteson agreed with these arguments, and ordered the opposing party to show cause why Cresswell should not be released by granting a rule nisi. The primary goal of Cresswell was to have the court rule on the contract, so he could not be proceeded against yet again.[51]

On 16 November the writ of habeas corpus was not decided because it was the last day of Cresswell's sentence, and he would be discharged before the writ could be sent to Stafford Gaol. The representatives of the magistrates asked that the certiorari be denied, and they not be required to bring up the records of the conviction because Cresswell's attorney had failed to give them the mandatory six days' notice of his intention to seek a certiorari. Patteson agreed that the failure to give the magistrates notice was fatal, but to demonstrate his displeasure with the magistrates' behavior, he refused to grant them any costs. They would be out-of-pocket for the costs of their attorneys, barristers and travel.[52] The legal error made by Cresswell's attorney in not giving the magistrate proper notice, and the short sentence given by the magistrate, thwarted Cresswell's efforts before Queen's Bench.

In industries that depended upon the contributions of highly skilled workers, such as the glass-making trade, the validity of contracts of employment was of critical importance. C. B. Barker estimates that at mid nineteenth century, there were fewer than 700 skilled glassmakers in all of Great Britain, including 200 glass-blowers of whom only 50 could blow sheet glass. These skilled men could command excellent wages, particularly if they were not under contract during periods of economic expansion. For this reason, it was not unusual for employers to lock up these scarce workers in multi-year contracts, some even as long as seven to 10 years. Because employers claimed that they needed flexibility to meet market conditions, however, they often wrote loopholes into these contracts that permitted employers to shirk their obligations to the skilled employees in times of economic recession. One such seven-year contract was agreed to by glass-maker Richard Pemberton and the Pilkington Brothers Glassworks on 3 March 1845.[53]

Barely a month after having signed this contract, a competitor of the Pilkington Brothers offered Pemberton a management position. The Pilkingtons were prepared to let Pemberton go if he could find a suitable replacement. He failed to do so, but left anyway. The Pilkingtons then demanded £100 compensation from their competitor for Pemberton, and when this was refused, they pursued Pemberton under the 1823 Act.

The hearing took place on 6 September 1845 before magistrate Samuel Taylor. Pemberton hired Roberts to represent him, and John Ansdelle appeared for the prosecution. When Ansdelle introduced the contract into evidence, Roberts

---

[51]   NA: KB 1/125/38; 'Ex Parte Cresswell', *JP* 8/46 (16 November 1844), p. 758.

[52]   'Ex Parte Cresswell', *JP* 8/49 (7 December 1844), p. 805.

[53]   NA: KB 1/143/2, KB 1/140/17; C. B. Barker, *The Pilkington Brothers and the Glass Industry* (London, 1960), Chapter 7; Barker, *Pilkington: The Rise of an International Company, 1826–1976* (London, 1977), pp. 81–95.

objected because the agreement was unstamped. Taylor overruled this objection. Roberts also argued that the agreement was not mutual in its advantages. It bound Pemberton exclusively to the Pilkingtons for seven years, which he could not terminate before its term had expired, in return for the piece rates for whatever he produced. The agreement allowed the Pilkingtons the right to fine Pemberton, and refuse him payment for sub-par work. During a depression in the trade his masters could reduce his pay to 'a moiety of his wages' upon two weeks' notice, could dismiss him outright with a month's notice, and should Pemberton become sick or lame, the masters retained the right to dismiss him immediately and entirely without pay. Taylor saw nothing wrong in this agreement. Ansdelle called James Varley, the cashier to the company, to testify to the terms of the agreement and Pemberton's breach. On cross-examination, Roberts got Varley to admit that Richard Pilkington had not signed the agreement on the third of March when Pemberton did, and in fact, said 'he could not swear' that the agreement was signed by Pilkington before August, long after Pemberton had left. Roberts demanded a dismissal of the charges because if Pilkington had not signed the agreement, it was not mutually or reciprocally binding, and therefore not an agreement that it was illegal to break. Taylor disagreed, sentencing Pemberton to one month at hard labor.[54]

Roberts immediately initiated a writ of habeas corpus and certiorari on the grounds that Taylor had exceeded his jurisdiction by enforcing a non-mutual employment agreement that it was not illegal to break. On 25 September 1845, counsel requested before Baron Platt that Pemberton and the conviction be brought up on writs of habeas corpus and certiorari. Opposing counsel argued that due to a legal error on one of Roberts' two affidavits, the request should not be granted. Platt decided that Roberts' one good affidavit was sufficient to demonstrate that there was not cause for detaining Pemberton, but he gave the respondents leave to raise the argument of Roberts' affidavits when the writs were returned to the full court.[55]

Although the case was far from over, Roberts used Pemberton's release in a series of speeches in early October to the unionized glassmakers as evidence that their contracts were not binding. This led to a mass exodus of Pilkington's workers, which only ended when the firm threatened to sue any masters employing their 'runaways' for enticement. Pilkingtons was forced to give a series of public addresses, purchase advertisements and send out circulars to demonstrate that their contracts were valid and binding.[56]

One of the enticement cases that they initiated eventually reached the Court of Exchequer. In the important case of *Pilkington v. Scott* (1846) the Pilkingtons sued a competitor for enticing a crown glass-maker away from their employment. Scott, the competitor, argued that the Pilkingtons' contracts lacked adequate consideration, because they bound the workers exclusively to them, but only

---

[54]   Ibid.

[55]   Ibid.

[56]   Ibid.

obliged the masters to pay piece rates, and not guarantee work or wages for the full term. It also gave them a wide freedom to reduce wages unilaterally, or with a month's notice terminate the agreement in times of depression. The Court of Exchequer ruled that the promise to pay part wages during a depression, as well as the provisions requiring the employer to make annual payments for housing and firing, when taken all together, provided adequate consideration for the servant's promise to work exclusively for the master.[57]

In late October 1845, the Pilkingtons re-negotiated contracts with some of the workers who had absconded, and one of the terms they insisted upon was a promise from the men to not engage Roberts in the future. Roberts had become an issue in collective bargaining. In July of 1846, Queen's Bench upheld the objections regarding the legal error in Roberts' affidavits, and quashed the certiorari for Pemberton. The Pilkingtons agreed, however, to not prosecute Pemberton again, and to accept £50 from him over two years in return for releasing him from his contract.[58]

In the fall of 1845, the Miners of South Staffordshire were again organizing, leading to a number of strikes in the region, and, of course, master and servant prosecutions. The Secretary of the No.1 Lodge of the Miners' Association in Wolverhampton, John Hammond, spent the autumn busily raising money for the law fund. He hoped to fund an action before Queen's Bench on behalf of a group of Bilston miners who recently had been convicted to two weeks' hard labor in Stafford Gaol. What Hammond might not have realized at the time was that the money he helped to raise for the law fund would soon be used to secure his own freedom.[59]

On 14 November 1845, John Hammond left the employment of a butty collier who was unable, or unwilling, to provide him with any work. His employer, Edward Brown, brought Hammond before magistrates Henry Hill and George Briscoe for leaving work without giving two weeks' notice, which he argued was the rule of the colliery. Hammond disputed this claim, insisting that neither his agreement nor the custom of the country stipulated a requirement to give a fortnight notice for his type of work, and that he could provide witnesses to that effect. Hammond said that he was not allowed to produce these witnesses, and his representatives later complained that the employer had done nothing to prove the existence of an

---

[57]   Steinfeld, *Coercion*, pp. 111–15. Also see another very similar case involving the enticement of another crown glass maker, *Hartley and Cummings v. Another* (1847), 5 C. B. 247.

[58]   Barker, *Pilkington Brothers*, pp. 104–7; T. C. Barker, *The Glassmakers* (London, 1977), pp. 84–9.

[59]   'Staffordshire Miners', *NS* (23 August 1845), p. 1; 'South Staffordshire Miners Delegate Meeting', *NS* (27 September 1845), p. 5; 'The Staffordshire Miners' and 'The Bilston Miners', *NS* (1 November 1845), p. 1; 'The Miners of Bilston to the Inhabitants of Bilston and its Surrounding Districts' and 'The Bilston Victim Fund Committee of the Miners Association', *NS* (15 November 1845), p. 1.

agreement, let alone one that required notice. He was convicted to one month's imprisonment at hard labor.[60] When workers signed contracts they were often held to have agreed to a set of rules of the firm and customs of the country that appeared nowhere in their agreement (and were often changed at the whim of the employer). Workers' attempts to argue that they had not explicitly agreed to, or were aware of, these rules almost always failed.[61]

A few months after Hammond's action before Queen's Bench was heard, a correspondent asked the *Justice of the Peace* about magistrates' jurisdiction to enforce the customary notice period of an employment agreement under 4 George IV, c.34 (1823). He stated that a local mine had a custom of demanding two weeks' notice to terminate an employment contract, but 'it often occurred that men, ignorant of the custom, [were] engaged without being made aware of it at the time the contract was entered into'. The *Justice of the Peace* responded that 'A conviction cannot take place ... unless it be proved on the part of the masters that the servant knew that [the notice] was the custom of the house'.[62]

By 21 November, Roberts was hired to win Hammond's freedom. The next day, Huddleston went before Mr Justice Patteson to have Hammond brought to Westminster on a habeas corpus. Huddleston made the novel argument that, because the warrant of commitment was the only instrument that justified this imprisonment, it was invalid for not setting out the evidence upon which the conviction was based. Patteson noted 'there will not ... be time to bring up the prisoner before the full court this term, and this ... argument is much too important to be argued at chambers before a single judge'. Patteson granted the writ, and allowed Hammond to be released on bail until the case was heard next term. Roberts paid the bail, claiming that Hammond was 'in extreme poverty'.[63] It would be nearly seven months before Hammond's case was heard.

In the meantime, Roberts returned to Lancashire. On 15 January 1846, Jacob Ogden was one of several miners brought before three magistrates at Leigh Petty Sessions for leaving their work under 4 George IV, c.34 (1823). Attorney John Barlow defended the miners, who were involved in a labor dispute with their employer, John Darlington of Tyldesley, Lancashire. Barlow argued that the miners' contract was not mutually binding, because it bound the men to work

---

[60]   NA: KB 1/141/42; 'The Colliers of Staffordshire', 'The Liberation of John Hammond' and 'To the Miners of South Staffordshire', *NS* (20 June 1846), pp. 4, 6.

[61]   Willibald Steinmetz, 'Was There a De-Juridification of Employment Relations in Britain?', in Willibald Steinmetz (ed.) *Private Law and Social Inequality in the Industrial Age: Comparing the Legal Cultures of in Britain, France, Germany, and the United States* (London, 2000), pp. 273–5.

[62]   'Practical Points', *JP* 10/41 (10 October 1846), p. 650.

[63]   NA: KB 1/141/42; 'Ex Parte John Hammond', *JP* 9/48 (29 November 1845), p. 773; 'In Re: John Hammond', *JP* 10/23 (6 June 1846), pp. 356–7; 'In Re: John Hammond', *JP* 10/36 (5 September 1846), p. 569; 'The Colliers of Staffordshire – Liberation of John Hammond', *NS* (20 June 1846), p. 4.

exclusively for Darlington, but did not oblige him to provide any work. Barlow also objected to the fact that the magistrates who heard the case were not the same ones who originally received the information against Ogden.[64] Despite Barlow's efforts, the three magistrates, James Pownall, John Green and Malcolm Ross, found Odgen (and the other miners) guilty and sentenced him to three months' imprisonment *without* hard labor.

Darlington, however, recognized the error in law that could provide Ogden with a means of escape and sought to remedy it by contacting Samuel Newton, the magistrate to whom he originally swore out the information against Ogden. Ogden was in the local lockup awaiting transportation to Kirkdale, when at 9 p.m. on 17 January he was taken, without any summons, warrant or explanation into a small room with Newton and two other men. Newton asked Ogden if he had signed an agreement with John Darlington. The prisoner said yes, and then Newton immediately convicted him to 75 days' imprisonment *with* hard labor. Within 15 minutes of being sent for, Ogden was back in his cell. Newton's commitment was the legal instrument used to justify Odgen's imprisonment at hard labor.

The union sent for Roberts on 20 January, and four days later he initiated a habeas corpus to release Ogden, and a certiorari to quash the conviction, arguing it was invalid because Newton had no jurisdiction to determine a case that had already been decided by another magistrate. Roberts also noted that Newton's conviction failed to state the evidence against Ogden. Huddleston argued the case before Mr Justice Wightman, who stated that although he could not enter into 'the irregularities and statements' of this case, he found the conviction sufficiently flawed to justify Ogden's release. The *Northern Star* characteristically responded with an article that praised Wightman, while condemning Newton for acting as a mere tool for the mine owners. The article observed that Ogden was the thirty-seventh miner that Roberts had freed from a master and servant conviction before the Queen's Bench in two years. The article warned Newton that he had 'not yet heard the last' of this case, as Roberts would pursue him for false imprisonment.[65]

Six days after Ogden's conviction, John Darlington prosecuted four other miners for leaving their employment without serving their notice. Like Ogden, the miners in this case, Seth Turner, Matthew Ollerton, Edward Potter and Thomas

---

[64]   According the writers at the *Justice of the Peace*, under 4 George IV, c.34, s.3 (1823), 'the same justice or justices must receive the information, issue the process, hear the complaint, and convict and commit. A committal by any other justice or justices would be illegal'. 'Practical Points', *JP* 8/23 (8 June 1844), p. 380; 'Of the Jurisdiction of Justices to Receive Informations or Complaints of the Same or Others, or Another, To Adjudicate Therein', *JP*, 9/16 (19 April 1845), p. 258; 'Practical Points', *JP* 9/4 (25 January 1845), p. 59.

[65]   NA: KB 1/145/55; 'Ex Parte Ogden', *JP* 10/7 (14 February 1846), p. 105; 'More Extraordinary Proceedings of the Lancashire Magistrates Under the Masters and Servants Act, and the Single Triumph of the Miners' Attorney General, W. P. Roberts, Esq.', *NS* (14 February 1846), p. 1.

Robinson, argued that their contract of employment was bad for want of mutuality, because it did not necessarily oblige Darlington to find work for them. They also claimed that Darlington had asked them to 'riddle' the coal, a practice that created more work without adding to their wages. They asserted that after their refusal to perform this task, Darlington angrily 'told them to go'. The magistrate, Thomas Sanderson, was unmoved by these arguments, and committed the miners to sentences ranging from one to three months' at hard labor. Roberts initiated a writ of habeas corpus to obtain the release of the men.

On 28 February 1846, Huddleston argued before Mr Justice Williams at Queen's Bench that the miners should be brought to Westminster because the convictions did not demonstrate that they were based upon informations charging the prisoners with an actual offense. He also argued that their contract with Darlington was bad for want of mutuality. The former argument was based upon the fact that the informations in this case charged the men with being absent from their employment, but did not explicitly charge them with being 'unlawfully absent'. Therefore, it failed to negate the possibility that the men had a lawful reason for not being at work, and thus did not charge them with an offense at all. The argument that Roberts, the miners, and certainly the *Northern Star*, were most interested in was the question of the validity of the men's contracts, as it had the potential to affect all of Darlington's men. Williams granted the writ, but finding that the question of the men's contract was one with important consequences, he felt that the full court should hear the case. He released the men on bail until the case could be heard at the beginning of the next term. The *Northern Star* celebrated the men's release on bail as another instance where 'the law of the land triumphed over "justices' law"', and reported on the miners' happy reunion with their families.[66]

On 1 June 1846, the court heard both arguments from Bodkin and Huddleston against the conviction. Lord Denman expressed great reluctance to enter into the issue of the contract's validity, feeling it was unnecessary for deciding the case. He stated that the easier question for the court to determine was 'whether the information states an offence for which the magistrates had the authority to commit the prisoner. I think it does not'. Because the information did not negate the possibility that the men had a lawful reason for their absence it 'charged no offence at all'. The prisoners were therefore discharged.[67]

---

[66]   'Mr. John Darlington of Channock Richard, Lancashire, and His Colliers, Again!', *NS* (7 March 1846), p. 1.

[67]   'Mr. John Darlington of Channock Richard, Lancashire, and His Colliers, Again!', *NS* (7 March 1846), p. 1; In the matter of Turner, Ollerton, and Others, 15 L. J. 140–143; 'In Re: Turner', *JP* 10/23 (6 June 1846), p. 357; 'In Re: Turner', *JP* 10/36 (5 September 1846), p. 571; Napier, 'Contract of Service', p. 123; Steinfeld, *Coercion*, pp. 115–17. In *R. v. Haines*, Roberts helped to win the freedom of Pikeman who refused to work as a miner for his employer on the same grounds. 'R v. John Haines', *JP* 11/7 (13 February 1847), p. 103.

Once again, if one merely looked at the case report, one might conclude that the judges of the Queen's Bench were engaged in 'technical quibbling' by demanding that the information explicitly state that the absence had been 'unlawful'. After all, could it not simply be assumed that the absence was unlawful? Why else would the employer have bothered to bring an information under the Master and Servant Act? A closer look at the context of this case reveals, however, that the defendants alleged that their employer had 'told them to go'. If true, this meant that there *actually had been a lawful excuse for being absent and the miners had committed no offense*. The objection was not technical at all.

On the same day the court heard In Re: *Turner et al.*, arguments were presented in the case of John Hammond, a case that provoked considerable excitement among magistrates. Bodkin and Huddleston argued that the instrument used to justify the imprisonment of Hammond purported to be both a conviction and a warrant of commitment in the same document. The order to the Keeper of the House of Correction did not recite a conviction that it was based upon, but simply stated on its face that Hammond was 'convicted'. Yet unlike a conviction, it did not set out the evidence taken under oath before the justices, and in the presence of the prisoner, and was therefore was invalid. Opposing counsel, Mr Pashley, argued that the document was a perfectly valid warrant of commitment that showed jurisdiction, an offence, and the fact of a conviction. Mr Justice Williams ruled that because a conviction had not been brought up, and the document before the court used the phrase 'convicted', it 'assumed a double shape: as a warrant, it may be sufficient authority to the gaoler, but it purported to be also a conviction'. Therefore it needed to set out the evidence taken before the justices.[68]

This case was significant because in ruling that warrants of commitment needed to recite the evidence, the court had gone further than ever before in the requirements for such documents. These requirements were contrary to the instructions found in many of the most widely used justices' manuals of the day. In Re: *Turner* was also frustrating for magistrates, because if the court would not even assume that the absence the master complained about was 'unlawful', then they clearly would assume nothing favorable to the magistrates' forms. In Re: *Hammond* and In Re: *Turner* can be interpreted as the high-water mark for high-court scrutiny of the forms of magistrates' summary hearings. Much of this scrutiny can be explained by the problem of expanding summary jurisdiction without legislation that satisfactorily answered the procedural concerns of jurists and civil libertarians.[69]

The *Northern Star* celebrated the victory, but lamented the degree to which this case was 'a specimen of the ordinary administration of "justices' justice" in the Staffordshire coal districts'. The author stressed that Hammond's victory was far from a technicality. The evidence of the case had not been set out in the

---

[68]   In the Matter of John Hammond, 15 L. J. 136–40; 'In Re: Hammond', *JP* 10/23 (6 June 1846), pp. 356–7; Steinfeld, *Coercion*, p. 156.

[69]   Ibid.

commitment, because, if Hammond was to be believed, *none had been provided at the hearing*. Hammond steadfastly insisted that he had not entered an agreement requiring notice to terminate, and in fact, had always exercised caution to avoid such a contract. He went on to argue that the employer provided no proof that such an agreement existed, and that his own attempts to introduce arguments and evidence fell on deaf ears, as 'the master [sat] on the bench chuckling with his brother magistrate'. The author thanked Queen's Bench for its 'most wholesome warning against magisterial incapacity and partiality'. The same issue contained an open letter from union secretary John Jones, encouraging the miners 'to strive to compel the magistrates to refund' the money spent winning Hammond's freedom by raising money to pursue them for false imprisonment.[70]

The Exchequer Chamber finally delivered a ruling in the case of *Lindsay v. Leigh* in 1848. Steinfeld identifies this case as signaling a shift in the attitude of the common law courts toward the formalities required in the warrant of commitment. The central issue in the case was whether the conviction Lindsay wrote after Leigh's release could be used to support the flawed commitment, and demonstrate that he had acted within his jurisdiction. The Exchequer Chamber ruled that the only instrument for authorizing imprisonment under the 1823 Act that the legislature had intended was a warrant of commitment. No conviction was either mentioned expressly or implied by the statute, which granted magistrates only the power 'to commit'. Therefore, the legality of the imprisonment depended upon sufficiency of the warrant of commitment alone, and need not be backed up by a valid conviction. Baron Parke stated that the warrant of commitment in this case was insufficient because it did not state that the contract had been entered into or was in writing, as the 1823 statute explicitly required to bring the case within magistrates' jurisdiction. Therefore Lindsay's new convictions did not remedy his flawed commitments.

Baron Parke and the court ruled narrowly in this case, noting that though 'some important questions were discussed, we think the commitment is bad upon grounds irrespective of some of those questions'. One of these important questions was whether the warrant of commitment needed to recite all the facts of the case like a conviction (as ruled In Re: *Hammond*), or could take the less rigorous form of an order. Robert Steinfeld observes that Baron Parke and Judge Patteson, however, both strongly hinted at a retreat from the position Queen's Bench took in *Hammond* by suggesting the warrant of commitment was, in fact, simply an order, and could take a looser form. They did not need to decide the matter in this case because the statute explicitly stated that magistrates had jurisdiction in cases where the contract was in writing or entered into by the accused, and this had not appeared in the commitment.[71] This decision, while a victory for labor, combined

---

[70] 'The Colliers of Staffordshire – Liberation of John Hammond' and 'To the Miners of South Staffordshire', *NS* (20 June 1844), pp. 4, 6.

[71] *Lindsay v. Leigh*, 116 E. R. 547, 17 L. J. 50; Steinfeld, *Coercion*, pp. 156–7.

with the 1848 Jervis Acts to close off a remedy for challenging unjust rulings by magistrates that trade unions had used to great effect during the 1840s.

The cases described in this chapter shaped both the law and popular politics in some important ways. Roberts' victories set precedents for material necessary in valid warrants of commitment and convictions. These precedents could be used to free workers in future cases. The building momentum of Roberts' campaign increased the pressure on Parliament to intervene to clarify procedures and forms and protect magistrates in the exercise of their judicial duties. This is described in Chapter 6.

This campaign also had a significant impact outside the courtroom. For Chartists and trade unionists the magistrates who enforced a high proportion of labor law became an important issue. Roberts' work illuminated the lack of procedural safeguards, conflicts of interest and legal errors that pervaded summary hearings. This exposure informed the protests and petitions initiated by labor and Chartists against the bad behavior of individual magistrates described in Chapters 4, 5 and 7.

Chapter 4

The Warrington Cases, 1846–1847:
'He might almost as well be without trial'

Introduction

This chapter examines the 1847 prosecution of six Warrington file-forgers under the 1823 Master and Servant Act, a case that highlights many of the strategies and tactics used by organized labor in its struggle against the penal characteristics of employment law. In mid nineteenth century Lancashire, an employer using master and servant law to prosecute skilled workmen during a labor dispute was an ordinary event. In this particular instance, however, W. P. Roberts engineered an extraordinary outcome by bringing the case to the attention of Parliament and the Home Secretary at a politically sensitive moment in the history of magistrates' summary jurisdiction. Amid considerable public discussion, Roberts convinced the Home Office and the Crown's law officers to grant the convicted file-forgers a pardon due to irregularities and legal errors in the hearing.

This case was the defining event of a labor dispute between Joseph Edelsten and his skilled workmen, and demonstrates the importance of the law in early industrial action. It also further illuminates the effect that trade unions' increasing use of solicitors had upon popular understandings of the law, as well as the political controversy over the English magistracy and the expansion of summary justice. The struggle over the fate of six Warrington file-forgers provides uniquely detailed insight into how many of the broader transformations in the relationship between labor and the law, as well as the development of the contract of employment, manifested themselves in the everyday experience of workers.[1] This case also sheds light on the great challenges faced by lay magistrates when trying to enforce complex laws.

In the context of Roberts' work before Queen's Bench, described in Chapter 3, this case was part of the persistent criticism of magistrates' administration of the law. Rather than make this case simply another instance of using writs of certiorari and habeas corpus, Roberts chose an even more public remedy. The explanation for Roberts' choice in tactics points once again toward the controversy surrounding the expansion of magistrates' summary powers. During 1847 Parliament was considering a measure that ultimately gave magistrates the authority to determine

---

[1] Raymond Challinor, *Radical Lawyer in Victorian England: W. P. Roberts and the Struggle for Workers' Rights* (London, 1990), pp. 142–4.

summarily cases of larceny under 5s committed by juveniles.[2] Roberts' open letter and petition raised a number of objections to the hasty and unfair process by which the Lancashire magistrates convicted his clients.[3] Roberts' objections echoed the concerns voiced by opponents to the further expansion of summary jurisdiction to Lord Brougham's Select Committee. During a 14-month period from April 1846 to June 1847 when Parliament was considering the expansion of magistrates' judicial powers, there were no fewer than five demands for Parliamentary inquiries into the misconduct of specific magistrates. Four of these arose from the magistrates' handling of labor cases.[4] The timing of these protests combined with the challenging of magistrates' convictions at Queen's Bench made many in Parliament realize that expansion of summary jurisdiction had to be accompanied by wider-ranging reform of the magistracy.

This case illuminates the effect that master and servant law had on maintaining an unequal employment relationship. Even in the mid nineteenth century, employment remained very much a relationship of status, and decidedly not one between equals who had reciprocal obligations toward one another.[5] The employer in this case, Joseph Edelsten, caused the dispute with his file-forgers because he wanted to obtain more work from his apprentices at the expense of his journeymen's customary and contractual rights. He dramatically and unilaterally

---

[2]   'First and Second Reports From the Select Committee of the House of Lords Appointed to Inquire Into the Execution of the Criminal Law, Especially Respecting Juvenile Offenders and Transportation; Together With the Minutes of Evidence Taken Before the Said Committee, and an Appendix (House of Lords, 1847)', *Parliamentary Papers*, Vol. VII (447), p. 534; *Hansard Debates*, Vol. 90, cols. 1012–22; Vol. 92, cols. 33–47; Vol. 93, cols. 2–6, 699–701; Thomas Sweeney, 'The Extension and Practice of Summary Jurisdiction in England, c.1790–1860' (PhD dissertation, Cambridge University, 1985), pp. 140–60; Bruce P. Smith, 'Circumventing the Jury: Petty Crime and Summary Justice in London and New York City, 1790–1855' (PhD dissertation, Yale University, 1996), pp. 421–48.

[3]   'A Copy of the Informations and Evidence Given Before the Magistrates Assembled in Petty Sessions at Warrington, On Monday 25th Day of January Last, On Which James Gerrard, Thomas Wyke, James Ireland and John Dobson Were Sentenced to Three Months Imprisonment With Hard Labour for Leaving the Service of Joseph Baxter Edelsten, File Manufacturer; Together With Copies of the Convictions and Warrants of Commitment, and of the Contracts Entered into by the Said Prisoners With the Said Joseph Baxter Edelsten', *Parliamentary Papers*, Vol. XLVI (78), p. 487; NA: HO 18/193/38; Challinor, *Radical Lawyer*, pp. 142–4.

[4]   See Chapter 5. Also: *Hansard Debates*, Vol. 85, cols. 470–478; Vol. 90, col. 1136; Vol. 92, cols. 1056–62; Vol. 93, cols. 120, 597–653.

[5]   Simon Deakin, 'The Contract of Employment, A Study in Legal Evolution', *Historical Studies in Industrial Relations* 11 (Spring 2001): 1–5, 7, 20–22; Otto Kahn-Freund, 'Blackstone's Neglected Child: The Contract of Employment', *The Law Quarterly Review* 92 (October 1977): 508–28.

altered the terms and conditions under which his employees worked, ignoring the specific terms of the contracts that should have governed their relationship.

During the previous four years, Edelsten had frequently used the Master and Servant Act against his employees, turning to magistrates to compel them to fulfill their agreements against the threat of imprisonment. Magistrates in these cases did not perceive Edelsten's alterations in the terms of work or his frequent violations of his contracts and indentures as repudiations of the agreements. In the eyes of the law, the obligations of employees to be obedient were far more open-ended than were Edelsten's to adhere to his agreement. Defending the Warrington file-forgers in this case, Roberts (and the file-forgers themselves) frequently attempted to bring the principles of classical contract doctrine into the case, only to have the arguments rejected by the magistrates.

Background to the Case, 1846–7

This case originated in the town of Warrington, Lancashire, which was notable for the production of high-quality saw-files and small precision tools. The dominant file manufacturer was Peter Stubs, who died in 1806, but his business continued to thrive under his sons. The Stubs firm was important in this master and servant prosecution: it had helped to establish many of the customs of the trade, and William Stubs, one of Peter's sons, was a magistrate involved in determining the case. William, who retired from an active role in the firm in 1841, 'was the architect of the success achieved by the concern after the death of Peter'.[6]

J. B. Edelsten was a competing, though much smaller, file manufacturer established in the mid 1830s. Little information is available about Edelsten and his business, beyond that he completed his legal apprenticeship as a file cutter. In Stubs' papers there is a reference in 1821 to the employment of an operative named Edelsten who produced saw-files. While this operative might have been a young J. B. Edelsten, a family connection to the industry is another possibility. E. Surrey Dane, in his history of Peter Stubs' business, makes a vague reference to a Warrington competitor of Stubs named Edelsten, who angered wholesalers by attempting to sell his files directly to small shops in Edinburgh.[7] In his defense of the file forgers, Roberts characterized Edelsten as 'a new man, poor and needy, who is endeavoring to get more work from his men at a lower rate of wages than other masters'.[8] Local business directories demonstrate that at no point before

---

[6] T. S. Ashton, *An Eighteenth Century Industrialist: Peter Stubs of Warrington, 1756–1806* (New York, 1970); E. Surrey Dane, *Peter Stubs and the Lancashire Hand Tool Industry* (New York, 1973), pp. 26–32.

[7] 'A Copy of the Informations and Evidence … (1847)', p. 9; NA: HO 18/193/38. Dane, *Peter Stubs*, 132, Appendix Ia, 207; 'File-Makers Turn Out', *Manchester Courier and Lancashire General Advertiser* (hereafter, *MCLGA*) (30 January 1847), p. 71.

[8] 'The Warrington Shallows Again', *NS* (13 February 1847), p. 4.

1851 did the Stubs firm have more than five small competitors in town.[9] Edelsten was probably a small master with little margin for losses, facing the challenge of competition with the more established Stubs. Daphne Simon suggests that master and servant law was often 'the weapon of the small master', who needed to prevent the loss of skilled labor to larger firms.[10]

The size of Edelsten's firm played a significant role in Roberts' defense. Edelsten's employment contracts stipulated that for certain tasks he would pay the prevailing prices in Warrington. Roberts attempted to show that because Edelsten was a marginal producer, he paid his men less than the Stubs firm for comparable tasks, and made his journeymen absorb expenses that were contrary to the custom of the trade.[11]

Employers in file manufacturing were heavily dependent upon skilled labor, and increasingly relied on the use of bounties or advances to lure journeymen into long-term agreements and bind many apprentices in restrictive indentures.[12] Edelsten bound his men to contracts for between three and five years, and other manufacturers in Sheffield went as high as seven.[13] E. S. Dane argues that the competition for labor between file manufacturers in Warrington and Sheffield was limited because they frequently corresponded, enquiring whether prospective workers were under contract elsewhere. Among masters in the trade there was a high sensitivity to the illegality of soliciting contracted workers. Other means of preventing bidding for workmen included advancing money ahead of pay settlements and providing cottages. A large proportion of Stubs' workforce was

---

[9]   Dane, *Peter Stubs*, p. 53.

[10]   Daphne Simon, 'Master and Servant', in J. Saville (ed.), *Democracy and the Labour Movement: Essays in Honour of Donna Torr* (London, 1954), pp. 190–194. For more on the use of master and servant law by small/large employers, and some qualifications of Simon's findings, see Douglas Hay, 'Master and Servant in England: Using the Law in the Eighteenth and Nineteenth Centuries', in Willibald Steinmetz (ed.), *Private Law and Social Inequality in the Industrial Age: Comparing the Legal Cultures of Britain, France, Germany, and the United States* (London, 2000), pp. 243–4; Robert Steinfeld, *Coercion, Contract and Free Labour in the Nineteenth Century* (Cambridge, 2001), p. 74; D. C. Woods, 'The Operation of the Master and Servants Act in the Black Country, 1858–1875', *Midlands History* 7 (1982): 109–10.

[11]   'A Copy of the Informations and Evidence ... (1847)', p. 9; NA: HO 18/193/38.

[12]   S. Pollard, *A History of Labour in Sheffield* (Liverpool, 1959), pp. 1, 3, 40, 50, 55, 65.

[13]   Ashton, *Eighteenth Century Industrialist*, pp. 27, 29; Dane, *Peter Stubs*, p. 59; 'A Copy of the Informations and Evidence ... (1847)', pp. 2, 4, 7, 10 (contracts of James Ireland, James Gerrard, John Dobson, and Indenture of Thomas Wyke); NA: HO 18/193/38; F. Hill, 'An Account of Trade Combinations in Sheffield', *Trades Societies and Strikes: A Report of the Committee on Trades Societies, Appointed by the National Association for the Promotion of Social Science* (London, 1860), reprinted (New York, 1968), p. 531. For a discussion of long contracts and master and servant law, see: Steinfeld, *Coercion*, pp. 58–62.

in debt to the firm. When file-forger James Gerrard needed an advance from Edelsten to pay for the burial of his child, the latter made the loan conditional upon Gerrard accepting a new five-year contract extension.[14] The efforts made by file manufacturers to impede the free movement of labor demonstrate that the loss of skilled workmen could have profound consequences for individual firms. This fact combined with Edelsten's status as a cost-cutting small manufacturer help to explain the importance of master and servant law and the aggressiveness with which he pursued absconding workmen.[15]

Edelsten's conflict with the union in 1846–1847 was caused by his decision to bind apprentices directly to himself and receive the benefit of their work. Previously, apprentices could bind themselves to journeymen in Edelsten's employ because traditionally both masters and journeymen in the industry took on apprentices. Journeymen accepted payment for the work done by their apprentices while teaching them the trade. As apprentices advanced in ability, they could claim a larger proportion of the price of their work, ultimately receiving 75 percent of a journeyman's rate.[16]

T. S. Ashton observes that in the hand-tool industry, 'by the end of the eighteenth century apprenticeship had lost much of its original justification as a system of technical training, and had become little more than a means of obtaining supplies of cheap, juvenile labour'. Both Ashton and Dane argue that by the early nineteenth century this relationship had become highly exploitative, causing Peter Stubs to break with the custom of the industry and have all apprentices bound directly to him and his successors. Ashton concludes that Peter did this out of 'sensibility and humanity', but there were economic advantages as well. Although there is evidence that apprenticeships to journeymen were exploitation of cheap labor without instruction in the trade, in some cases this was mitigated by the frequency with which workmen took their own sons or relatives as apprentices. Ashton finds that the rest of the industry did not follow Stubs' policy, and among most of the other firms in the industry, the practice of journeymen taking apprentices increased.[17] Edelsten's policy was contrary to the custom of the industry as a whole, but it was the same as that of the country's largest manufacturer.

On 28 September 1846, with the support of the union, five of Edelsten's journeymen and apprentices broke their contracts and absconded from Warrington. On the same day a deputation of union delegates approached Edelsten, asking him to change his policy of binding apprentices to himself. They accused Edelsten of overworking apprentices and giving them tasks more appropriate for journeymen. They argued that losing the benefit of apprentices' work, and the tasks he gave to

---

[14]   'The Warrington Shallows Again', *NS* (13 February 1847), p. 4; Ashton, *Eighteenth Century Industrialist*, pp. 32–6; Dane, *Peter Stubs*, pp. 62, 70–71, 90–96, 101.

[15]   'A Copy of the Informations and Evidence … (1847)', p. 16; NA: HO 18/193/38.

[16]   Dane, *Peter Stubs*, pp. 103–4; Ashton, *Eighteenth Century Industrialist*, p. 28.

[17]   Dane, *Peter Stubs*, p. 101; Ashton, *Eighteenth Century Industrialist*, pp. 28–9; Hill, 'Trade Combinations in Sheffield', p. 533.

them, were extremely costly to journeymen and contrary to their agreements. They also claimed that Edelsten violated his contracts with his men by paying them less than the prevailing Warrington prices for particular kinds of work. Edelsten replied that because he had served an apprenticeship it was his right to train his workers, and he was entitled to the benefit of their work. He denied the allegation that he paid his men less than the Warrington rates.[18]

The five men who fled from Edelsten's employment split into two groups. File-striker James Ireland and file-forger James Gerrard traveled to Scotland. File-cutters John Dobson and Samuel Wilcock, and apprentice Thomas Wyke, went to the Sheffield area. The workmen and their families were supported by payments from the union totaling 35s per week each.[19]

Edelsten swore out informations under 4 George IV, c.34 (1823) against his five workmen for absconding from their work. He chose not to prosecute union leaders for conspiring to violate the 1825 Combination Laws Repeal Amendment Act, even though the elements of that charge appear to have been present. In all probability, his choice can be explained by the fact that master and servant offences were usually less expensive to pursue, easier to prove, and more likely to result in a speedy return to work.[20] Armed with warrants for the arrest of Ireland and Gerrard, deputy constable Jones captured the two in Scotland and brought them back to Warrington.

On 10 October, Ireland and Gerrard were tried before magistrate James Greenhall. It does not appear that the men had legal representation at this hearing. Edelsten testified about his meeting with the union representatives and the men's breach of contract. Greenhall 'expressed astonishment at this behaviour' and, believing Gerrard to be a union ringleader, sentenced him to two months imprisonment with hard labor. At the urging of Edelsten, Greenhall allowed Ireland to return to his work, conditional upon paying half the expenses of his capture and conviction. Greenhall's clerk determined that these expenses amounted to £6 9s

---

[18] 'Filemakers' Turn-Out', *MCLGA* (30 January 1847), p. 71; 'A Copy of the Informations and Evidence … (1847)', pp. 9, 16; NA: HO 18/193/38; 'The Warrington Shallows Again', *NS* (13 February 1847), p. 4.

[19] 'A Copy of the Informations and Evidence … (1847)', pp. 16–17, 20; NA: HO 18/193/38.

[20] Within months of Edelsten's decision not to pursue a conspiracy charge against his workmen, other Warrington employers, John Jones and Arthur Potts, brought an important (and famous) conspiracy case against 27 of their striking employees. W. P. Roberts was engaged for the defense in that case, which was eventually known as *R. v. Selsby* (1847). See: J. Jones, *Selsby and Others on the Prosecution of Jones and Potts, Narrative, Introduction, &c.* (London, 1847), Goldsmith-Kress Library of Economic Literature, Reel 35390; NA: KB 1/157/65; John Orth, *Combination and Conspiracy: A Legal History of Trade Unionism, 1721–1906* (Oxford, 1991), pp. 95–6; Challinor, *Radical Lawyer*, pp. 151–4. For more on the merits of master and servant over conspiracy: Hay, 'Master and Servant in England', pp. 254–5.

2d. The constables intercepted a letter from the union to the men containing £2 for their maintenance, and this was applied toward Ireland's debt to Edelsten.[21]

This first case of *R. v. Gerrard and Ireland* illuminates some important points about the use of master and servant law in industrial relations. It was very common for masters to prosecute workers under these statutes, not for the purpose of imprisonment, but to use the threat of prison to force them back to work.[22] To fight industrial action and restore production at his firm, Edelsten needed his skilled workers in the workshop, not the House of Correction. Ireland was forced back to work against the threat of imprisonment, and in debt to his employer in multiple ways. Edelsten sought a prison sentence for Gerrard because he perceived him to be a union 'ringleader', whose imprisonment would alert workers to the consequences of breaking their contracts.

After only four days at Kirkdale House of Correction, Gerrard began to complain of painful rheumatism in his shoulders. On 14 October he wrote to his employer:

> Dear Mr. Edelsten,
> I write these few lines hoping they find you in good, as they leave me very poorly at present, and likely to remain without you will fetch me out. I am willing to pay all expenses. I never thought you would have picked me out as the ring-leader. I never attended but the first general meeting, and Ireland has been on the committee every Saturday night, and took all our money. I have nobody to blame but him. I hope and trust you will fetch me out tomorrow if it is possible; I can hardly write this letter, I am so put out of the way; but never will I be led away any more if you will but fetch me out this time soon as ever you can, for I am very poorly.
> So no more at present from your humble servant,
> James Gerrard.[23]

After receiving this letter, Edelsten asked Greenhall's clerk about the possibility of a discharge from prison, and an application was sent to the Home Office. On 27 October 1846 the Home Office approved a free pardon for Gerrard, who promised to pay Edelsten the expenses of the case and return to work.[24]

---

[21] 'Warrington', *ME* (17 October 1846); 'Filemakers' Turn-Out', *MCLGA* (27 January 1847), 71; 'A Copy of the Informations and Evidence…(1847)', pp. 16, 21; NA: HO 18/193/38.

[22] Hay, 'Master and Servant in England', pp. 233–4, 238; Woods, 'Master and Servant', p. 106. For more on the use of master and servant law to compel specific performance of the contract of employment, see: Steinfeld, *Coercion*, pp. 58–72.

[23] 'A Copy of the Informations and Evidence … (1847)', p. 21; NA: HO 18/193/38; 'The Warrington Shallows Again', *NS* (13 February 1847), p. 4; 'The File Cutters Turn-Out', *MG* (30 January 1847), p. 8.

[24] Ibid.

Peace between Edelsten and Gerrard did not last long. Gerrard was either unable or unwilling to re-enter Edelsten's service. The file-forger claimed that the pain in his shoulders was too severe for him to work, but a doctor paid by Edelsten declared that he was 'shamming'. Edelsten demanded that Gerrard promise to return to work the following Monday (2 November). Gerrard later told Roberts that he feared if Edelsten charged him with neglect of work no one would accept his word against a doctor's testimony. On November first, Gerrard again fled Warrington. Apparently he no longer harbored bad feelings toward Ireland because the two once again joined together, along with apprentice John Baxter. The three met the still-uncaptured group of Edelsten's employees hiding in Sheffield since 28 September.[25]

Edelsten advertised a £20 reward for the capture of his workmen in several English newspapers. Edelsten was so determined that police officers were sent to Wales, Staffordshire, Warwickshire and throughout Lancashire to search for the missing workers. After receiving a tip, and obtaining assistance from the local magistrates, Constable James Branwood found the six men hiding in a cottage near West Handley, a small town nine miles from Sheffield.[26] At 5:30 a.m. on 24 January 1847, Bramwood and three constables burst into the cottage with cutlasses drawn to find Edelsten's six workmen sound asleep. Bramwood later claimed that the men made a series of incriminating statements, including a confession that they had fled on orders from the union. He testified that the men defiantly hoped it had cost Edelsten £200 to catch them, and that they would break him because their union, affiliated with the National Association of United Trades for the Protection of Labour, had a treasury of over £9,000. He said that they claimed they would rather 'climb Jacob's ladder', by which they meant walk the treadmill, than submit to Edelsten's terms.[27]

The constables shackled the six and took them to Sheffield, where they remained until 5 p.m. when they boarded a train to Manchester. They arrived in Manchester at 8 p.m., and slept overnight in the New Bailey. They claimed that they were not permitted to see visitors, or obtain counsel, though Bramwood testified that they had 'every opportunity of having communication with anyone'. Aside from a 'friend' at Sheffield, there is no evidence that the prisoners spoke

---

[25] Ibid.

[26] 'A Copy of the Informations and Evidence … (1847)', pp. 6, 17; NA: HO 18/193/38. The magistrate who authorized the execution of the Warrant for Gerrard et al. in the West Riding was none other than Wilson Overend, no friend of trade unions, and the subject of Chapter 5.

[27] 'A Copy of the Informations and Evidence … (1847)', pp. 9, 15, 17; NA: HO 18/193/38; 'The File-Makers' Turn-Out', *MCLGA* (30 January 1847), p. 71; 'To T. S. Duncombe, M.P., 8 Princess Street, Manchester, 29 January 1847', *NS* (6 February 1847), p. 4; 'The Spring Knife Cutters and the National Association', *SRI* (24 April 1847), p. 5. The National Association of United Trades claimed a membership of over 50,000 in 1846–1847. Malcolm Chase, *Chartism: A New History* (Manchester, 2007), p. 247.

to anyone prior to their arrival in Warrington at 8:30 a.m. on 25 January. William Wood, Secretary of the Warrington local, and Joseph Davies, General Secretary of the union, received word of the men's capture late in the evening of the 24th. A messenger was sent very early the next morning from Warrington to Manchester to hire Roberts to defend the men in a hearing that was to begin at 11 a.m. that same day.[28] Roberts, who had been very busy over the previous two months, barely had been home in Manchester a day when word of the file-forgers' arrest reached him. It was after 9 a.m., less than two hours before Edelsten's men were to be tried miles away in Warrington.[29]

Magistrates Thomas Lyon and William Stubs

The magistrates called upon to determine this case received considerable public abuse. Both men were deeply stung by this criticism and the lack of support they received from the government.[30] Thomas Lyon and William Stubs were community leaders in Warrington for whom the magistracy was an important mark of status. On 25 January 1847, they heard what must have appeared to them as an open-and-shut case. Roberts' arguments in court and to the press made it appear that they were unfamiliar with the law and partial toward the employer, a judgment that in some circles was confirmed by the government's reversal of their ruling. This was particularly curious because there is no reason to believe that their relationship with organized labor was an antagonistic one and, in fact, there is evidence that Stubs had been on excellent terms with local workmen. This highlights the difficult, and oftentimes unfair, situation faced by magistrates when attempting to administer the law during a bitter labor dispute.

Thomas Lyon was a small landowner, brewer, banker and investor, who had been an active magistrate since 1819. Through partnerships, investments in railways and brewing, and his marriage into the wealthy Parr family, Lyon was

---

[28] 'A Copy of the Informations and Evidence … (1847)', pp. 9, 16–17, 20; NA: HO 18/193/38; 'To T. S. Duncombe, M.P., 8 Princess Street, Manchester, 29 January 1847', *NS* (6 February 1847), p. 4; for the National Association of United Trades for the Protection of Labour, see: S. and B. Webb, *The History of Trade Unionism* (London, 1902), pp. 168–77.

[29] On 23 January 1847 Roberts was in Gateshead defending striking glass-blowers against a master and servant prosecution. See *Proceedings at the Gateshead Police Court, Saturday January 23, 1847, In the Case of John Coulson, Glassmaker, Charged With Unlawfully Leaving His Masters' Service* (Newcastle upon Tyne, 1847). This case was printed by the Glassmakers' Union, and was another method of publicizing the issues and injustices of master and servant law. For his heavy involvement in a carpenters' strike of December 1846, see: 'Rochdale and Middleton: Turn Out Joiners Serious Charges', *ME* (26 December 1846), p. 7.

[30] The articles in the *Northern Star* bothered the pair so much, they complained to the Home Office, sending copies of the offending articles, see NA: HO 43/73, 17 February 1847; 'The File Cutters' Turn Out', *MCGLA* (20 March 1847), p. 183.

well-connected to the elite industrial families of the region. He was appointed to the bench on the basis of his small landholdings, but likely identified more with the commercial and industrial men later appointed to the bench in large numbers. In 1819, the appointment of a largely commercial man to the magistracy represented a significant social coup. He was a 'consistent and active' supporter of the Conservative party, but still probably expected greater support from the Home Secretary in this case than he ultimately received.[31] Having sat on the bench for 28 years, the presence of attorneys at Petty Sessions might have represented a new phenomenon for him, as he was the allegedly more hostile of the two magistrates to Roberts. Lyon and William Stubs were long-time acquaintances. Since 1802 Lyon had been a landlord and creditor to the Stubs firm.[32]

William Stubs, the seventh of Peter Stubs' 18 children, expanded the family business with his brothers John and Joseph after the death of their father in 1806. In his early years in the business, William traveled widely across England marketing the Stubs products. The business thrived under the guidance of William and Joseph, and in 1840 they secured a lucrative contract to produce files for the Admiralty. A year later, the firm employed over 200 men in the shop and had an extensive network of out-workers, a six-fold increase in the number of employees since 1821. William was appointed to the magistracy in 1836, perhaps as the result of Lord Stanley's 1835 request for the appointment of more liberal men to the Lancashire bench. William, a liberal, was active in politics, in regular contact with local MPs and on one occasion invited to stand for Parliament.[33]

William and Joseph Stubs appear to have enjoyed very good relations with their workmen. There is some evidence that, in the radical language used by skilled workmen since the eighteenth century, William Stubs was an honorable master, who cooperated with his workmen to maintain their status while taking his just profits.[34] In late 1840 and early 1841, Stubs' workmen held a series of meetings to plan a dinner and gift for William and Joseph to thank them for fostering 'a good understanding between the employer and employed'. They resolved to honor

---

[31]   T. C. Barker and J. R. Harris, *A Merseyside Town in the Industrial Revolution, St. Helens, 1750–1950* (London, 1953), pp. 103, 186; David Foster, 'The Social and Political Composition of the Lancashire Magistracy, 1821–1851' (PhD dissertation, University of Lancaster, 1972), p. 231.

[32]   'To T. S. Duncombe, M.P., 8 Princess St., Manchester, 29 January 1847', *NS* (6 February 1847), p. 4. Lyon also rented a garden to William's mother, Mary. Barker and Harris, *A Merseyside Town*, pp. 103, 186; Dane, *Peter Stubs*, pp. 58, 72, 74–5; Ashton, *Eighteenth Century Industrialist*, pp. 26, 114.

[33]   Manchester Public Library: MS L24/1, Box 26, 'An Account of the Dinner and Presentation of Plate to Mr. W & J Stubs by Their Workmen, 1841'; Dane, *Peter Stubs*, pp. 60, 66, 133–7, 170–174; Foster, 'Lancashire Magistracy', pp. 211–12.

[34]   I. Prothero, *Artisans and Politics in Early Nineteenth Century London: John Gast and His Times* (Kent, 1979), p. 226; Richard Price, *Labour in British Society: An Interpretive History* (London, 1986), p. 51.

the brothers for their 'sturdy sense of justice' and 'boundless liberality towards their workmen'. The workmen raised subscriptions to purchase a pair of four-quart silver gilt cups costing 60 guineas each. They were inscribed 'Presented to William [Joseph] Stubs esquire, by his workmen at Warrington and Rotherham as a testimony of their esteem for his honourable conduct towards them as employer, 1841'.[35]

Over 200 workmen and a number of local notables attended Warrington Town Hall on 3 April 1841 to honor William and Joseph. After a series of toasts made with freely-flowing Warrington Ale, or lemonade and ginger beer for those seated under the teetotal banner, the two most senior employees presented the silver cups to William and Joseph. They also thanked the pair for paying the best wages in the region, and avoiding layoffs even in difficult periods. The speakers stressed this last point:

> No, these alternatives you have never made use of, but have left them to be embraced by those narrow-minded manufacturers, who will employ all they can meet with when trade is flourishing, and even take on numbers of apprentices, to be discharged at the least appearance of gloom.[36]

One can detect the elements of 'artisan political economy' in this praise, such as the distinction between good and bad masters, the need to regulate production, and the importance of maintaining skill and trade standards.[37] William had recently removed himself from an active role in the firm to pursue his work as a magistrate.[38] The workmen toasted 'May you, sir, long live to fulfill those duties which have been imposed upon you in your magisterial capacity ... and which you have hitherto performed with so much credit'.

William received the cups and gave a paternalistic speech in which he extolled the value of education and self-discipline. He also declared that his intent was to set aside his own personal aggrandizement and work for the welfare of the whole

---

[35] Manchester Public Library: MS L24/1, Box 26, 'An Account of the Dinner and Presentation of Plate to Mr. W. & J. Stubs by Their Workmen, 1841', and 'A Public Meeting of the Workmen and File Makers, 14 December 1840 and 2 February 1841'; Dane, *Peter Stubs*, p. 37; Ashton, *Eighteenth Century Industrialist*, p. 141. These types of celebrations of good employers were not uncommon. For a couple examples, see: 'Merthyr: Public Meeting', *MM* (29 June 1844), p. 4; 'An Example for Masters and Workmen', *Sheffield Free Press* (1 November 1851), p. 8; 'Dinner to Workmen', *Sheffield Free Press* (15 May 1852), p. 4.

[36] Ibid.

[37] Prothero, *Artisans and Politics*, p. 226; Price, *Labour in British Society*, p. 51.

[38] Manchester Public Library: MS L24/1, Box 1, 'Agreement as to the Dissolution of Partnership'. William removed himself from active participation in the firm in 1841, and on 31 March 1845 sold his interest in the business to his brother Joseph.

community in his role as magistrate.[39] Roberts managed to severely puncture this paternalistic relationship with local file-forgers. Within six years, these same working men and women of Warrington were drunkenly lampooning William Stubs as a tyrant while celebrating the liberation of Edelsten's employees.[40]

In previous chapters it has been shown that Roberts' appellate actions burdened magistrates with costs, damages and embarrassment. This case study shows that it could also undermine their authority and status in a broader sense. In an earlier era, neither Lyon nor Stubs could have taken their appointment to the magistracy for granted, because both were primarily men of industry and commerce. Both were community leaders, and their appointment to the bench was a recognition or legitimation of their social position. Stubs wanted to adopt the role of paternalistic community leader. Roberts and the *Northern Star* constructed the magistrates in such a way as to undermine any paternal authority they had among workers. They rejected the portrayal of magistrates as neutral community arbitrators and conciliators, but instead firmly linked them with the interests of industrial employers. The pardon issued to the men was treated as a further rebuke to Lyon and Stubs' local authority from no less than the Crown's representatives. Both felt so undermined by the government that they refused to sit at Warrington Petty Sessions, claiming they no longer commanded the legitimacy necessary to do their jobs.[41]

The Hearing of *Edelsten v. Gerrard et al.*, 25 January 1847

On the morning of 25 January 1847, a large crowd assembled across the street from the Sessions House in Warrington, as rumors circulated that the prisoners were to be defended by the 'Miners' Attorney-General'. The accused arrived in town at 8:30 a.m. At 11 a.m. the courtroom opened, and filled immediately, leaving three-quarters of the crowd still outside, unable to get in.[42]

Solicitors Mr Beaumont and James Nicholson, representing Edelsten, began the hearing by proposing that the six cases be heard separately, a proposal that was granted by the magistrates. At this point the prisoners had no legal representation. The first case heard was that of apprentice file-cutter Thomas Wyke. The prosecution submitted that John Wyke, shortly before his death in February 1844, apprenticed his 17-year-old son to Edelsten for a period of four years. Thomas was required to serve and obey Edelsten in return for room, board, clothes and an education in the trade of file-cutting. Edelsten was also bound to pay Wyke a minimum of 5s per

---

[39]   Manchester Public Library: MS L24/1, Box 26.

[40]   'Warrington Justices' Retirement into Private Life', *NS* (13 March 1847), p. 5; 'Warrington Breach of Contract Case', *MG* (6 March 1847), p. 3.

[41]   'The File Cutters' Turn Out', *MCGLA* (30 January 1847), p. 183.

[42]   'File-Cutters' Turn-Out', *MG* (30 January 1847), p. 8.

week in the first year, 6s per week in the second, 7s per week in the third and 8s per week in his fourth year.[43]

This was not Wyke's first appearance before magistrates. On two prior occasions Edelsten had disciplined Wyke using master and servant law. Two years earlier, Wyke missed a quarter-day's work because he woke up too stiff to get out of bed, blaming his condition on the long hours of labor demanded of him. Edelsten had him taken into custody and held overnight in the local bridewell. The next morning, Edelsten requested the magistrates to 'forgive' the offence and release Wyke back into his service. A similar episode occurred in June 1846, when Wyke missed several days in one week due to pain from long hours of labor. Wyke was again brought before magistrates, reprimanded and released to Edelsten.[44]

Edelsten's solicitors called him to testify to the terms of Wyke's indenture, and his violation of it by absconding. Edelsten emphasized his good treatment of Wyke by pointing out that the apprentice had earned 18s 3½d in overtime pay during the week before he absconded. Wyke did not cross-examine Edelsten, and thus was unable to raise the fact that he had worked 95 hours during that particular week.[45]

Lyon and Stubs asked Wyke what he had to say in his defense. Wyke argued that Edelsten had violated his indenture by forcing him to pay for his own tools and taking deductions that were neither in his indenture nor customs of the trade. He argued that Edelsten had broken the indenture first, thereby repudiating the agreement. Implicit in this argument was a strain of contract law – the notion that the precise terms of the contract should be equally binding upon both parties. Lyon asked Wyke if he had made a formal complaint to Edelsten about these deductions before absconding. The apprentice had not. After a brief deliberation, the magistrates sentenced Wyke to three months' imprisonment with hard labor. This case did not take 10 minutes of the court's time.[46]

What is striking about Wyke's defense was that many of the arguments he raised were similar to ones a solicitor would have made. Where Wyke was at a disadvantage was in his lack of knowledge of legal process and an inability to

---

[43] 'Copies of the Informations and Evidence … (1847)', p. 5; NA: HO 18/193/38.

[44] 'The Warrington Shallows Again', *NS* (13 February 1847), p. 4; 'A Copy of the Informations and Evidence … (1847)', p. 5; NA: HO 18/193/38.

[45] It was later alleged that Edelsten used leverage other than the law in this struggle with Thomas over his hours of work. Wyke's widowed mother had two younger children, leaving her heavily dependent upon his contributions and assistance from poor relief. In a public letter to Thomas Duncombe after the hearing, Roberts accused Edelsten of having used his position as poor law guardian to threaten Wyke with 'stopping his mother's pay' unless he worked the required overtime. 'The Warrington Shallows Again', *NS* (13 February 1847), p. 4; Challinor, *Radical Lawyer*, p. 143.

[46] 'A Copy of the Informations and Evidence … (1847)', pp. 5–7; NA: HO 18/193/38; 'The File Cutters' Turn Out', *MG* (30 January 1847), p. 8; 'The File Makers' Turn Out', *MCGLA* (30 January 1847), p. 71; 'The Warrington Shallows Again', *NS* (13 February 1847), p. 4.

challenge forms and procedures used against him. On the 'merits' of the case, he had a solid argument. Roberts used a similar line of defense a year later when defending a group of apprentices in the glass-blowing trade in Birmingham. Between 200 and 300 glass-makers were on strike against Mr Harris to protest his alteration in the form of manufacture from the slow and labor-intensive process of cutting glass to the simpler process of pressing glass into molds. Harris charged a group of apprentices with leaving their work under 4 George IV, c.34 (1823). In a hearing that lasted over three hours, Roberts successfully argued that the apprentices' indenture stipulated that Harris would teach them the art and mystery of glass blowing and cutting, and because Harris was making them do press-work, he was not fulfilling this obligation, repudiating the indenture. The magistrates accepted this argument and the charges were dismissed. In another case that took place one month earlier, however, this argument did not move the magistrates, and the men had been forced to return to work.

Workers representing themselves in master and servant cases often presented good defenses, even if magistrates rarely accepted their arguments. In 1848, a glass-blower was charged by his employer with misbehavior under the 1823 Act for disobeying his employers' demand that he make glass cylinders at 13 ounces per square foot. The defendant had signed a 10-year agreement in 1844 that explicitly stated that he was to make cylinders at 12 ounces per foot. The worker, representing himself, argued that he was following the precise terms of his contract. The heavier cylinders would cost him money because he could not produce as many of them in a week. His master, however, replied that industry standards had changed since the agreement was signed and he needed to make heavier cylinders. The magistrates, far from rewarding the worker for his strict adherence to the contract, reprimanded him for his 'insolence' and disobedience. The magistrates abated nearly 14s of his wages, made him pay all costs and forced him to apologize to his employers.[47]

Roberts had still not arrived when James Gerrard's hearing began. Edelsten produced Gerrard's five-year contract, and testified that Gerrard had twice absconded. He also provided the details of Gerrard's earlier absence, and his efforts to secure a pardon for Gerrard. He further stated that, contrary to Gerrard's claims, his doctor had found the prisoner fit for work. When asked to speak in his defense, like Wyke, Gerrard displayed some sense of contract law. He argued that his contract did not represent a true meeting of minds because he had felt coerced into signing it the previous April, needing a loan from Edelsten to bury his child. This fell far short of demonstrating coercion, but it was an informed argument nonetheless. Roberts had successfully used a similar defense seven months earlier in Oldham. He argued that the employment contract entered into by a group of joiners did not represent a true meeting of minds because the employer had

---

[47]   'Mr. Harris' Glass Works', *Birmingham Journal* (hereafter, *BJ*) (24 June 1848), p. 5; 'Glass Makers' Strike', *BJ* (22 July 1848), p. 7; 'Disobedience of Orders by a Workman', *BJ* (29 January 1848), p. 7.

misled the men by neglecting to tell them that he was hiring them as replacement workers to break a strike. This argument did not work for Gerrard, however, as the magistrates sentenced him to three months' imprisonment with hard labor. By now they had been sitting for barely 20 minutes.[48]

James Ireland's case was next, and after the examination of two witnesses it was conforming to the pattern of the previous two hearings. At 11:40 a.m., the magistrates were about to conclude the case when they:

> were interrupted by the most unseemly disturbance, a burst of huzzas accompanied by clapping of hands, stamping of feet, and other marks of popular excitement, which was carried on to such an extent that we felt bound, for the decent conduct of the business of the court, indeed, to enable us to proceed at all, to require that it should be closed.[49]

The crowd was responding to the dramatic entry of Roberts, who had paid a carriage driver double fees to expedite his arrival in Warrington. The magistrates cleared and closed the courtroom.[50]

Roberts introduced himself and asked the magistrates to permit the audience to return. The magistrates refused and the courtroom was closed to the public for the remaining hearings. Roberts requested that the magistrates re-hear the cases of Wyke and Gerrard, citing the 1836 Prisoners' Counsel Act, which stated that in cases of summary conviction prisoners were entitled to have a solicitor conduct their defense and cross-examine witnesses. Roberts argued that he had received word of the hearing only two hours earlier, and the prisoners had not had adequate opportunity to engage counsel, or even speak with anyone, during their captivity, violating the spirit of that act.[51]

This fact loomed large in light of subsequent irregularities and omissions that Roberts uncovered in the cases of Ireland and Dobson. Wyke and Gerrard had been unable to cross-examine any of the witnesses against them or raise objections to the hasty and informal process of their rapid hearings. In contrast, with Roberts conducting the defense, James Ireland's case consumed nearly three hours, and came much closer to what a modern observer might consider an adversarial trial.

---

[48]   Ibid.; 'Charge Against Two Carpenters', *ME* (2 May 1846), p. 5.

[49]   Ibid.

[50]   Challinor, *Radical Lawyer*, p. 142; 'The File Cutters' Turn Out', *MG* (30 January 1847), p. 8; John Belcham and James Epstein, 'The Nineteenth Century Gentleman Leader Revisited', *Social History* 22/2 (1997): 174–93.

[51]   'To T. S. Duncombe, M.P. 8 Princess Street, Manchester, 29 January 1847', *NS* (6 February 1847), p. 4; 'A Copy of the Informations and Evidence … (1847)', p. 18; NA: HO 18/193/38; 'The File Cutters' Turn Out', *MG* (30 January 1847), p. 8 'The File Makers' Turn Out', *MCGLA* (30 January 1847), p. 71; 6 & 7 William IV, c.114, s.2 (1836).

The magistrates correctly decided that it would have been irregular and illegal to re-hear a case in which they had already delivered a judgment.[52] Lyon and Stubs agreed to start Ireland's case from the beginning, giving Roberts 15 minutes to confer with his client.[53] After a brief discussion with Ireland, Roberts requested to see the information against Ireland. This was the formal complaint, the statement under oath that informed the magistrate of an offence within his jurisdiction. It was usually in written form, and it contained the charge which the defendant was to answer. Sections 1 and 3 of 4 George IV, c.34 (1823) explicitly required the information be made under oath by the complainant before the same magistrate who ultimately determined the case.[54] Three months earlier, Edelsten had sworn out informations against his workmen before magistrate William Hall, who had since left the region. According to the *Justice of the Peace* (and the law officers of the crown), the proper course of action would have been for Edelsten to have withdrawn the old informations against the defendants, and then sworn out new ones before the sitting magistrates. The clerk was forced to admit to Roberts that the information in this case, and those from the two preceding ones, were not in the court.[55] This meant that Wyke and Gerrard had been convicted in the absence of an information against them. Their hearing had been so informal that the precise charge against them, sworn out by Edelsten, had not been read to them.

This point was of considerable significance. Queen's Bench required that convictions contain all facts necessary to demonstrate the magistrates' jurisdiction. Without the information required by the statute, there was no charge or offense. If there was no offense within the magistrates' jurisdiction then obviously any conviction was invalid.[56] A conviction could be lost due to errors on the information,

---

[52]   Ibid. A year earlier, Roberts had initiated a certiorari and habeas corpus in a similar case, see In the matter of Ogden (1846), described in Chapter 3.

[53]   Ibid. There was some dispute on this point. Roberts claimed he was only granted 15 minutes to talk to Ireland, but the magistrates stated that they offered a two-hour adjournment and Roberts only wanted 15 minutes.

[54]   'Of the Jurisdiction of Justices to Receive Informations or Complaints of the Same or Others, or Another, To Adjudicate Them', *JP* 9/16 (16 April 1845), p. 258, and 'Practical Points', *JP* 9/4 (25 January 1845), p. 59, 'the same justice or justices must receive the information, issue the process, hear the complaint, and convict and commit. A committal by any other justice of justices would be illegal'. It was upon this ground that the file-makers ultimately won their pardon, see NA: HO 18/193/38.

[55]   Challinor, *Radical Lawyer*, p. 143; 'A Copy of the Informations and Evidence ... (1847)', p. 18; NA: HO 18/193/38; 'To T. S. Duncombe, M.P., 8 Princess Street, 29 January 1847', *NS* (6 February 1847), p. 4.

[56]   W. R. Cornish and G. de N. Clark, *Law and Society in England 1750–1950* (London, 1989), p. 35. Informations, like convictions, were required by the courts to be precise. Convictions could be overturned if the information failed to specify the location of the offense, or in cases where the accused had contracted with a partnership, if it failed to list every partner's name. 'Practical Points', *JP* 10/33 (15 August 1846), p. 522; 'Practical Points', *JP* 10/38 (19 September 1846), pp. 603–4.

as in Seth Turner's Case (1846) which was described in Chapter 3. In February 1847, at the Lancashire Assizes, another of Roberts' clients brought a charge of trespass and false imprisonment against a magistrate who had convicted him under 4 George IV, c.34 (1823) two years earlier. In that case Roberts won the release of the prisoner with a writ of habeas corpus because the warrant of commitment failed to state that an information or formal complaint had been sworn against the accused, and thus it failed to establish the magistrates' jurisdiction.[57] Roberts argued that this technicality was 'no mere matter of form' because 'if the doctrine is admitted in these cases a man might be tried for murder without an indictment'. In Roberts' experience, if a formal information charging an offense within the magistrates' jurisdiction was not required, those officers would, and in fact often did, rule in cases where they had no jurisdiction at all. This point really comes down to competing visions of summary procedure, whether the process would conform to the Benthamite vision of an efficient machine for speedy convictions, or Roberts' vision of a real trial with some constitutional protections for the accused.[58]

The information was delivered to court, but was *not* read, and the trial proceeded. Edelsten testified to the existence of a five-year contract between himself and Ireland, which the latter had broken twice. Roberts cross-examined Edelsten aggressively about the terms of this contract. In particular, Roberts emphasized the clause that stated 'Edelsten agrees to pay him [Ireland] for every dozen inch half-rounds, the sum of 8d, and for striking all other sizes the usual prices paid by the trade by the other masters in Warrington'. Edelsten testified that he paid 1½d per dozen for the task of straightening old files. Roberts forced him to admit that he had not investigated what other masters paid for this task and was unable to name another master who paid the same rate. Roberts informed Edelsten that the firm of Stubs paid their men 2d per dozen for the same task. Edelsten first denied being aware of this, but then admitted that a deputation from the union had brought it to his attention. At this point an uncomfortable magistrate Stubs intervened, ruling that the point was immaterial because 'the amount was scarcely worth talking about, so few had to be done'. Stubs argued that not every breach of agreement on the part of an employer was so fundamental as to be a repudiation of the contract. Roberts countered with an appeal to classic contract doctrine, stating that contracts had to be fulfilled to the letter, not merely the parts

---

[57]   Seth Turner's Case (1846), 115 E. R. 1206–10. Five days after Edlesten and Gerrard et al., another of Roberts' clients, a pikeman who was convicted for refusing to work as a miner, was freed by the Queen's Bench on nearly the same grounds, see 'Reg v. John Haines', *JP* 11/7 (13 February 1847), p. 103; 'An Action Against a Magistrate for False Imprisonment', *MG* (24 Feburary 1847), p. 5.

[58]   'A Copy of the Informations and Evidence ... (1847)', p. 18; NA: HO 18/193/38; 'To T. S. Duncombe, M.P., 8 Princess Street, 29 January 1847', *NS* (6 February 1847), p. 4; Sweeney, 'Summary Jurisdiction', pp. 94–101; Smith, 'Circumventing the Jury', pp. 75–9.

one party deems 'worth speaking about'. Roberts was making substantially the same argument as Wyke, that Edelsten had so consistently broken and ignored his agreements with his men that these documents had ceased to govern their relationship before they absconded. According to prevailing case law, had Ireland 'misbehaved', demonstrated incompetence or violated the contract then Edelsten could have summarily dismissed him.[59] Workers, however, were not free to summarily determine contracts when their employers refused to fulfill the terms.

Joseph Bramwood, the constable who captured the men, testified to the inflammatory statements he heard them make at their arrest. Roberts' strategy on cross-examination was to establish the chronology of the men's arrest and transportation to Warrington, so he could later expose the policy of isolating the prisoners and convicting them quickly. Bramwood argued that the men 'had every opportunity of having communication with anyone', but then testified that with the exception of a friend in Sheffield, 'they did not see any person apart from him while in his custody'. Ireland saw his wife immediately before the hearing, but had no other visitors.[60]

In presenting Ireland's defense, Roberts returned to the information, requesting a copy, perhaps to exploit inconsistencies between the testimony, warrants and the information.[61] His request was denied. Roberts then asked if the information could be read slowly so he could copy it by hand. The magistrates refused to allow Roberts to hold the information, having the clerk read it out at 'the normal speed'. The magistrates were reluctant to allow Roberts to see the information because he might spot a legal error. If they had, Roberts likely would have noticed that the information had been sworn before William Hall, and not the magistrates who were currently hearing the case.

The *Justice of the Peace* often fielded questions related to the defendant's right of access to the informations. The editors of that journal always insisted that magistrates were not required to give a copy of the information to the defense, and strongly advised against it in cases where the accused was represented by counsel. In 1845, the *Justice of the Peace* told a correspondent that magistrates should give a copy of the information to the defense only 'when it is to be used for a legitimate purpose', but not when 'it is merely to enable the defendant to take advantage of a defect in form'. Two weeks later a correspondent asked if he could refuse to read

---

[59]   *Spain v. Arnott* (1817), 117 E. R. 638; *Amor v. Fearson* (1839), 9 A. & E. 548; *Turner v. Mason* (1845), 153 E. R. 411; *Mercer v. Whall* (1845), 114 E. R. 1314; *Lilley v. Elwin* (1848), 135 E. R. 1201; *Harmer v. Cornelius* (1858), 28 L. J. C. P. 85.

[60]   It is possible that Ireland and his wife discussed the condition of their sick child, who died shortly after Ireland was committed to the House of Correction. 'A Copy of the Informations and Evidence … (1847)', pp. 9–10, 14–15; NA: HO 18/193/38; 'The File Makers' Turn-Out', *MCLGA* (30 January 1847), p. 71; 'The File Cutters' Turn Out', *MG* (30 January 1847), p. 8; 'To T. S. Duncombe, M.P., 8 Princess Street, Manchester, 29 January 1847', *NS* (6 February 1847), p. 4.

[61]   Smith, 'Circumventing the Jury', pp. 186–91.

the information or show it in court. The editors emphasized that 'it is obligatory on him to cause that it [the information] be so read, that the … defendant may know with what offence he is charged'. They further stressed that the information had 'to be seen in open court by the defendant', even if granting a copy to the prisoner or his/her lawyer was at the discretion of the magistrate.[62]

Roberts then attempted, without being certain of its contents, to raise objections about the information, suggesting that it failed to show the terms of the contract. He was unsuccessful, and later argued that 'there remained many legal points for observation, but argument after this would have been idleness'. Ireland was convicted to three months' imprisonment with hard labor.[63]

Edelsten, perhaps weary from the three-hour ordeal, offered to withdraw the charges against apprentice John Baxter provided he express remorse and return to work. At first, Baxter declined, but after some discussion agreed and was discharged. John Dobson was the next man to be tried. Edelsten offered to withdraw all charges and give him the choice of returning to work or being discharged from his contract, provided he admitted his guilt and paid part of the expense of his capture and trial. The clerk determined that these costs were £4 1s 8½d. Dobson could not afford this sum, and was unable to accept this offer. The union, which later in the day paid Roberts £20 for handling the cases, could have paid these expenses for Dobson. It is possible that Roberts advised Dobson and the union that there were a number of strong grounds for a certiorari or habeas corpus.[64] Dobson and the union were both confronted with the choice of conviction with the possibility of being released by Queen's Bench, or immediate freedom while conceding the validity of Edelsten's policies. This difficult choice was later rhetorically exploited by Roberts and the *Northern Star*, arguing that 'Dobson … is now at the tread-wheel, not as a misdemeanant, but as a debtor to the amount of £4 1s 8½d'.[65] The magistrates later stated that Dobson's failure to pay the costs was of less significance to them than his 'obstinately and pertinaciously refusing' to acknowledge his guilt.

Stubs and Lyon offered to adjourn Dobson's case for two days, or even a week, but without bail, likely because he had proven himself to be a flight risk. The defense refused the magistrates' offer, and court was adjourned for 15 minutes. Roberts used this time to deliver a speech to the assembled workmen and women outside about what was occurring inside the Sessions House, 'creating a great

---

[62] 'Practical Points', *JP* 7/6 (11 February 1843), p. 54; 'Practical Points', *JP* 9/21 (24 May 1845), p. 332; 'Practical Points', *JP* 9/23 (7 June 1845), p. 351; Smith, 'Circumventing the Jury', pp. 186–91.

[63] 'A Copy of the Informations and Evidence … (1847)', pp. 18–19; NA: HO 18/193/38; 'To T. S. Duncombe, M.P., 8 Princess St, Manchester, 29 January 1847', *NS* (6 February 1847), p. 4; 'File Cutters' Turn Out', *MG* (30 January 1847), p. 8.

[64] Ibid.

[65] 'Ruin Them With Expenses', *NS* (6 February 1847), p. 4.

disturbance in the street'.[66] Roberts had transformed the courtroom into a site of class confrontation.

When the hearing resumed, Roberts applied for a copy of the information. Not only was Dobson's information absent from the court, but it had been lost entirely. Roberts demanded Dobson's immediate release, as there was no charge for him to answer. The magistrates asked Edelsten to swear out a new information against Dobson. Roberts again demanded that Dobson be discharged because this was irregular, and the new informations 'neither agreed with the contract nor with the warrant under which the prisoner was apprehended'. The magistrates overruled his objections.[67]

The new information was read out in court 'in the usual way', which was too fast for Roberts to copy any of it down. Roberts 'urged various objections' to the contract between Edelsten and Dobson, which were ineffective and not specified in the record. Roberts later observed that without access to the defendant's information, 'it was uphill work'.[68]

In his cross-examination of Edelsten, Roberts argued Dobson had absorbed expenses for preparing old files for re-cutting, which was contrary to his contract and the custom of the trade. Roberts also proved that Edelsten paid Dobson less than the Warrington rate for particular tasks. As with Ireland, these objections were ineffective. Dobson was sentenced to three months' imprisonment with hard labor. The remaining prisoner, Samuel Wilcock, accepted Edelsten's offer to withdraw the charges against him if he admitted that he had acted wrongly.[69]

The narrative of the hearing once again illuminates the importance of master and servant law to a small producer in a competitive industry. Edelsten had brought several of the prisoners before magistrates as many as two or three times each, usually using the threat of imprisonment to coerce them into performing their contracts. It further illuminates that workers were expected to maintain much closer conformity with the precise terms of their agreements than their employers. The magistrates felt that as a matter of law, Edelsten's refusal to pay the prevailing Warrington rates as his agreements stipulated, or the expenses of his workers that were customs of the trade, were not nearly as serious as a tired apprentice missing

---

[66] 'A Copy of the Informations and Evidence ... (1847)', pp. 19–20; NA: HO 18/193/38; 'The Warrington Shallow Again', *NS* (13 February 1847), p. 4; 'To T. S. Duncombe, M.P., 8 Princess Street, Manchester, 29 January 1847', *NS* (6 February 1847), p. 4; Challinor, *Radical Lawyer*, p. 143.

[67] Ibid. Roberts also argued that Dobson should be able to settle his case at a discount, since 'on the information actually tried against Dobson no costs whatever had been incurred except a shilling or two – the information on which he was brought from Derbyshire [and £4 8s 1/2d incurred] was lost'.

[68] Ibid. One of these objections might have been that Dobson's contract with Edelsten did not specify the date it was to commence.

[69] Ibid.

a morning of work. Roberts, and the file-forgers themselves, repeatedly attempted to shift the focus of the hearing toward Edelsten's broken promises.

It also demonstrates the benefits and limitations of the Prisoners' Counsel Act and having a solicitor present at Petty Sessions. Although Wyke and Gerrard made legally informed arguments in their defense, their hasty and informal hearings lasted less than 10 minutes each. Roberts forced the issues of the case to be explored more deeply, and raised procedural objections that created opportunities for a favorable settlement in two of the cases. Magistrates and employers frequently circumvented the right to an attorney by holding hearings immediately after late-night arrests, as was clearly attempted here.[70] Even when attorneys gained access to Petty Sessions, these hearings show that solicitors still faced an uphill battle, as magistrates were not required to consider their arguments and could withhold documents to make it more difficult to present a full defense. Although Roberts exposed a number of grounds to challenge the judgments, his clients still suffered the same fate as Wyke and Gerrard.

These cases also reveal the importance of Roberts' struggle to establish case law that shaped summary procedure into a more formal process with greater protections for the accused. It might appear that his objections about the informations were merely 'technicalities' because the prisoners were obviously guilty in the spirit of the act. However, not bothering to have the formal charges present in the courtroom, or in the case of Dobson, not having them at all, exposed a sense that the burden lay not with Edelsten to prove the men's guilt, but with the prisoners to prove their innocence.[71] It implies that the magistrates already knew the outcome of the case, and the hearing was merely a troublesome formality.

Roberts' Demand for a Parliamentary Inquiry

On 29 January 1847, Roberts sent a letter and a petition signed by the prisoners' wives and mothers complaining of the procedural irregularities of this case to T. S. Duncombe in Parliament. Roberts justified his pursuit of a parliamentary inquiry into the magistrates' ruling instead of a certiorari to Queen's Bench on the grounds that public exposure on the nation's largest political stage might draw some attention to disturbing practices in magistrates' hearings.[72] The *Northern Star* disagreed with this strategy. 'Much as we rely on Mr. Roberts' judgment and zeal, we should have preferred the inevitable exposure of a certiorari to the mock sentimentality of the Home Secretary; or the farce of Parliamentary Debate'. Doubting Roberts' chance of success, 'we fear the indifference of OUR Home

---

[70] Challinor, *Radical Lawyer*, pp. 142–4.

[71] See Bruce P. Smith, 'The Presumption of Guilt and the English Law of Theft, 1750–1850', *Law and History Review* 23/1 (Spring 2003): 133–71.

[72] 'To T. S. Duncombe, MP, 9 Princess Street, Manchester 29 January 1847', *NS* (6 February 1847), p. 4.

Secretary and the apathy of the people will allow a further precedent' of magisterial tyranny. Roberts' court challenges were used to critique corrupt patronage politics (the magistrates), reinforcing the Chartist faith in the constitution and institutions of 'real law', represented by Queen's Bench. The *Northern Star* challenged the legitimacy of magistrates, warning that their 'standing was being daily weakened and undermined by a brutal exercise of irresponsible power'.[73] Obtaining relief from an unreformed Parliament would undercut the Chartist argument by showing that justice could be obtained from that institution.[74]

Aware that members of Parliament were unlikely to sympathize with trade unionists who absconded from their contracts to the potential ruin of their master, Roberts' letter focused on flaws in the process of the hearing. 'The petitions do not go into the merits of the cases ... I carefully steered clear of that rock. What the petitions charge is this – and to this argument should be confined – that the men did not have a fair trial'.[75] Roberts not only emphasized his strongest arguments, but also placed the case within the context of recently renewed discussion regarding the expansion of magistrates' summary powers. In 1847, Parliament revisited the old proposal of allowing magistrates to determine summarily cases of small larcenies by juveniles.[76] Roberts' letter was the first of three demands for Parliamentary inquiries into the conduct of magistrates in master and servant and combination cases between February and June 1847, the same period Parliament was considering the Juvenile Justice Bill.

After narrating the particulars of the case, Roberts' letter drew attention to three flaws in the hearing. His first objection was the common practice of rushing the summary process to prevent the accused from obtaining legal counsel:

> The principle evil, however, which the parties are desirous of bringing before Parliament is the unjust and indecent haste with which these summary jurisdiction cases are disposed of. In ninety-nine cases out of a hundred, the accused are tried and convicted within an hour or two after he is in custody.

Roberts argued that this not only kept prisoners from obtaining counsel, but also prevented them from gathering witnesses and evidence to build a defense. Roberts argued that the benefits conferred by the 1836 Prisoners' Counsel Act were 'altogether useless, unless the accused have some time' to obtain a lawyer.[77] Roberts stressed that the prisoners' request to see a Sheffield attorney immediately

---

[73]   'The Warrington Shallows Again', *NS* (6 February 1847), p. 4.

[74]   Gareth Stedman Jones, *The Languages of Class: Studies in Working Class History, 1832–1982* (London, 1983), pp. 102–6, 109.

[75]   'To T. S. Duncombe, MP, 9 Princess Street, Manchester 29 January 1847', *NS* (6 Feburary 1847), p. 4.

[76]   See Chapter 5, below. Sweeney, 'Summary Jurisdiction', pp. 152–60.

[77]   'To T. S. Duncombe, MP, 8 Princess Street, Manchester, 29 January 1847', *NS* (6 February 1847), p. 4; Challinor, *Radical Lawyer*, p. 142.

after their capture was ignored and they were prevented from seeing friends prior to their hearing. Consequently, two of the cases were disposed of before he arrived.[78] There was nothing in the 1836 Act to prevent a hasty trial, or guarantee an adjournment of a hearing so the defendant could find an attorney. Yet the narrative of the men's capture, transportation and trial was clearly contrary to the spirit of the act. This complaint had resonance in Parliament, as one of the arguments made against the 1847 Juvenile Justice Bill was that it was 'most dangerous to the liberty of the subject, upsetting the great principle of trial by jury, and substituting for it a secret tribunal, where [in practice] no counsel could be heard'.[79]

To stress that this was not an isolated event, Roberts alluded to the case of a Rochdale man tried and convicted under the 1825 Combination Laws Repeal Amendment Act within an hour of his arrest. More shocking still was the case of a group of boys who were arrested, tried and committed to a week's incarceration for skipping a day of work. Their arrest and trial were carried out with such haste that many of their parents were unaware of the proceeding until it was over and the children were being shipped to prison.[80]

Roberts' second objection was two-fold. Two of the trials took place in the absence of informations charging the defendants with an offense. In three of the cases 'the same magistrate before whom the said informations were laid ought in law to have tried your petitioners, and consequently your petitioners have not had a fair trial'. Roberts had been unaware of this fact at the trial because the magistrates had refused to allow him to see or hear the information. Roberts explained that the information sworn under oath was explicitly required under the 1823 Act and was absolutely necessary for providing an adequate defense to the charge. The lack of informations in Wyke's and Gerrard's cases, and the fact that in the first three cases the informations had been signed by a different magistrate, clearly made their convictions illegal under the 1823 Act. Roberts challenged the conventional wisdom that magistrates were within their discretion not to allow solicitors to see copies of the informations, asking 'if informations are not to be produced, why need they be laid?'. He reminded his readers that in cases of felony it was established

---

[78]   'A Copy of the Informations and Evidence … (1847)', p. 17; NA: HO 18/193/38; 'To T. S. Duncombe MP, 8 Princess Street, Manchester, 29 January 1847', *NS* (6 February 1847), p. 4.

[79]   Sweeney, 'Summary Jurisdiction', p. 158; Smith, 'Circumventing the Jury', pp. 416–19, 426–7, 430, 433.

[80]   The 10 Ashton boys worked as 'piecers' for Samuel Carpenter, and were charged with playing 'hooky' to attend the Stalybridge Wakes. Roberts reported that the boys were summoned, kept at work until the magistrates were prepared to hear the case, and then sentenced to seven days imprisonment each. Months later Roberts was engaged to initiate a certiorari on behalf of one of them, James Armitage, perhaps to prepare a case of trespass and false imprisonment against the magistrate 'To T. S. Duncombe, MP, 8 Princess Street, Manchester, 29 January 1847', *NS* (6 February 1847), p. 4; NA: KB 1/153/42; 'Ashton', *ME* (25 July 1846), p. 5.

practice to have the indictment read slowly enough for it to be copied at the request of the prisoner. Why should summary hearings have a lower standard in this regard when they already contained fewer protections for the accused?

Roberts also objected to Dobson's imprisonment for his failure to pay costs. This was less a legal argument than a rhetorical one, as Edelsten could have prosecuted Dobson to the full extent of the law without regard to the payment of costs. Roberts and the *Northern Star* emphasized this point, because in practice the threat of prison was often used to compel workers to complete their contracts saddled with additional debt from the costs of the proceedings. Edelsten often used master and servant law, but only when pushed did he pursue the imprisonment of his workers. Imprisonment might inconvenience an employer, but the threat of imprisonment and debt for costs was highly useful.

Roberts closed his letter by anticipating opponents criticizing him for seizing upon 'technicalities':

> A moment's reflection, however, will show that these points are not technical, – on the contrary they are most substantial. If the prisoner is to be deprived of their benefit, he might almost as well be without trial. In cases of summary jurisdiction – deprived of the protection of TRIAL BY JURY – one might be tempted to contend that the accused was entitled to even more stringent application in his favour of the rules of law.[81]

Roberts was again attempting to tap into opposition to the expansion of summary jurisdiction at the expense of 'our ancient rights of trial by jury', just as he had in the protest against the 1844 bill described in Chapter 2. Roberts was strategically positioning labor within law reform debates, as his language was remarkably similar to that of opponents of the 1847 Juvenile Justice Bill. No fewer than six witnesses testified before Lord Brougham's Select Committee on Juvenile Justice that they opposed giving magistrates summary powers to determine these matters because they were 'entirely against anything that takes away the jurisdiction of the jury'.[82] Roberts also touched on another common criticism of the magistracy, by observing that the case was heard by 'the celebrated file manufacturer' William Stubs. He highlighted the conflicts of interest that were all too common when magistrates adjudicated in master and servant cases. The strong criticism of the practice of summary justice contained in this petition and letter was inconvenient for supporters of expanding magistrates' judicial powers, and they probably hoped to dispose of it as quickly as possible. The petitions closed with a plea for mercy,

---

[81] 'To T. S. Duncombe, MP, 8 Princess Street, Manchester, 29 January 1847', *NS* (6 February 1847), p. 4; NA: HO 18/193/38.

[82] 'First and Second Reports … Respecting Juvenile Offenders … (1847)', Charles Ewan Law, Question 33; John Adams, Questions 126–9; Charles Phillips, Questions 1564–5; James Manning, Question 2339; Captain A. Maconochie, Question 2555; Charles Pearson, Question 2868.

informing the crown that Gerrard, Ireland and Dobson each had wives and small children, and Wyke had a poor mother and small siblings who were all dependent upon their earnings.[83]

On 7 February, Roberts wrote a second letter to Duncombe, accompanied by more petitions. After re-emphasizing some of the points from his first letter, Roberts attempted to delve into the 'merits' of the cases. This was done to emphasize that if the process had been fair, each of the workers had a reasonable defense to the charge. He accused Edelsten of using his leverage as poor-law guardian to threaten Wyke's mother with a loss of benefits unless her son worked more overtime. He charged Edelsten with exploiting Gerrard's need for money to bury his child to coerce him into a long-term agreement. Most importantly, he claimed that Edelsten had consistently violated his contracts by making men pay for their own tools, absorb certain work expenses and receive less than the Warrington rate for particular tasks. He alleged that Edelsten had taken deductions from Wyke's pay that were not sanctioned by his indenture. Roberts' purpose with this letter was to demonstrate that had the process been fair, 'in each of the cases, I had a good defence. The master had not performed his part of the contract'.[84] Once again, Roberts is expressing a vision of the employment relationship in which the parties had mutual, and equally binding, obligations to one another. Roberts asked Duncombe to have his letters 'printed and circulated freely' among members of Parliament. On 3 February, J. W. Patten, MP, made Lyon and Stubs aware of the letters.[85]

The Response of Thomas Lyon and William Stubs

On 4 February 1847, Lyon and Stubs responded to Roberts' charges against them in a letter to Home Secretary, Sir George Grey. They presented a broader narrative of the trade union's 'continual persecution and annoyance' of J. B. Edelsten, casting him in the role of the victim. In their letter they portrayed Roberts as an interloping mercenary, seeking to generate fees through delay and seizing upon legal loopholes without the slightest concern to the 'merits' of the case.

Their choice to focus on the larger context of the case is consistent with the 'common sense' approach that lay magistrates often used to defend their lack of legal training. Years later, clerk Thomas Part argued that legal knowledge was rarely needed in master and servant cases. He testified that because most master and servant prosecutions turned upon 'questions of fact' rather than 'questions

---

[83] 'To T. S. Duncombe, MP, 8 Princess Street, Manchester, 29 January 1847', *NS* (6 February 1847), p. 4; NA: HO 18/193/38.

[84] 'The Warrington Shallows Again', *NS* (13 February 1847), p. 4; 'To T. S. Duncombe, MP, 8 Princess Street, Manchester, 29 January 1847', *NS* (6 February 1847), p. 4.

[85] 'Warrington: The File Cutters Turn-Out', *MCLGA* (13 February 1847), p. 108. 'The File Cutters' Turn-Out', *MG* (13 February 1847), p. 8.

of law', it was more important for the magistrate to have a 'practical knowledge' of the local trade in question.[86] More important than quibbling over form was a familiarity with local circumstances and a sturdy sense of 'fair and foul'. In fact, proponents of expanding summary jurisdiction had always justified it as a means to escape 'rules-bound justice', and get to the facts of the case.[87]

Lyon and Stubs established what they saw as the 'practical facts of the case'. They described the dispute between Edelsten and the union over apprentices, emphasizing how the union issued an ultimatum to Edelsten after paying his men 35s per week to break their contracts and abscond. Their narrative described Ireland's and Gerrard's first conviction before Greenhall, and Edelsten's mercy toward both men. For good measure they sent the Home Secretary a copy of Gerrard's groveling letter asking to be released. The magistrates then explained the great expense Edelsten endured when these men absconded a second time and were absent for nearly three months. Both the *Manchester Guardian* and the *Manchester Courier* repeated these arguments, reporting that it would be a great injustice to free clearly guilty workers on frivolous objections.[88]

The magistrates denied that they prevented the men from obtaining counsel. Lyon and Stubs argued that on the morning of the hearing the men were escorted from the train station to the bridewell 'by a large number of their relatives, friends and fellow workmen'. Once at the bridewell 'they had ... the means of verbally communicating with their friends through the iron grating enclosing the bridewell'. The magistrates argued that at no point did Wyke or Gerrard ask for counsel or an adjournment.[89]

Lyon and Stubs also sought to defend their actions by describing Roberts as 'a sharp practitioner', the same strategy pursued by northern coal-owners. Roberts' zealous efforts on behalf of his clients were interpreted as attempts to cause delay and raise fees through technicalities. In this construction, Roberts' legal acumen actually plays as evidence of his shadiness rather than competence. Lyon and Stubs hoped to take advantage of the low opinion that much of the public had of the lower branch of the legal profession. In his study of nineteenth-century Birmingham solicitors, Andrew Rowley demonstrates that 'sharp practice', professional misconduct and the existence of unqualified attorneys were widely perceived by solicitors and non-solicitors alike as the most serious obstacles to elevating the social status of the profession. In cant, a sharper is a cheat, one to take advantage to protect his own interests. In the mid nineteenth century attorneys

---

[86] 'Report From the Select Committee on Master and Servant (1866)', 115, Questions 2400–3. *Parliamentary Papers* (1866), Vol. XIII (449), p. 1.

[87] Sweeney, 'Summary Jurisdiction', pp. 86, 94, 98–9.

[88] 'A Copy of the Informations and Evidence ... (1847)'; NA: HO 18/193/38; 'The File Cutters' Turn Out', *MG* (13 February 1847), p. 8; 'Warrington: The File Cutters' Turn Out', *MCLGA* (13 February 1847), p. 108.

[89] 'A Copy of the Informations and Evidence ... (1847)', pp. 17–18; NA: HO 18/193/38.

sought to improve this through 'professionalism as a strategy ... dominated by ready-to-hand contemporary notions of gentlemanliness, character and honour rather than technical expertise'.[90]

They stressed that Roberts was retained by the trade union, for a fee of £20, and was never asked for by the men. They pointed out that after their arrest the men requested an attorney in Sheffield, not Roberts, though they failed to explain why this attorney never met with the prisoners. They argued that if left to their own devices, without the outside interference of Roberts and the Union, the men would have neither absconded nor engaged a lawyer. By portraying Roberts as a divisive and greedy interloper the magistrates were describing behavior that was ungentlemanly and unprofessional.

The magistrates argued that the missing informations were a mere oversight that was quickly corrected. They suggested that Roberts had every opportunity to use the information to cross-examine witnesses and only requested a copy when all of his other arguments failed, again consistent with a scheming lawyer seeking out technicalities. They stated:

> It was perfectly manifest from his demeanor that his object was solely that of vexation and annoyance to the bench, and to occasion delay, and we feel called upon to state that his conduct throughout the inquiry was most disrespectful, and many of his observations to the bench were personally offensive and impertinent.[91]

It was in just such situations that the *Justice of the Peace* recommended that magistrates withhold informations from counsel. 'Practical Points' sometimes received queries on the powers of magistrates to arrest attorneys for contempt or remove them from the courtroom for disrespectful behavior. The editors replied that magistrates had no power to hold for contempt, but could remove an insulting attorney from the courtroom: 'give the attorney liberal allowance, and if he abuse it, expel him'.[92] Lyon and Stubs told the Home Secretary that they gave such allowance, 'hoping he would see the propriety of ... apologising for intemperate language made use of by him'.[93] Their indulgence of Roberts' tiresome and ungentlemanly behavior was calculated to demonstrate their fair-mindedness toward the prisoners. The magistrates insisted that they had performed

---

[90]   Arthur S. Rowley, 'Professions, Class, and Society: Solicitors in Nineteenth Century Birmingham' (PhD dissertation, University of Aston in Birmingham, 1988), pp. 100–111; Allyson May, *The Bar and the Old Bailey, 1750–1850* (Chapel Hill, 2003), pp. 124–5.

[91]   'A Copy of the Informations and Evidence ... (1847)', pp. 16–21; NA: HO 18/193/38.

[92]   'Practical Points', *JP* 10/24 (13 June 1846), p. 377; 'Practical Points', *JP* 7/11 (18 March 1843), p. 139.

[93]   'A Copy of the Informations and Evidence ... (1847)', pp. 19, 21; NA: HO 18/193/38.

their duty honestly and fairly, and trusted 'that we shall not look to you in vain for your justification and support ... against the unwarrantable attack which has been made against us'.[94] The Home Secretary informed Lyon and Stubs that their statement gave him 'much satisfaction' and that he would lay it before the House of Commons.[95]

The Home Office Pardon and Community Reaction

During February 1847, Thomas Duncombe presented six petitions on the subject of Edelsten's workmen, and made repeated attempts to have their case discussed in the House of Commons. He succeeded in having a motion for an inquiry into the case scheduled for 2 March. In February, a rumor began to circulate that Lyon and Stubs intended to resign if their ruling was overturned.[96]

On 2 March Duncombe was informed that a pardon for the four prisoners had been granted. Duncombe rose in the House to confirm this, and Grey replied that this pardon:

> had nothing whatever to do with the merits of the case. A second petition which his Hon. Member had presented contained an allegation complaining of informality in the mode adopted and in the cases of the four men alluded to in the first petition, who were charged with absenting themselves from the employment of Mr. Edelsten, of Warrington. The law officers had pronounced the objection valid ... He begged the Hon. Member to understand that the pardon had nothing to do with the merits of the case.[97]

The precise grounds for the pardon were that the informations against the prisoners were sworn before magistrate William Hall, but tried before Lyon and Stubs, contrary to the statute.[98]

The pardon set off a polarized reaction in the Warrington community. When the four released prisoners returned home on the evening of 3 March they were met by 'some hundreds of working men, with every demonstration of joy'. This procession included flags, banners, music, songs and abundant alcohol. Two elderly women dressed as 'Thomas' and 'Billy' mockingly re-enacted the magistrates' hearing. The celebration was so boisterous that Mr Jones, the local constable, later summoned a local landlord for 'suffering people to be drunk on the premises'. The

---

[94]   Ibid.

[95]   NA: HO 43/73, 6 February 1847.

[96]   In early February 1847, William's brother Joseph was appointed to the Lancashire Bench.

[97]   'The House of Commons', *MG* (6 March 1847), p. 4; *Hansard Debates*, Vol. 90, p. 679.

[98]   NA: HO 18/193/38.

Manchester Courier bitterly complained that 'we are sorry to remark that since the return of the men from Kirkdale, the greatest portion of the file cutters have given themselves over to rioting and drunkenness to commemorate their triumph over the law'.[99]

On 15 March, a delegation from the union met with Edelsten to resolve the dispute. As a matter of law, there was nothing to keep Edelsten from prosecuting his men a second time if they refused to return to work. After two days of negotiations, the union agreed to buy-out the contracts of Ireland, Gerrard and Dobson for £22 13s. Edesten, however, insisted on retaining Wyke's indenture.[100]

The *Northern Star* used familiar rhetoric to describe this case. Its headline read 'Another Triumph of Right Over Might: Release of the Four Warrington Victims'. The article claimed 'we can never recollect a case exhibiting more reckless and indecent contempt for the forms and solemnities of justice'. It went on to threaten the magistrates with other legal action from Roberts in what it termed 'A Higher Tribunal! What a phrase it is – how significant – how extremely unpleasant to the reckless magistrate – what retribution threatens tyranny'! It went on to warn Thomas Lyon, 'Rely on it, Thomas, you will be watched for some time to come. Be careful: Another Blunder! And you go to the right-about'. One of the important benefits of Roberts' legal work was that a small number of victories could have a large impact as cautionary tales to other magistrates. The journal commented that if Roberts, 'the purifier of the Bench', who 'had destroyed the appetite of many a justice', could force Lyon and Stubs to retire, it would rank among his greatest accomplishments. Lyon and Stubs did not retire, but refused to sit in Warrington Petty Sessions. The article remonstrated, 'Foolish men! So they hope, by getting into Cheshire, to be out the Attorney-General's reach. Vain hope – he'll be after them – he'll find them out, let them take our word for it'.[101]

The response from other inhabitants of Warrington was less celebratory. The *Manchester Courier* lamented the loss of the magistrates' services in Warrington, and argued that the Home Secretary 'should be called upon to give an account of … the discourtesy shown to the two worthy magistrates'. The article also questioned Grey's haste issuing the pardon because 'several honourable members … were in possession of the real facts of the case, and would have liked an opportunity of speaking on the subject' to defend the magistrates. The magistrates' clerks expressed dismay over the ruling of the crown's law officers, pointing out that

---

[99]   'The Breach of Contract Case', *MG* (6 March 1847), p. 8; 'Turn Out of the File Cutters', *MCLGA* (6 March 1847), p. 108; 'Another Triumph of Right Over Might: The Release of the Four Warrington Victims', *NS* (6 March 1847), p. 5; 'The Warrington Justices' Retirement into Private Life', *NS* (13 March 1847), p. 5.

[100]   In Re: William Baker, 2 H. & N. 219–41; 'The File Cutters' Turn Out', *MCLGA* (20 March 1847), p. 183.

[101]   'Another Triumph of Right Over Might', *NS* (6 March 1847), p. 5; 'The Warrington Justices' Retirement into Private Life', *NS* (13 March 1847), p. 5.

William Hall had ceased to live in Warrington before the men were apprehended, and that Dobson had been tried upon an information signed by Lyon and Stubs.[102]

On 9 March 1847, several hundred inhabitants of Warrington signed a memorial addressed to Thomas Lyon and William Stubs. The letter began by stating,

> We deeply regret the course of action the Secretary of State has deemed it his duty to take in the matter, by which, instead of upholding and vindicating the law, he has been, we are sorry to observe, the means of enabling the misguided men … openly to triumph and exhault over it.

The memorial conceded that three of the men had been erroneously convicted 'as a mere matter of form is concerned'. It warned that the Home Secretary's decision would have a negative impact on respect for the law and the legitimacy of the magistrates' office. Many propertied individuals were beginning to see the need for Parliament to provide better guidance and protection for the unpaid volunteers on whom so much local order and governance depended.

The memorial expressed the 'debt of gratitude' owed to Lyon and Stubs by the community for 30 and 10 years, respectively, of unpaid service. This tribute hoped that the Home Secretary's pardon would not discourage 'other men of independent minds' from serving in the future. It begged Lyon and Stubs 'for the sake of the neighbourhood' not to retire because 'you possess our full and entire confidence and respect'.[103]

Lyon and Stubs responded a week later, thanking the inhabitants for their kindness. They clarified the terms of their retirement:

> It has never been our intention to retire from the commission of the peace for the county of Lancaster, but we are grieved to state that the prejudice raised against us (by the extra-judicial decision of the Home Secretary) amongst that class of persons, whom in a populous town, we have been chiefly called upon to act, would so greatly impair our usefulness that we shall feel obliged to absent ourselves in the future from Warrington Petty Sessions.

They added that if anything could have changed their minds it would have been the kind words of the memorial.[104]

The *Northern Star* could not resist responding to this memorial with their most disrespectful article on the subject to date, titled 'The Warrington Just-Asses'. It argued that Lyon and Stubs' 'doings have been of a nature that the more they are stirred the more they stink', and claimed that 'you must know that nothing could

---

102   'The Secretary of State and the Turn-Out File Cutters', *MCLGA* (13 March 1847), p. 167; 'The Retirement of Magistrates', *MG* (17 March 1847), p. 5. NA: HO 18/193/38.

103   'The Secretary of State and the Turn-Out File Cutters', *MCLGA* (13 March 1847), p. 167.

104   'The File Cutters' Turn Out', *MCLGA* (20 March 1847), p. 183.

be easier than the collection of three times three thousand signatures in Warrington requesting that you remain in "retirement"'.[105]

The diverse reactions to this remarkable event reveal several consequences of trade unions' engagement with the law. Laborers showed an intense interest, as demonstrated by the crowds assembled at the courthouse, their outburst at Roberts' arrival, and celebrations upon the release of the men. The publicity given to the perceived injustices in the magistrates' hearing undermined the legitimacy of master and servant law and Edelsten's claim upon it, making this clearly a counter-productive use of the coercive laws available to an employer. Many respectable members of the Warrington community pledged their support to the embattled magistrates, showing that contempt for summary jurisdiction was far from universal. They expressed fear that the government's failure to support the magistrates would have an adverse effect on the maintenance of law and order in their town. These diverse reactions hint at the successes and failures of the law in mediating mid-Victorian social relations.

This case underscores the significance of master and servant legislation in the lives of skilled workers. Joseph Edelsten had his skilled workmen exclusively bound to himself with contracts of between three and seven years, staggered so that they would expire at different times, making collective action on their part difficult. These contracts were clearly more binding upon the employees than on Edelsten, as he felt free to alter the conditions under which his journeymen worked, and ignore aspects of the agreement that were not convenient for him to fulfill. The obedience required of his apprentices and workers was considerably more open-ended, to the point where a young apprentice could not refuse a 95-hour workweek. Edelsten frequently used the Master and Servant Acts to enforce the terms of these contracts by bringing his workers before magistrates who were favorably disposed toward him. These magistrates pressed the reluctant workmen or apprentices to return to work and pay the costs of the proceedings. Some of Edelsten's workers had been brought before the magistrates at least three times.

This case also illuminates the consequences of labor's growing legal resistance to these prosecutions during the 1840s. If nothing else, Roberts' presence in the courtroom eliminated the speed and convenience that made Master and Servant Acts so attractive to employers, as exemplified by Ireland's three-hour hearing. His presence also raised the level of legal formality, and fairness, of magistrates' hearings. In cases against Wyke and Gerrard, the formal charges against the prisoners were not read, and neither defendant was given the opportunity to cross-examine the only witness against them. This explains why Edelsten was so anxious to have a quick hearing in order to exclude Roberts, a common practice in Lancashire and elsewhere.[106]

The publicity given to Roberts' victories at Petty Sessions and before the Court of Queen's Bench in master and servant cases had important consequences

---

[105] 'The Warrington Just-Asses', *NS* (20 March 1847), p. 5.

[106] Challinor, *Radical Lawyer*, pp. 142–4.

for the magistracy. Roberts' work in challenging master and servant convictions exposed magistrates to costs, embarrassment and civil proceedings for false imprisonment.[107] They also informed a growing critique of the bias and legal ignorance of the new industrial magistrates. This critique drew labor into debates over the expansion of magistrates' authority to determine certain types of offences summarily. This case, along with the protest of the Sheffield artisans, described in Chapter 5, must be considered in that context. Roberts raised concerns about the procedural fairness and bias of his clients' hearings. Within months labor-directed protests would bring the actions of another magistrate, Wilson Overend, before the consideration of Parliament. In a little over a year, the cumulative weight of cases such as this one, and the labor-directed protests that they inspired, influenced the final shape of the Jervis Acts.[108]

---

[107]   In August 1844 a group of Durham magistrates settled 18 charges of false imprisonment by paying Roberts and his clients £200 and all legal costs. Eight months later, he successfully sued magistrate Colin Lindsay for £30 and all legal costs for falsely convicting a miner under the Master and Servants Act. In 1851, Roberts forced Thomas B. Rose to pay his own legal costs in a criminal information against that magistrate for not bothering to hear the defense of a miner charged under the Master and Servant Act. Not to be outdone, Welsh attorney John Owen won £120 and all legal costs against magistrates who falsely imprisoned seven Rhondda colliers in 1843. See: J. H. Morris and L. J. Williams, *The South Wales Coal Industry, 1841–1875* (Cardiff, 1958); NA: KB 1/190/23; KB 1/191/60; HO 43/67, 13 July 1844, 3 September 1844 and 19 October 1844; *NS*, 12 April 1845, pp. 4, 8.

[108]   Smith, 'Circumventing the Jury', pp. 444–5, 450–453, 463–6; Steinfeld, *Coercion*, pp. 159–61.

Chapter 5

Trades of Sheffield against Dr Wilson Overend, 1842–1847: 'I hope his prescriptions are better than his law'

Introduction: Three Levels of Law

The 'Sheffield Outrages' of the 1860s occupy an important place in nineteenth-century trade union history. On 8 October 1866 a canister of gunpowder was used to destroy the house of a former member of the Saw Grinders' Union in Sheffield. One could argue that it was the timing of this event as much as its nature which caused considerable public alarm and condemnation, provoking a Parliamentary investigation chaired by Sheffield Barrister William Overend. This investigation revealed strong union organization in the light metal trades of Sheffield and willingness by a minority of unions to enforce their policies with tactics ranging from the theft or destruction of tools to physical violence.[1] In the 1860s, opponents of organized labor and parliamentary reform had hoped to use this investigation to discredit trade unionists before the meeting of Mr Justice Erle's Parliamentary Commission on Trade Unions, but the larger London-based new model unions and their supporters were ultimately successful in marginalizing the Sheffield unionists and presenting a much different image to the public, one which paved the way for an improvement of their legal status in the late 1860s and 1870s.[2] The conflict of over the power and tactics of Sheffield trade unions did not begin in the 1860s. It had been a vigorous struggle fought for decades and much of it took place in local courts. This chapter will focus upon the form the conflict took in the

---

[1]   S. Pollard (ed.), *The Sheffield Outrages: Report Presented to the Trades Union Commissioners in 1867 With an Introduction by Sidney Pollard* (New York, 1971) (London, 1867), p. vii; J. H. Stainton, *The Making of Sheffield, 1865–1914* (Sheffield, 1924) pp. 24–40, 261–2; Richard Price, *Labour in British Society: An Interpretive History* (London, 1986), pp. 86–7; Frank Hill, 'An Account of Trade Combinations in Sheffield, Trades Societies and Strikes: A Report of the Committee on Trades Societies, Appointed by the National Association for the Promotion of Social Science' (London, 1860), pp. 531, 534; D. Smith, *Conflict and Compromise: Class Formation in English Society, 1830–1914: A Comparative Study of Birmingham and Sheffield* (London, 1982), pp. xi, 32, 64–9.

[2]   Mark Curthoys, *Governments, Labour and the Law in Mid-Victorian Britain: The Trade Union Legislation of the 1870s* (Oxford, 2004), pp. 65–6. Keith Laybourne, *A History of British Trade Unionism* (London, 1997), pp. 48–9.

earlier period between 1842 and 1847, and how the struggle intersected with larger national trends.

Specifically, this chapter examines the local and national implications of the protest by Sheffield trades unions in May 1847 against the older brother of William Overend, magistrate Dr Wilson Overend. Local union leaders petitioned Parliament and the Town Council, and also held a massive public meeting advocating the removal of Overend from the Bench. They claimed he had displayed bias against unionists and made convictions against the statute and the evidence when adjudicating cases under the 1825 Combination Laws Repeal Amendment Act.[3] This statute made it legal for workers to combine to raise wages or reduce hours of labor. It also granted two magistrates the power to convict summarily and imprison for up to three months with hard labor any person who threatened, intimidated, obstructed or molested employers, fellow-workers or replacement workers to achieve these ends. In 1847, the legal meaning of these terms was not a fully settled matter, yet by the early 1850s the higher courts gave them a broad definition.[4]

The dispute between the artisans of Sheffield and Overend demonstrates the interaction and conflicts between three different types of law. This first type of law was the customary rules, expectations and understandings of a unique community of artisans and small masters regarding entry into the trade, the regulation of labor and the process of negotiating price lists. These rules originally had a basis in statute law, particularly the 1562 Statute of Artificers and related case law. After much of that statute was repealed in 1814, unlike the rest of the country where such regulations soon became a distant memory, trades' law enforced primarily by specialized unions maintained its legitimacy in Sheffield, and indeed, actually became stronger right up to the 1860s. It drew its legitimacy from long usage and its success in maintaining a high standard of living for the Sheffield artisan.

During the 1840s some local employers attempted to supplant the authority of 'the trade', with the support of local institutions of justice. Some of these masters came together and formed a prosecution society and turned to a second type of the law, that administered by local magistrates who were sympathetic to their desire to displace customary practices. In particular, these employers funded cases brought under the 1825 Combination Laws Repeal Amendment Act (1825) before Overend.[5] Between 1842 and 1847, Overend oversaw the convictions of 18 men at Sheffield Petty Sessions for using threats or intimidation against their employers or other workers. In all but one of these cases, Overend inflicted the maximum sentence permitted: three months' imprisonment with hard labor.

---

[3]   6 George IV, c.129 (1825).

[4]   J. Orth, *Combination and Conspiracy: A Legal History of Trade Unionism, 1721–1906* (Oxford, 1991); Curthoys, *Goverments, Labour and the Law*.

[5]   Hill, 'Trade Combinations in Sheffield', pp. 543–6; Smith, *Conflict and Compromise*, pp. 57–8.

In each of these cases, local trade unions paid solicitors to defend their members against these charges at Petty Sessions. They provided vigorous defenses, challenging evidence and Overend's interpretation of the statute, but they always had to resort to another level of law to defeat this local partnership of employer and magistrate. This type of law was based on the precedents, interpretations and formalism determined by the higher courts with less fluid procedures. Section 12 of the act allowed anyone convicted under its provisions to be released upon bail and appeal the ruling to the next Quarter Sessions. To use this provision the prisoner had to provide immediately a £10 recognizance and two £10 sureties. In each of the 18 cases, local unions provided the funds for such an appeal. At Quarter Sessions, 17 of those convictions were subsequently overturned, and the prosecutor withdrew the other before an appeal could be heard.[6]

In 1847, trade union supporters argued that the harsh sentences delivered by Overend, the continual reversal of his rulings on appeal and his injudicious statements from the bench meant that at the very least he 'ought not to adjudicate upon trades union cases'. They soon demanded the extreme remedy of his removal from office because of his cooperation with employer-funded prosecution societies, which sought to use the courts to undermine traditional practices. Although justices of the peace served at the pleasure of the Lord Chancellor, they were not often removed. The local artisans and their supporters expressed their displeasure through a massive public meeting, a memorial to the town council and a petition to Parliament.[7]

As in Chapter 4, the timing and language of the Sheffield trade unions' mobilization against Overend occurred in the context of the controversy over magistrates' summary jurisdiction. Just as in the protest against the 1844 Master and Servant Bill, the victories before Queen's Bench and the protest against the Warrington magistrates, the trades of Sheffield also added to the debate over further expanding the summary powers of magistrates. Duncombe raised the issue of Overend's conduct before Parliament less than three months after Home Secretary

---

[6] 'A Return of the Date and Number of Convictions Under the Combination Act that Have Taken Place at Sheffield Petty Sessions from the 1st Day of January 1842 to the Present Time; Specifying Those Quashed on Appeal; Showing the Sentence Passed in Each Case, with the Name of the Magistrate or Magistrates by Whom Such Sentences Were Passed', *Parliamentary Papers* Vol. 156 (541), p. 184.

[7] John Knipe, 'Justice of the Peace in Yorkshire, 1820–1914: A Social Study' (PhD dissertation, University of Southern California, 1970), p. 59; 'The Spring Knife Cutlers and the National Trades Association', *SRI* (24 April 1847); 'Special Meeting of the Town Council', *The Sheffield Times* (hereafter, *ST*) (8 May 1847), p. 6; 'Public Meeting Respecting the Magisterial Conduct of Wilson Overend', *ST* (8 May 1847), pp. 6–7; 'The Case of the Workmen of Sheffield Against Mr. Overend as it Occurred in the House of Commons', *ST* (22 May 1847), p. 2.

Grey had pardoned the four Warrington file-forgers described in Chapter 4.[8] The Sheffield artisans' petition, just like that of the Warrington file-forgers, arrived when Parliament was debating a bill to allow magistrates to determine summarily petty larcenies committed by juveniles. Overend's supporters in Parliament, however, were far better prepared than the defenders of Lyon and Stubs, and they successfully shifted the focus away from the magistrate's rulings and toward the frightening behavior of Sheffield trade unions.

During the previous year, Parliament had received at least five other petitions demanding inquiries into the conduct of magistrates, which contributed to doubts about the ability of the magistracy to administer the law consistently with the rulings of the higher courts.[9] The proportion of Overend's rulings in labor cases that were quashed upon appeal, often for defects in form, added to existing pressure on Parliament to formulate clearer guidelines for magistrates to follow and afford them greater protection. Overend's supporters utilized familiar rhetoric emphasizing the difference between errors in form and malicious mistakes, which became so prominent in the discussions over the Jervis Acts.

The Sheffield protest also had great local significance. Due to the unique historical development and economic structure of the light metal trades in Sheffield, several narrowly specialized unions had a strong bargaining position relative to the numerous small-scale manufacturers. In Sheffield, closely-knit communities of artisans engaged in a variety of trades adhered to, and were prepared to enforce, the rules which they perceived as being essential to the preservation of their status. Dennis Smith observed that in this Sheffield artisan community, within specified limits, there was 'widespread toleration of physical sanctions against anyone who disobeyed the norms of the local community'.[10]

The most common of these sanctions was 'rattening', the theft of tools or the expensive bands used to connect grinding wheels with their power source, preventing the offender from working until his or her conflict with 'the trade' was resolved. Persistent violations could result in more violent punishments, such as

---

[8]   In fact, the protest against Overend was initiated at a public meeting in Sheffield where several local unions in the metal trades voted to join the National Association of United Trades, the same national union to which the Warrington file-forgers belonged. 'The Spring Knife Cutlers and the National Trades' Association', *SRI* (24 April 1847).

[9]   *Hansard Debates*, Vol. 85, cols. 470–478; Vol. 90, col. 1136; Vol. 92, cols. 1056–62; Vol. 93, cols. 120, 597–603.

[10]   Quote from: Smith, *Conflict and Compromise*, pp. xi, 42, 44, 45, 55, 64; Sidney Pollard, *A History of Labour in Sheffield* (Liverpool, 1959), 65–8, 156–7; S. Pollard, J. Mendelson, W. Owen and V. M. Thornes, *The Sheffield Trades and Labour Council, 1858–1958* (Sheffield, 1958), p. 13; Price, *Labour in British Society*, pp. 86–7; Hill, 'Trade Combinations in Sheffield', pp. 531, 534; E. Thompson, *The Making of the English Working Class* (London, 1963), p. 286.

those uncovered by the famous Sheffield outrages inquiry of 1867. The inquiry demonstrated that the conflict over 'outrages' had a long history in Sheffield.[11]

Overend was personally committed to fighting the community's conspiracy of silence about local union tactics. To balance the scales against union power, he often convicted offenders on rather thin and highly circumstantial evidence. He interpreted the terms 'threats, intimidation, obstruction and molestation' expansively, in a manner completely at odds with community values, but in a way that foreshadowed how the high courts would eventually define these phrases with Mr Justice Erle's decision in *R. v. Duffield, R. v. Rowlands* (1851).[12] Overend's statements from the bench suggest that he viewed these cases as important opportunities to educate the larger community. His rulings and speeches made him a controversial figure in Sheffield. Employers in Sheffield attempted to use laws and magistrates favorable to their interests to impose their will upon labor. Labor's representatives, however, showed themselves to be adept at finding ways to gain protection through the forums of law that had greater protections for the accused.

Trade Union Power in Sheffield, 1814–1867

In the first half of the nineteenth century Sheffield enjoyed a near-monopoly in the tool-making, cutlery and metal working trades. These were largely in the hands of small firms engaged in production according to customary practices; the variety of patterns and qualities of products required many different skills and did not lend themselves easily to machine production. As a result, skilled labor remained 'by far the most important factor of production'.[13] There was considerably less social distance between the fluid categories of masters and skilled journeymen in Sheffield than elsewhere in England. In fact, several Sheffield manufacturers were radicals in politics, and many willingly contributed to the funds of trades' societies to help maintain customary standards.[14]

---

[11] Smith, *Conflict and Compromise*, pp. xi, 32, 45–6, 64–9; Hill, 'Trade Combinations in Sheffield', p. 541; Pollard, *History of Labour in Sheffield*, pp. 71–2; *The Sheffield Outrages*, p. vii; Stainton, *Making of Sheffield*, pp. 24–49, 261–2; Price, *Labour in British Society*, pp. 86–7; Thompson, *Making of the English Working Class*, p. 286.

[12] *R. v. Rowlands, R. v. Duffield* (1851), 5 Cox Criminal Cases 404, 465. NA: KB 1/199/59–60; KB 1/203/662–3; 1/204/51.

[13] Smith, *Conflict and Compromise*, p. 23; Hill, 'Trade Combinations in Sheffield', pp. 521, 531; Pollard et al., *Sheffield Trades and Labour Council*, pp. 7, 13; Smith, *Conflict and Compromise*, 32, 35–7, 40, 67–9, 85, 88–92; Pollard, *Labour in Sheffield*, pp. 1, 3, 40, 50, 55, 65. Pollard estimates that in 1850 there were only six manufacturers in the trade who employed more than 100 workmen.

[14] Hill, 'Trade Combinations in Sheffield', pp. 532–5, 542; Pollard, *Labour in Sheffield*, pp. 3–4, 40–41, 56–7; Mendelson et al., *Sheffield Trades and Labour Council*,

Artisans in these trades enjoyed considerable autonomy in their work. Most grinding work was done at 'public wheels', which contained many 'troughs' that were rented to artisans or employers. A 'trough' consisted of a grinding wheel connected by a wheel band to a power source. The landlords of these public wheels often rented troughs directly to workmen while the master merely provided the material. This autonomy was not limited to grinders, as related trades were most commonly performed off-premises in the home of artisans. The independence and solidarity of the artisan community was re-enforced by kinship and settlement patterns in Sheffield, where 'the overlap between the workplace and household was exceptionally great, producing exceptionally strong control by the local community over its members'.[15]

Sheffield had a large number of small and highly specialized unions. For example, different trade societies existed for grinders of edge-tools, fenders, forks, pens and pocket knifes, saws, scythes and table knives. Each of these societies carefully guarded their rights to particular types of work, but they also cooperated to maintain each other's rules and price lists. These different trades had long traditions of offering mutual support during labor disputes.[16] In times of conflict it was not easy for employers to find skilled replacement workers from other regions. These unions established a strong negotiating position with respect to price lists and preserving custom.

Regulation in the cutlery trade was historically legitimated by custom and a 1624 Act of Parliament that gave the Company of Cutlers the authority to regulate apprentices, admit freemen into the company, collect money for the poor of their trade, protect craft standards and quality, prevent the forgery of marks and set standard prices. As in many other skilled trades, these practices came under attack from around the mid eighteenth century by advocates of classical political economy. The freemen of Sheffield unsuccessfully appealed to the law for protection of their customary (and statutory) status and standards. The growth of trade unions in Sheffield coincided with the relaxation of trade regulations by the Company of Cutlers. In 1814, Parliament repealed the apprenticeship clauses of the Statute of Artificers, as well as the authority of the Company. This did not result in de-skilling or the disappearance of customary trade practices in Sheffield. Frank H. Hill found that after 1814, 'a policy of exclusion and protection, which the masters had ... finally abandoned, was adopted by the artisans. The workmen began to attempt by combinations, not merely to secure what they deemed fair ...

---

pp. 7–9, 13–14; G. I. H. Lloyd, *The Cutlery Trades: A Historical Essay in the Economics of Small Scale Production* (London, 1913).

[15] Quote from: Smith, *Conflict and Compromise*, pp. 26–7, 30–31, 37, 42; Hill, 'Trade Combinations in Sheffield', pp. 532–3; Pollard, *Labour in Sheffield*, pp. 56–7.

[16] Pollard, *Labour in Sheffield*, pp. 1, 50; Pollard et al., *Sheffield Trades and Labour Council*, pp. 13–14; Smith, *Conflict and Compromise*, pp. 24, 35, 39, 40, 45; *Sheffield Outrages*, pp. 3, 41 Questions 46, 2038–41.

but to aim at regulating by minute and stringent legislation, the conduct of their respective trades'.[17]

Organized labor in Sheffield performed 'not only the ordinary industrial functions of a trade union, but also a host of social and political functions, and at times it claimed an extensive share in the control of the industry as a whole'. The key to the success of these unions was their careful control entry into the trade and the supply of labor. Men from out of town had to be approved by the trade and pay dues in order to work. Members of these unions and small masters paid into a general fund, part of which was used to maintain men 'on the box' during slack times in the trade. This fund allowed artisans to maintain high wages by restricting the number of workers available. During one four-and-a-half year span, 10 unions in Sheffield paid out over £29,000 to maintain members on the box, while the parish paid out merely £16,000 in poor relief. It was desirable to keep men off parish relief, because otherwise the parish might force them to take work under price from local masters.[18]

This control was often enforced through the application of sanctions against workmen or employers who violated the rules of the trade or failed to pay their dues to the union. Rattening dates at least as far back as 1821 in Sheffield, and continued for another 25 years after the 1867 inquiry into the Sheffield outrages brought it nationwide condemnation. Local unions often publicly disavowed the practice and the inquiry concluded that by the 1860s only 12 of 60 local unions actually engaged in it. Nonetheless, there is evidence that it was seen by much of the community as a legitimate penalty for those who violated trade rules and threatened people's livelihoods.[19] These attacks 'were not the work of hotheads' but were 'directed ... systematically against men whose only offences were offences against union regulations'.[20] William Overend lamented that rattening was a 'common thing ... which is hardly considered a crime at all in this town apparently'. He went on to state that 'there is no doubt' that local unionists 'consider it [rattening] no sin'. Many saw it as the enforcement of 'a private legal code'.[21]

---

[17]   Smith, *Conflict and Compromise*, pp. 26–46, 50–51, 55, 64; Hill, 'Trade Combinations in Sheffield', pp. 523–32, 534–45, 541–3; Pollard, *Labour in Sheffield*, pp. 65–77; Thompson, *Making of the English Working Class*, p. 286; R. E. Leader, *History of the Company of Cutlers in Hallamshire* (2 vols., Sheffield, 1905), pp. 18–38, 79–91; Pollard et al., *Sheffield Trades and Labour Council*, pp. 7–8, 13.

[18]   *The Sheffield Outrages*, pp. 2–10, Testimony of John Platt, pp. 89–91, Questions 4611–14. Pollard, *Labour in Sheffield*, pp. 65–71; Smith, *Conflict and Compromise*, pp. 39, 45; Hill, 'Trade Combinations in Sheffield', pp. 531, 536–40, 555.

[19]   Leader, *Company of Cutlers*, p. 98; Pollard, *Labour in Sheffield*, p. 44; Pollard et al., *Sheffield Trades and Labour Commission*, p. 31.

[20]   Pollard, *Labour in Sheffield*, p. 44; Hill, 'Trade Combinations in Sheffield', p. 583; *Sheffield Outrages*, p. ix.

[21]   *Sheffield Outrages*, pp. ix, xiii, 317, Questions 16633–4.

The legitimacy of rattening was strengthened by the feeling that those who received benefits from their union had an obligation to make contributions and follow the rules. In an 1840 conflict between table-knife grinders and a defaulting member, a Sheffield magistrate expressed the opinion at Sessions that regardless of the law on the subject, members were 'morally obliged to pay' their union dues.[22] In October of 1843, scissor manufacturer Thomas Lillyman prosecuted Abraham Hall under 6 George IV, c.129 (1825) before Overend for attempting to intimidate him by stealing his wheel-bands. Lillyman had refused to contribute to the common fund and had violated regulations of the trade. A group of between 20 and 40 men went to the wheel where Lillyman's employees worked and removed their wheel-bands. Hall unapologetically told the magistrates that although he did not take any of the bands personally, 'the plaintiff knew where to come for his band if he was willing to pay his contribution – he was party to the measure resolved [by the union], having held up his hand in favour of the regulation'. Hall's candor on the subject earned him a sentence of two months' imprisonment. He was later freed and awarded costs on an uncontested appeal to Quarter Sessions.[23]

In Sheffield, trade regulations and customs, agreed to by union members, with traditions going back to the Company of Cutlers, had the force of law:

> With regard to commonplace rattening it must be admitted that it is a branch of unwritten law, and it has been the system to enforce obedience by that sort of distraint. Very little interest attaches to that part of the subject. Outsiders may represent these things as something horrible and marvelous, but to those who know the usages of the Sheffield trades, there will not appear to be anything more wonderful about them than the executions put into force every week by the bailiffs of the County Court, except that the law of the land sanctions the one and forbids the other.[24]

Sheffield radical town councilor Isaac Ironside stated that journeymen and masters had an ethical obligation to obey trade rules. He went on to blame rattenings on one-sided laws that prevented trades from enforcing the rules that protected Sheffield artisans' property in their skill. These sentiments were often repeated by Sheffield union representatives.[25]

Part of the legitimacy of trades' law within the artisan community came from the knowledge that trade regulation contributed to a higher standard of living for their families than those of the same class from other regions. In 1839, a magistrate writing to the Home Office observed that the working classes in Sheffield earned

[22]   Hill, 'Trade Combinations in Sheffield', p. 539.

[23]   'Rev. W. Alderson, Overend, William Bagshaw', *ST* (7 October 1843), p. 2; 'Quarter Sessions', *ST* (28 October 1843), p. 6.

[24]   *SRI* (18 May 1867) as quoted in Pollard, *Labour in Sheffield*, p. 154.

[25]   *Sheffield Outrages*, pp. x, 28–9, 34, 42, 317, Questions 1457–60, 1467–77, 1690–1694, 2063–8, 16633–4; Pollard, *Labour in Sheffield*, pp. 153–4.

the best wages in the kingdom. In 1851, a metal worker estimated that a grinder in Sheffield could make three times the wages that a grinder in Birmingham earned, which he credited to the 'more general' presence of unions.[26] In 1859, Hill observed that 'a greater proportion of workmen in Sheffield are householders and have votes for members of Parliament than is the case with the same class in any other town'. He went on to express 'no doubt' that when one considered 'the elements of physical wellbeing, and in intellectual activity and cultivation, they [Sheffield artisans] are quite at the head of their class in England'.[27] It is worth noting that grinding work was very dangerous and many men in this profession died young from occupational disease. However, the careful regulation of labor by unions in Sheffield was widely perceived as being responsible for their unequalled standard of living.[28]

The treatment of trades' rules as well-established local law is suggested by the curiously matter-of-fact testimony by employers and workmen before the 1867 outrages inquiry. John Platts, who was a member of the Scissor Grinders' Union for 18 years before becoming a manufacturer, told the committee of a case in which he had six bands stolen. He immediately went to the union leadership, not the police, to enquire about recovering his bands. The union secretary denied knowledge of the theft, but reminded him that his contributions were in arrears. After paying his dues, he received an anonymous note telling him where he could locate his bands. Platt told this story as though the sequence of events was neither extraordinary nor surprising.[29]

Other descriptions of rattening closely followed this familiar ritual. Victims of rattening usually understood why their bands had been taken as well as the steps they needed to take to recover them. Saw-file manufacturer R. T. Eadon testified that he did not go to the police on one occasion where his employees were rattened for not paying their contributions because it was less trouble to send the workers to the union. He repeatedly stated that because 'it was simply a trade dispute, they had no dispute with us', he was content to allow the men to handle it amongst themselves. There appears to have been an acceptance, or at least a grudging recognition, of a separate law that existed between workmen. Eadon chose to intervene personally in a case where one of his workers who was in good standing with the union was rattened by mistake. Instead of going to the police or magistrates, Eadon demanded payment from the union for the inconvenience that they had caused, not because of the rattening itself, but because they had rattened the wrong man. The union secretary did not admit any knowledge of the theft, but paid Eadon 2s 6d 'to avoid unpleasantness'.[30]

---

[26] Pollard, *Labour in Sheffield*, p. 45; Thompson, *Making of the English Working Class*, p. 354; Smith, *Conflict and Compromise*, p. 43.

[27] Hill, 'Trade Combinations in Sheffield', p. 534.

[28] *Sheffield Outrages*, p. 54, Question 2696.

[29] *Sheffield Outrages*, pp. 2–10, Testimony of John Platts.

[30] *Sheffield Outrages*, pp. 14–17, Testimony of Robert Thomas Eadon.

Because of the protection which the community afforded those who carried out the rattenings, an appeal to the authorities was often useless. When eight of Eadon's grinders were in arrears to the union, he anticipated a rattening and engaged three police officers to guard the wheel where they worked. In spite of this protection, his men were still rattened. The grinders went to the union and paid their arrears, to which were added *the expenses of carrying out the rattening*.[31]

Many of the intimidation cases brought before Wilson Overend were, in fact, conducted by outsiders, for whom the rituals of rattening were not a part of their shared heritage with the community. The ineffectiveness of the state in protecting victims and prosecuting offenders is suggestive of the legitimacy, within certain prescribed limits, of these actions among the community. Hill lamented 'the mere fact that it is impossible … to trace the authors of such crime, shows that they are efficiently protected and screened'.[32] Despite the many rattenings and violent physical attacks carried out between 1820 and 1867, and offers of rewards that sometimes reached over £1,000 for testimony, successful prosecutions were exceedingly rare.[33] Prosecutions under the Combination Laws Repeal Amendment Act were an outside interference with community norms and the result of a breakdown in the established system of trade rules and practices.

When these rules consistently produced outcomes that were unfavorable to employers, however, there was always the possibility of recourse to the state and a set of locally administered laws that were heavily weighted toward their advantage. Rules and practices for bargaining established within trades were always significantly shaped by an awareness of the possibilities of the statute law. In several of the cases discussed below, workers expressed an expectation that the conflicts should have been settled through negotiation and custom rather than the courts. In these instances, masters rejected one set of local trade rules for the more advantageous protection of the largely unsupervised magistracy. The 1840s were a period of significant trade union aggressiveness in which workers tried to limit the advantage of coercive laws administered summarily by magistrates. The trades of Sheffield were no strangers to the legal work of Roberts, and demonstrated an adeptness for fighting magistrate-enforced labor law.[34]

---

31   Ibid.; Smith, *Conflict and Compromise*, p. 58.

32   Hill, 'Trade Combinations in Sheffield', p. 583.

33   Hill, 'Trade Combinations in Sheffield', p. 577; *Sheffield Outrages*, p. 86; Pollard, *Labour in Sheffield*, p. 67.

34   Roberts often worked in Yorkshire during his long legal career. For a few cases between 1842 and 1847, see NA: KB 1/119/28, 29, KB 1/123/39; 'Rotherham', *SRI* (18 May 1844), p. 2; 'The Colliers', *SRI* (8 June 1844), p. 8. Roberts and Mr Broomhead were highly active in 1844 in fighting against the use of truck in local mining operations, see: 'Colliery Cases', *SRI* (25 May 1844), p. 2; 'Justice Room, Hemsworth', *SRI* (15 June 1844), p. 5; 'Paying Colliers in Stuff', *SRI* (15 June 1844), p. 8; 'Justice Room, Eckington', *SRI* (29 June 1844); 'Paying Colliers in Stuff', *SRI* (6 July 1844), p. 3. In 1847, Roberts also attended the coroner's inquest in the case of the Barnsley Colliery Explosion on behalf of

Prosecutions under 6 George IV, c.129 (1825) before Wilson Overend, 1842–1847

Dr Overend, called 'one of the most accomplished and expert surgeons in the provinces', was appointed to the bench in 1842 and was a very active magistrate until his death 23 years later. Throughout his career, Overend opposed the illegal enforcement of trade regulations and sought to penetrate the veil of secrecy behind which these acts were carried out.[35] The repeated quashing of his rulings at Quarter Session confirmed in the eyes of many that he was a vindictive and partial arbiter. Overend's lack of legitimacy was exacerbated by the fact that his family was already infamous in Sheffield before he was appointed to the bench.

Like Lyon and Stubs of Warrington, Overend was a 'new magistrate', from a class that only a generation earlier had very little representation on the bench. The dearth of local landed men, 'created a status vacuum at the top of Sheffield society which avidly sucked in professional men', notably the Overends. Like his father and older brother John, Wilson Overend went into medicine, assisted teaching anatomy and surgery at the family's medical school and at 24 was appointed surgeon to the local infirmary. In 1846 he and his brother-in-law opened a highly successful medical practice in town.[36]

Wilson Overend and his father achieved a degree of infamy in Sheffield through their medical school. In the first half of the nineteenth century it was difficult to legally obtain cadavers to use in the instruction of medical students. It was rumored in Sheffield that the Overends went on 'resurrection expeditions' to 'obtain subjects for their students at great personal risk from the law and populace'.[37] In 1835, 'an infuriated mob' burned the Overends' medical school to the ground and rioted in front of Wilson's house until troops dispersed them.[38] With this event engraved in

---

the victim's families, see: 'Colliery Explosion at Barnsley: Adjourned Inquest', *SRI* (20 March 1847), p. 6.

[35]   J. Furness, *Municipal Affairs in Sheffield* (Sheffield, 1893), p. 131; J. Leader and S. Snell, *Sheffield General Infirmary, Now, by the Favour of the Queen, the Sheffield Royal Infirmary: A Brief Sketch of a Century's Work* (Sheffield, 1897), pp. 114–16; W. Smith Porter, M.D., *The Medical School in Sheffield, 1828–1928* (Sheffield, 1928), p. 10; 'Sheffield Christmas and Intermediate Sessions', *SRI* (4 March 1862); 'Mr. Overend and the Trade Unions', *SRI* (5 March 1862); 'Mr. Overend and the Trade Unions', *SRI* (8 March 1862); Smith, *Conflict and Compromise*, p. 55.

[36]   Quote from Smith, *Conflict and Compromise*, p. 154. Wilson's father, Hall Overend, became a local medical practitioner, creator of a natural history museum, and founder of a medical school where he taught anatomy and surgery. Wilson's younger brother William became a barrister, Queen's Counsel, candidate for Parliament in 1857, and eventually chair of the outrages inquiry in 1867. Leader and Snell, *Sheffield General Infirmary*, pp. 114–16; Porter, *Medical School in Sheffield*, pp. 6–10.

[37]   Ibid.

[38]   Ibid.

public memory, it is possible that Overend was despised among the class of people whose cases he was most frequently called to adjudicate.

Overend was also at odds with prevailing community values regarding the trades' right to enforce their rules. His determination to break this underground law was expressed in some remarks to the Grand Jury at the Quarter Sessions in 1862. He drew their attention 'to those horrible deeds that are called trade outrages, which have made Sheffield remarkable and infamous throughout England'. He asserted 'we all know … where they emanate from. The difficulty is only how to prove them'. He charged

> Every person knows – there is not a single person in the town that does not know – that they do emanate from trade unions. There is not a single man living in town that believes the statements which are made that they do not emanate from those unions; and persons who make statements of that kind do not deceive the public, but only deceive themselves.

He accused unions of 'arbitrary conduct' by preventing men from working, and masters from hiring, as they pleased. He told the Grand Jury that he hoped 'the disgust and horror which [outrages] excite in all well constituted minds' would influence them to prevent such acts from occurring in the future.[39] This assumption of a conspiracy of silence is important for understanding Overend's rulings from the 1840s, in which he sometimes convicted individuals on weak evidence.

The *Sheffield and Rotherham Independent* wrote an editorial criticizing Overend's 1862 remarks, suggesting that he had brought the impartiality of the magistracy into question:

> If after this a man be charged at our Town Hall before Mr. Overend, with any act that can be made to wear the appearance of arising from a union, what will be his confidence in the impartiality of a gentleman who has publicly committed himself by the dictum we have quoted?

The author lamented that it would be unfortunate if workers developed distrust of the magistracy and its administration of labor law. The paper published the editorial because 'We regard this as affecting so much the popular estimation of our magistrates'.[40]

A letter from 'A Trade Unionist' printed in the same newspaper three days later was more pointed:

> I believe the strength of the magistracy *has* frequently been weakened by Mr. Overend's pre-judging both trade unions and other classes that have come before him, and his judicial opinions and administration of the law in both these and

---

[39]   'Charge to the Grand Jury', *SRI* (4 March 1862), p. 5.

[40]   'Mr. Overend and the Trade Unions', *SRI* (5 March 1862), p. 5.

other cases have not always been such as to secure the general confidence of the public in his impartiality.

He argued that among working people, Overend's conduct as magistrate 'provoked such an amount of public disgust as, I believe, was never manifested against any other magistrate in this town'. He suggested that in two decades on the bench, 'it is evident from the cases … Mr. Overend did not, nor does he now, enjoy the confidence of the town in general as having discharged his duties as a magistrate impartially'.[41]

The same charge was made in the 1847 protest against Overend, and forced the Clerk of Sheffield Petty Sessions to produce a return to Parliament of all the cases heard by that magistrate under 6 George IV, c.129 (1825) since his appointment to the bench. This return revealed that none of these convictions had withstood the scrutiny of Quarter Sessions. It appears that the protest against Overend was provoked primarily by his ruling in an intimidation case initiated by the Masters' Protection Society in the spring of 1847. An examination of some of his cases between 1842 and 1847 demonstrates employers' use of the statute law to transform traditional trade practices and forms of negotiation, as well as the skill and vigor with which local unions used the resources of the legal system to protect their interests. Overend repeatedly articulated the conviction that the law was an instrument for educating and changing the norms of the populace, but in the end he clearly undermined the legitimacy of summary justice in Sheffield.

Eleven cases from the clerk's return originated in the spring of 1844. Eight of these 11 convictions were the result of a single trade dispute that represented a failure of the traditional practices of negotiation. In March 1844, a conflict developed between stove manufacturers Stuart, Smith and Co. and their 29 fender and stove-grate fitters. The company imposed a new price list without negotiation and relied on local legal institutions to assist them. The union attempted without success to initiate negotiations with their employers, causing a rise in tension between the parties. This manifested itself when one of the partners, 'who was unfortunate in having an irritable temper', slammed a journeyman against a wall and thrust a brass ornament down his throat.[42] Despite this hostility, most workers still anticipated a negotiated settlement according to established practices. George Hepworth, a union stove grate-fitter, later noted 'we had no idea of leaving our employment', but only wanted to 'meet as to prices, and establish a regular rate of wages'. Stuart, Smith and Co. provoked 'great excitement' and solidarity in the community which forced the firm to import workers from Birmingham and London, and hire police to protect them, 'or their whole establishment must

---

[41]   Ibid.

[42]   Town councilor Isaac Ironside, himself a stove grate manufacturer, offered on multiple occasions to mediate the conflict, only to be turned away by management. 'Address to the Public on Behalf of the Stove Grate and Fender Makers of Sheffield', *NS* (11 May 1844), p. 6.

have been at a stand'. These outsiders were met by large jeering crowds at the railway station and were warned by their employers to minimize contact with the community.[43]

On 23 April 1844, two of the first replacement workers hired by the firm, Samuel Mortimer and George Wilkinson, charged Jason Goddard, George Morton, Matthias Thompson and John Wadsworth under 6 George IV, c.129 (1825) with having used threats and intimidation to force them to leave their jobs. Two attorneys, Mr Palfreyman and Mr Dixon, presented the case. Messrs. Broomhead, Senior and Junior, represented the defendants before Wilson Overend and four other magistrates. Overend was by far the most active and vocal magistrate during the hearing.[44]

Mortimer was the first witness called and testified that while working as a replacement worker during the previous five weeks he was frequently 'annoyed' by people shaking fists and calling him 'knobstick'. He stated that on 16 April, he and George Wilkinson were walking home from work when the four defendants, 'with many others', blocked their way. He estimated that over 200 people had assembled to jeer at them. He claimed that Goddard raised his fist at him, called him 'a bloody rogue and a thief' and shouted 'he would have my life'. Mortimer and Wilkinson plowed forward through chants of 'knobstick' and considerable 'hooting and hissing'. Mortimer testified that Goddard then grabbed Wilkinson, pushed him against a wall, grabbed one of his ears and hit him while 'saying he should like to kill him'.[45]

The strategy for the defense was revealed in the cross-examination of Mortimer. They intended to separate Goddard from the other three defendants, against whom the cases were comparatively weak, and prove that the prosecutors had provoked Goddard with violent words or actions. They also attacked the character of the complainants. The community was predisposed to believe, as did city Councilman Ironside, that 'knobsticks ... are the scum of society, entirely destitute of morality, who would on other occasions not be touched by the masters even with ... a pair of tongs'.[46]

Broomhead asked Mortimer where the other defendants were during Wilkinson's encounter with Goddard to establish that they were nowhere near the action. Mortimer insisted that the 'defendants were part of the crowd all the way'. The witness denied having challenged anyone to a fight or provoking the defendants. Broomhead then asked him about his own criminal record, forcing the witness to admit that he had once been convicted of stealing lead from the railway though he denied having served six months for stealing forks. Broomhead

---

[43] 'Intimidation of Workmen', *SRI* (27 April 1844), p. 2; 'Assault', *SRI* (27 April 1844), p. 5.

[44] Ibid.

[45] 'Intimidation of Workmen', *SRI* (27 April 1844), p. 2; 'Address to the Public on Behalf of the Stove Grate and Fender Makers of Sheffield', *NS* (11 May 1844), p. 6.

[46] Ibid.

was about to present evidence of this conviction when Overend declared this line of questioning immaterial. The prosecution next called Mr Raynor, a local police officer, who described the chaos caused by the turnout and the crowd of men standing on the street on the day of the assault. On cross-examination he admitted that although he saw Goddard, he did not see him commit any crimes, and he did not remember seeing any of the other defendants at all. A second police officer also conceded that he had not seen the four defendants in the crowd.[47]

The prosecution rested their case, which appeared to be insufficient to convict at least three of the defendants. Broomhead argued as much to the bench, contending that 'no offence under the act of Parliament had been made out' against them. Overend replied that, on the contrary, 'a good case had been made out', and another magistrate found the evidence 'quite straight-forward'.[48]

Broomhead called witnesses to prove that three of the defendants were not present when the offense took place. Stove-grate fitter Edward Coates testified that he was in Rotherham on the day of the assault and saw the defendant Wadsworth gardening with his mother-in-law between noon and 7:30 p.m. On cross-examination, Palfreyman tried to discredit the witness by suggesting a friendship between him and the defendant. He was only able to prove that the witness was an apprentice in the same trade, but not a member of the same union. He asked the witness if Broomhead had coached him on his testimony, which Coates denied. John Heath was called next, and confirmed Coates' testimony. At this point Overend intervened, questioning the witness himself. He asked if the he and Coates had traveled to Sheffield together. Heath said that they were on the same coach, but did not sit together. Overend also asked who examined him at the Broomheads' office, and the witness replied that he had spoken with their clerk. Overend's skeptical treatment of this witness for the defense is suggestive of his assumptions about the case, as he did not cross-examine any prosecution witnesses. Alibi witnesses were called for Morton and Thompson and they were treated the same way by the bench. Broomhead then called two witnesses to prove that the prosecutors had violently attacked Goddard first.[49] The bench disregarded their testimony, and that of all witnesses for the defense.

---

[47] Ibid. It was also revealed on cross-examination that replacement workers carried hammers with them when traveling to and from work.

[48] Ibid.

[49] The next two alibi witnesses were William Raines and John Smith, who both testified that they saw the defendant Morton gardening in the Army Hotel Garden between 4 p.m. and 9 p.m. on the day of the assault. Broomhead then called rod-roller Edward Shepherd to testify that he and the defendant Thompson went drinking together at several taverns in Rotherham, and did not part company until nearly seven o'clock. Clement Deakin, a fender maker, and Thomas Eyre, a stove grate fitter, both testified that the prosecutors attacked Goddard first. 'Intimidation of Workmen', *SRI* (27 April 1844), p. 2; Pollard, *Labour in Sheffield*, pp. 17, 28.

Palfreyman rose to make his closing argument when Overend stopped him, saying

> He might save him the trouble ... They were of the opinion that the case was fully made out, and they considered it such a case, that under existing circumstances, it was necessary to make an example to the town. They had therefore decided to commit each of the defendants to three months, to the House of Correction, to hard labour.[50]

Making matters worse, Goddard was also indicted for assault, to be heard at the next Quarter Sessions. Broomhead gave notice of appeal under George IV, c.129, s.12 (1825), which stated that defendants may appeal the magistrates' rulings to the next Quarter Sessions by immediately entering into a £10 recognizance and two £10 sureties. At this point Mr. Smith, the employer, rose and reminded the court that each defendant had to present sureties and recognizance immediately. Broomhead confirmed that they had sureties present.[51] The next Quarter Sessions were not until July.

There are a number of reasons why both this charge and the conviction were unpopular among the artisan community. The employers who had paid for the prosecution had refused to enter into customary negotiations with their employees. They instead used the magistracy to support the importation of unpopular 'outsiders' to take the jobs of local men. The hearing itself appeared one-sided, with the defense witnesses being disregarded by the magistrates. If middle-class observers felt that alibis provided by artisans in the same trade as the defendants were suspect, to a working-class audience it was dubious to send a man to prison on the testimony of a convicted thief who also acted as a scab. Overend and the other magistrates took no time to deliberate or hear closing arguments, which gave the appearance that they had pre-judged the case. This evidence appeared to be paper-thin against at least three of the defendants. Overend's emphasis on the use of Petty Sessions to educate the public underscored the foreignness of his interpretation of the Act's provisions to the community.

Three days later the defendants Thompson and Morton were once again charged under 6 George IV, c.129 (1825), this time with fellow stove-grate fitters, William Mason and Thomas Freeman. Replacement workers George Vickers and Samuel Mortimer accused them of using threats and intimidation to make them leave their jobs with Stuart, Smith and Co. Attorneys Palfreyman and Dixon again argued the cases for the prosecutors, and the defendants' case was again managed by the Broomheads. Wilson Overend and one other magistrate determined this case.

Vickers and Mortimer, both replacement workers, testified that on 18 April 1844 they were walking home when the defendants and a large crowd wielding 'thick sticks' blocked their path, called them 'knobsticks' and 'thieves and rogues',

---

[50] Ibid.

[51] Ibid.

pushed them and knocked their hats off. Neither sustained any injuries. Broomhead, on cross-examination, again tried to prove that the prosecutors had provoked the defendants by challenging them to a fight, which the witnesses denied.[52]

Broomhead then asked Overend if he had a case to answer, because no threats had been made. Overend replied 'there was proof of both intimidating, threatening, and obstructing, and as to the object, it was clearly made out by the use of the word "knobstick"', which established that the crowd was victimizing the men for acting as replacement workers. He stated that 'unless Mr. Broomhead had evidence to disprove the connection of these parties with the word knobstick, they should hold that the case was clearly proved'. Broomhead, showing some signs of frustration with Overend, replied 'it was of no use his calling witnesses, though he had witnesses, yet he saw it was a waste of time to bring them forward'. Overend convicted the four artisans to three months in the house of correction, with hard labor. Broomhead gave notice of an appeal, and the defendants entered into more recognizances and sureties to have their case heard at Quarter Sessions in July.[53]

Broomhead's opinion of Overend's impartiality was suggested by another hearing on the same day in which two replacement workers charged five apprentice turnouts from Stuart, Smith and Co. with common assault. Dixon and Palfreymen moved that because the defendants 'were influenced in their conduct by others older than themselves', they wanted the information laid under 9 George IV, c.31, s.27 (1829). This act allowed two magistrates to rule summarily in cases of common assault and carried a maximum penalty (with costs) of £5.[54] Broomhead requested that the case to be heard before a jury at Quarter Sessions because the defendants 'would have a chance of having the case heard by parties who were a stranger to it'. He argued that because the magistrates' 'minds could not help receiving some impression from the prejudicial rumours that came to their ears', it would be more just to indict the defendants for assault and have the case heard in July. Overend replied that 'these remarks were dictated by a want of proper respect to the bench'. The fact that Broomhead was prepared to expose his clients to far more serious penalties just to remove the case from Overend's authority speaks volumes about his opinion of that magistrate's impartiality and the lack of procedural protections in his hearings. Overend insisted on determining the case and delivered his ruling by stating that the magistrates 'deemed this case so important to the town', at which point a frustrated Broomhead interrupted by shouting 'Ah! There it is!'. Overend convicted the five apprentices and fined them £5 apiece or two months' imprisonment in default. Overend instructed Broomhead that his clients could appeal to Quarter Sessions, but the defense attorney informed the magistrate that the statute, in fact, allowed no such appeal.[55]

---

[52]   'The Roscoe Place Workmen', *SRI* (27 April 1844), p. 5.

[53]   Ibid. Ironside provided the sureties.

[54]   'An Act for Consolidating and Amending the Statutes in England Relative to Offences Against the Person', 9 George IV, c.31, s.27 (1829).

[55]   'Assault', *SRI* (27 April 1844), p. 5.

The last of the cases from the spring of 1844 in the return was a rattening in the razor-grinding trade. It did not arise out of a conflict between an employer and the union, but rather a conflict within the union over a recently adopted policy. On 30 April 1844, in response to a new rule adopted by the Razor Grinders' Union that reduced the hours members were allowed to work, 16 members left the union.[56] They continued to work longer hours than the union allowed. On 5 May 1844, former union members Samuel Sharpe, William Sykes and Luke Jarvis charged union leaders William Hawksley, Benjamin Turner and Samuel Bagshawe with having used threats and intimidation to prevent them from carrying on their work. Overend and the Reverend Mr Alderson heard the case. Palfreyman conducted the prosecution, and Broomhead the defense.[57]

Broomhead started the proceedings by objecting that the defendants had not received 24 hours' notice of the charge as required by the statute. Palfreyman argued that notice was only necessary when the accused had been summoned and in this case they had been brought up by warrant. He alleged that two of his key witnesses were intimidated the night before at a public house commonly frequented by razor grinders. Palfreyman called two witnesses to prove that the union summoned them to ask what they planned to testify. Overend ruled that under these circumstances, the case could be postponed only if the defendants were held without bail. Broomhead replied that 'he would risk the case, and not have the defendants kept in custody'.[58]

Palfreyman called razor-grinder Samuel Sharpe to testify, who described leaving the union with 16 others on the 30 April and subsequently having an order delivered to him from the union listing the hours he was allowed to work. At 6 a.m. on 3 May, he was working in one of his troughs with two others when Hawksley and Turner arrived. He recalled that Turner said 'I'm surprised you cannot be content working the hours the trade allows', to which he replied that he was no longer a member of the union. Turner then warned him that 'means shall be taken to make you a member'. He testified that Hawksley informed him that 'thou knows thou'lt not work here any more after this week'. Turner and Hawksley then left, and later that weekend, Sharpe was rattened with 'injury done to the wheel to a great extent'.[59]

Broomhead's strategy for the defense was to emphasize that there was no direct evidence that any of his clients ordered the taking of Sharpe's wheel-bands or the damaging of his trough. Every witness for the prosecution admitted upon cross-examination that he had only strong suspicions, but no direct evidence to prove

---

56   The new rule limited grinders to working between 10 a.m. to 12 p.m., and 1:30 p.m. to 4:30 p.m. on Mondays; from 8 a.m. to 12 p.m. on Tuesdays; from 8 a.m. to 12 p.m. and 1:30 p.m. to 6:30 p.m. on Wednesdays, Thursdays and Fridays; and from 7 a.m. to 12 p.m., and 1 p.m. to 5 p.m. on Saturdays.

57   'The Razor Grinders' Trade', *SRI* (11 May 1844), p. 5.

58   Ibid. The witnesses were grinders Richard Crosland and Charles Pass.

59   Ibid. Pass and Crossland confirmed this testimony.

that the defendants were actually responsible.[60] Hawksley's and Turner's vague warnings could be considered threats, particularly if one was familiar with trade practices, but the possibility of multiple interpretations of their words made the case against them shaky. The case against Bagshawe appeared especially weak.

Overend was 'satisfied that the evidence was sufficient to convict upon', but offered to remand the case until Tuesday, while holding the defendants in prison, so that Broomhead could prepare a more thorough defense. Broomhead rejected the offer, informing the bench that he had sureties present for an appeal. The men were convicted to three months' hard labor, and immediately entered into recognizances and sureties for an appeal to Quarter Sessions.[61]

At the West Riding Mid-Summer Quarter Sessions at Rotherham on 8 July 1844, 11 appellate actions were pending against convictions made by Overend under 6 George IV, c.129 (1825). The three convictions against razor-grinders William Hawksley, Samuel Bagshaw and Benjamin Turner were overturned because no one appeared at the hearing to support the prosecution. It is possible that this was because the parties had reached a private settlement, the prosecutors feared losing the appeal or they simply wanted to avoid the costs of preparing and presenting a response to the appeal.[62]

The next appeal heard was that of stove-grate fitter, Joseph Goddard, which had been pending since the previous April. William Overend and Mr Monteith defended the conviction, while Mr Pickering and Mr Wilkins presented the appeal. Wilkins argued that Goddard had been improperly convicted according to Section 7 of 6 George IV, c.129 (1825), which stated that the conviction had to be based upon either a confession by the defendant or evidence taken upon the oath of one or more credible witnesses. Because the written conviction explicitly stated neither of these things Wilkins suggested that to allow it to stand would represent 'gross tyranny'. Pickering cited In Re: *Tordoft* (1844), described in Chapter 3. Wilkins made an appeal to both 'Blackstone's Palladium of British Liberty', and the strict legal formalism that was the defendants' only protection in cases determined summarily. He reminded the bench that in these cases 'the ordinary right of trial by jury was dispensed with, and therefore the law most wisely and strictly guarded against its abuse'.[63] He was making an appeal to a precedent set by a higher legal authority than the magistracy.

Mr Monteith responded that 'The objection was about the silliest he ever heard'. He and Overend argued that the conviction closely followed the form set out in the act. The Bench disagreed, and ruled that the conviction was bad, and as a result overturned eight others written in the same form by Overend. In one

---

[60] Ibid.

[61] Ibid.

[62] 'West Riding Midsummer Sessions', *SRI* (13 July 1844), p. 2.

[63] Re Tordoft, 1 New Sessions Cases 171; 'West Riding Midsummer Sessions', *SRI* (13 July 1844), p. 2.

morning, Overend had lost 11 convictions. The workers were freed on precedents set in the high courts by previous union-funded legal actions.

Goddard still faced trial for assaulting George Wilkinson, which took place in a very crowded courtroom at Quarter Sessions. William Overend conducted the prosecution, while Wilkins and Pickering defended Goddard. The prosecution and defense presented were largely the same as that of the 23 April intimidation case. The jury found Goddard guilty, and the Chairman declared that because the defendant was 'part of a system of intimidation carried on in this county to a great extent … we … find it our duty to administer the law, as to protect the property and lives of all parties involved'. In order to 'deter others from the course you have pursued' the chairman sentenced Goddard to six months in the House of Correction, at which point the crowd began loudly booing and hissing to such an extent that the chair had to threaten to take anyone making noise into custody.[64] The Chairman of Sessions, like Overend, sought to use the law to instruct the community, but reaction in the courtroom suggests that they rejected his message.

The antagonistic relationship between the artisan community and the magistracy increased when some saw and file manufacturers formed 'The Sheffield Manufacturers and Tradesmen's Protection Society' on 13 November 1844. This idea was proposed in an open letter to the *Sheffield and Rotherham Independent* in May of 1844, calling for 'a determined resistance on our part to that worst of all tyrannies, the tyranny of the mob'. It proposed compensating victims of 'outrages', or other union action, and paying for the prosecution of those who carried them out. It also proposed mutual assistance for employers facing industrial action. It closed 'again, manufacturers of Sheffield I call upon you to meet forthwith and adopt some plan for the extinction of labour combinations'.[65] The Protection Society also lobbied borough MP, H. G. Ward, for greater government support, describing the interference of local unions in the hiring practices of masters and the 'numerous outrages … perpetrated at the instigation, or with the connivance of, trades' societies'.[66]

The formation of the Protection Society confirmed the worst fears of Sheffield artisans. Earlier chapters have shown how Roberts and the *Northern Star* skillfully fostered the perception of a corrupt partnership between magistrates and masters. The Trades of Sheffield made the same argument about the Protection Society and Overend. They complained that in the cases funded by the Society, 'the testimony of the lowest witnesses was received, whom even the constables said would not believe on their oaths'. They argued that in intimidation cases magistrates convicted defendants on very thin evidence, interpreting the law in a way at odds with both local values and the precedents of the higher courts. Local unions used reports of workers arrested in bed in the middle of the night and prosecuted at the

---

[64]   Ibid.

[65]   'Trades Unions', *SRI* (25 May 1844), p. 6.

[66]   Hill, 'Trade Combinations in Sheffield', pp. 543–7; Pollard, *Labour in Sheffield*, pp. 68–72.

behest of the employers' combination to mobilize and unify trades societies in Sheffield.[67]

By mid 1845, the trades of Sheffield had determined to fight against the Protection Society by obtaining 'real law'. On 5 June 1845 a group of trade delegates met and resolved to use all 'legal and moral means' to defend workers against the manufacturers' combination.[68] The meeting agreed to a subscription of 1/2d per member to create a law fund. The number of cases actually funded by the employers' prosecution society was small, but its actions aroused considerable resentment.

The Return of Combination Act Convictions at Sheffield Petty Sessions lists five convictions between October 1846 and the protest in April–May of 1847 that were either withdrawn by the prosecutors or quashed upon appeal to Quarter Sessions. The Manufacturers and Tradesmen's Protection Society funded four of these cases, increasing its visibility within the community. The prosecutions reveal not only willingness on the part of magistrates to interpret generously evidence for the prosecution, but also to adopt an expansive definition of intimidation, obstruction and molestation.

On 27 October 1846, William Graham, one of the owners of the Milton Ironworks, charged union secretary, Jonathan Davy, with having used threats and intimidation to deprive him of the services of iron-molder, George Beanland. In this case the bench openly expressed doubt as to the legality of convicting the defendant, but did so nonetheless, forcing him to appeal to Quarter Sessions. Graham's firm was under contract to deliver a quantity of piping to a client by a certain date. His foreman and six iron-molders exploited Graham's vulnerable position by demanding a raise. Graham agreed to their price, but gave the foreman one-month's notice of dismissal. The men refused to continue working without the foreman and upon Graham's refusal to retain him, they walked off the job. Graham hired new workers to complete the contract, but one, George Beanland, left after receiving his first pay packet and a note from the union. This note said:

> 9 October 1846
> The purpose of this note is to inform you that if you continue work at Milton for Belk, you will be fined according to the 6th bye-law.
> I remain yours, J. Davy, Secretary.[69]

The sixth bye-law of the Iron Moulders' Society stipulated that any member working at a firm where employees were on strike would be subject to fines of £1 6s 2d per day and be excluded from all benefits of the society.

After Graham testified to these facts he was cross-examined by Broomhead, who tried to demonstrate that Graham lacked the standing to bring this case

---

[67] Ibid.
[68] Ibid.
[69] 'Tuesday', *ST* (31 October 1846), p. 5.

because Beanland was actually employed by a subcontractor named Belk. Graham denied that this was true. Broomhead then pointed out that as the note threatened to fine Beanland only if he continued to work for Belk, it suggested no sanctions for working for the witness. No threat had been made concerning Graham at all. Broomhead also tried to demonstrate that Beanland had been under no legal obligation to continue working for Graham longer than he did, intimating that the note might have played no role in his leaving. When presenting his defense, Broomhead also submitted that no evidence had been produced to demonstrate that Davy had actually written the note or that it was in his handwriting. One of the curious silences in this case is that of George Beanland, who did not testify. The case report said that he was 'not forthcoming'.[70]

Overend acknowledged that the case before him was a legally weak one, suggesting 'the case would have been a different one if the name of Graham had been on the note', but he 'had no doubt that the sending of the note was an act of interference'. Overend repeated his concern that the note might not sufficiently prove intimidation to a man working for Graham, but that 'on the merits of the case he was prepared to convict'. His clerk then suggested that it would be a good case to be heard at Quarter Sessions. Overend then convicted Davy to three months' imprisonment. Broomhead gave notice of an appeal. Clearly, not everyone thought the case was a good one for appeal, as the parties settled it privately, and Davy served no prison time.[71] Overend's assumptions about the activities of local trade unions allowed him to make a conviction that the evidence did not support. Overend was applying the 'common sense' justice that supporters of summary justice advocated. Overend 'knew' the defendant was guilty even if the prosecutor could not produce sufficient evidence.

On 29 December 1846, The Manufacturers and Tradesmen's Protection Society supported a prosecution by scissor manufacturer, Mrs Shackley, against scissor-grinder John Wreaks.[72] Her employment of two non-union grinders brought her into conflict with the defendant, who warned her on 16 December 1846 that unless she discharged them her tools would be destroyed. She refused to comply with Wreaks' demands and her tools were subsequently destroyed in a rattening. Wreaks was convicted by Overend and another magistrate, and appealed against the conviction to the Quarter Sessions.

At the Quarter Sessions in April of 1847, Mr Pashley and Mr Pickering, counsel for Wreaks, objected to the conviction on the grounds that it violated Section 13 of 6 George IV, c.129 (1825). That section stated that no magistrate who was a master in, or was concerned with, the trade in which the offense was alleged to have been committed could adjudicate. Clauses like this one had been introduced

---

[70]   Ibid.

[71]   Ibid.

[72]   In 1847 there were over 200 women working in the file trades, despite repeated attempts by the file unions 'to prohibit it altogether'. Hill, 'Trade Combinations in Sheffield', p. 555.

into a number of other statutes also conferring summary jurisdiction, such as the 1831 Truck Act. One of the magistrates in this particular case, Mr Butcher, was a dealer in hardware, who manufactured edge-tools and razors, and sometimes contracted-out scissors that he stamped with his name.

Hall and Johnson, barristers for the respondents, objected that the linkage between Butcher and the scissor trade was exceedingly weak. They called witnesses, many who were also members of the Protection Society, to prove that the magistrate was not really a manufacturer of scissors. Pashley responded by appealing for the preservation of the law's legitimacy, emphasizing 'the jealousy with which the laws kept watch over the administration of justice, in order that it may be kept pure and above all suspicion'. His argument carried the day and the conviction was overturned.[73]

Of the cases supported by the Manufacturers and Tradesmen's Protection Society, the most contentious was that of saw manufacturer *Samuel Newbould v. William Ashby, James Bacon and Michael Slinn*. On 23 March 1847, Newbould charged the three defendants with having used threats and intimidation to force him to limit the description of workers he employed. The case was profoundly offensive to the trades of Sheffield because it sought to expand the definition of intimidation to include union members warning masters of 'moral unpleasantness' that might result from employing non-union workers. Worse still, no evidence was presented to prove that after the 'threat' was made the prosecutor experienced any unpleasantness from any union member, moral or otherwise. If left unchallenged, this prosecution would have seriously undermined the ability of unions to bargain collectively and redress grievances with employers. Overend's interpretation in this case anticipated, however, the controversial 1851 ruling of Mr Justice Erle in *R. v. Rowlands* and *R. v. Duffield* (1851), in which union leaders were convicted for conspiring to obstruct and molest an employer by peacefully convincing workers not to accept employment from him.[74]

A. C. Branson conducted the case for the prosecution and Mr Unwin defended the accused before Overend and three other magistrates. Branson suggested to the bench that Newbould was taking 'the mildest course which was open to him', as he could have indicted the parties for conspiracy at Common Law. Newbould testified that on 19 February 1847 the three defendants waited upon him and informed him that one of his 24 employees was in arrears to the union, and asked him if he could 'use his influence' to convince the man to pay his contribution. Newbould informed the deputation that he opposed unions and would use his influence to convince Allen not to pay. The deputation then informed him that he employed another man who was 'not in the trade', and that unless Newbould discharged him there would be 'considerable unpleasantness'. Newbould asked the three if he was to be 'blown up'. Ashby assured him that no one would resort

---

[73] 'Thursday', *ST* (10 April 1847), p. 8.

[74] *R. v. Rowlands, R. v. Duffield* (1851), 5 Cox Criminal Cases 404, 465. NA: KB 1/199/59–60; KB 1/203/662–663; 1/204/51.

to physical violence, but he might face the 'moral unpleasantness' of having his men turn out. Newbould turned them away, arguing 'as long as he paid the wages he had a right to employ whomsoever he saw fit'.[75] Unwin's strategy on cross-examination was to emphasize that the deputation used civil and non-threatening language, suggesting that they were merely asking him for assistance rather than dictating terms.

Unwin then submitted to the bench that there was no case against the defendants. There was no evidence that Newbould had lost a single workman, or suffered 'unpleasantness' of any type as a result of this conversation. He argued there was no proof of any attempt to limit Newbould's right to carry on his trade as he liked. Overend replied that the charges only concerned the threats themselves, 'they had nothing to do with the result'. Overend lamented that as unions had developed in Sheffield, 'they were ... framed as to interfere with the interest of trade, and they led to an excess of crime which caused them to be regarded with a degree of horror, which in their original state they did not deserve'. He ruled that the 'deputation had waited upon Mr. Newbould in a way which brought them within the act of Parliament', so he found them guilty and sentenced them to be imprisoned for three months. Unwin gave notice of an appeal.[76] Trade unionists would have disagreed with Overend's assessment of their role, as they often asserted that *they protected* the interests of the trade. Overend equated 'the interests of the trade' with the interests of employers. The *Northern Star* reported that 'there is a rumour in the town that Mr. Roberts is to be sent for to appeal this case'. Roberts did not represent the men, but the artisans of Sheffield heeded the advice to protest.[77]

The appeal was heard at the Quarter Sessions on 5 April 1847. Hall and Ingram acted as counsel for the defendants, Pashley and Pickering represented the respondents. Pashley and Pickering argued that the evidence showed that the prisoners used threats and intimidation to force Newbould to limit the description of his workmen. They examined Newbould, who gave the same testimony as in the original hearing. On cross-examination Hall made Newbould acknowledge that he had often received deputations of workers in the past, and that he had peacefully arranged differences through this method. He conceded that although he opposed unions, he was a member of an employers' union, the Manufacturers' Protection Society. Hall further established that during the meeting the men spoke in civil manner, and at no time was Newbould alarmed.[78]

Hall then submitted to the bench that 'no case whatever had been made out to sustain a conviction'. He pointed out the obvious fact that no witness had ever alleged that two of the defendants, Slinn and Beighton, had said or done anything before, during, or after the meeting with Newbould. He also stressed that Newbould himself conceded that 'what was said to him by the appellants did

---

[75] 'Charge of Intimidation', *ST* (27 March 1847), p. 3.

[76] Ibid. Chartist Isaac Ironside again provided sureties for the prisoners.

[77] 'Conspiracy of the Sheffield Masters', *NS* (3 April 1847), p. 4.

[78] 'Intimidation Case at Sheffield', *ST* (10 April 1847), p. 8.

not excite any fear or apprehension in his mind that he would suffer injury', and thus was not a threat. He then asserted that the men were right not to work with a man who had not served an apprenticeship, arguing 'irregular education had filled the bar with pettifoggers – the medical profession with empirics – and the church with bigots'. He suggested to the chairman that if he permitted untrained men to plead at Quarter Sessions, 'that powerful union – the British Bar – would not work with them'. If the Chairman allowed these men to plead, and then asked the bar members 'whether he would be blown up, they would assuredly tell him … that he *would* be blown up'. Hall's hyperbole provoked laughter in the courtroom. Hall closed by warning that if this case was upheld it would criminalize peaceful deputations for the settling of differences, and unions would go underground, leading to 'greater violence'. The Chair 'at once said the conviction was quashed *on its merits'.*[79]

Hall humorously emphasized the legitimacy of union actions by putting them in a context that a middle-class audience could understand – a professional organization. Both regulated entry into the profession, standards and fees, as well as penalized members who violated their rules. While one organization was legitimate to the middle-class, the other was accepted by Sheffield artisans. Hall's cross-examination of Newbould stressed the regularity of negotiations between the trade and employers. A set of rules and practices for negotiations had developed in many Sheffield trades, whereby artisans had a strong bargaining position. In many of the cases described in this section, masters turned to the magistracy to overturn these established practices. Hall's mocking tone highlighted the weak case against his clients, which would have applied to many others heard by Overend. In fact, if a Manufacturers' Protection Society had not supported some of these cases, it is unlikely they would have been presented at all.

Finally, the Chairman's immediate quashing of Overend's ruling demonstrates the impact of a successful appeal on the public perception of the administration of the law. As in Roberts' successful actions, it made little difference whether cases were overturned on matters of form, abandonment by the prosecutor, or the 'merits of the case' (though in this most public of cases, the Chairman emphasized that the conviction was bad on its merits), as all served to undermine the credibility of Overend. His open partnership with employers, repeated reversal of his rulings and statements from the bench made it easy to argue Overend was a partial and vindictive magistrate.

The Sheffield Trades' Protest against Wilson Overend, April–May 1847

By the end of April 1847 workers in several trades, as well as some middle-class radicals, were disturbed by the case of Ashby, Slinn and Beighton. They organized a protest against Overend, which divided the town mostly along class lines. The

---

[79]   Ibid.

town also sharply divided over the meaning to be drawn from the refusal of Overend's rulings. Locally, this protest was as much about deference, authority, the role of the law and democracy as it was about Overend himself.

On 20 April 1847 workmen in four branches of the pen and pocket-knife trades met to discuss the merits of joining the National Association of United Trades. Although it was not on the agenda of the meeting, the recently determined case of Ashby, Slinn and Beighton was in the thoughts of many. Mr Parker, who spoke at length about the many benefits of the National Association, ended by stressing the importance of having Duncombe as its president:

> He mentioned the prompt attention given by Sir George Grey, the Home Secretary, to the representation made by Mr. Duncombe in the House of Commons, of the case of three men committed for three months by two Warrington magistrates. Sir George Grey at once sent down an order for the discharge of these men. There had been three men lately committed from this town for waiting upon one of the manufacturers to advise with him. The conviction had certainly been quashed; but the law remained the same, and if it would touch men for doing what they were committed for, it was time it was altered. He advised that they should put into the hands of Mr. Duncombe a statement of the particulars of that case, which he would bring before the house, with a view to getting Mr. Overend discharged from the commission.

Another speaker, Mr Stocks, agreed, insisting, 'the working men were not to be made the victims of either the manufacturers or the magistrate, who oppressed and persecuted them, without some cognisance being taken of their proceedings'.[80]

The next speaker was local radical Isaac Ironside, who expressed disgust at the prosecution of Ashby, Slinn and Beighton. He also reported that because Overend often publicly condemned unions, he should not determine cases involving unionists. Yet, to the contrary, Overend, he argued, actually sought out these cases, to which someone in the crowd added 'Aye, when he's made his mind up aforehand'. He urged them to report the facts of this case to either Duncombe or the Home Secretary, and ask them to have Overend removed from the commission.[81]

Mr Sykes informed the crowd that the effort was already underway. A delegation of trades had determined to ask the Mayor to call a meeting to consider the propriety of memorializing the Home Secretary to remove Overend from the bench. They anticipated that the Mayor would reject this proposal, in which case they would hold a public meeting themselves. Sykes assured the crowd that other trades were also offended by Overend's actions and the meeting would be well-attended.[82]

---

[80] 'The Spring Knife Cutlers and the National Association', *SRI* (24 April 1847), p. 5.

[81] 'The Spring Knife Cutlers and the National Association', *SRI* (24 April 1847), p. 5.

[82] Ibid.

Two deputations of workers met with the Mayor, and both were turned away because the Mayor disapproved of singling out an individual magistrate for condemnation. He called a meeting of the Town Council, however, when approached by a group of councilors who were defenders of Overend. Because the unions of Sheffield were planning to hold a public meeting on 3 May 1847, they felt it important that the Council conduct one of its own so that the trades' meeting would not be Sheffield's only voice on the subject.[83]

Defenders of Overend stressed a distinction between a ruling being incorrect on its 'merits', and in its 'form'. The latter was acceptable, because it demonstrated no malice, and was understandable given the complexity of the judicial system. They argued that Overend's rulings were usually quashed due to mistakes in form. The councilors clearly had more confidence in the ability of local summary courts to get to the 'real facts' of the case than more formal forms of rules-based justice.

The Mayor opened the meeting on 3 May, three hours before the workers were scheduled to convene. Ironside objected to the meeting because it was illegal to hold it without proper notice. The Mayor disregarded Ironside's objections, and proceeded to defend Overend's character and motives and expressed confidence that the magistrate would be exonerated. Alderman Lowe asserted 'none of the difficulties magistrates had to contend with were greater than those which are caused by the frequent disputes arising between masters and workmen', and that Overend heard more of these cases than any other magistrate. He then moved a resolution to be delivered to the Home Secretary, stating that the council regretted that the working classes of Sheffield felt dissatisfied with Overend's rulings, but found 'no real grounds exist for such dissatisfaction'. The resolution went on to proclaim 'full confidence' that Overend had 'acted with the strictest honesty and impartiality'. Alderman Dunn moved to amend the resolution to say 'unquestioned honesty and impartiality'.[84]

Alderman Bright supported the motion, distinguishing between cases quashed on their 'merits' or for 'defects in form'. Due to the 'glorious uncertainty of the law', it was not alarming that Overend's convictions were sometimes quashed. He asserted that anyone 'who read the law reports from the proceedings of magistrates in Petty Sessions … would see that judgments were frequently reversed'. The continual emphasis in this meeting on the acceptability of 'mere errors in form', reveals a shared assumption with Overend that the accused parties were always actually guilty. Mr Rodgers rose and condemned the public meeting of workers as an attempt to 'intimidate the magistrates', and argued that it would 'create in the minds of the lower classes a spirit diametrically opposed to what they ought to entertain towards those who are placed in authority'.[85]

---

[83]   The Mayor stated that the Town Council would act as Overend's 'defense counsel'. 'Special Meeting of the Town Council', *ST* (8 May 1847), p. 6.

[84]   Ibid.

[85]   Ibid.

Two of Overend's three opponents on the Town Council made their voices heard as well. Mr Briggs moved to amend the resolution to state that 'the council had no confidence either in Mr. Overend, or the government who appointed him'. Briggs recognized that he had an uphill battle, arguing that the council 'that met to try Mr. Overend, was a packed jury – they were magistrates to try a magistrate'. He recommended they attend the public meeting, which would demonstrate 'if they were to admit working men into that jury for trying Mr. Overend the vote of confidence would not be passed'. Briggs was reiterating the Chartist argument that in a more democratic society there would be neither laws like the 1825 Combination Act nor men like Dr Overend enforcing them. He praised the workers for organizing the protest which would act as a check on magistrates, who 'would not, in the future, be in a hurry in coming to conclusions, and they would carefully study and weigh over what was laid before them'. He expressed hope that one day men would democratically elect magistrates.[86]

Ironside also appealed to democratic principles. He warned the council that they were putting themselves in direct opposition to the opinions of the overwhelming majority of Sheffield's inhabitants. He argued that the Council existed to represent the people; it was 'the town in miniature' and 'ought not to contravene the expression of the town in its collective capacity'. He cautioned the councilors that 'they were taking up a position which would not reflect credit upon' them. Ironside quoted Overend's statements against unionists, and commented on his own observations of the magistrate's bias:

> I am sorry to observe an unseemly and unbecoming zeal on the part of the magistrates and their clerk in identifying themselves with the master, and helping on his case. I particularly noticed one expression that fell from Mr. Overend. The master's attorney wished to put a letter in as evidence, to which the other attorney objected, showing most clearly by the rules of evidence it was inadmissible. The magistrates took the letter, read it, and after a short private consultation, Mr. Overend returned it to the master's attorney, saying, in a very significant manner, 'never mind the letter, we can do without it'.[87]

Ironside recommended that the Council withdraw their resolution and attend the public meeting and make their feelings known there. Briggs and Ironside could not prevent the Council from passing the resolution supporting Overend's character and conduct.[88]

Despite pouring rain, an estimated 8,000 workers attended the public meeting that took place later that day. They adopted a petition informing Parliament that 'their confidence in the wisdom, prudence, and justice displayed in the magisterial conduct of Wilson Overend, Esq., ... has been greatly shaken'. The

---

[86]   Ibid.

[87]   Ibid.

[88]   Ibid.

petition described numerous successful appeals against his rulings, as well as the particulars of the case against Ashby et al. The petition charged Overend with 'an unseemly anxiety to convict when they were charged with violating the law, and to let the employers escape when they were the parties accused'. It asked for a strict Parliamentary inquiry into his conduct because his 'decisions in all cases between the employer and employed have now no moral effect'.[89]

Speakers at this meeting returned to a number of similar themes. They accused Overend of colluding with the Manufacturers' Protection Society, displaying gross bias and attempting to use the law to crush trade unions and the values of the artisan community. Ironside chaired the meeting, and urged that the speakers adopt a respectful tone.

William Broadbent told the assembled crowd that 'as he conceived that Wilson Overend and the Protection Society had identified themselves as one and the same person, the working classes need never expect justice at his hands'. He also condemned the debate in the Town Council, calling it 'another specimen of the sort of justice they were to expect from manufacturers, merchants and Protection Society men'. Joshua Sykes asserted that 'in the administration of the law it was now firmly believed that he [Overend] had made himself the agent ... of the Protection Society'. He accused Overend of riding to and from court with prosecutors in cases that organization sponsored.[90] Speakers repeatedly expressed the sentiment that Overend and the employers of the Protection Society were in partnership with one another.

Other speakers accused Overend of a more general class bias. Thomas Wells argued that Sheffield should be provided by with a stipendiary magistrate because Overend's 'conduct had given them cause to think that he was influenced by sectional views, sectional feelings, and by class interests'. File-grinder, J. Hodgson, made an argument that the *Northern Star* and Roberts often made with respect to the judicial authority of magistrates. This was the distinction between 'real law' and 'magistrates' law'. Hodgson informed his audience that 'the law itself was one thing, and the administration of law was another'. He continued, 'where the law itself was just, the proceedings had been marked by an unjust administration, and thus the law itself had been rendered null and void'. He argued that this was because Overend bent to 'class interests and class views'. Mr Sykes argued that Overend 'had lain himself open to all the suspicions they could possibly entertain' because 'he was a partial man in his adjudications on trades union cases'. William Hawksworth praised Ironside and Briggs, but condemned the class bias of the rest of the Town Council, which protected Overend. Hawksworth's remarks were met with chants of 'We'll turn them out!'.[91]

---

[89] 'Public Meeting Respecting the Magisterial Conduct of W. Overend, Esq.', *ST* (8 May 1847), pp. 6–7.

[90] Ibid.

[91] Ibid. Brush-maker Henry Hill asked 'did it not seem likely that the greatest bulk of his [Overend's] practice, and by far the greatest reward, came from the rich; and on an

Other speakers condemned Overend because he represented an attempt to crush the enforcement of trades' rules and regulations. Wells argued

> One main point with trades unions was that they took into consideration, and provided themselves with laws and means for maintaining a fair remuneration for the labour they performed. And, he would ask, was there anything wrong in this sort of procedure? The manufacturers and merchants and professional men did not think it wrong to combine and interfere in this way.

The protest against Overend was essential for the trades to maintain 'their own rights, privileges and interests'. Hawksworth described a few of Overend's rulings and exclaimed, 'surely these proceedings were not in accordance with the custom of the town, which, however, would be altered *in toto* if they were to be guided by the views of Mr. Overend'. He went on to describe the conviction of Jonathan Davy for warning a worker that he was in violation of the sixth bye-law of their union. He asked 'what cause was there in this that the man should be committed for three months?' The crowd answered his question with chants of 'None! None! Shame! Shame!' Joshua Sykes complained that

> Wilson Overend had endeavoured to destroy, by the power of the law, their position as trades unionists, and their first reason arriving at this conclusion was because in the most trivial instances where it was conceived an offence had been committed – in point of fact without having reference to the motives of the individuals against whom the charges were laid – the utmost penalty allowed by law had been invariably inflicted upon the parties accused.

Sykes continued that the trades 'not only had just grounds of complaint for an attempt to injure these men, but also the whole order to which they belong'.[92]

The accusations of magistrates displaying class bias and conspiring with employers against trade unions would have been quite familiar to Northumberland and Durham miners, Lancashire file-forgers or Staffordshire potters. In the Sheffield protest unions were struggling to maintain their authority over the trade in the face of an attack from their employers and local law administered by magistrates allied with those employers.

The Debate in Parliament, May 1847

After the Trades of Sheffield sent their petition to Duncombe, several respectable Sheffield citizens came forward to defend Overend. The Town Council, the Mayor,

---

acknowledged principle that self interest was a deceiver of the eyes … it was certain that many intimate preferences and friendships arose as the consequence'?
[92]   Ibid.

the Trustees of Sheffield, the Company of Cutlers and the Church Burgesses all sent memorials to Parliament praising the character and conduct of the embattled magistrate. On Thursday, 13 May 1847, a deputation from Sheffield, including Earl Fitzwilliam and Lord Wharncliffe, accompanied Overend to a meeting with Home Secretary Sir George Grey. They had a long meeting with Grey, and they informed him that 'unions had seriously interfered with the proper freedom of both workmen and masters', and now 'sought to intimidate the whole bench'. Grey assured the deputation that he would give the issues they discussed his full attention.[93]

The conflict between unionists in Sheffield and Overend occurred at an important moment in the legislative history of summary justice in England. The growth in the business of the criminal justice system, the inconvenience and costs of jury trials for small offences, as well as a desire to make the penalties for petty crimes more humane (but also more certain) all necessitated the expansion of the summary jurisdiction of magistrates. In the spring of 1847, Parliament had begun consideration of a bill that eventually expanded the authority of magistrates to determine summarily cases of small larcenies committed by juveniles.[94] Several members of Parliament continued to cling to the ideal of the jury trial, and expressed doubts about the ability of the magistracy to administer the law correctly.

Just a few weeks before Overend's conduct was discussed in Parliament, Mr Roebuck objected to the second reading of the Juvenile Offenders Bill because 'these extraordinary powers were not to be given to a learned judge, but to a fox-hunting justice'. E. B. Denison agreed because the bill was 'most dangerous to the liberty of the subject; upsetting that great principle of trial by jury'. He argued that magistrates should not want such powers because 'even the most competent of that class often found themselves exceedingly embarrassed without the aid of skillful and learned counsel'. Another opponent, Mr Henley, 'was by no means anxious to see any more power entrusted into the hands of magistrates'.[95]

On 2 June 1847, Mr Thomas Wakley attempted to amend the bill to eliminate the powers of magistrates to administer 'a good wholesome flogging' to juveniles charged with petty thefts.[96] Wakley argued, 'The magistrates of this country were not a very wise or discreet body of men, nor were they always selected on account of their love of justice; he had seen enough of their conduct to tremble at a proposal to place more power in their hands'. Wakley recounted a story of a vindictive magistrate to argue that these officials were unfit to administer such a brutal punishment. Wakley was unsuccessful by a vote of 55 to 7.[97]

---

[93]   'The Magisterial Conduct of Mr. Overend', *ST* (15 May 1847), p. 4.

[94]   Thomas Sweeney, 'The Extension and Practice of Summary Jurisdiction in England, c.1790–1860' (PhD dissertation, Cambridge University, 1985), pp. 158–60.

[95]   *Hansard Debates*, Vol. 92, cols. 33–48.

[96]   The phrase was used by Viscount Sandon, *Hansard Debates*, Vol. 93, cols. 2–6.

[97]   *Hansard Debates*, Vol. 93, cols. 4–5.

The significant volume of successful actions and protests against the rulings of magistrates created anxiety about the conduct of magistrates. In April 1846, Duncombe, armed with petitions from the people of Dundee, demanded a select committee to investigate the 'illegal trial and imprisonment' of six 'unfortunate and unprotected factory girls' who were convicted for absenting themselves from their work. Duncombe alleged that the young women were kept in isolation until their trial and forced to sign a confession. Furthermore, the prosecutor had secret communications with the convicting magistrate before he sentenced the women, aged 14 to 20, to 10 days' imprisonment with hard labor. Duncombe was unsuccessful in obtaining a select committee, but the long debate undoubtedly brought unwelcome publicity to a Dundee magistrate and manufacturer.[98]

On 11 March 1847, Lord Brougham demanded an inquiry into the conduct of a magistrate who indicted a group of 10-year-old boys for taking their friend's hat and throwing it into a field.[99] In June of 1847, Mr Ferrand demanded the Home Secretary produce his correspondence with a group of magistrates who had wrongfully convicted a woman named Mary Dawson from Keighley, Yorkshire, under the Worsted Embezzlement Act for neglect of her work. The magistrates had incorrectly decided the case, and then denied her father a copy of the warrant of committal. By the time Ferrand was able to get a pardon from the Home Secretary, Dawson had been walking the treadmill for three straight weeks. He claimed that 'she was so weakened by the labor on the treadmill that she could not walk without assistance'. Grey refused to produce the desired correspondence. Ferrand consoled himself by observing 'the magistrate was a very good mark for some skillful attorney to aim at; and he had no doubt that there were plenty of attorneys who, when they saw the report of tonight's proceedings ... would feel considerable commiseration for the poor girl'.[100]

Duncombe presented his motion on 18 May 1847, describing the consistency and severity with which Overend ruled for employers over employees in labor cases, as well as the regularity with which they were quashed upon appeal. He joked 'I hope his prescriptions are better than his law'. He accused Overend, 'who was thought to be adept at putting down combinations amongst the workmen', of deliberately seeking to hear these cases. Duncombe related the facts of *Newbould v. Ashby et al.*, claiming that when the prisoners arrived at the Town Hall there were three magistrates ready to hear the case, but the prosecutors refused to begin until Overend arrived. He argued that the defendants were 'most severely and unjustly dealt with' and had to spend £50 to appeal their case. He observed 'that it should give rise to complaints of partiality in his administration of justice against the men, and in favour of the masters, was not surprising'. The radical MP recommended

---

[98]   *Hansard Debates*, Vol. 85, cols. 470–480.

[99]   *Hansard Debates*, Vol. 90, col. 1136.

[100]   *Hansard Debates*, Vol. 93, cols. 120, 947–53; Richard Soderlund, '"Intended as a Terror to the Idle and Profligate": Embezzlement and the Origins of Policing in the Yorkshire Worsted Industry, c.1750–1777', *Journal of Social History* 31/3 (1998): 647–70.

the appointment of a stipendiary magistrate for Sheffield, who would impartially determine cases. Duncombe argued that Parliament should produce a return so that they could determine whether Overend should be removed from the bench.[101]

Sir George Grey assured Duncombe that he did not oppose the return, but moved to amend the motion to include the printing of the many memorials that he had received praising the character and diligence of Overend. He informed the House of the 'fearful system of intimidation that existed in Sheffield, under which the magistrates were obliged to act in circumstances of great difficulty and much peril'. E. B. Dennison concurred with Grey, saying 'the town of Sheffield was afflicted with a system of combination … occasioning great loss and inconvenience on masters, and imposing great difficulties on magistrates'. James Wortley, the son of Lord Wharncliffe, added 'the state of things in Sheffield was actually frightful' with respect to unions. He informed the House of masters offering £1,000 rewards for information leading to the conviction of the authors of outrages, to no avail. He knew of a case where a 'gentleman of extensive capital' considered setting up an establishment for the manufacture of railroad engines in Sheffield, but fearful of 'the terrible state of society there' took his capital elsewhere. Wortley pleaded with Duncombe, the president of two trade unions, to use his power to stop such outrages.[102]

Supporters of Overend painted such a fearful picture of Sheffield trade unions that it appeared acceptable for a magistrate to stretch the law in combating them. Sheffield MP Mr Ward, claimed that he had risked his seat 'by his attempts to bring home to the working men of Sheffield the evils they entertained upon themselves by the extent to which they carried their associations'. He felt that their activities 'were destructive to all proper subordination, and fraught with ruin to the trade of the town'.[103]

Mr Henley warned that a return of Overend's convictions would not necessarily prove corruption or malice on his part, but rather the complexity of a difficult law that a layman was called upon to enforce. Alluding to recent appeals of magistrates' rulings, he argued 'there was no conviction so clear that a man might not be found to pick a hole in it; but the Government in this case sat quietly down, and gave the magistrate no protection whatsoever'. He warned against Parliament investigating judicial proceedings, as 'this course was a direct premium to tempt persons to make that House the judge in matters with which … it had nothing at all to do'.[104]

It was clear by the end of the debate that although Parliament would authorize the publication of the return and the memorials, Overend had nothing to fear. As distrustful as some members of Parliament were of magistrates over-reaching

---

[101]   'The Case of the Workmen of Sheffield Against Mr. Overend, as It Occurred in the House of Commons on Tuesday May 18', *ST* (22 May 1847), p. 2; *Hansard Debates*, Vol. 92, cols. 1056–62.

[102]   Ibid.

[103]   Ibid.

[104]   Ibid.

their authority, they feared powerful trade unions more. Many in the House of Commons might have begun to feel that magistrates needed greater government support and guidance in the performance of their duties to protect them from this type of action.

In conclusion, the protest against Wilson Overend highlights the important role that trade unions' legal activities and direct action had in fighting the administration of unjust labor laws and contributing to law reform debates during the mid nineteenth century. The protest also, however, is useful for examining the interaction of three different types of law and authority in Sheffield. By the 1840s, the local expectations and customs for regulating trade and negotiating prices had assumed a force of law among artisans and many small masters in Sheffield, despite the repeal of the statute and case law that had once underpinned its legitimacy. These traditions were highly favorable to Sheffield artisans, provoking some employers in Sheffield to use statutes that were heavily weighted to their advantage, and locally administered by friendly magistrates, to upset this system of bargaining and control of the trade. Indeed, the master and servant statutes and 1825 Combination Laws Repeal Amendment Act were both at their core designed to limit the framework and boundaries within which bargaining could take place to advantage employers and limit the freedom of workers.[105] In the industrial regions magistrates were often not seen as neutral arbiters, but rather as agents of the employers.

Earlier chapters have shown that trade union representatives demonstrated great skill in mobilizing the precedents and formalism of the higher courts to fight back against the coercive elements of magistrate-administered labor law. Trade unions in Sheffield showed themselves equal to this challenge as well, hiring skilled attorneys who made strong arguments at the Petty Sessions and were prepared to contest magistrates' rulings at the Quarter Sessions. These lawyers used every available legal method (including the precedents developed by previous union-funded litigation) to impede the use of these acts. As Roberts did in Warrington three months earlier, these representatives eventually felt that a more public remedy was needed to expose the partnership between Overend and the Manufacturers' Protection Society. They hoped both to exploit, and contribute to, concerns regarding the enforcement of law at the local level by lay magistrates. In this case, however, Overend had more accurately anticipated than did labor where the high courts and Parliament were going with respect to trade union law. Parliament showed itself to be far more afraid of powerful unions than arbitrary magistrates, and its response signals the beginnings of the reform of summary justice.

---

[105]   Hay and Craven, 'Introduction', in *Masters, Servants, and Magistrates in Britain and the Empire, 1562–1955* (London, 1977), p. 36.

Chapter 6

The Reform of Magistrates' Summary Jurisdiction, 1843–1854: 'The imperious necessity of affording greater protection to justices'

Introduction

Previous chapters have demonstrated that it could be difficult to be a magistrate. Most lacked formal legal training, yet were expected to administer complex statutes defined by an ever-expanding body of confusing higher court case-law. They had responsibility for preserving peace and order, but few resources to assist them in these efforts. As the individuals who enforced most local labor law, they adjudicated disputes of the most bitter and divisive nature, and sometimes their personal background made it hard to maintain the perception that they were neutral rather than a party to the conflict. Parliament passed statutes granting them summary jurisdiction for the explicit purpose of providing fast, cheap and certain prosecutions, yet the higher courts exposed them to damages and embarrassment when they overlooked proper procedures and forms. Additionally, unlike judges of the higher courts, they were vulnerable to serious consequences for their errors or bad behavior and could be proceeded against with civil actions. The only saving grace for justices of the peace had been that in previous eras only in the rarest instances were their decisions scrutinized by the higher courts, so they could operate with a high degree of autonomy and discretion. Even in the 1840s, their rulings were, in fact, not often challenged. These challenges were increasing, however, and publicity that Roberts brought with every successful certiorari and habeas corpus greatly amplified the impact of every victory. A small number of successful suits for false imprisonment against magistrates could cause considerable concern for the entire bench. The Home Office pardon of the Warrington File forgers and the mass protest against Dr Overend were cautionary tales that made magistrates nervous when executing their judicial duties. The dangers of costs, damages and public humiliation appeared to be more immediate threats to magistrates after 1843. Throughout the 1840s justices of the peace and members of the legal community began to demand greater guidance and protection from Parliament.

In 1848 Attorney-General Sir John Jervis brought forward four bills to clarify and consolidate the forms and procedures to be followed by magistrates in their judicial duties. The Summary Proceedings Bill was especially helpful because it included template forms of warrants, summonses, informations, convictions and committals in its schedules, making them much more difficult to challenge for technical errors. These acts were passed in 1848–1849.[1] The *Justice of the Peace* heavily promoted the Jervis Acts, but soon expressed doubts and anxiety over whether Queen's Bench would interpret the template form for a warrant of commitment that appeared in the schedules of the Summary Jurisdiction Act as applying to master and servant commitments. This anxiety was soon relieved because the higher courts followed Parliament's intentions. By the mid-1850s they were much more reluctant to overturn magistrates' rulings due to errors of form. The impact of the loss of labor's ability to use certiorari and habeas corpus effectively is illuminated by the case study of *R. v. Collier* and *R. v. Bailey* (1854). This case demonstrates that this transformation did not simply protect magistrates from 'technical quibbling', but also prevented workers from redressing very serious injustices.

The Magistrates' Reaction to High Court Scrutiny

The litigation funded by organized labor was part of a larger increase in the scrutiny of magistrates' summary rulings. Many blamed this increase on the legal profession, for whom it had become a 'lucrative source of practice to dispute magistrates' proceedings'.[2] Perhaps a sign of the times, *The New Practice of Attournies in the Courts of Law at Westminster, With Forms* (1844) promised its readers that it would 'aid the younger members of the profession in detecting technical errors in the forms of their adversaries, and will at once indicate the mode of taking advantage of such errors'. A reviewer for the *Justice of the Peace*, writing for an audience that frequently suffered from these errors, opened with the disclaimer 'we shall of course be understood, not to be speaking of a commendation of a system for which such instruction is necessary'.[3]

In another 1844 book review of a *Guide to the Crown Side of Queen's Bench*, the author was 'inclined to believe that the extraordinary increase in the business of the Crown Side of Queen's Bench' was due to the growth of the solicitors' profession. He lamented that 'one most obvious effect is that technical objections to summary proceedings have increased, is increasing, and it is for the public to say, whether it ought to be diminished'. He called his readers to action, suggesting 'if the public does not, magistrates ought to bestir themselves to attain an alteration of the law in this particular'. In what could be a reference to both the work of Roberts and the reporting of the *Northern Star*, the author complained:

---

[1]   11 & 12 Victoria, c.42, 43, 44 (1848); 12 & 13 Victoria, c.18.

[2]   'Notices of New Works', *JP* 8/25 (23 June 1844), p. 423.

[3]   'Notices of New Works', *JP* 8/16 (20 April 1844), p. 268.

a justice of the peace is in danger ... from merely attempting to carry out the ill-expressed intentions of the legislature; and such is the ignorance of the public that it hails with satisfaction a decision against him, though the offender has been discharged on mere technical grounds, and eluded the punishment due to his misconduct ... We apprehend ... that the practice of attorneys will soon prove to be so vexatious that individuals will be obliged to decline the acceptance of the office, rather than be martyrs for the public good. The forms of conviction and commitment are ... as intricate as the forms in the courts of common law; and yet, in those courts, a functionary is not visited with damages for adopting an incorrect form.

He argued for a distinction between technical errors and corrupt or malicious ones, with only the latter as grounds for actions.[4]

The rulings from labor-funded litigation added to magistrates' frustration with the increasing high-court scrutiny. Chapter 1 described magistrates' frequent complaints over the higher courts' confusing interpretation of the scope of master and servant law. They also regularly expressed dismay over the rulings of Queen's Bench regarding the form of valid warrants of commitment in these cases. From their perspective, just as they learned the rules for making proper commitments, the rules were changed. Between 1843 and 1846, magistrates learned that their warrants of commitment would be found defective if they failed to state explicitly that the evidence had been given under oath, or that the prisoner had been present when the evidence was heard. Other cases informed them their commitments needed to state that the agreement had been entered into by the prisoner or that the contract was in writing; or that the magistrate was acting in the county where he had jurisdiction; or that the servant's absence was in fact an 'unlawful' one. It was a lot to remember, and in many cases it appeared that magistrates were being asked to anticipate the higher courts. One author lamented that being exposed to damages based upon these fluid rules was like being convicted under an '*ex post*

---

[4] 'Notices of New Works', *JP* 8/25 (23 June 1844), p. 423. Some were skeptical of the argument that summary hearings should be held to a higher standard because the accused was deprived of the protection of the petty jury. One correspondent to the *Justice of the Peace*, observed that historically 'Trial by jury has been well known to be the palladium, etc., of English Liberty ... although all along the jurors were abundantly ignorant'. He argued that 'in truth, the whole jury system is founded on the principle of ignorance or being ignorant'. He described the paradox of having 'a case is prepared by a skilled attorney, is conducted by learned counsel, and ... summed up by a learned judge; but the decision on all this is left to ignorant men'. According to this analysis, 'ignorant' jurors were at least as likely to make an erroneous judgment as lay magistrates, but the jury system was invested with deep reverence from the public. 'To the Editors of the Justice of the Peace', *JP* 9/17 (26 April 1845), p. 287.

facto law.[5] Roberts' cases of *Tordoft* (1844), *Hammond* (1846) and *Leigh* (1848) created particular vexation among magistrates and legal commentators.

R. v. Tordoft (1844) was troublesome because the convicting magistrates had used the form for commitment provided in the commonly-used justices' manuals *Burns's Justice of the Peace* and *D'Oyly & Williams Justice of the Peace*. The *Justice of the Peace* journal reported Tordoft with several other recent master and servant discharges by Queen's Bench, complaining:

> These ill-conditioned statutes, which seem to serve no other purpose than to put costs into attorneys' pockets and extract them from justices', have afforded, during the last term, numerous instances of the unsuccessful application of them. We are really almost disposed to recommend justices have nothing to do with them.[6]

The journal warned its readers that the commitment forms in popular manuals could no longer safely be used. The author expressed fear that the Queen's Bench ruling that commitments needed to state that the prisoner was present during the hearing of evidence given under oath meant, 'not one commitment out of ten will stand good or be sustainable, in cases where a good conviction is not produced'.[7]

Magistrates writing to the *Justice of the Peace* expressed similar opinions about the 1844 rulings of Queen's Bench in master and servant cases. One magistrate, after reading about another discharge, argued that 'the state of the law is awful, and justices should come to a general understanding to petition Parliament for greater protection in cases where their well-intentioned proceedings are upset by what really appears in many instances to be the almost capricious quibbling of the judges'.[8] The courts were adding requirements to the warrant of commitment that were contrary to the longstanding practice of magistrates. For example, the writers at the *Justice of the Peace* observed that Wightman 'has decided contrary to the general practice' that the warrant of commitment needed to state that the magistrate signed the document in the county where he had jurisdiction. They complained that this 'had never been the usual' procedure. The author suggested that 'it will now, of course, be advisable to adopt' the practice.[9]

Tordoft represented a surprise for magistrates, but Hammond (1846) was shocking to much of the legal community. When the habeas corpus was reported in December 1845, the *Justice of the Peace* exclaimed, 'we cannot believe that the Court of Queen's Bench would propound and establish the doctrine that the evidence must be set out in the commitment'. The law experts felt that the

---

[5] 'Notices of New Works', *JP* 8/25 (23 June 1844), p. 423.

[6] 'The Recent Discharges On Writs of Habeas Corpus, of Persons Committed Under the Statutes Relating to Servants, Artificers, Etc.', *JP* 8/20 (18 May 1844), p. 323.

[7] Ibid.

[8] 'Practical Points', *JP* 8/23 (8 June 1844), pp. 381–2.

[9] 'Practical Points', *JP* 8/20 (18 May 1844) p. 333.

commitment should not have to recite the evidence because 'by no very forced implication' it could be understood that this material was stated in a conviction form, even when one was not presented. The author regretted that the quashing of commitments was becoming 'too common, and calculated to produce in the law all the obscurity and surprisal which prevailed before the law reports were published as they are at present'. He also warned the judges to consider 'that it is very dangerous and very injurious to call into question settled decisions; it is most unjust to magistrates, and most injurious to those parties whose remedy is thus causelessly allowed to be questioned'.[10]

In Re: *Hammond* produced a number of letters to the editor to the *Justice of the Peace*. One letter similar to the alarmist response to Tordoft expressed concern that 'the validity of almost every warrant of commitment now in force under this statute will be questioned should those before the court be declared bad'. Magistrates and their clerks were not in the habit of reciting the evidence in the warrant of commitment. The editorial staff predicted that the court would uphold Hammond's commitment, telling the correspondent not worry because 'we can hardly believe that such an objection was taken, still less, that it was called one of importance'. They asked 'what lawyer or practical man ever set out the evidence in the warrant of commitment?'[11] The judges of Queen's Bench provided a surprising answer.

By June of 1846, the *Justice of the Peace* had learned more about the peculiar construction of the warrant of commitment in Hammond's case, which did not refer to, or recite, a previous conviction, and purported on its face to 'convict'. The journal explained the ruling to its readers, while expressing dissatisfaction with the decision. The author observed that because the document presented in this case blended the conviction and the commitment, the court ruled that it needed to have all of the information required for both. It made the recommendation that magistrates should always have both an instrument of conviction and a warrant of commitment ready to send up to the higher courts as protection. This practice adopted, then *Lindsay v. Leigh* (1848) made it obsolete with the ruling that the warrant of commitment was the only instrument that the 1823 Act intended for justifying the imprisonment, and a conviction form was not required. After 1848, the validity of the imprisonment depended upon the legality of the warrant commitment alone, raising the question of the form this document should take.[12]

The confusing state of the law had costly implications for active magistrates. In the summer of 1844, Roberts settled actions of false imprisonment against a group of Durham magistrates for £200 and all legal costs. A year later he won £30

---

[10]   'Servants – Form of Commitment – Railway Labourers, Whether Within the Acts', *JP* 9/49 (6 December 1845), pp. 785–6.

[11]   'To The Editors of the Justice of the Peace – Ex Parte John Hammond', *JP* 9/49 (6 December 1845), p. 799; 'To the Editors of the Justice of the Peace – Servants – Commitment', *JP* 9/52 (27 December 1845), p. 847.

[12]   'Commitments under the Master and Servants Act', *JP* 10/23 (6 June 1846), pp. 353–4.

and all costs from Col. Lindsay. In September of 1846, John Owen won £120 and costs against magistrates who imprisoned seven Rhondda colliers with informal warrants of commitment.[13] Given the complexity of master and servant law, and the publicity that these damages received, it is not surprising that magistrates increasingly demanded greater indemnity from Parliament for 'honest' errors committed when carrying out their duties.

In early 1845, after four South Staffordshire miners had their convictions overturned by Queen's Bench, the *Justice of the Peace* led with an article on 'The Liability of Justices of the Peace to Actions in the Exercise of Summary Jurisdiction'. The article complained that the parties most responsible for the 'error and confusion' of summary hearings were not the ones exposed to civil damages. The statutes that magistrates were asked to interpret contained 'the most inapposite provisions conveyed in language committing every possible offence against orthography and syntactical arrangement'. Rather than clarify the situation, the higher courts had done 'more than their due share' to make the law 'the converse of certainty'. Magistrates were the only judicial officials subject to damages for erroneous judgments, causing the author to complain 'not to speak disrespectfully, error absolutely pervades the superior courts; but the judges sit far out of reach of consequences, unharmed and fearless of actions for damages'.

He argued that the law should prohibit suits against magistrates based upon 'errors in form or technical inaccuracies' that 'do not touch the merits' of a case, and provide relief only when a party could prove he or she was 'oppressively or maliciously dealt with'. After all, 'why should a person be freed from the just punishment of an offence … because there is some insignificant technical error in the proceedings, or a misunderstanding of the precise meaning of an act of Parliament?' He insisted that, 'some measure should be adopted to protect not only magistrates and their clerks, who are frequently responsible in pocket for unavoidable errors, but the public itself for the injury inflicted by such a state of law'. The article concluded with a reminder that the public suffered when summary proceedings were quashed on a technical flaw because the injured party lost the remedy promised by the law, diluting confidence in its institutions.[14]

A month later, a jury's award of heavy damages against a magistrate for a technical error in a game-law prosecution prompted the *Justice of the Peace* to again assert 'the imperious necessity of affording greater protection to justices in the multifarious duties of their office'. Though responding to a poacher's legal victory over a magistrate, the article addressed the state of magistrates' summary proceedings in general, including those under master and servant statutes. The article complained that 'it is almost incredible that … a magistrate should be subject to heavy damages and costs for the omission of a single word in the form

---

[13]   NA: HO 43/67, 17 July 1844, 3 September 1844; J. H. Morris and L. J. Williams, *The South Wales Coal Industry, 1841–1875* (Cardiff, 1958), pp. 267–8.

[14]   'Liability of Justices of the Peace To Actions in the Exercise of The Summary Jurisdiction', *JP* 9/5 (1 February 1845), pp. 65–6.

of his adjudication, which with such omission was just as intelligible to any reader of common sense'. The author then described 'the whole of summary jurisdiction' as a snare used by poachers [attorneys] 'to trap unwary justices'. He criticized those writers who celebrated victories over magistrates, or portrayed civil actions against these officers 'as commending the ingredients of the poisoned chalice to the lips of the poisoner'. He tied the interests of magistrates with the public, warning 'every offender who escapes on a technical flaw is … thereby encouraged'. The prisoner freed on a technicality was not in terror of the law, but 'pocketed some score of pounds of justices' money and received the congratulations of his friends'. The *Justice of the Peace* insisted that 'we strongly recommend that justices take some steps to secure to themselves better protection than they now receive in their onerous office' as it 'cannot … much longer remain in this ineffective condition'.[15]

The *Justice of the Peace* revisited the issue of defective warrants again in July 1845. In yet another article on the subject, the journal demanded greater protection for magistrates who issued defective warrants of commitment in cases where 'their good faith was manifest'. The author suggested that because acts of Parliament were so confusing,

> so doubtful, indeed, that one court after another may be divided as to the construction to be given to them, it is a little too much to say that … [magistrates] should be liable to actions for damages if, in carrying out their honest intention, should they commit some small error in form.

Justices, according to the article, were 'made accountable for the most petty informality of statement'. They were entitled to protection when acting in good faith, and should agitate for reform.[16] The *Justice of the Peace* warned its readers that 'If justices continue to submit to this legal martyrdom, they have, we verily believe, only themselves to blame. They might obtain an equitable adjustment in the law, if they would exert themselves'.[17]

Another article complained that given the higher courts' dislike of summary proceedings, and the closeness with which they scrutinized magistrates' forms, 'there is little hope … of any allowance being made for errors on the face of the conviction'. Other articles in that journal alluded to the factors discouraging magistrates from acting, including the frequent reports and newspaper articles criticizing their rulings.[18] A common theme in these articles was that by freeing

---

[15] 'Actions against Justices for Technical Errors', *JP* 9/12 (22 March 1845), pp. 177–8.

[16] 'Liability of Justices on Matters of Form; Bona Fides', *JP* 9/29 (19 July 1845), pp. 451–2.

[17] 'For What Offences Justices Cannot Commit Servants Under the Master and Servant Acts', *JP* 10/43 (24 October 1846), pp. 674–5.

[18] 'Claim of Right as a Defense to Summary Convictions', *JP* 11/45 (6 November 1847), pp. 785–6; 'Magistrates Bound to Exercise Discretion and Judgment in All Cases',

prisoners on technical flaws in warrants, the high courts were diminishing the dread of punishment, and encouraging them to re-offend.[19]

Correspondents to the *Justice of the Peace* also contributed suggestions for reform. One writer included among his list of 'Suggestions for an Act for Improving the Summary Jurisdiction of Justices of the Peace' that 'Justices should not be answerable for error in judgment or informality in proceedings'. Another writer included a list of 28 suggestions for an act of Parliament to improve the summary hearings of magistrates. Suggestion 13 was that the act should include official template forms of informations, summonses, convictions, warrants and commitments to help magistrates. Number 22 proposed an increase in the amount of the sureties required for an appeal to Quarter Sessions, insisting that prosecutors and magistrates be given a one-week notice of such appeals. Item 25 requested that

> No action to be brought against any justice for any conviction, or any thing done in connection therewith, unless the justice shall have convicted the party of some offence not punishable by summary conviction, or in some penalty not authorised to be imposed for the offence of which he has been guilty, or unless it be alleged and proved that the proceedings of the justice were done maliciously and without probable cause.

The correspondent stressed the importance and necessity of these reforms, observing:

> The reports of cases in Queen's Bench every succeeding term, show that the commitments, warrants, convictions and orders of justices, though drawn up in many instances by barristers of first reputation, are constantly quashed on some unimportant technical error, the merits being wholly untouched. Great expense is hereby incurred by Justices, whilst the purity of their motives and intentions is never questioned.

Previous chapters have demonstrated that the purity of the magistrates' motives were, in fact, regularly and loudly questioned. The author concluded his letter by reminding readers that not only magistrates, but the public at large suffered from the uncertainty created when 'summary convictions are quashed for want of form at the instance of one party'.[20] Many of the suggestions in this letter are strikingly

---

JP 9/32 (9 August 1845), pp. 500–501; 'The Kingswinford Case: Necessities of Summary Jurisdiction', *JP* 9/33 (16 August 1845), pp. 513–14; 'Notice of the Intention to Sue Out a Writ of Certiorari', *JP* 9/34 (23 August 1845), pp. 529–30. In one case of gross magisterial error in Staffordshire, the journal lamented that 'the press has not failed to exaggerate and denounce the whole business in its usual style'.

[19]   'Society for Promoting the Amendment of the Law', *JP* 11/9 (27 February 1847), pp. 147–8.

[20]   'To the Editors of the Justice of the Peace', *JP* 9/40 (4 October 1845), p. 655; 'To the Editors of the Justice of the Peace', *JP* 9/47 (22 November 1845), p. 767.

similar to clauses that appeared in the Summary Justice Act and Vexatious Actions Act of 1848.

The Jervis Acts, 1846–1848

In May of 1846, Lord Brougham brought a bill to protect justices against vexatious actions brought against them for the performance of their duty. The *Justice of the Peace* commented that, although 'we were in hopes that some more effectual protection would have been proposed by the bill than it will give', Brougham's bill provided more 'than the small amount of protection they already receive'. The bill proposed to increase the notice magistrates received of actions against them, and gave prosecutors only six months to commence such suits. It also made it easier for magistrates to recover costs in cases where they successfully defended themselves. A year later a version of the bill passed the House of Lords, only to languish in committee in the House of Commons.[21] By the end of the year, however, Attorney-General Sir John Jervis was prepared to offer a more comprehensive solution to the difficulties magistrates confronted. He gave notice of his intention to bring forward four bills to consolidate and clarify the rules and forms relating to commitments for indictable offences, summary hearings, actions against magistrates and the holding of Petty Sessions.

On 3 February 1848, Jervis brought the four bills before Parliament. He sought to steer clear of the controversy over expanding magistrates' summary jurisdiction, stating 'though there might be difference of opinion in the House as to the expediency of intrusting to the unpaid magistracy the large powers they now possessed, all must agree that it was [Parliament's] … duty to afford all possible assistance to the gentlemen who discharged such duties'. He informed the House that his intent was to consolidate in a few acts, the rules, forms and procedures of magistrates' various judicial functions, which were spread across numerous statutes and high-court rulings. He insisted that the Indictable Offences Bill and the Summary Proceedings Bill contained nothing new, but merely collected and clarified established rules, and appended a useful schedule of official forms. These two bills were for the most part well-received by Parliament.

The third of the Jervis Acts, the Vexatious Actions Against Justices Bill, also received a mostly favorable reception in the House of Commons. Mr Cripps argued forcefully in favor of giving magistrates greater civil immunity in their judicial duties. In what was possibly a reference to Roberts, he complained 'it was becoming common practice to bring actions against magistrates, for the mere purpose of harassing them, for what the parties were pleased to call illegal

---

[21]   'Vexatious Actions, Protection Against', *JP* 10/21 (23 May 1846), p. 325; 'A Bill, Intitled an Act For Protecting From Vexatious Actions Persons Discharging Public Duties', *JP* 11/26 (26 June 1847), pp. 451–2; 'Legislative Intelligence', *JP* 11/28 (10 July 1847), pp. 497–9.

commitments'. Cripps warned that he knew of three 'most respectable and highly intelligent magistrates' who were on the verge of resigning their commissions 'because they had been harassed with actions'. He added that even when these magistrates successfully defended their rulings, 'they were put to £15 or £20 expense, and worried for merely doing their duty'.

The only member who spoke against giving additional protection to magistrates was Joseph Hume, who expressed doubts regarding the competence and fairness of the magistracy, doubts which Roberts' work reinforced. He argued 'that if the public were not to have the protection of the law, or of the dread of the law, against improper proceedings of the Justices of the Peace, the Government ... should prevent any one being appointed a justice till he ... was known to be qualified'. He stated that out of his duty to 'protect the liberties of the people' he would 'protest any protection being granted to these unpaid magistrates, unless there was some regulation regarding their qualifications and acquaintance with the law'. Hume agreed, however, with the two consolidation bills, which he felt were 'very proper'.[22]

The *Justice of the Peace* gave considerable coverage to the content of these bills, as 'subjects of greater interest to ... our readers ... could scarcely be suggested'. The editors were for the most part pleased with the bills' content, and informed Jervis that 'we wish him all imaginable success'.[23] Between February and April 1848, the journal devoted four cover articles to explaining the proposals in the acts, and contained several other articles making recommendations for amendment.[24] The Summary Proceedings Bill and the Protection of Justices from Vexatious Actions Bill passed in the House of Commons on 16 June 1848. A little over a month later the House of Lords passed the bills, which received Royal Assent on 14 August 1848.

The first section of the Vexatious Actions Act stated that any action against a magistrate for things done in the execution of his duty had to allege expressly that the magistrate had behaved maliciously, and without any reasonable or probable case. The second clause gave a cause of action without an allegation of malice only in cases where a justice acted without any jurisdiction, or delivered a sentence

---

[22]   *Hansard Debates*, Vol. 96, cols. 4–7; 'The House of Commons – The Law Relating to Magistrates', *JP* 12/6 (5 February 1848), p. 84.

[23]   'Jurisdiction of Justices of the Peace Out of Sessions With Respect to Indorsing Warrants of Apprehension', *JP* 12/2 (8 January 1848), pp. 17–18.

[24]   'The Administration of Justice Bill (No.1)', and 'Courts of Special and Petty Sessions Bill', *JP* 12/8 (19 February 1848), pp. 113–15; 'The Administration of Justice Bill (No.2)' and 'Protection of Justices From Vexatious Actions Bill', *JP* 12/9 (26 February 1848), pp. 129–30, 132–3; 'The Administration of Justice Bill, (No.2)', *JP* 12/10 (4 March 1848), pp. 145–6; 'Protection of Justices from Vexatious Actions', and 'The Attorney-General's New Bills', *JP* 12/14 (1 April 1848), pp. 209–10. Some recommendations made by the *Justice of the Peace* were adopted, including one that clarified the language of Section 10 of the final act.

which exceeded the statue he was acting under, but only if the conviction or order was first quashed by Queen's Bench. The act also required that prosecutors give magistrates a one-month notice of any action against them, and placed a statute of limitations of six months on suits against these officials. Section 13 of the act limited the damages for imprisonment under a bad conviction or order to only two pence without costs if it was proven that the plaintiff was actually guilty of the offence of which he or she was convicted.[25] One can see many of the magistrates' recommendations for greater protection in this bill, particularly the distinction between 'technicalities' and the 'merits of the case' implied by Sections 1 and 13.

Osborne argues that the Summary Proceedings Act used material salvaged from scores of statutes and high court rulings to create a 'great highway' for guiding summary hearings. He exclaims that 'it is not possible to exaggerate the importance and significance of the legislation of 1848' because it paved the way for 'the tremendous expansion of summary jurisdiction which developed in the nineteenth century'.[26] In addition to clearly consolidating and describing the proper procedures to follow in summary hearings, the schedule of this act contained 37 fill-in-the-blanks short template forms for different types of summons, warrant, order, information, conviction, commitment and certificate. Section 17 of the act authorized the use of its forms of conviction and orders for acts that did not specify a precise form, which was thought at the time to include master and servant statutes.[27] These short forms reduced the value of certiorari by including very little information about the case on their face. The *Justice of the Peace* praised the three Jervis Acts (the Act Regulating Petty Sessions passed in May 1849), suggesting that the 1848 session of Parliament, 'in regard to effective reforms in matters connected with the criminal law, it may fearlessly challenge competition with any of its predecessors'.[28]

A case initiated by Roberts, however, created doubts about the value of these acts. In *Lindsay v. Leigh* (1848), the court ruled that a conviction form was unnecessary under the 1823 Act, and that a commitment was the only instrument Parliament intended for justifying imprisonment. The schedules of Summary Justice Act, 11 & 12 Victoria, c.43 (1848), contained a form for a conviction (form I.3), and a form for a warrant of commitment based upon a conviction (form

---

[25] 11 & 12 Victoria, c.44 (1848), s.1, 2, 8, 9, 13.

[26] Bertram Osborne, *The Justice of the Peace, 1361–1848: A History of the Justices of the Peace for the Counties of England* (Dorset, 1960), pp. 225–8. These sentiments are echoed in Sir Thomas Skyrme, *History of the Justice of the Peace* (3 vols., Chichester, 1991), Vol. 2, p. 177 and Bruce P. Smith, 'Circumventing the Jury: Petty Crime and Summary Justice in London and New York City, 1790–1855' (PhD dissertation, Yale University, 1996), pp. 463–6. Smith also suggests that the legitimacy conferred by the Jervis Acts eased the further expansion of magistrates' summary jurisdiction.

[27] Robert Steinfeld, *Coercion, Contract and Free Labour in the Nineteenth Century* (Cambridge, 2001), p. 158.

[28] 'Administration of Criminal Justice', *JP* 12/38 (16 September 1848), pp. 609–10.

O.1), but there was no form for a warrant of commitment issued alone in the first instance.[29] So conditioned were magistrates to harsh scrutiny from Queen's Bench, that many expressed doubt as to the applicability of the Jervis Acts' forms to master and servant proceedings, even though it was repeatedly acknowledged that the legislature clearly intended them to apply. In a review of a book explaining the Jervis Acts, the reviewer stated 'whatever the intention of the legislature may have been, there are various duties of a justice ... which it is presumed do not come within these enactments'. Among these duties was 'the commitment of a servant under 4 George IV, c.34 (1823)'. The editors responded to several letters to 'Practical Points' on this subject in the months after the Jervis Acts passed. The editors explained to readers that in *Lindsay v. Leigh* (1848) 'the court said that it clearly appeared that the commitment, by whatever name it is called, is the only instrument ... to exist in such cases', and 'the recent statute ... has no application to cases in which a commitment issues in the first instance, without the intervention of a conviction', so the Jervis Acts did not apply to master and servant convictions under 4 George IV, c.34 (1823).[30]

On 7 October 1848 the issue of the *Justice of the Peace* led with an article describing the new dilemma magistrates faced when enforcing the 'ill-omened' Master and Servant Acts, the question of the applicability of the forms in 11 & 12 Victoria, c.43 (1848). Although the Jervis Act 'was no doubt intended to be of universal application, and to comprehend these proceedings', it appeared that because of *Lindsay v. Leigh* magistrates would have to continue using the old confusing form of the warrant of commitment. 'Owing to some extraordinary obliquity of vision' Parliament had not considered this ruling. Magistrates could use the order forms in the Summary Proceedings Act for wage orders brought under 4 George IV, c.34 (1823), but the Act's useful forms did not apply to the imprisonment of workers. After describing the current state of master and servant law, the article closed by observing 'the difficulties of obtaining the summary punishment of a servant were already sufficiently great'. The discovery that the Jervis Acts would not apply to these cases was 'a most unfortunate omission, and one which will be seriously felt'.[31] As late as 1860, magistrates continued to write to the law officers of the crown, asking whether the 11 & 12 Victoria, c.43 applied

---

[29] 'Of a Warrant of Commitment Under the Master and Servant Acts', *JP* 12/12 (18 March 1848), p. 178.

[30] In answer to another letter, the editors stated that it 'appears from Lindsay v. Leigh the commitment is the only instrument required in such cases ... they cannot fall within this statute [11 & 12 Victoria, c.43] which only applies to those cases in which either a conviction or an order has been made'. 'Notices of New Works', and 'Practical Points', *JP* 12/39 (23 September 1848), pp. 631, 636–9; 'Practical Points', *JP* 12/40 (30 September 1848), p. 652; 'Practical Points', *JP* 12/41 (7 October 1848), p. 667.

[31] 'Proceedings in Matters Relating to Servants', *JP* 12/41 (7 October 1848), pp. 658–9; David Philips, *Crime and Authority in Victorian England: The Black Country, 1835–1860* (London, 1978), pp. 132–6.

to cases under the Master and Servant Acts, requesting further legislation to clarify the matter. The law officers responded that they had no doubts whatsoever that the forms in the Jervis Acts did apply to master and servant proceedings.[32]

In this instance, the *Justice of the Peace* incorrectly anticipated the higher courts. Steinfeld has observed that the replacement of Lord Denman with Lord Campbell at Queen's Bench coincided with a changed approach toward reading the forms from magistrates' summary hearings. Parliament continued to expand the types of cases that magistrates could hear and determine summarily, passing acts in 1847, 1853 and 1855, which gave them jurisdiction over most juvenile thefts, juvenile assaults and simple larcenies.[33] As the judicial system grew more dependent upon magistrates acting summarily, and the legislature appointed more professional stipendiary magistrates and gave these officers clearer guidelines for forms and procedures, the Courts in Westminster became more inclined to support magistrates' rulings. In Re: *Geswood* (1853), the Queen's Bench asserted that the warrant of commitment in master and servant convictions did not need to set out the evidence, and that Section 17 of 11 & 12 Victoria, c.43 (1848) did, in fact, apply. Magistrates who used the forms in the schedule of that act for commitments under the master and servant law would now be safe from being overturned.[34] The Court of Queen's Bench was even more emphatic in the case of Re: Bailey, Re: Collier (1854).

Re: *Bailey*, Re: *Collier* (1854)

Although Roberts promised that he would contest every attempt by mine-owners to use master and servant law to discipline their employees, and though to contemporaries 'he seemed to be everywhere at once', there were practical limits to the number of cases he could challenge.[35] Taking the rulings of magistrates before Queen's Bench was an expensive proposition, and unions had to choose where to make their stand. The cases that unions chose to challenge were ones in which there was unfairness in the magistrates' hearing. The legal rules that governed writs of certiorari and habeas corpus sometimes forced Roberts to argue points which were not obviously connected to this unfairness, but he nonetheless was often able to free his clients. As long as the courts gave a strict reading to the warrants of commitment in a very high proportion of cases there were usually at least some grounds for quashing magistrates' rulings on 'technical flaws'. This provided an imperfect remedy that labor could use to correct outcomes from a

---

[32] NA: HO 45/7003.

[33] Skyrme, *History of the Justice of the Peace*, Vol. 2, p. 178; 16 & 17 Victoria, c.30; 18 & 19 Victoria, c.126.

[34] Steinfeld, *Coercion*, p. 158.

[35] Friedrich Engels, *The Conditions of the Working Class in England* (London, 1845), p. 189.

few of the worst conducted summary proceedings, even if it could not afford to challenge every single conviction. In the 1840s this had been a valuable safety valve for labor.

Labor lost the war by winning too many battles. As Steinfeld notes, 'It became apparent to the Courts by the 1850s that matters had gotten out of hand'.[36] Instead of preserving the law's legitimacy, members of Parliament recognized that the actions of Roberts were undermining the magistrates who conducted much of the business of the criminal justice system. With the Jervis Acts, Parliament provided better guidance and protection for magistrates, and the higher courts soon followed suit by taking a less rigorous view of magistrates' forms. Legal historians argue that the legitimacy of summary jurisdiction improved with the enactment of Jervis Acts.[37] But were summary hearings between employer and employee conducted with greater fairness after 1848? Here the answer is much more doubtful.

One decisive defeat for organized labor on each of the three fronts of the 'struggle over the rules' of master and servant case law was In Re: *Bailey* and In Re: *Collier* (1854), a case involving the conviction of two Welsh butty colliers.[38] All of the traditional arguments that labor solicitors and barristers had used to great effect during the 1840s were strongly rejected by a different Queen's Bench. As in some of the worst cases described in Chapter 3, the defendants in this case were prevented by a magistrate who had a conflict of interest from making their full defense and answer to the charges. Unlike the cases described above, Queen's Bench no longer provided a simple means of redress.

In early December 1853, over 60 miners working at Messrs. Marshall and Knowles' White Rose Colliery and Coke Works in Bedwelty left their employment without giving the required one month's notice. They claimed that their contract stipulated that they were to be paid the same as miners working at Messrs. Protheros' colliery, who had been given a raise on 1 December 1853. Marshall refused to match this raise, claiming that the agreement stated that his miners' wages were to match those paid by other collieries in the district generally, and not those at Messrs. Protheros' colliery specifically.

George Bailey and John Collier were butty colliers working at Messrs. Marshall's pits who had joined the strike. In many mining areas, including parts of South Wales and South Staffordshire, mine owners contracted with subcontractors called 'butties' to mine coal at a fixed rate per ton. The butty would then hire the workers and provide the small supplies. These subcontractors had usually been

---

[36]   Steinfeld, *Coercion*, p. 162.

[37]   Smith, 'Circumventing the Jury', pp. 463–6; Osborne, *Justice of the Peace*, pp. 227–8; Skyrme, *History of the Justice of the Peace*, p. 177. Though not among workers, see Willibald Steinmetz, 'Was There a De-Juridification of Employment Relations in Britain?', in Willibald Steinmetz (ed.) *Private Law and Social Inequality in the Industrial Age: Comparing the Legal Cultures of in Britain, France, Germany, and the United States* (London: Oxford University Press, 2000).

[38]   Steinfeld, *Coercion*, pp. 119–21, 144–5, 158–9.

seen by the courts as being outside of the definition of a contract of service. In fact, for the next several decades, the higher courts continued to rule that butty colliers were not servants under the 1831 Truck Act, and therefore had no ability to use that law to prosecute or claim wages against mine owners who paid them with goods, or truck, from company stores.[39]

On 9 December Bailey and Collier, who were on strike, went to the colliery office at the White Rose Colliery to collect November's pay, which Marshall still held in hand. Policemen arrested and handcuffed them at the office, keeping them in isolation in the local lockup overnight. The miners' friends hired solicitor John Owen to defend them, and at 10 a.m. the next day he went to the lockup and demanded to see his clients. The constable refused to permit him access to the prisoners.

At noon, the defendants, along with four other miners, were brought before magistrate George Homfray, the son of Samuel Homfray, a fellow magistrate and managing partner of the Tredgar Iron Works. They were charged with leaving their work without notice under 4 George IV, c.34 (1823). Owen, seeing his clients for the first time, demanded an adjournment so that he could confer with them and summon witnesses for their defense, particularly one of the agents of the works, Evan Jenkins. Owen offered to give bail personally for the defendants. According to Bailey and Collier, Homfray replied 'I will not adjourn it, the interests of the masters must be attended to'. Homfray denied making this statement, but acknowledged that he refused to adjourn the hearing. Owen threatened to withdraw from the case, stating that he could not provide a defense without being permitted to confer with his clients and summon witnesses. He insisted that Jenkins could give testimony about his clients' contract that would prove their innocence. He reminded Homfray that the 1823 statute, unlike the 1825 Combination Laws Repeal Amendment Act, did not allow for an appeal to Quarter Sessions. Because of this, it 'would be most unjust to convict a prisoner without giving him the opportunity to prove his innocence'. Homfray was unmoved, and insisted that the hearing go forward.

G. H. Hutchinson, an agent for Marshall and Knowles, was the only witness to testify, and he was cross-examined by Owen. One conflict in this case was whether the masters had voided the contract by failing to adhere to its terms. Another was a dispute over whether the contractual obligations of Bailey and Collier made them 'servants' within the statute. Owen tried to highlight these distinctions in his cross-examination of Hutchinson. Bailey and Collier, both butty colliers, claimed that they were not bound to any specific hours of working, nor obliged to cut a specific quantity of coal for their employers, and that no allowance was made for them when the trade was slack or the mine closed by accident. Hutchinson disputed this, stressing that the men were exclusively bound to the company, and

---

[39]   *Riley v. Warden* (1848); *Sharman v. Sanders* (1853); *SA* (15 November 1862), p. 7; Brian Napier, 'The Contract of Service: The Concept and Its Application' (D.Phil thesis, Cambridge University, 1975), pp. 113–14.

the company considered itself obliged in the event of an accident to provide the defendants with work or pay, and therefore they were servants.[40] Owen insisted that the higher courts had repeatedly excluded subcontractors from the scope of Master and Servant Acts. Owen also attempted to raise the fact that the employers had not lived up to their promise to pay the same wages as the Protheros' colliery. Hutchinson insisted that the (conveniently verbal) agreement stipulated that the miners would be paid the same rates as other mines in the neighborhood generally. In both instances, the magistrate believed Hutchinson. The two pitmen were sentenced to two months' imprisonment with hard labor without being allowed to summon witnesses to testify in their defense. Recognizing he was before a hostile tribunal, Owen negotiated with the employers for two of the other miners' return to work on the best terms he could obtain.[41] The employers had used the law to defeat a strike.

Owen initiated a habeas corpus to Queen's Bench. Collier and Bailey had already served over half of their sentence by the time Mr Justice Erle released them on recognizance pending the hearing of their case by the full court. He found the question of whether Bailey and Collier's agreements were valid mutually binding contracts a particularly difficult question that he should not determine alone.

On 1 May 1854 barrister Mr Smythies moved for the discharge of the prisoners, and Huddleston argued that they should be remanded to serve their full sentence. Smythies made three familiar arguments during the hearing. He argued that the magistrate did not have jurisdiction because there was not a mutually binding contract between the parties. Bailey and Collier's contracts did not oblige the employers to find work for the prisoners. Roberts had succeeded in quashing the conviction of James Lord (1848), using the established rule that minors could enter only beneficial contracts. Lord's contract was ruled 'inequitable and wholly void' by Lord Denman because it bound him to be available at all times during the term, but allowed the master to stop his work and wages any time it was convenient for him.[42] It was not clear if the court would accept such an argument in a case involving an adult. Recent precedents, such as *Pilkington v. Scott* (1846) and *R. v. Welch and Another* (1853), suggested that the Judges were prepared to read an obligation on the part of employers to find reasonable work, 'according to the state of the trade', into the contract of employment even if it was not explicitly stated. This would be sufficient consideration for the servant's promise to work exclusively for the employer.[43] Lord Campbell rejected Smythies' argument, finding that it could be assumed that Bailey's and Collier's contracts contained

---

[40]   This statement is actually double underlined in Hutchinson's affidavit. NA: KB 1/223/46.

[41]   NA: KB 1/222/9,10, 30, 31, KB 1/223/46, 47; Steinfeld, *Coercion*, pp. 119–22, 144–5, 158–9; In the Matter of George Bailey, In the Matter of John Collier, 118 E. R. 1269–75, 18 J. P. 630; 'Magistrates' Office', *MM* (16 December 1853), p. 5.

[42]   Steinfeld, *Coercion*, pp. 116–17.

[43]   Ibid.

an obligation on the part of the employers to employ the men, 'not necessarily ... day by day', but to provide enough work to 'continue the relation of master and servant'. Campbell suggested that if the employer 'causelessly' refused to find work for the men while the mine was operating, he would have voided the contract. This implied obligation, Campbell ruled, 'would be ample consideration for the servant's promise'.[44]

Related to the first argument, Smythies also suggested that the contract did not create a relationship of service, as was necessary to give the magistrate jurisdiction. He used affidavits from Bailey and Collier to prove that as subcontractors, the 'prisoners were at liberty to work or not to work as they pleased' and their agreement was not an exclusive one. Huddleston presented affidavits from Hutchinson and Homfray, and reminded the court that the question was not whether the magistrate drew the right conclusions from the evidence, but whether he could have reasonably inferred from that evidence that he had jurisdiction. Campbell agreed, noting 'if they [Bailey and Collier] showed that there was no evidence before the justice on which he was warranted in coming to the conclusion that there was a contract of service and a breach of it ... this would show he exceeded his jurisdiction'. But in the present case he found that there was enough evidence which 'fully warranted in inferring that there was a contract of service'.[45] Not raised was the fact that the defense had not been permitted to summon witnesses who would have clearly demonstrated that these butties were not in a relationship of service.

The final argument was that the warrant of commitment in this case was a commitment and a conviction in the same document, and was therefore deficient because it did not set out the evidence, or state on its face that the evidence was taken under oath and in the presence of the prisoners. Smythies cited a wide range of Roberts' cases, including *Lindsay v. Leigh* (1848), In Re: *Gray* (1844), and *R. v. Tordoft* (1844). Huddleston's argument is interesting considering that he had been the victorious counsel in all of these cases. He argued that the instrument in this case was not a hybrid conviction/commitment, but a simple warrant of commitment founded upon a prior good conviction (which had not been presented to the court). Therefore, it was merely an order, and required none of the strict formalities of a conviction, citing a case in which he was the losing barrister, *R. v. Richards* (1844).

The Judges, in a clear break with the past, agreed with Huddleston. Mr Justice Erle ruled 'They who administer this law, have been repeatedly defeated by points of form, which no acuteness can foresee. The tendency of our decision will be to relieve them from peril as to many matters of form which on other occasions they have been found vulnerable'.[46] Mr Justice Campbell turned Smythies' argument on its head, by stating that though the commitment did not stipulate the defendants were present when the evidence was heard under oath, there 'was nothing to show

---

[44]   118 E. R. 1273–74; Steinfeld, *Coercion*, pp. 121–2.

[45]   Napier, 'Contract of Service', p. 113; 118 E. R. 1273.

[46]   18 J. P. 631–2.

that the witnesses were not, in point of fact, sworn, and examined in the presence of the prisoners'. He went on to note that there was nothing to show that 'the prisoners had not in fact had the full benefit of everything to which they were entitled'.[47]

Of course, the real tragedy of this case is that the prisoners did not get everything to which they were entitled. They did not get the opportunity to present a full defense and answer to the charges by calling the witnesses they required. By mid-century it was far more difficult to challenge injustices from magistrates' summary hearings. By 1857, it soon became apparent to legislators that the Common Law courts and Parliament had gone too far in one direction. Parliament decided to correct this imbalance, and passed 'An Act to Improve the Administration of the Law so Far as Respects Summary Proceedings before Justices of the Peace' (1857). This act gave parties who felt aggrieved by a magistrate's ruling the right to apply within three days for the magistrate to sign and state a case. This meant setting out the facts and evidence upon which the decision was based, and submitting it for opinion to one of the Superior Courts of Law in Westminster. This act allowed litigants in summary cases to get opinions from the high courts on questions of law without appearing to be punitive in tone toward magistrates. Sir George Grey felt that this act was necessary for maintaining the legitimacy that justified further expansion of magistrates' jurisdiction.[48]

In conclusion, between 1843 and 1848, Roberts often succeeded in challenging magistrates' rulings in master and servant cases because it gave Queen's Bench the opportunity to assert greater authority and control over magistrates' summary proceedings. By applying high legal standards to warrants of commitment and convictions judges were compensating for the lack of procedural protections in magistrates' summary hearings. These actions undermined the legitimacy of the magistracy and made their summary jurisdiction an important part of labor's critique of master and servant law. Roberts' legal campaign informed Chartist rhetoric and popular protests against the actions of individual magistrates. Justices of the peace complained that they were being unfairly victimized by being made responsible for the inevitable results of poorly constructed laws and confusing and contradictory rulings from the higher courts. They demanded better guidance and protection from Parliament, and legislators realized that if the inexpensive, speedy and certain remedies of summary jurisdiction were going to continue to expand, they would have to oblige. The Jervis Acts clarified the forms and procedures of magistrates' judicial duties, and provided them with civil immunity from all but the most egregious abuses of their powers. These acts and the changing interpretations of the higher courts closed off a remedy used by unions to challenge unjust convictions under coercive labor laws. Roberts and his colleagues would have to find other resourceful ways to oppose imprisonment for breach of contract.

---

[47]   18 ER 1273.

[48]   20 & 21 Victoria, c.43 (1857); W. R. Cornish and G. de N. Clark, *Law and Society in England 1750–1950* (London: Sweet and Maxwell, 1989), p. 35.

Chapter 7

The Trades of Staffordshire against T. B. Rose, 1842–1851: 'Let but one of them come before me and I'll commit him'

Introduction

Labor-directed public protests and petitioning against the actions of specific magistrates, and the courtroom efforts of Roberts, contributed to the pressure on Parliament to guide and protect these officials by passing the Jervis Acts in 1848.[1] This chapter explores some of the implications of these acts for subsequent trade union legal efforts to fight coercive labor laws and discipline hostile magistrates. To many, these acts answered critics of summary hearings by creating the perception that magistrates were conducting more uniform proceedings that were less likely to be overturned at Westminster Hall. Bruce Smith argues that these acts, combined with the recruitment of more legally trained stipendiary magistrates and better Home Office supervision, served to strengthen the legitimacy of magistrates' judicial powers.[2] Despite initial doubts about the applicability of the Jervis Acts to master and servant proceedings, by 1853 the Queen's Bench was more protective of magistrates who used the forms in its schedules.[3] For the remainder of the nineteenth century, organized labor would not again enjoy a period of success in litigation comparable to that of 1843–1848. Yet, the Jervis Acts neither dramatically improved the legitimacy of summary procedure with workers, nor made these hearings more equitable.[4]

---

[1]   11 & 12 Victoria, c.42, 43, 44 (1848).

[2]   Bruce P. Smith, 'Circumventing the Jury: Petty Crime and Summary Justice in London and New York City, 1790–1855' (PhD dissertation, Yale University, 1996), pp. 81, 119, 441–66.

[3]   R. Steinfeld, *Coercion, Contract and Free Labour in the Nineteenth Century* (Cambridge, 2001), p. 158; In the Matter of Geswood (1853), 23 L. J. 53 and Ex Parte Bailey, Ex Parte Collier (1854) 118 E. R. 1269; 'Practical Points', *JP* 12/39, (30 September 1848) pp. 634–7; 'Proceedings Relating to Masters and Servants', *JP* 12/41 (7 October 1848), pp. 657–8; 'On the Present State of the Law of Master and Servant', *JP* 12/44 (28 October 1848), pp. 705–6.

[4]   Steinfeld, *Coercion*, pp. 157–9; Willibald Steinmetz, 'Was There a De-Juridification of Employment Relations in Britain?', in Willibald Steinmetz (ed.), *Private Law and Social*

Specifically, this chapter explores the career of Thomas Bailey Rose, the first stipendiary magistrate appointed to the North Staffordshire Potteries district, and the development of his adversarial relationship with trade unionists and Chartists. It illuminates the level of misconduct that Queen's Bench was prepared to accept from magistrates in the changed legal climate of the 1850s. It also shows how trade union legal representatives continued to search for new methods of resisting coercive labor laws and making those who administered them more accountable. Disciplining magistrates who displayed disregard for the law had never been an easy matter. Roberts initiated a number of successful civil actions for false imprisonment in the 1840s that were costly to magistrates, but the Jervis Acts made these more difficult to bring. Another method the Court of Queen's Bench provided for punishing magistrates who abused their power was the criminal information. Douglas Hay argues that in the eighteenth century, this mode of proceeding was difficult, risky and rarely successful.[5] These patterns are consistent with the use of criminal informations in the 1850s as well. Despite having decided three high-profile cases incorrectly within a 13-month period, and frequently having displayed bias and malice, Rose faced small consequences for his actions. Miner Robert Greaves made the most serious allegation of misconduct against Rose by an application for a criminal information in 1850, which alleged that the magistrate maliciously convicted him for breach of contract under 4 George IV, c.34 (1823) without hearing his full defense.[6]

Rose displayed consistent malice toward Chartists and trade unionists during his long and active career as a magistrate. He often made statements from the bench that brought his impartiality into question. Profoundly disliked by workers in Staffordshire, Rose was the target of riots by colliers in 1842, as well as public protest, petitions and letters to Parliament by unionists in 1843, 1845 and 1851.[7] Roberts frequently clashed with Rose, and brought at least six of these confrontations before the Court of Queen's Bench, three of them within a 13-

---

Inequality in the Industrial Age: Comparing the Legal Cultures of in Britain, France, Germany, and the United States (London, 2000). Steinmetz argues that although the quality of magistrates' hearings actually improved in the last quarter of the nineteenth century, with fewer egregious examples of class-bias, there is strong evidence that fewer and fewer employees sought redress through the courts against their employers.

[5]   Douglas Hay, 'Dread of the Crown Office: The Magistracy and the King's Bench, 1740–1800', in N. Landau (ed.), *Law, Crime, and English Society, 1660–1830* (Cambridge: Cambridge University Press, 2002), pp. 21–5, 26–30.

[6]   NA: KB 1/190/22, KB 1/191/60.

[7]   R. Fyson, 'The Crisis of 1842: Chartism, The Colliers' Strike, and the Outbreak in The Potteries', in Dorothy Thompson and James Epstein (eds), *The Chartist Experience: Studies in Working Class Radicalism and Culture, 1830–1860* (London: Macmillan, 1982), p. 210.

month period in 1850–1851.[8] Each of these cases demonstrates the difficulties workers faced with employer-dominated local legal institutions, as well as the legal and political strategies that unions pursued for redress. These cases provide examples of how locally administered labor law enforced by magistrates, particularly the use of the 1823 Master and Servant Act, the 1825 Combination Laws Repeal Amendment Act, and the 1831 Truck Act, shaped Staffordshire labor markets and industrial relations. Marc Steinberg has persuasively shown that in mid-Victorian Staffordshire, pottery masters utilized annual contracts that bound workers exclusively to a single employer while allowing manufacturers a wide freedom to control labor costs by the payment of piece rates, and the ability to determine custom and judge the quality of ware. These contracts were maintained with master and servant statutes administered by local magistrates who had strong political, social and economic ties to the pottery manufacturers. Similar arrangements existed for miners and ironworkers in the region. This chapter will confirm many of Steinberg's observations while drawing attention to what his work neglects, which is the continued organized resistance by workers to this regime.[9]

Early Confrontations between Rose and Labor, 1842–1845

In 1839, Thomas Bailey Rose, an experienced barrister, began his career as a stipendiary magistrate during a period of social unrest in the Potteries. It is possible that Rose's attitude toward organized labor and Chartists was shaped during the tense early years of his tenure. In 1834 and 1836 strikes in the Potteries shut down 75 percent of the trade, and the region suffered serious riots in 1837, 1841 and 1842.[10] In the summer of 1838, deputations from different districts of the Potteries met to petition Parliament for special legislation appointing a stipendiary magistrate and creating a police force for the borough of Stoke-on-Trent. The nearly 40 petitioners included some of the county's most important master potters, coal owners, manufacturers and magistrates, highlighting the cohesion of local elites and magistrates. They requested the appointment of Rose specifically to

---

[8]   Four are discussed in this chapter. The fifth and sixth were In Re: *Geswood* (1853) and In Re: *William Baker* (1857) see 23 L. J. 35 and 2 H. & N. 219. Also see: 'Breach of Agreement', *SA* (16 May 1857), p. 2; Steinfeld, *Coercion*, pp. 57–60, 158.

[9]   Marc Steinberg, 'Capitalist Development, Labour Process and the Law', *American Journal of Sociology* 109/2 (2003): 445–95.

[10]   J. Wedgwood, *The Staffordshire Pottery and its History* (London, 1913); J. Ginswick (ed.), *Labour and the Poor In England and Wales, 1849–1851: The Letters to The Morning Chronicle from the Correspondents in the Manufacturing and Mining Districts, the Towns of Liverpool and Birmingham, and the Rural Districts* (3 vols., London, 1983), Vol. 2, pp. 111–13; Fyson, 'The Crisis of 1842', p. 196.

maintain order and protect property in the face of an increasingly unruly working-class population.[11]

Rose immediately became one of the region's busiest magistrates. His clerk estimated that between 1839 and 1850 Rose heard an average of 800 cases per year, a high proportion of which were labor cases.[12] A minority of the magistrates handled the overwhelming majority of the judicial business in England. Because of his heavy caseload, Rose was a significant presence among local workers. In his memoirs, 'An Old Potter' named Charles Shaw remembered 'the stipendiary magistrate, Bailie Rose, ruled as the Jove of the pottery district. He was certainly a terror to evil-doers, but only a terror', and not a beloved figure in the community.[13] The magistrate was a highly visible symbol of authority in the region, making him one of the first targets in periods when authority was challenged.

One such period of disorder was during the depression in the summer of 1842. That summer over 4,000 miners were on strike against wage cuts initiated by coal owners. These colliers forcibly turned-out other mines and collieries, pulling plugs from boilers to stop work. The large Chartist presence in northern Staffordshire, as well as disorder in other parts of the country, added to the concern of local authorities. On 13 August, Rose warned the Home Office of the need for more troops to put down the growing number of seditious meetings. He reported that at these meetings, 'the most dangerous doctrines are instilled into the minds of the lower orders and all their proceedings aim at the subversion of every kind of authority and order'.[14] Two days later, Rose's fears were realized when a speech by Chartist Thomas Cooper, and word from Manchester of a resolution to strike for the Charter, led to two days of destructive rioting in the Potteries.[15]

Local elites bore the brunt of the crowd's displeasure. Police stations, workhouses, mine offices and the homes of mine owners, pottery manufacturers

---

[11] Staffordshire Record Office: D 593/L/3/25, 'Meeting of Deputations from Different Districts of the Potteries Held at White Sheaf Inn Stoke-Upon-Trent, Monday, September 3, 1838'; Steinberg, 'Capitalist Development'; Smith, 'Circumventing the Jury', p. 405.

[12] NA: KB/1/191/60.

[13] Charles Shaw, *When I Was A Child* (London: Caliban Books, 1903), p. 41.

[14] Quote from: NA: HO 45/260, 222–6; W. H. Sparrow, the Earl of Granville, made particularly deep cuts in wages. Fyson, 'The Crisis of 1842', pp. 197–8, 200–203; Raymond Challinor, *Radical Lawyer in Victorian England: W. P. Roberts and the Struggle for Workers' Rights* (London, 1990), p. 63; F. C. Mather, 'The General Strike of 1842: A Study in Leadership, Organization and the Threat of Revolution During the Plug Riots', in R. Quinault and J. Stevenson (eds), *Popular Protest and Public Order: Six Studies in British History, 1790–1920* (New York, 1974); S. H. Palmer, *Police and Protest in England and Ireland, 1780–1850* (Cambridge, 1988), pp. 455–61.

[15] NA: HO 45/260, 236–49, 474–85; Shaw, *When I Was A Child*, pp. 155–71; T. Cooper, *The Life of Thomas Cooper*, ed. John Saville (New York, 1971, originally 1872), pp. 186–219; Fyson, 'The Crisis of 1842', pp. 207–14; Challinor, *Radical Lawyer*, pp. 64–7.

and magistrates were all attacked and destroyed.[16] Rose's own home in Penkhill was sacked and burned while he was leading troops to quell the disorder. He told the Home Secretary, 'we could not arrive in time to prevent them <u>destroying everything I possess</u>. My wife and children escaped with their lives, but that is all. They broke every window and destroyed <u>everything</u>'.[17] It appears that the crowd was selective in its targets and it is highly unlikely that the destruction of Rose's home was a mere opportunist 'whim' of the crowd.[18] The magistracy was the form of state authority that workers were the most likely to experience, and thus it is hardly surprising that these office-holders 'were customarily the first target in a riot'.[19]

The magistrates and troops withdrew and surrendered Hanley to the crowd during the evenings of the 15 and 16 August, a decision for which the Home Office later severely criticized Rose. Home Secretary Sir James Graham told the Queen that 'he was by no means satisfied with the activity of the magistrates ... [who] had shown a want of proper spirit in defending their property'. Lord Lieutenant Talbot defended Rose against the censure, arguing to the Home Secretary that despite the 'difficult position in which Mr. Rose was placed' one could 'not find that he was wanting in activity or exertion to quell the riots'.[20] It is interesting to observe the relative ease with which a magistrate could earn a rebuke for failing to protect property, compared to their remarkable immunity from penalties for abusing their power over workers at Petty Sessions.

Magistrate Captain Powys finally suppressed the disorder with considerable force and mass arrests followed. Over 703 men and women were arrested, 276 were put on trial, 116 were imprisoned and 49 were transported. Despite questions about the limits of Rose's territorial jurisdiction, he sat at Newcastle-under-Lyme

---

[16]   Challinor, *Radical Lawyer*, p. 65.

[17]   Emphasis in original. The crowd destroyed police offices in Hanley and Fenton, the coal office of the Earl of Granville, the home of master potter Charles Mason and the homes of magistrates William Parker, Thomas Allen, Reverend R. E. Aitken and T. B. Rose. NA: HO 45/260, pp. 236–49, 474–85; Fyson, 'Crisis of 1842', pp. 207–10; Shaw, *When I Was A Child*, pp. 155–71; Cooper, *The Life of Thomas Cooper*, pp. 186–219.

[18]   Fyson disagrees, hypothesizing that 'isolation, vulnerability or the chance whim', might have played an equally significant role in the crowd's choices. He suggests 'it would be rash to assume that all those whose property was attacked were necessarily the most hated men in the Potteries'. Fyson concedes, however, that Rose 'was always deeply unpopular with the working classes'. Fyson, 'The Crisis of 1842', pp. 210–211; Jacqueline Fellague Ariouat, 'Rethinking Partisanship in the Conduct of Chartist Trials, 1839–1848', *Albion* 29/4 (Winter 1998): 601.

[19]   Challinor, *Radical Lawyer*, 79; D. Jones, 'Thomas Campbell Foster and the Rural Labourer: Incendiarism in East Anglia in the 1840s', *Social History* 1 (1976): 5–43; J. Archer, *By a Flash and a Scare: Incendiarism, Animal Maiming and Poaching in East Anglia 1815–1870* (Oxford, 1990).

[20]   NA: HO 45/260, pp. 483–85; J. T. Ward, *Sir James Graham* (London 1967), pp. 190–191; Fyson, 'The Crisis of 1842', p. 214.

with the magistrates who examined and committed prisoners, some of whom had participated in the sacking of his own house.[21] It was reported that at one of these hearings, a lawyer named Mr Allen representing the prisoners objected to Rose's conduct in the hearings. Rose asked the lawyer 'do you know that I have been in the profession for twenty years?'. Allen replied, 'Yes, sir. I know you have; but what I complain of is that you have stood still in the profession, and not progressed with the march of mind'.[22]

In 1842, Rose was the target of rioting colliers, and in 1843–1845 he became the subject of criticism by local unions. In December 1843, potters employed at Mr Hackwood's firm went on strike, questioning the legal validity of their contracts because they lacked reciprocity. These contracts gave the employers exclusive rights to their labor, the right to refuse to pay them for 'dirty ware' (and then sell it at discounted prices), and the unlimited power to fine. Some employers operated an allowance system, whereby under the contract they were 'allowed' to deduct 2d to 4d from every shilling a potter earned. The *Potters' Examiner* called this system 'nothing short of a felony – yea, a felony of the very worst description; as it is perpetrated on helpless poverty; which does not, as justice is at present administered in this neighbourhood, come within the jurisdiction of "The Law"'.[23] This contract stipulated that workers would be paid by the piece, but obliged employers to find work for them only as 'they conveniently can'. Potters complained that 'if an operative potter be starving on two days work per week, and a situation be offered him at which he might earn a comfortable living he dare not

---

[21]   NA: HO 45/260, pp. 366–71 and Staffordshire Record Office: D 5567/ 1–6 for correspondence regarding whether it was illegal for Rose to sit at Newcastle, because the act appointing him specified his jurisdiction as 'Stoke-upon-Trent and certain places adjoining'. Though Thomas Cooper represented himself at both trials, he met with Roberts before the first hearing and took his advice on defense strategy. See Cooper, *The Life of Thomas Cooper*, pp. 214–17. At Dudley some magistrates refused to take bail from certain prisoners, which resulted in a criminal information against the justices. The rule was discharged, but the Judges of the Queen's Bench were critical of the magistrates' conduct and required them to pay the costs of both the prosecution and their own defense. See 'The Queen v. Badger and Cartwright: Criminal Information – Magistrates Refusing Bail', *JP* 7/11 (18 March 1843), pp. 128–30; 'Rejecting Bail on Insufficient Grounds', *JP* 7/23 (10 June 1843), pp. 317–18. Also see: 'Copies of the Several Affidavits Filed in the Court of Queen's Bench, on the Application Made in Michaelmas Term Last, at the Instance of Arthur George O'Neill, for a Criminal Information Against Thomas Badger, Esq. And the Rev. W.H. Cartwright, Magistrates for the County of Stafford', *Parliamentary Papers*, Vol. XLIV (195).

[22]   'Constitutional Law versus Justices' Justice', *NS* (8 February 1845), p. 4.

[23]   William H. Warburton, *The History of Trade Union Organization in the North Staffordshire Potteries* (London, 1931), pp. 44–6, 90–98, 105; 'To the Potters' Examiner', *PEWA* 1/6 (6 January 1844), p. 44.

accept it in defiance of his employers'.[24] Josiah Wedgwood, of the famous pottery family, wrote 'An employer could keep a man tied to a situation which gave him but one day's work a week, yet if the man left he might be prosecuted'.[25] Steinfeld argues that the struggle over the consideration required in contracts of employment was a critical front in the legal 'struggle over the rules' of master and servant law during the mid nineteenth century. He finds that for much of that period, the courts ruled that contracts where the employer bound the employee to work for him or her exclusively, but did not explicitly promise to provide a reasonable quantity of work, were bad for want of adequate consideration. Beginning in the mid 1840s, however, the court reversed itself, ruling that a promise to provide reasonable work 'according to the state of the trade' could be inferred in any contract of employment, and this implicit promise would be adequate consideration.[26] The degree to which the high court's rulings in these cases were mirrored by the reality of magistrates' enforcement of contracts of employment at the local level, of course, remains open to question.

The *Potters' Examiner* repeatedly challenged the legality of these one-sided agreements. This paper criticized Rose's ruling in Hackwood's prosecution of potter Joseph Clarke for breaking his contract under 4 George IV, c.34 (1823) because the contract was an 'unblushing mockery at anything like reciprocity of interest … making it appear more like a caricature upon common sense than a legal bond'. It promised its readers that 'steps are now being taken to ascertain the legality of the agreement'.[27] Two weeks later an editorial called the potters' bond 'a vile African slave bond, without a shadow of reciprocal interest or legal validity, concocted by West Indian planters, for the especial use of North Staffordshire Pot masters. Thus saith morality; but she is almost afraid to speak for fear of the "law"'.[28] By challenging the validity of these contracts, the potters were directly challenging a central pillar of the pottery masters' factory regime based upon legal coercion.

On 16 December, Mr Hackwood prosecuted Edgar Steele before Rose under 4 George IV, c.34 (1823) for breaking his contract. In his defense, Steele told

---

[24] 'To The Editor of the Potters' Examiner and Workman's Advocate', *PEWA* 1/2 (9 December 1843), p. 11; '16 December 1843', *PEWA* 1/3 (16 December 1843), p. 20.

[25] Wedgewood, *Staffordshire Pottery*, p. 170.

[26] Steinfeld, *Coercion*, pp. 104–23. See *Sykes v. Dixon* (1839) 8 L. J. 102; *Beeston v. Collier* (1827) 130 E. R. 786; *Fawcett v. Cash* (1834) 110 E. R. 1026; *Williams v. Byrne* (1837), 6 L. J. 239; *Lees v. Whitcombe* (1828) 130 E. R. 972; *Williamson v. Taylor* (1843) 114 E. R. 1214; *Pilkington v. Scott* (1846) 153 E. R. 1014; *Aspdin v. Austin* (1844) 114 E. R. 1402; *Dunn v. Sayles* (1844) 114 E. R. 1408.

[27] '16 December 1843', *PEWA* 1/3 (16 December 1843), p. 20.

[28] 'To The Editor of the Potters' Examiner', *PEWA* 1/5 (30 December 1843), p. 34. For use of rhetoric comparing 'American Slavery' with 'English Slavery', see Marcus Cunliffe, *Chattel Slavery and Wage Slavery: The Anglo-American Context, 1830–1860* (Athens, 1979), pp. 8–16.

Rose that he feared consequences from the union if he returned to work. Rose demanded the names of union members who had intimidated him. Steele did not give any. Rose suspected that Steele 'knew more than he chose to admit about the confederation of the turn-outs', and sentenced him to three months imprisonment at hard labor. He upheld Hackwood's contracts, warning:

> There is a set of idle vagabonds about, I know, trying to induce colliers and potters to absent themselves from work ... let but one of them come before me, and I'll commit him – I'll send him to the House of Correction for three calendar months, to hard labour or commit him for trial at the assizes.[29]

The Potters' Union interpreted Rose's remarks as a sign of his bias in favor of employers during industrial disputes, asking 'Does Mr. Rose require a charge only to put his threat into execution? Or does he require evidence also, to substantiate the charge?'. The editors suggested that in light of his threat, Rose could no longer present himself as an impartial judge. 'We are afraid that Mr. Rose's mind would not be sufficiently calm to investigate the facts of the case; and consequently the ends of justice may be thwarted by this man'. The editorial questioned his calling union leaders 'idle vagabonds', asking, 'is a man idle for wishing to raise himself and family in the scale of social existence by improving the price of his labour?'.[30]

Between December 1843 and May 1844, the statement 'Let one of them come before me, and I'll commit him' became a rallying cry for potters. In a five-month period, Rose's warning was quoted in nine separate articles in the *Potters' Examiner*, and during that same period the paper published many articles discussing the importance of the impartial administration of the law. Encouraged by Roberts' victories at Queen's Bench, the paper soon adopted the same argument as the Miners' Union and the *Northern Star*, that one-sided and illegal employment contracts were enforced with the threat of imprisonment by magistrates who were either employers themselves, or in confederation with employers.[31]

---

[29]   'Neglect of Work: The Potters' Turn-Out', *SA* (16 December 1843), p. 2; 'The Potters' Examiner and Workman's Advocate', *PEWA* 1/4 (23 December 1843), p. 29; Rose commonly made similar warnings to the wider community when issuing rulings from the bench. See: 'A Charge of Vagrancy', *SA* (6 September 1851), p. 4; 'Stoke-Upon-Trent', *SA* (12 July 1851), p. 4.

[30]   'The Potters' Examiner and Workman's Advocate', *PEWA* 1/4 (23 December 1843), p. 29.

[31]   They also adopted the same praise and reverence for 'patriarchs of the law' at Queen's Bench who granted Roberts' victories. 'The Potters' Examiner and Workman's Advocate', *PEWA* 1/4 (23 December 1843), p. 29; 'To The Editor of the Potters' Examiner', *PEWA* 1/5 (30 December 1843), pp. 33–4; 'The Potters' Examiner and Workman's Advocate', *PEWA* 1/6 (6 January 1844), p. 44; 'To C. J. Mason, Esq.', *PEWA* 1/8 (20 January 1844), pp. 57–8; 'To Mr. Mason's Turn-Outs', *PEWA* 1/12 (17 February 1844), pp. 89–90; 'To the Editor

Rose's threat was used as a short-hand proof of this argument. When Mr Mason's potters turned out, the *Potters' Examiner* accused the employer of 'exercising your tyranny under the apathy of "the law" – that "law" which says "let but one of them (not you of course, but those who complain of your tyranny) ... be brought before me and I'll commit him"'.[32] In a letter to Mr Mason's turnouts, the journal discussed the legal disadvantage of trade unions, arguing

> should we complain of, or seek to remedy, those evils, or to improve our condition by legal or constitutional means, the harpies of 'the law' are hounded upon us: ... if we send a deputation to any branch of our trade, we are called 'idle vagabonds', and are threatened with three months' imprisonment to hard labour.[33]

A Longton printer wrote to complain that if a potter turned-out for a less one-sided agreement, he 'incurred the censure of his superiors, and the anger of the accommodating "law-maker" and dispenser, who brands him ... "an idle vagabond", and who exclaims, with all the arrogance of an aristocratic despot "I'll send him to the house of correction for three calendar months"'. An editorial describing the potters' bond quoted Rose's warning, and then boldly asserted that it was only the collusion of magistrates and pottery masters that made it enforceable. It argued that 'The hiring system of the Potteries owes its existence ... to the connivance of unprincipled magistrates', who were 'perverters of national justice'.[34]

In March of 1844, Rose released two colliers he had imprisoned under 4 George IV, c.34 (1823) for breaking their contracts, pre-empting union-funded writs of certiorari and habeas corpus. The *Potters' Examiner* wrote an open letter to Rose stating that if he had acted in a more dispassionate manner he might have

> Avoided the disgrace which must inevitably stain your professional character from the circumstance of your being compelled, for fear of a higher tribunal, to release two poor colliers lately imprisoned by you. The circumstance proves clearly that the two colliers, in question, were unjustly punished by you. Either you were ignorant of the law, or were actuated by vindictive or malevolent feeling; in either of which case you proved yourself unfit to fill the high judicial station you at present occupy.

---

of the Potters' Examiner', *PEWA* 1/15 (9 March 1844), p. 116; 'To T.B. Rose, Stipendiary Magistrate For the Borough of Stoke-Upon-Trent', *PEWA* 1/18 (30 March 1844), pp. 137–9; 'The Hiring System, To the United Branches of Operative Potters', *PEWA* 1/19 (6 April 1844), pp. 145–6; 'To the Editors of the Potters' Examiner', *PEWA* 1/22 (27 April 1844), pp. 174–5.

[32] 'To C. J. Mason, Esq.', *PEWA* 1/8 (20 January 1844), pp. 57–8.

[33] 'To Mr. Mason's Turn-Outs', *PEWA* 1/12 (17 February 1844), pp. 89–90.

[34] 'To the Editors of the Potters' Examiner', *PEWA* 1/22 (27 April 1844), pp. 174–5.

The article also claimed that the potters had obtained the opinion of barristers that their contract, 'containing no stamp and no reciprocity of interest … is not valid in law'. This meant that 'there has been a frightful perversion of law in all such cases which have been brought before you … men have been imprisoned; domestic comfort has been destroyed; and all done in the most cruel and illegal manner'. It then alluded to Roberts' recent victories and warned 'that actions, for false imprisonment, may be commenced', subjecting Rose 'to penalties and disgrace of a very serious nature'.[35]

The article once again quoted Rose's earlier warning, which by this point must have been very familiar to readers of the *Potters' Examiner*. It commented

> This language, Sir, is anything but the calm, dignified expression of an impartial judge, and displays a vindictive recklessness of feeling highly disparaging to an intelligent mind. There is a thoughtless defiance in your words, that borders on a total disregard of all law.

The contrast with the paper's reverence for 'the patriarchs of the law' who sat in the higher courts, is striking. It further observed that such 'foolish and cruel displays of passion' were a 'peculiar feature in your magisterial career'. It commented on his impact on the legitimacy of the law, asking 'how can they reasonably expect that the masses will treat with awe, that which magistrates administer with contempt?'.[36]

In early 1845, Rose once again found himself the subject of labor propaganda, deciding the master and servant case against four Longton colliers that opened this book. Roberts initiated the writs of habeas corpus and certiorari that resulted in the quashing of the conviction. In 'Constitutional Law versus Justices' Justice', the *Northern Star* offered Roberts 'congratulations for the additional victory, rendered doubly important by the fact of Mr. Bailey Rose belonging to the legal profession, and his services being called in to insure such a triumph for the masters as would defy the scrutiny of Mr. Roberts'. The linkage between the interests of employers and the magistracy is notable. The miners celebrated the release of the four prisoners with a large public meeting with bands and processions.[37]

The *Potters' Examiner* turned Rose's own words to attack the fairness and legality of the contract and its enforcement. These events undermined Rose's credibility with workmen and women in the Potteries. It is clear that by 1845 Rose

---

[35] 'To T.B. Rose, Stipendiary Magistrate For the Borough of Stoke-Upon-Trent', *PEWA* 1/18 (30 March 1844), pp. 137–9.

[36] Ibid.

[37] NA: KB 1/131/42; 'Constitutional Law Versus Justices' Justice', *NS* (8 February 1845), p. 4; 'Great Rejoicing of the Staffordshire Miners', *NS* (15 February 1845), p. 1; 'Ex Parte John Williams', *JP* 9/5 (1 February 1845), p. 84; 'Judge's Chambers, Sergeant's Inn, Saturday – The Pitmen's Strike in the Potteries', *NS* (8 February 1845), p. 8.

had already formed an adversarial relationship with organized labor and Chartists, which only deteriorated further.

R. v. William Austin (1850)

Over 13 months in 1850–1851, Roberts brought three actions before the Court of Queen's Bench based upon rulings made by Rose. By 1851, these cases again made Rose the subject of protest by local working people. These cases demonstrate the role of the magistracy in industrial relations, the class barriers created for workers when they were faced with legal coercion, as well as the strategies unions used to resist these harsh laws.

The first of these three cases, *R. v. William Austin*, was heard by Rose and Edward Wood on 2 May 1850. A replacement worker named William Weston charged iron-hoop maker William Austin under the Combination Laws Repeal Amendment Act with having used threats and intimidation to prevent him from entering his agreement at the Roondale Ironworks.[38] Through his defense of union officials charged with conspiring to violate the 1825 Act, Roberts was important in the establishing much of the case law that defined the terms 'threats, intimidation, obstruction and molestation' in the act. In fact, Roberts acted as solicitor in nearly every case of conspiracy to violate the 1825 Act that occurred during his professional life. In 1847 he had been the solicitor in the case of 26 Warrington mechanics charged with conspiring to violate the 1825 Act by using pickets to warn replacement workers that they would be known as a 'knobsticks'. In this case, *R. v. Selsby* (1847), Baron Rolfe defined an illegal threat as one that communicated the possibility of bodily harm.[39] This case was widely seen as a victory for organized labor. The words 'obstruction' and 'molestation' remained vague until the conspiracy cases of *R. v. Rowlands* and *R. v. Duffield* (1851), in which Mr Justice Erle defined them in the 'broadest possible terms'. Erle told a jury at the Staffordshire Assizes that conspiring to take away all of the plaintiff's workmen qualified as obstruction and molestation under the 1825 Act.[40] After 1851, 6 George IV, c.129 made it legal for men to combine to raise wages or reduce hours, but criminalized any effective tactics for achieving these ends, such as the information picket. The 1825 Act, combined with the magistrates' control of the local police forces, could seriously impair the ability of workers to picket

---

[38]   6 George IV, c.129 (1825); John Orth, *Combination and Conspiracy: A Legal History of Trade Unionism, 1721–1906* (Oxford, 1991), pp. 87–90. The Roondale works were owned by Mr Heath, Mr Welsh and Mr Higgins.

[39]   NA: KB 1/157/65; Orth, *Combination and Conspiracy*, pp. 95–6; Challinor, *Radical Lawyer*, pp. 150–154; J. Jones, *Selsby and Others on the Prosecution of Jones and Potts, Narrative, Introduction, &c.* (London, 1847), Goldsmith-Kress Library of Economic Literature, Reel #35390.

[40]   Orth, *Combination and Conspiracy*, pp. 97–8.

effectively. This ruling led to political agitation by labor that ultimately resulted in the 1859 Molestation of Workmen Act, which brought only very limited relief.[41]

Three witnesses testified against Austin. Weston swore that on the 19 April he agreed to act as a replacement worker beginning the following Monday. Three days later, he and other replacement workers arrived at the railway station in Longport, and were greeted by a crowd of between 30 and 40 jeering men and women. Weston claimed that the defendant yelled, 'You're a pretty bugger to come into a county and take men's jobs of them under price' and 'You shall have your buggering skull scraped for you'. Weston said he responded to these threats with one of his own, 'I shall see you again'. James Ward and Daniel Parkes, two other replacement workers, confirmed Weston's testimony, adding that Austin offered them each a sovereign to return home. The workers were either so frightened by the crowd, or so enticed by the sovereign, or some combination of both, that they refused to enter their new jobs.[42]

Austin's attorney, William Heaton, objected to the form of the information against his client, which Rose overruled. Heaton called two witnesses. The first was John Nack, who swore he was next to Austin during the confrontation, and heard him call the workers 'shabby hands' who would do themselves no good working under price. He assured the court that he heard nothing about 'skulls'. Police officer John Ross testified that he knew Austin and felt 'his character is good'. After the testimony of Ross, and before the trial was completed, Heaton hastily left the court 'in consequence of pressing business'.[43]

This had important consequences for Austin. Rose and Wood convicted him to three months' imprisonment with hard labor. As noted in Chapter 5, Section 12 of the 1825 Combination Act gave prisoners who 'felt aggrieved' by the ruling of the magistrates the right to be released on bail and appeal the conviction to Quarter Sessions by 'immediately' entering into a £10 recognizance and two £10 sureties. Not many laborers had £10 savings, or two friends who had this sum.[44] Heaton was not present to initiate an appeal, and he failed to instruct his client that he had this right. The magistrates were under no obligation to inform Austin of his right to appeal. Heaton later justified this omission by stating that he saw no possible grounds for an appeal, and that if Austin had not been guided by 'outside forces', meaning Roberts and the Union, the prisoner would not have desired an appeal.[45]

---

[41]   NA: KB 1/199/59–60, KB 1/203/62–63, KB 1/204/50–51, KB 21/68; Orth, 'English Law and Striking Workmen, the Molestation of Workmen Act, 1859', *The Journal of Legal History* 2 (1981): 238–57.

[42]   NA: KB 1/190/4, 29; 'Tunstall', *SA* (4 May 1850), p. 4; 'The Late Case of Intimidation of Workmen', *SA* (11 May 1850), p. 4.

[43]   NA: KB 1/190/ 4, 29.

[44]   Section twelve also allows for evidence to be re-heard in the appeal to Quarter Sessions, not just technical points on the face of the conviction.

[45]   NA: KB 1/190/29; NA: KB 1/190/4; 'The Late Case of Intimidation of Workmen', *SA* (11 May 1850), p. 4; 'Practical Points', *JP* 7/46 (18 November 1843), p. 695.

It is important to note the difference in political commitment of attorneys such as Roberts and John Owen on the one hand, and Heaton on the other. Heaton was an active solicitor in Staffordshire, who often handled labor cases, representing both employers and workers. Heaton's later statements imply that he believed that Austin was guilty.[46] Roberts' professional investment in one political cause, labor, was unique for solicitors at this time. Roberts' conviction that labor law was unfairly biased toward capital meant that he was prepared to exhaust all legal options when defending workers, particularly when the issues at stake might have wider relevance for organized labor. Roberts saw grounds for an appeal that were not apparent to Heaton.

On 6 May, Roberts appeared before Rose in Hanley to inform him that he had been retained by Austin, and gave notice of his client's intention to appeal his conviction to Quarter Sessions. Rose refused to accept the recognizance and sureties because they had not been made 'immediately'. Roberts reminded Rose that Austin's attorney had not been present at the conviction and argued that this was the first time Rose had been available in the four days since the hearing. He also stated that he knew of a similar appeal in which Baron Alderson had ruled 'that magistrates had the power to admit bail after a "reasonable period"'.[47] Roberts claimed that this ruling meant that magistrates had to look at the circumstances of the case and consider the difficulties 'people in some conditions of life' had in finding sureties. Rose said he would consult with Wood and give his ruling the next day.[48]

Roberts chose not to follow Rose to the Burslem Petty Sessions to hear his ruling, perhaps sensing the direction Rose was leaning. He instead prepared affidavits for an action to Queen's Bench. On 7 May, Rose 'very decidedly addressed himself to Mr. Heaton', stating that although 'he would naturally favour an appeal to a superior tribunal', he had no power to accept the recognizance of Austin because the punishment had commenced. Although he did not consult with Edward Wood as he promised Roberts, he expressed 'no doubt of the court's concurrence' with his decision because the matter was 'so clear'. Rose also insisted that if Austin truly felt aggrieved 'under the Jervis Acts the prisoner could still appeal to the highest tribunal'.[49] Heaton assured Rose that he was in full agreement with his decision.

---

[46]   NA: KB 1/190/29.

[47]   NA: KB 1/190/4; 'The Late Case of Intimidation of Workmen', *SA* (11 May 1850), p. 4. Roberts was probably referring to *Thompson v. Gibson and Another* (1841). In the appeal in this case to the Exchequer, Baron Alderson endorsed a definition of 'immediately afterwards' that stretched to 'within such convenient time as is requisite for doing the thing'. *Thompson v. Gibson and Another* (1841) 8 M. & W. 282–90. Roberts' Barrister, Huddleston, cited a number of cases to support Austin's motion at the Queen's Bench, but this was the only one that involved Baron Alderson.

[48]   NA: KB 1/190/29; 'The Late Case of Intimidation of Workmen', *SA* (11 May 1850), p. 4.

[49]   Ibid.

He disavowed any connection with the 'outside forces' that were currently giving William Austin legal advice.[50]

Rose was referring to Section 5 of 'An Act to Protect Justices of the Peace from Vexatious Actions for Acts Done by them in Execution of their Office', 11 & 12 Victoria c.44 (1848). That section of the act allowed individuals to apply to the Court of Queen's Bench to compel magistrates who 'shall refuse to do any act relating to the duties of his or their office'. This was attractive to Rose because it also stated that if the application was successful 'no action or proceeding whatsoever shall be commenced or prosecuted against such justice'.[51] If Austin appealed under this act, Rose was protected from any future civil action for false imprisonment. This was an important protection because as recently as the summer of 1848, a Norfolk magistrate was pursued in civil action for not accepting the bail of a defendant.[52]

On 23 May Roberts submitted the warrant of commitment and an affidavit describing the facts of the case to the Court of Queen's Bench, requesting it force the magistrates to accept Austin's recognizance. In his affidavit, Roberts described Heaton's absence at the time of Austin's conviction, his own encounter with Rose on 6 May, and related the fact that Austin was illiterate and 'in very poor circumstances'. This last point was intended to stress that the prisoner was incapable of initiating an appeal himself, and to demonstrate the difficulty he faced in collecting sureties. On 5 June, Rose replied by sending a copy of the minutes of the case, and affidavits of William Cooper, who acted as Weston's attorney, and Rose's clerk, John Randolf Rose. These affidavits stressed that Austin was 'not in poor circumstances but respectable for his station in life'. They also emphasized that Austin had enjoyed 'able legal counsel', who believed that had he been 'left to his own discretion the matter would not have been heard of'. Yet again, Roberts' opponents used the stereotype of the 'sharp practitioner' to discredit his legal arguments. They reiterated Rose's inability to accept Austin's recognizance under the statute.[53]

On 8 June opposing counsel argued the case before Mr Justice Wightman. T. Jones, Rose's barrister, showed cause why the magistrate should not allow Austin to appeal to the Quarter Sessions. He argued that 'immediately' meant as soon as the judgment was pronounced, or at least before the commencement of the sentence. He noted that otherwise a prisoner could spend more time in prison than he was sentenced to serve. The 1825 Act provided that in the event of an unsuccessful appeal, Quarter Sessions was to commit the prisoner to prison for

---

[50]   NA: KB 1/190/29; KB 1/190/4 .

[51]   11 & 12 Victoria, c.44, s.5 (1848).

[52]   'The Queen v. Bager and Cartwright: Criminal Information – Magistrates Refusing Bail', *JP* 7/11 (18 March 1843), pp. 128–30; 'Rejecting Bail on Insufficient Grounds', *JP* 7/23 (10 June 1843), pp. 317–18; 'Lindford v. Fitzroy', *JP* 12/30 (22 July 1848), p. 469. Also see: 'Copies of the Several Affidavits … Arthur George O'Neill …'.

[53]   Ibid.

the full sentence of the original conviction. If a prisoner had served time before initiating an appeal, Jones argued that this would not count toward that sentence.

Huddleston, who often took briefs from Roberts, argued Austin's case. He suggested that if the Court accepted Rose's interpretation of Section 12 of the act, it would 'for all practical purposes' deprive workers of its intended benefit. Workers usually did not have the £10 in their pocket, and needed time to secure two £10 sureties. Huddleston suggested that 'It would be to hold (in effect) that the defendant is to go to the hearing provided with sureties, as if he anticipated a conviction against him'. He then cited seven cases in which the higher courts had construed the word 'immediately' in other statues to mean 'without such delay as cannot be satisfactorily accounted for'.

Wightman expressed 'difficulty in reconciling the object of the statute with its strict words'. He agreed with Huddleston's argument that if a 'literal construction of the words be adopted, in the majority of cases, the benefit intended by the statue would be perfectly illusory'. If the prisoner 'did not anticipate a conviction he may not have been prepared with' sureties. Wightman then recited the chronology of Austin's conviction, emphasizing that Austin's attorney left before the judgment was given, and that while in prison the worker had to find and arrange sureties and consult with an attorney. He also observed that Austin lost two days because magistrates did not sit at the weekend. He 'came to the conclusion that this application was not too late', ordering Rose and Wood to release Austin and accept his recognizance and sureties. He also disputed Jones' notion that the part of his sentence Austin had already served would not count toward the whole if his conviction was confirmed by Quarter Sessions. On 1 July Huddleston argued Austin's appeal at Staffordshire Quarter Sessions. The grounds do not appear in the record, but the form of the warrant of committal might have been an issue because it did not match the form of the conviction required by the statute. Quarter Sessions quashed the conviction.[54]

There were no allegations of poor conduct in this case against Rose, as his interpretation of the act was a perfectly plausible one. The case does, however, demonstrate the difficulty that class barriers created for workers when confronted with the legal system. Rose could not, or would not, appreciate the difficulties workers faced in obtaining sureties, and chose to interpret that section of the statute in the way least favorable toward labor. Class barriers clearly created problems between the prisoner and his own attorney, who saw no grounds for pursuing an appeal, and in fact, actively discouraged him. This case was legally important as well. Chapter 5 demonstrates that workers often successfully appealed magistrates' rulings under 6 George IV, c.129 (1825) to Quarter Sessions. Had Rose's interpretation of the act held, it would have made such efforts much more difficult. It is also important to stress the relevance of the Jervis Acts in making

---

[54] 'Reg v. Austin', *JP* 15/1 (4 January 1851), pp. 9–10; NA: KB 21/68, 8 June 1850; *County of Staffordshire, Orders of Sessions*, Q/SO, Vol. 37: Microfilm Copy at Osgoode Law Library, York University, Toronto.

it more difficult to punish magistrates for errors in judgment. Had Rose not been protected from civil suit by the Vexatious Actions Act (1848), he might have chosen to err on the side of caution and release Austin on bail. Instead, Austin spent three weeks in prison, contrary to the statute.

R. v. T. B. Rose Esq. (1851)

If it is possible to defend the behavior of Rose in the case of William Austin, in the case of Robert Greaves it certainly is not. Greaves' criminal information against Rose produced seven conflicting sworn affidavits, three newspaper articles and a multiplicity of different interests among the participants. Nonetheless, even if these documents are interpreted in a way most generous to Rose, it appears that he wrongfully sent a miner to prison, and made statements that were unprofessional given the frequency with which he was required to adjudicate cases arising from labor disputes. His behavior was deemed so bad that the miners' union took the very unusual step of attempting to prosecute him under a criminal information.

In February 1850, butty collier and provisions dealer, John Caton, hired Robert Greaves to work as a miner at Golden Hill Colliery in Wolstanton, which was owned by Mr Williamson. Greaves was to be paid 3s per day for getting coal, and he later claimed that neither side was required to give notice when terminating the contract. After a month, this relationship deteriorated because Caton paid Greaves most of his wages in truck redeemable at a shop run by Caton's wife. Greaves claimed that Caton deducted 6d at every reckoning for drink, even when Greaves refused to accept any. According to Greaves, he complained repeatedly about this illegal practice.[55]

Paying workers in truck, or goods, was widespread in the iron, coal, cutlery, pottery and nail-making trades in Staffordshire during the mid nineteenth century.[56] Truck often took the form of advances on wages in goods from a local shop. These shops were sometimes owned by the employers themselves, or by shopkeepers who paid them for the business they provided. In the 1830s truck was so common in the region that landlords complained that they sometimes had to accept goods for rent because their tenants had no currency.[57] According to a correspondent of the *Morning Chronicle* writing from Staffordshire between 1849–1851, 'not a few magistrates themselves are notorious truck store keepers'. Sometimes the owners of these establishments were of more humble origin, as when several butty

---

[55]   NA: KB 1/190/22; 'Neglect of Work', *SA* (16 March 1850), p. 5; 'Convictions Under The Truck Act, Tunstall', *SA* (18 May 1850), p. 7.

[56]   G. W. Hinton, *The Truck System: Including A History of the British Truck Acts, 1465–1960* (Cambridge, 1960), pp. 31–3, 121–4.

[57]   'Cases of Distress and Oppression in the Staffordshire Potteries; By Labourers Wages Being Paid in Truck' (Burslem, 1830), pp. 4–12, Goldsmith-Kress Library of Economic Literature, Reel #26355.

(subcontractors) colliers would join together to run a truck shop, or a public house. Mine owners used long pay-periods to compel workers to take advances in the form of goods at the shop, which would later be deducted from their wages. Goods at the shop were sometimes 25–150 percent more expensive than similar products that could be purchased elsewhere.[58]

In 1831 Parliament passed the Truck Act, which made it illegal to pay employees in anything but the current coin of the realm. The act covered servants in a variety of trades, including mining, iron and steel manufacture, pottery, textiles, lace-making and the cutlery trades, but specifically excluding domestic servants and agricultural workers. The act allowed workers in the listed trades who were paid in truck to bring an action before two magistrates, neither of whom could be engaged as the same trade as the plaintiff. The magistrates could award the worker the full monetary value of any wages paid in truck, and could fine the offending employer £5 to £10 for the first offence, between £10 and £20 for the second offence, and up to £100 for a third violation. Magistrates had the discretion to award half of the fine, up to £20, to the informer.[59]

The Truck Act was widely considered a failure. Because of the large presence of mine-owner magistrates in Staffordshire, it was not always easy for a miner to find two magistrates who could hear a case. Workers who were able to bring suit successfully were usually fired and often blacklisted in the region. Magistrates' attitudes toward truck were highly variable, some being greatly offended by the practice, and others showing great reluctance to convict or punish offenders. The Act's provisions proved easy to evade, as many truck masters adopted the practice making advances in actual money to technically comply with the statute, but with the understanding that if the employee spent the currency outside of the company store he/she would be refused future advances or, worse, discharged.[60]

In 1849 and 1851, large employers and local shopkeepers, both of whom resented the unfair competition of truck-paying employers and company stores, made common cause with workers, creating Anti-Truck Societies in at least eight different communities in Staffordshire. The South Staffordshire Anti-Truck Association, an umbrella organization which oftentimes engaged solicitor William Henry Duignan, secured over 250 convictions of truck masters in 1850 and 1851

---

[58] 'Reflections on the Injustice of the Truck System by a Staffordshire Morelander' (London, 1830), pp. 13, 15, 17, Goldsmith-Kress Library of Economic Literature, Reel #26435; *Labour and the Poor in England and Wales, 1849–51...,* Vol. 2, pp. 105–8; Hinton, *Truck System*, pp. 35–6.

[59] 1 & 2 Will 4, c.37, s.1,3,4–5, 9, 19–21 (1831); Hinton, *Truck System*, pp. 109–11.

[60] Hinton, *Truck System*, pp. 121, 128; J. H. Morris and L. J. Williams, *The South Wales Coal Industry, 1841–1875* (Cardiff, 1958), 269; Roger Swift, 'The English Urban Magistracy and the Administration of Justice During the Early Nineteenth Century: Wolverhampton, 1815–1860', *Midlands History* 17 (1992): 75–92.

under the Truck Act. In spite of his many courtroom victories, Duignan himself was skeptical of the impact they had on eradicating truck wages.[61]

The conflict between Greaves and Caton reached its breaking point on 2 March. In that pay settlement, 6s 6d of Greaves' wages were paid to him in truck. Greaves demanded that these wages be paid to him in cash. Caton, perhaps aware of the activity of Anti-Truck societies in the region, agreed to pay Greaves in currency in return for Greaves signing a document stating that he had never been paid in provisions. Greaves refused, and two days later again demanded the money owed to him and to be paid only in currency in the future. Caton told him he must accept his wages as the other miners did. Greaves replied that he would no longer work for him if he was not paid in currency.[62]

On 5 March, Greaves approached William Daniels, a lecturer and organizer for the Miners' Union, and asked him how he could collect his unpaid wages. Daniels and Greaves went to the provision shop and confronted Caton's wife. Like her husband, she offered to pay Greaves his wages if he signed a document saying that he had never received truck. Greaves again refused. On the next day, Daniels took Greaves to the Hanley County Court Office and took out a summons against Caton for £1 18s, the total of the truck wages he had received.[63]

Late in the evening of 11 March, Greaves was arrested and taken to Burslem under an arrest warrant signed by Rose charging him with unlawful absence under 4 George IV, c.34 (1823). When this news reached Daniels, he immediately collected three witnesses to testify to the terms of the contracts at Golden Hill Colliery, as well as the practice of paying men's wages in beer and bacon from Caton's shop. Daniels then engaged solicitor John Turton of Tunstall to defend Greaves.[64]

William Heaton, who had defended Austin, conducted Caton's prosecution of Greaves. Caton testified that his contract with Greaves could only be determined with a fortnight notice on either side. He claimed to have posted a copy of the contract in his office, and distributed 50 copies to the colliers in his employ. On cross-examination, however, Caton was unable to produce a single copy of this agreement. Greaves denied this contract, and he and Daniels later both swore in affidavits for the criminal information against Rose that they had three witnesses present at the hearing prepared to contradict Caton's testimony.[65] Rose, Heaton,

---

[61] Hinton, *Truck System*, pp. 121–31.

[62] NA: KB 1/190/22; 'Neglect of Work', *SA* (16 March 1850), p. 5; 'Convictions Under The Truck Act, Tunstall', *SA* (18 May 1850), p. 7.

[63] Ibid.

[64] Ibid.

[65] NA: KB 1/190/22, KB 1/191/60; because Greaves had already entered into Caton's service, parole evidence was sufficient to prove a contract under 4 George IV, c.34. C. M. Smith, *A Treatise on the Law of Master and Servant, Including Therein Masters and Workmen in Every Description of Trade and Occupation; With an Appendix of Statutes* (London, 1852), p. 313.

and Rose's clerk, each swore that Caton 'clearly proved' the contract and its requirement of 14 days' notice to end, as well as the fact that Greaves left 'without leave, notice or reason'.[66]

Sworn accounts of what happened when Mr Turton began to cross-examine Caton also conflict with one another. According to Daniels and Greaves, Turton asked Caton if he had been summoned to County Court by Greaves to recover wages paid in truck. They claimed that Rose intervened, declaring the question 'wholly irrelevant'. They swore under oath that Heaton, Caton's attorney, told Rose 'this Sir is a union case', to which the magistrate replied, 'Oh, I see'. Rose then turned to Greaves and said 'you stand committed to the House of Correction for a month'. When Turton stated that he still had witnesses to call, Rose replied, 'he did not believe anything of the defense set up and that it was all pretence'. As Turton argued, Rose shouted him down, saying 'call the next case!'.[67]

Rose, his clerk, a police superintendent, and Heaton all swore affidavits that explicitly denied the magistrate made any of those statements at the 12 March hearing. Yet their accounts conflict with one another in some important ways. Rose and Heaton each claimed that Turton did not ask Caton about truck under cross-examination. Rose's clerk, John Randolf Rose, however, swore that Turton asked Caton about the payment of wages in truck, and Caton testified that Greaves had never refused to accept truck. John Rose's affidavit states that the magistrate then dismissed this defense, stating that Greaves should have entered into proceedings to receive his wages in currency (which, in fact, Greaves had done) and not left work without notice.[68]

If J. R. Rose's testimony is truthful, then Greaves was very dubiously sent to prison. According to Section 1 of the 1831 Truck Act, 'if any such contract whole or any part of such wages shall be made payable in any other manner than in the current coin aforesaid, such contract shall be and is hereby declared illegal, null and void'. Had Turton proved that Caton paid Greaves any portion of his wages in truck, it would have made the contract void. Whether Greaves had agreed to accept truck was completely irrelevant, because truck was illegal whether he consented or not. Rose might have exceeded his jurisdiction because there was not a valid contract between the parties.[69]

---

[66]   Ibid.

[67]   Ibid.

[68]   I strongly suspect that John Randolf Rose is a relation of Thomas Bailey Rose, but I cannot confirm this. NA: KB 1/191/60.

[69]   1 & 2 William IV, c.37, s.1, 3, 4, 6 (1831). Sections 3 and 4 of the same act make all payments in truck illegal, the same as if Caton had never paid Greaves at all. If Rose did not know this, Roberts taught him. In November 1851, a miner was brought before Rose charged with leaving his work without proper notice under 4 George IV, c.34 (1823). Roberts represented the man and proved that the miner had been paid in a public house owned by a group of butty colliers (which was illegal under 5 & 6 Victoria, c.69), who

In his examination of a sample of master and servant cases from the 1850s, however, Steinmetz finds that magistrates were rarely sympathetic to workers charged under the Master and Servant Acts who defended themselves by arguing that their employer had voided the contract through illegal behavior.[70] This does not seem consistent with the wording of the statute, or the opinion that the law officers of the crown expressed in 1845.

In 1845, a similar case in Glamorgan had been brought to the attention of the Home Office. A group of miners walked off their jobs to protest against the practice of compelling workers to accept advances of price-inflated goods at a truck shop by 'holding wages in hand'. In some cases miners' wages were nine weeks in arrears. Their employers swore informations under 4 George IV, c.34 (1823), and magistrates issued a large number of arrest warrants. Six of the miners were tried on 16 August 1845, and were found guilty despite the defense proving that the employer had violated both the contract and the custom of the trade. The custom of the trade was to pay four weeks' wages when five were due, but the employers were paying four weeks' wages when seven or eight were due, holding a greater amount in hand and forcing the miners to accept advances in truck. The magistrates gave the miners one day to return to work or be sentenced to one month at hard labor, and the miners returned to work. A miner wrote a letter to Home Secretary, Sir James Graham, complaining of the case. Graham was bothered by the conviction, and wrote:

> I am not altogether satisfied with this case. It is doubtful whether the masters fulfilled their portion of the contract by the payment of wages due at exact periods stipulated: if the masters so failed to fulfill their engagement, then the question arises whether the workmen were not absolved from their contract also and at liberty to strike or withdraw from their employment without a month's notice.

Graham dispatched Mines Inspector Seymour Tremenheere to the district to investigate allegations of truck in the region, and asked Mr Phillipps to give his opinion on the above point of law. Phillipps' reply was unequivocal:

> I have no doubt that if the master does not fulfill his part of the contract by the due payment of wages, the workman may quit the service without giving a month's notice. The non-payment of wages is a violation of the contract and may be treated as a determination of the contract.

---

forced him to accept 6d of every pay packet in drink. Rose dismissed the charges against the miner. See 'Colliers' Wages', *SA* (18 January 1851), p. 5.

[70]   Steinmetz, 'De-Juridification', p. 276.

The Home Office pardoned the convicted miners.[71] It does not require a great leap of reasoning to argue that if not paying wages on time voids a contract of employment, then illegally refusing to pay wages in currency should as well. According to the wording of the Truck Act, paying a worker in truck was the same as not paying him/her at all.

The report of this case in the *Staffordshire Advertiser*, seems to confirm the clerk's affidavit, stating that Mr Turton introduced into evidence that 'an information was laid against the employer under the Truck Act'. T. B. Rose and Heaton claimed that Turton only mentioned truck in his closing, but had not introduced any evidence of it during the hearing.[72] It is unlikely that Turton would fail to ask Caton about such a relevant point, especially if he planned to use it as his client's defense.

The final point of dispute in the affidavits was the one that was the most important for the success of the criminal information. Did Rose, after making the malicious statements Daniels and Greaves attributed to him, refuse to permit the defense to call witnesses? Both Roses, Heaton, and police superintendent Povey, all swore that Turton simply chose, without obstruction or coercion, not to call any witnesses. Richard Heaton emphasized that Turton had the 'full opportunity' to present a defense.[73] This seems unlikely. Turton was paid to present a defense for Greaves, and had a good one available. Daniels was present at the hearing, and could have testified to the existence of the 'Tommy shop', as could three other witnesses. It is curious that Turton did not provide an affidavit for either side in the criminal information against Rose, and it is a glaring hole in attempts to reconstruct this case. Did Roberts omit an affidavit from Turton because he would not have corroborated Daniels and Greaves? If that was true, however, then why did Rose fail to use an affidavit from Turton in his defense? Rose received all of the plaintiff's affidavits before he was required to submit any in his defense, so he would have been aware of this omission in the case against him. It is possible that Turton, whose practice was concentrated in the Potteries, was not anxious to participate in a criminal information against one of the region's most active magistrates.

There are some reasons to believe the affidavits of Greaves and Daniels. Rose had a history of indiscrete statements and an adversarial relationship with trade unions. Rose's home had been destroyed and his family endangered by unionized miners eight years earlier. A rush to judge a union miner charged with breaking his contract, and bellicose statements, appear consistent with other behavior demonstrated during his career. Rose actually confessed to making some inappropriate statements toward the same parties a month later, when they appeared before him to file an information against Caton under the Truck Act.

---

[71]   NA: HO 45/994; 'Brigend Petty Sessions', *The Cardiff and Merthyr Guardian* (23 August 1845), p. 5.

[72]   NA: KB 1/191/60; 'Neglect of Work', *SA* (16 March 1850), p. 5

[73]   Ibid.

Not in dispute was the fact that Greaves went to prison. While Greaves was walking on the treadmill in the House of Correction, John Caton paid £1 18s and costs into the County Court to avoid a hearing. After his release, Greaves and the Miners' Union decided to prosecute Caton criminally under the Truck Act. On 25 April Daniels attended Tunstall Petty Sessions to swear out the necessary information against Caton.

Daniels claimed that when delivering the information to Rose, the magistrate asked police superintendent Povey, 'Who is he, what is he?'. Povey replied, 'He's a Chartist union lecturer'. Daniels swore that Rose then turned to him and said 'You are a destructive, a firebrand, you go about to make disturbances and to set the miners against their masters – what you are – who you are – you're a seditious fellow'. He then added 'If I had it in my power I would send such fellows as you out of the country'. Daniels replied, 'I think, Sir, this anger and abuse quite uncalled for, we are prepared to prove that the law has been grossly violated; you are an administrator of the law; you ought not to abuse those who wish to see the law carried out'. Daniels' affidavit states that Rose replied 'very well – what magistrates is it to be tried by? I'll let them know – I shall give you no support or countenance – I would send all of you out of the country if I could'.[74]

Rose's affidavit actually differs very little from that of Daniels', the only dispute being where Rose was standing when he made his provocative statements. Rose claimed that after he accepted the information, he stepped down from the bench, and told Daniels that he 'created much discontent among the miners of this district by his uncalled for interference'. He conceded that he 'rebuked … William Daniels for meddling with the affairs of others and causing much mischief in the neighbourhood'. Povey was more vague in his affidavit, testifying that Rose addressed Daniels 'with some words of rebuke and remonstrance for interfering between masters and men'. John Rose swore that the magistrate:

> Told him that he was a mischievous fellow and that it was men like himself who stirred up the people to revolt and that he had no business to interfere with other working men who were satisfied with their wages and if Thomas Bailey Rose had the power to do so, he would cause all such mischievous persons to be driven out of the country.

Rose defended his remarks by emphasizing that he had stepped down from the magisterial bench when making them, and was no longer acting in an official capacity.[75]

On 15 May 1850, Roberts appeared before Rose and two other magistrates at Longton Petty Sessions to prosecute Caton for paying Greaves in truck. Nine days earlier, Rose had refused to accept a recognizance and sureties from Roberts for Austin. Heaton appeared to defend Caton. Roberts introduced his case by

---

[74] NA: KB 1/190/22.

[75] NA: KB 1/191/60.

stating that Greaves had been imprisoned under 4 George IV, c.34 (1823) before he could prosecute Caton under the Truck Act. The response of those present was very peculiar when one considers that Roberts was the only person involved in this hearing who had not been present when Caton prosecuted Greaves. Heaton, who represented Caton in the earlier hearing, objected and asked if Roberts was prepared to prove that this had actually happened. An incredulous Rose then asked Roberts 'Do you say that the man has been in prison a month under the circumstances you have stated?'. Roberts told him that he had. Rose demanded to know the name of the magistrate who had committed him, and Roberts replied 'Yourself, Sir'. Rose expressed disbelief, and emphasized his strong disapproval of truck. He said if he had known, 'the man most certainly would not have been committed'.[76] Rose's surprise does not appear to be consistent with either the affidavits from the criminal information or the earlier newspaper report of Greaves' prosecution under 4 George IV, c.34 (1823). Rose had heard the case only two months earlier. That even a magistrate as busy as Rose would have completely forgotten this case is astonishing. It is possible, indeed likely, that with the arrival of Roberts, Rose became aware of the possible consequences of his actions and chose to act carefully.

Roberts called Greaves to testify to the payment of wages in truck, and his persistent complaints and meetings with Caton and his wife on the subject. Heaton objected to the introduction of Greaves' encounter with Mrs Caton, as the actions of a wife were not binding upon the husband. Heaton asked Greaves if anyone had heard him complain about the payment of truck wages, and Greaves stated that James Dunning, a fellow miner, had been present on one such occasion. Heaton then asked him if he belonged to the miners' union, which drew an objection from Roberts. In his closing argument, Heaton argued that 'the information had been laid by a Chartist delegate and the matter had been further encouraged by the delivery of some inflammatory harangues'. Heaton's choice to raise this issue is interesting, because it appears consistent with the allegation by Daniels and Greaves that in the March hearing he told Rose 'this Sir is a union case'. Roberts rose to reply, but was stopped by the bench, who informed Heaton that his observations were not relevant. The court fined Caton £5 and costs. When Roberts applied to have half the fine given to the informer, the Bench refused.[77]

The next day Greaves' representatives presented Rose with notice of his intent to apply to the Court of Queen's Bench for a rule to show cause why a criminal information should not be exhibited for committing 'certain misdemeanors in unlawfully and maliciously and corruptly and contrary to your duty … refusing to hear witnesses on the part of the said Robert Greaves'. The law required that magistrates receive sufficient notice of a prosecutor's intent to pursue a criminal information. This gave Rose the opportunity to prepare a defense.[78]

---

[76]   'Information Under the Truck Act at Longton', *SA* (18 May 1850), p. 7.

[77]   Ibid.

[78]   Hay, 'Dread of the Crown Office', pp. 26–8.

A criminal information was an expensive and risky method of pursuing justice, testimony to the miners' frustration with Rose.[79] The costs of this action were considerable due to its multiple stages, requiring the coordination of local attorneys and a barrister at Westminster. To initiate a criminal information, the prosecutor had to give the magistrate advance notice of the grounds for the charge. A local attorney then prepared all affidavits for the plaintiff's case, and sent them to Westminster, where a barrister used them to obtain a rule nisi from the court. A rule nisi meant that the court found sufficient grounds to require the defendant to answer with his own affidavits. Barristers for both sides then argued the case before Queen's Bench. If the prosecutor was successful, the court granted a rule absolute. This, however, only meant that there were grounds for holding an actual trial before a special jury at the next local assizes. If a prosecutor lost, at any stage, he or she could be saddled with paying the costs of both parties. Hay argues that these cases rarely advanced far because prosecutors were required to prove a high level of malicious misconduct. In the eighteenth century, he notes, there was 'a great tolerance by the high court judges for ignorant, mistaken, abusive, or even … what clearly appears to be malicious conduct' by magistrates.[80]

Yet, there were reasons for Rose to be afraid. In another 1850 criminal information against a magistrate, Mr Justice Campbell described the level of misconduct a prosecutor had to prove before the Queen's Bench would send it before a jury at the assizes:

> I am of the opinion that … a magistrate is properly answerable to a charge of misconduct in his office, though in such misconduct he may not be actuated by any motive of pecuniary interest and though he may not mean maliciously to injure any individual. If he gives way to passion in doing anything connected with the administration of justice or if he is guilty of any impropriety of demeanor, so as to affect the due discharge of his duties, this court may direct that the case against him shall be laid before a jury.[81]

The affidavits of Greaves and Daniels suggest this standard had been met.

Furthermore, while the judges of the Court of Queen's Bench had demonstrated a reluctance to send criminal informations against justices of the peace to special juries at the assizes, they were willing to use the sanction of costs to rebuke magistrates. Between 1820 and 1838, returns to Parliament list 36 criminal informations against magistrates in which Queen's Bench issued a rule nisi. In only two of these cases was a rule absolute granted, sending the case before a

---

[79]   Ibid., pp. 21–4, 26–30.

[80]   Ibid.

[81]   'Reg v. Barton – Criminal Information – Motion against a Justice of the Peace', *JP* 14/47 (23 November 1850), p. 47; 'Reg v. Barton – Criminal Information – Motion Against a Justice of the Peace', *JP* 14/48 (30 November 1850), pp. 738–9.

special jury at the assizes.[82] Four others were withdrawn, privately settled or referred to arbitration. In 10 cases, the rule was discharged with costs, meaning that the unsuccessful prosecutor was required to pay the costs of the magistrate. Twelve cases were discharged without costs, meaning that the magistrate was left out-of-pocket for the costs of his own defense. In eight cases, the court discharged the rule, but found the case serious enough that it made the magistrate pay the costs of the prosecution.[83] Although there were not a large number of these cases, their outcome is suggestive of how the court used the degree of costs granted, rejected or imposed as a means of sanction.

This was still a risky proceeding for Greaves and the Union. In addition to the expenses of affidavits, travel, solicitor's and barrister's fees, and all the filing and court fees, choosing to pursue Rose by criminal information meant that Greaves sacrificed his right to proceed civilly against Rose.[84] It was not enough, or even necessary, to prove that Rose decided the case incorrectly. Roberts had to demonstrate that from excess passion, or ill-will, Rose's personal feelings had impeded the due administration of his duties.

On 30 May the affidavits of Roberts, Greaves and Daniels were filed with the Master of the Crown Office, and the next day Huddleston obtained a rule nisi from the Court. This meant that Rose had to answer the charge, and would begin to build up legal expenses. On 7 June, the affidavits of T. B. Rose, J. R. Rose, Richard Heaton and Thomas Povey were sworn at an office in Staffordshire and sent to Westminster.

On 12 June, Huddleston and Whitmore appeared before Mr Justice Wightman to argue whether he should grant a rule absolute, which would allow the case to be heard by a special jury.[85] Four days earlier, Wightman had ordered the release of William Austin on recognizance. The *Staffordshire Advertiser* reported that 'the affidavits were of a contradictory character'. Because of this Wightman felt he had little choice but to rule for Rose. In his ruling, however, he expressed dissatisfaction with Rose's behavior:

---

[82] 'Return of all Applications In the Court of Queen's Bench For Criminal Informations Against Justices of the Peace in Which a Rule Nisi Was Granted, January 1820–December 1830', *Parliamentary Papers* (1831) Vol. XV (87); 'Return of All Applications In the Court of Queen's Bench For Criminal Informations Against Justices of the Peace in Which a Rule Nisi was Granted, January 1831-December 1833', *Parliamentary Papers* (1834) Vol. XLVIII (249); 'Return of All Applications in the Court of Queen's Bench For Criminal Informations Against Justices of the Peace in Which a Rule Nisi was Granted, January 1834-December 1838', *Parliamentary Papers* (1839) Vol. LXIII (431). In the two cases in which a rule absolute was granted, the assize juries granted one acquittal and one conviction. In the Easter Assizes of 1833, Pembrokeshire J. P. Samuel Harris was convicted and fined £500 and costs.

[83] Ibid.

[84] Hay, 'Dread of the Crown Office', pp. 27–30.

[85] Ibid.

Although the case had required some explanation, the affidavits in support had been answered; at the same time he thought certain expressions had been used by Mr. Rose, which to say the least of them, were indiscreet. He thought that the rule should be discharged, but under the circumstances, not with costs.[86]

Rose could take little satisfaction from this victory, as he had to pay his own considerable legal costs. Roberts and Huddleston were unable to penalize Rose with the full rebuke of a criminal information, but they did succeed in obtaining the indirect sanctions of legal costs and Wightman's public questioning of his conduct, which was reported in the most widely-read county newspaper in Staffordshire as well as the labor press.

R. v. Joseph Askew (1851)

A year after Rose suffered the indignity of paying costs in a criminal information, Roberts initiated a habeas corpus against another of his rulings under 4 George IV, c.34 (1823). The participants in this case were the familiar actors of Rose, Heaton, Turton, Roberts and Judge Wightman. According to Steinfeld, soon after the victory In Re: *Askew*, the high courts became much more reluctant to overturn convictions, determining in 1853 that magistrates using the general forms in the Jervis Acts would be protected.[87] The ruling of the Queen's Bench in this case was interpreted by local potters and miners as confirmation that Rose was a partial and vindictive magistrate. This led to widespread protest and petitioning against his conduct, further undermining his legitimacy.

On 7 June 1851, the Mayer brothers prosecuted potter Joseph Askew before Rose for giving an invalid notice to quit work under 4 George IV, c.34 (1823). Heaton represented the Mayers, and Turton defended Askew. Mayer and his manager, Mr Challinor, both testified that Askew's agreement with the firm stipulated that if they failed to provide Askew with 16 days' work during any four-week period, he could terminate the contract with a month's notice.[88] Askew had presented his employers with a written one-month's notice to end his employment, which expired on 2 June, but he did not claim that they had failed to provide the required work. Heaton argued that Askew's notice was therefore invalid.[89] This

---

[86] 'R. v. Rose: Bail Court', *SA* (15 June 1850), p. 5; NA: KB 21/68 (12 June 1850).

[87] Steinfeld, *Coercion*, pp. 158–9, see In Re *Geswood*, 23 L. J. 53. See Chapter 6 and *Lindsey v. Leigh* (1848), 17 L. J. 50; 'Proceedings in Matters Relating to Servants', *JP* 12/41 (7 October 1848), pp. 657–8; 'On The Present State of Master and Servant Law', *JP* 12/44 (28 October 1848), pp. 705–6; 'Practical Points', *JP* 12/39 (30 September 1848), pp. 634–7; 'Practical Points', *JP* 15/14 (5 April 1851), p. 234.

[88] The agreement also stipulated that this failure to provide work could not be caused by a turn-out.

[89] 'Invalid Notice to Quit Work', *SA* (7 June 1851), p. 4.

agreement gave the master the freedom to determine the contract with a month's notice, and complete control over the employee's right to do the same.

Turton cross-examined Challinor, asking whether he ever discharged workers at a month's notice, and Challinor said that he had. At this point Rose intervened, stating that Turton had to 'confine himself to the agreement; anything extra could not be considered'. Turton argued that if the employers could determine the agreement with a month's notice, it was perfectly reasonable for Askew to feel 'he might do the same'. Turton argued that this was not a case of unlawful absence, but of honest error.[90]

Rose was 'about to inflict a fine and payment of costs', when he asked Askew if he would return to work. Askew refused. Rose then remarked 'with some warmth' that it was his duty to send Askew to prison, 'as an example that the office of the magistracy must not be trifled with, nor the interests of employers injured with impunity'. He sentenced Askew to a month in prison with hard labor.[91] Once again, Rose's injudicious statements drew him into controversy. The apparent relish with which he punished Askew made it hard for potters to believe that he was an impartial arbiter. Quite often the most desirable outcome for an employer in a master and servant case was to have the magistrate make the worker pay the costs and force him back to work against the threat of imprisonment. Hay and Steinfeld have argued that for most of the nineteenth century the higher courts supported the use of master and servant law to compel specific performance of the contract of employment by repeatedly ruling that a conviction under these acts did not terminate the contract. If a worker refused to return to work after serving his or her prison sentence, he or she could be convicted again.[92] Rose could not disguise his anger at Askew's refusal to play his role in this familiar ritual.

The Potters' Union took up this case, outraged at what they called the 'oppressive and illegal' commitment of Askew. The day after Askew's hearing, the Union engaged Roberts to prepare the habeas corpus, and he quickly found a flaw in the conviction.[93] The warrant of committal failed to state that the contract between the parties was in writing, or that Askew had already commenced upon the agreement, as required by Section 3 of the 1823 Master and Servant Act.[94] It

---

[90]   Ibid.

[91]   Ibid. The 1823 Act did not permit magistrates to fine. Newspaper reports often confused the awarding of costs or the abatement of wages with a fine.

[92]   Douglas Hay, 'England, 1562–1875: The Law and its Uses', in Douglas Hay and Paul Craven (eds.), *Masters, Servants, and Magistrates in Britain and the Empire, 1562–1955* (Chapel Hill, 2004), pp. 59–60; Steinfeld, *Coercion*, pp. 57–60. Rose and Roberts were involved in one of the most important cases on this point, In Re: *Baker* (1857), 2 H. & N. 219, 'Breach of Agreement', *SA* (16 May 1857), p. 2.

[93]   'Burslem: Invalid Notice to Quit Work', *SA* (21 June 1851), p. 4.

[94]   4 George IV, c.34, s.3 (1823); Charles Manley Smith, *A Treatise on the Law of Master and Servant, Including Therein Masters and Workmen in Every Description of*

is clear from the newspaper reports that Askew's contract was in writing, and he had entered into the service of the Mayer brothers. This did not matter, however, because it was not stated on the face of the warrant of commitment. According to Seth Turner's case (1846), described in Chapter 3, a conviction or committal had to negate the possibility of a lawful excuse for leaving or not entering one's employment in order to establish the magistrate's jurisdiction. Had the employment contract been verbal, and Askew not yet commenced upon it, there would have been a lawful reason for Askew's actions, and the case would have been beyond Rose's jurisdiction. Roberts was aware of this because in another appeal he had initiated, *Lindsay v. Leigh* (1848), the Court of Queen's Bench and the Exchequer Chamber had ruled on precisely this point. Before the end of 8 June, Roberts sent an affidavit and a copy of the conviction to Huddleston.[95]

On 10 June 1851, Huddleston secured a writ of habeas corpus to bring Askew to Westminster. Three days later, Huddleston and Mr Pashley argued before Mr Justice Wightman whether or not to quash the conviction. Huddleston argued that the conviction did not demonstrate an offence, according to Section 3 of the 1823 Master and Servant Act, In Re: *Turner* (1846), and *Lindsey v. Leigh* (1848). He argued that this last case was precisely on the point, as that miner's conviction had been quashed because the warrant of committal failed to stipulate explicitly that the contract was in writing or that the miner had commenced it.

Pashley argued that these facts were implicit in the conviction, which stated that the offence occurred on 2 June, and that the contract between the parties was to commence seven months prior to that date. Pashley argued, not unreasonably, that

> there is considerable evidence by implication on the face of the document that the misconduct took place after Askew had entered into and upon his service to Messrs. Mayers, and outside Westminster Hall no one would have a doubt on the subject.

Pashley's statement is representative of many of the complaints from magistrates seen in Chapters 1 and 6, respecting the strict legal formalism with which these documents were read by the higher courts. The statement, however, foreshadowed where Queen's Bench would soon go with respect to these cases. From a 'common sense' perspective, it is clear that Askew had commenced upon his service, and that Rose had jurisdiction to determine the matter. It is equally clear, however, that there were wrongs in this case that the law and legal process prevented labor's representatives from raising in court. Magistrates felt that they were frequently the victims of legal sophistry and technical quibbles brought by sharp attorneys like Roberts. However, employees like Askew, who was trapped in a highly unequal

---

Trade and Occupation: With an Appendix of Statutes (London, 1852), p. 313.

[95]   NA: KB 1/199/47. Also see In Re: *Turner* (1846), 10 J. P. 570 and *Lindsey v. Leigh* (1848), 11 Q. B. 454.

contract, felt that collusion between magistrates and employers shaped the administration and interpretation of a highly coercive statue, and this represented a far greater injustice.

Responding to Pashley, Mr Justice Wightman declared 'You say that what is stated is equivalent to stating an entry [into service]; but I always distrust equivalents'.[96] The higher courts held instruments of conviction to a very high standard, requiring that they explicitly state all facts necessary to demonstrate the jurisdiction of the magistrate. Wightman ruled that he 'cannot distinguish this case from that in the Exchequer Chamber (Lindsey v. Leigh), a court of higher authority than this one'. Because 'Lindsey v. Leigh is a governing authority', he discharged the defendant.[97]

The *Staffordshire Advertiser* reported that this case 'excited considerable interest amongst the working potters generally'. Rose had a turbulent history with workers in the region, and having three of his rulings questioned by Queen's Bench in 13 months further undermined his standing. During the week of Askew's release, potters throughout the region placarded walls with handbills 'condemning in no measured terms the conduct of Mr. Rose', and held public meetings against Rose in Tunstall, Stoke, Longton, Burslem, Hanley and Fenton, all of which were 'numerously attended'. At these meetings speakers took turns condemning Rose, and passed resolutions for the creation of a legal fund to assist workers in proceedings against his rulings.[98]

These cases occurred during an era of transition, between a period when the Court of Queen's Bench had applied vigorous legal formalism to magistrates' proceedings, prepared to overturn them on the slightest technical flaw, and one in which the same courts gave greater latitude to the 'great unpaid'. The courts were faced with the difficult question of how best to preserve the legitimacy of the summary proceedings of magistrates with the class of people who experienced them the most.

These three cases from 1850–1851 demonstrate some of the ways that the law was used in everyday industrial relations at the local level, as well as the class barriers that workers faced when engaging the legal system. In the first case, not only did the magistrate support a highly restrictive view of 6 George IV, c.129 (1825), one which demonstrated a lack of understanding of workers' experiences, but so did the defendant's attorney. In the second case, a miner attempted to use the law to recover wages that were illegally paid to him in truck, but found himself outmaneuvered by his employer's use of the master and servant statute. Even though the employer had clearly violated the law and the contract of employment, his transgressions were not perceived by the magistrate as serious enough to end the

---

[96]   'Ex Parte Askew', *JP* 15/26 (28 June 1851), pp. 418–19; 'Reg v. Askew', *JP* 15/30 (26 July 1851), pp. 485–6; NA: KB 1/199/47; 'Burslem: Invalid Notice to Quit Work', *SA* (21 June 1851), p. 8; 'Queen v. Askew', *SA* (21 June 1851), p. 8.

[97]   'Reg v. Askew', *JP* 15/30 (26 July 1851), pp. 485–6.

[98]   'Burslem: Invalid Notice to Quit Work', *SA* (21 June 1851), p. 8.

servant's broad obligation of obedience. In the third case, an employer attempted to use the threat of imprisonment before a magistrate well-disposed toward himself in order to compel a potter to continue work under a highly one-sided and barely reciprocal agreement. In all of these cases, the 'indiscreet' statements that Rose made from the bench with near-impunity communicated the message that employers had a greater claim upon the laws of England than their employees.

These cases also demonstrate, however, the tremendous difference that trade-union-funded legal resistance continued to make in seemingly hopeless cases before biased magistrates. In Austin's case, not only did Roberts win the worker's freedom, but he created a precedent that ensured it would remain feasible for workers to appeal to Quarter Sessions convictions under the 1825 Combination Act. In Askew's case, Roberts used legal precedents, to which his work on behalf of unionists contributed, to win his client's freedom. The reaction of the potters in the aftermath of this case (and in the protests of 1843 and 1845) show that Roberts' cases severely undermined Rose's credibility with workers, and gave unionists a language for expressing their grievances. In Greaves' case, Roberts won belated justice against his client's employer, and attempted to make Rose face consequences for his behavior. The cases also make it clear that magistrates faced less serious consequences for incorrectly administering the law than they did in the 1840s, but the resourcefulness of trade union attorneys was not to be underestimated. Rose faced no civil suit in *R. v. Austin* thanks to the Vexatious Actions Act. In Greaves' case, Roberts had to settle for the indirect sanctions of costs and embarrassment due to the high level of magisterial misconduct the courts were prepared to accept from magistrates.

Conclusion

'We certainly ought not to let a mere technical slip … decide such a case'

'Constitutional Law versus Justices' Justice' Revisited, *R. v. Biggins* (1861–1862)

Sixteen years after the four Longton colliers were dragged from their beds in the dead of a cold January night, workers continued to suffer injustices under the Master and Servant Acts. What had changed was that in the years after the liberation of those miners, attorneys found it increasingly difficult to void the summary convictions of magistrates and, indeed, by 1865, a few of the most powerful unions in the country had become much more selective about trying. Campaigns led by radicals who systematically turned every master and servant prosecution into an apocalyptic public struggle between the people and the powerful, were no longer consistent with the larger goals of many trade unions. So-called new model craft unions that emerged in the 1850s and 1860s were distinct from their predecessors in their more centralized organizational structure and their larger treasuries that paid a variety of benefits to members. The leaders of these unions placed even greater emphasis than earlier unions had on their members' aspirations to middle-class notions of respectable manhood, and their desire for more stable relations with their employers and government. Organizations like the Amalgamated Society of Engineers (formed in 1851), the Amalgamated Society of Carpenters and Joiners (formed in 1860), and the Miners' Association (re-launched in 1858 and 1863) hoped to become accepted as part of the capitalist order and win favorable legislation to support this position. These unions expressed a desire to avoid strikes and, although they were not always successful in this effort, their leaders worked to project a non-threatening image and adopt less confrontational rhetoric. What was new about so-called new model unions was not their desire to have good relations with employers, avoid strikes or conform to middle-class notions of respectable masculinity, but rather the higher degree of success they achieved toward these ends and their greater recognition from the state for their efforts.

Yet, right up to his death, Roberts continued to defend workers in master and servant cases with obstructionist attacks on form and process, blistering cross-examinations of employers and their agents, inflammatory closing arguments publicizing workplace grievances and illegal behavior by the prosecutors and speeches to the public in which he denounced 'tyrannical' collusion between employers and local institutions of justice. Some union leaders felt that this type of activity hardened the positions of employers and the state, making them less willing to adopt a conciliatory stance toward organized labor. As a result, union leaders engaged men like Roberts much more rarely, and in the many instances where they still sought to pursue their interests through the courts, they utilized less controversial legal counsel. In his biography of Roberts, Raymond Challinor describes the very difficult struggle between Alexander MacDonald and the Council of the Miners' Association against several the local branches over the removal of Roberts as legal advisor. MacDonald was ultimately successful, though branches continued to hire Roberts from time-to-time, and parts of the rank-and-file remained bitter with MacDonald for years.[1]

Part of the logic behind this shift in tactics was the fact that by the late 1850s it had become clear that a growing number of politicians no longer regarded the 1832 Reform Act as necessarily permanent. The possibility of working-class voters meant that there was also the potential to use the political system to create a Britain in which workers could not be imprisoned for breach of contract. Rather than impede, obstruct and expose the administration of highly coercive labor laws by unsupervised magistrates, it seemed less far-fetched that workers could hope for more, and fight to have these hated statutes repealed altogether. Respectable and politically connected middle-class barristers, like Frederick Harrison and Arthur Edgar, forcefully argued in the 1860s that contracts of employment should be treated the same as all other civil contracts, with no imprisonment for breach or compulsion of specific performance.[2] These new possibilities, when combined with the closing of many of the legal avenues that unions used in the struggle against master and servant law during the 1840s and 1850s, made it unsurprising that some of the larger centralized unions began to channel their energies toward institutions of the state that offered the greatest prospects for success. It must be understood that those conducting Parliamentary lobbying for an end to the penal sanctions of employment law were, in fact, more deeply indebted than they would have cared to admit to the radical solicitors who used every legal and political strategy at their disposal to prevent workers from being imprisoned for breach of contract. By contesting prosecutions under the Master and Servant Acts, trade union legal counsel shone a spotlight on countless examples of injustice in the administration of these statutes that would have otherwise remained in the dark. The legal arguments formulated by these lawyers in the 1840s provided

---

[1]   Raymond Challinor, *Radical Lawyer in Victorian England: W. P. Roberts and the Struggle for Workers' Rights* (London, 1990), Chapter 14; Keith Laybourne, *A History of British Trade Unionism* (London, 1997), Chapter 2.

[2]   F. Harrison, 'Imprisonment for Breach of Contract or the Master and Servant Act', in E. Frow and M. Katanka (eds), *1868: Year of the Unions: A Documentary Survey* (London, 1968, originally 1868), p. 142; A. Edgar, 'On the Jurisdiction of Justices of the Peace in Disputes between Employers and Employed Arising From Breach of Contract', in G. W. Hastings (ed.), *Transactions of the National Association for the Promotion of Social Science, 1859* (London, 1860), p. 687.

the language and the examples for subsequent lobbying efforts. This book has demonstrated that the current historiography, which at times seems to suppose that organized efforts to repeal master and servant law emerged out of thin air in the 1860s, is in need of revision.

Yet, it would be wrong to suggest that organized labor abandoned the notion of pursuing and defending its interests in the courtroom. Trade unions continued to engage lawyers to defend workers in master and servant cases, and to represent them on a whole range of other issues, including prosecuting employers for paying truck wages, funding civil suits in cases of workplace injury or death, hiring legal counsel to attend coroner's inquests, and using attorneys to protect trade unionists' right to picket. Reform of the magistracy and summary justice remained an issue of great interest to trade unions for the remainder of the century. As the following case study will show, when unions felt their members were treated with considerable unfairness in master and servant proceedings, they were still sometimes prepared to engage the most aggressive attorneys and exhaust all legal options for making the magistrates accountable. Despite being viewed by many union leaders as a radical from another era, Roberts was still hired to work on a number of important cases in the 1850s and 1860s, and he remained popular among rank-and-file unionists in the north. Among these workers, there is a good deal of evidence that optimism about the potential of 'constitutional law' lived much longer than the results merited. Roberts continued to be active in the courts on behalf of unions in master and servant cases, truck, Combination Act offences, conspiracy, embezzlement of union funds, and worker injury after 1850.[3]

---

[3]   See Challinor, *Radical Lawyer*, Chapter 14. Also see *R. v. Baker* (1857), 2 H. & N. 241; *R. v. Rowlands* (1851), *R. v. Duffield* (1851), 5 Cox Criminal Cases 404, 466; NA: KB 1/199/59–60, KB 1/203/662–3, KB 1/204/51; W. Highfield, 'Great Tin-Plate Workers' Strike', *The Blackcountryman* 5 (April 1972): 49–57; *R. v. Walsby* (1861), 3 El. & El. 516; Challinor, *Radical Lawyer*, pp. 211, 255; *R. v. O'Neil & Galbraith* (1863), 4 B. & S. 376, 389; The Working Class Movement Library, Salford: *Trade Reports of the Boiler Makers and Shipbuilders Society, 1859–1868*; J. Orth, 'English Law and Striking Workmen: The Molestation of Workmen Act, 1859', *The Journal of Legal History* 2 (1981): 238–57; Orth, *Combination and Conspiracy: A Legal History of Trade Unionism, 1721–1906* (Oxford, 1991); J. McIlroy, 'Financial Malpractice in British Trade Unions, 1800–1930: The Background to, and Consequences of, Hornby v. Close', *Historical Studies in Industrial Relations* 6 (Autumn 1998): 1–64; *Hornby v. Close* (1867), 2 Q. B. 153. Also see: *R. v. Welton and Hickie* (1868), *R. v. John Ellis* (1868), Warwick University Modern Records Centre: MSS.78.OS.4.1.33; *Farrar v. Close* (1869), 10 Cox Criminal Cases 393. See Jamie Bronstein, *Caught in the Machinery: Workplace Accidents and Injured Workers in Nineteenth Century Britain* (Stanford, 2008); Haswell Colliery Explosion and Coxlodge Colliery Explosion (1844), NA: HO 45/631; 'Haswell Colliery Explosion: The United Miners Protection and Mutual Benefit Society', *MA* 1/21 (19 October 1844), p. 181; 'Coxlodge Explosion', 'The Late Explosion at Coxlodge', *MA* 1/22 (16 November 1844), pp. 193, 195; W. P. Roberts, *The Haswell Colliery Explosion, 28 September 1844, Narrative, Report of the Proceedings at the Coroner's Inquest and Plan of that Part of the Colliery in which*

This conclusion uses a case study of a master and servant prosecution from 1861–1862 to illuminate the transformation of the legal climate that had occurred during the period covered by this book. It also explores the continued engagement of organized labor with the legal system at both the local and national levels in spite of the changing attitudes of judges and policy makers and the new political opportunities for trade unions. It considers the long-term consequences of the trade unions' legal and political campaign against the penal characteristics of employment law.

In the summer of 1861, stonemasons Thomas Biggins, William Rogers, Robert Reed, Thomas Davies, Thomas Fawcett, William Nicholson and Robert Nicholson were under an agreement to work for subcontractor Henry Weaver 'for an indefinite period', terminable with one full day's notice. Along with Weaver's 200 other employees, they were building the Gannless Viaduct for the South Durham and Lancashire Union Railway near Cockfield, close to the Yorkshire–Durham boarder. On 18 June 1861, a stonemason in the employ of Weaver was late for work after having received an earlier warning about his punctuality. Weaver dismissed the man, who was a member of the union. The seven stonemasons informed Weaver that unless the man was re-hired, they would not continue to work for him. They considered this conditional notice to be sufficient for ending the agreement. The next morning the masons arrived at work and were informed that Weaver had no intention of re-engaging the often-tardy employee. The men then refused to begin the day's work, and demanded the unpaid wages that Weaver had in hand for each of them, which he refused.[4]

Later the same day a messenger from Weaver told the seven masons that if they wanted to receive their unpaid wages they should go to a nearby public house. When the men arrived at this pub, waiting constables ambushed them. The prisoners were very roughly treated, shackled and then made to march on foot three miles to the town of Staindrop, in Yorkshire. Here the seven were divided and placed in two separate damp cells, where they were forced to spend the night without beds or blankets. Between the moment of their arrest and the time of their

---

the Accident Took Place (Newcastle upon Tyne, 1845); *Full and Authentic Particulars of the Dreadful Explosion at Haswell Colliery On Saturday, September 28th, 1844, By Which Ninety-Five Lives Were Lost* (Sunderland, 1844); The Working Class Movement Library, Salford: F 62, Box 10, 'The Haswell Catastrophe!'; Challinor, *Radical Lawyer*, pp. 133–6. Kirkless Colliery Accident (1847), NA: HO 45/1830; Patricroft Colliery Accident (1847), NA: HO 45/1873; Ince Colliery Accident (1854), NA: HO 45/5588; Cassop Colliery and Burnhope Colliery, NA: HO 45/758; Burradon Colliery (1860), NA: HO 45/7007; *Mary Taylor v. Carr and Porter* (1861), 121 E. R. 1098, and *Alice Taylor v. Carr and Porter* (1862), 2 B. & S. 335; NA: KB 1/263/35, KB 1/264/26; Robert Steinfeld, *Coercion, Contract and Free Labour in the Nineteenth Century* (Cambridge, 2001), pp. 149–50.

[4] Warwick University Modern Records Centre: MSS.78.OS.4.1.20, MSS.78.OS.4.1.22; NA: KB 1/264/37; R. Challinor, *Radical Lawyer*, p. 211.

hearing the following morning, they were not given any food, or permitted to speak with anyone.[5]

At 7:30 a.m. on 20 June 1861 the stonemasons were brought before a magistrate, the Rev. Henry Lipscombe. Lipscombe had been an active magistrate in Durham between 1848 and 1859, but feeling that magisterial business was eating into the time needed for his parochial duties, he had withdrawn from hearing cases. Weaver claimed that he chose this particular magistrate because all magistrates in the southwest division of Darlington Ward were unavailable. The employees felt his intent was to remove the masons from their friends and families and try them rapidly in order to lessen the possibility of their obtaining legal representation. Lipscombe later swore in an affidavit that prior to this incident he had never met any of the parties involved with the case.

Lipscombe informed the seven that they were charged under 4 George IV, c.34 (1823) with leaving work without giving proper notice. The defendants asked for an adjournment so that they could obtain an attorney to represent them and summon witnesses for their defense. Lipscombe refused on the grounds that he could see 'no dispute of any matter of fact between them'. Of course, it is extremely doubtful that an attorney such as Roberts or John Owen would have agreed with this assessment. Lipsombe made that common distinction between 'matters of fact' in the case, which he felt no attorney could dispute, and 'matters of form', which a crafty solicitor might use for advantage. Supporters of summary justice had used this argument to great effect during the previous 20 years, and as this case study will demonstrate, were now pleased to see that it was a distinction adopted by the judges of the higher courts as well.

The masons then asked to be tried separately because they claimed that their cases were different from one another. Lipscombe refused because he felt that the 'material facts' were the same in every case. In practice, this meant that the defendants could not act as witnesses for one another. Lipscombe then heard two witnesses, Henry Weaver, and the superintendent of the works, Thomas Simpson. Neither witness was cross-examined. The stonemasons presented no defense. Lipsombe told the stonemasons that he was inclined to fine all of them and order them back to work. 4 George IV, c.34 (1823) did not actually give magistrates the power to fine workers. The magistrate could assign costs, or abate wages, which in practice acted as fines. Newspaper reports often misreported this distinction when covering master and servant cases, and it appears that Lipscombe had misspoke, and meant assigning costs and forcing the defendants back to work. Biggins and the others said that they would rather go to jail, at which point Weaver told Lipscombe that he owed each of the masons at least 10s in unpaid wages. Lipscombe then abated 10s of wages from each of the masons, warning them that Weaver could have requested three months' imprisonment with hard

---

[5]   Ibid.

labor. Weaver, hoping he could avoid alienating his masons and convince them to return to work, agreed to pay the costs of the proceedings.[6]

The Central Committee of the Operative Stone Masons was disturbed by this case, and after much correspondence with the Barnard Castle Lodge of the union, they showed little interest in being conciliatory toward this employer and magistrate. They contacted Roberts for an opinion on their legal options. On 25 September 1861, Roberts wrote to the union describing these options in discouraging terms. He was unsure of the union's chances of obtaining redress in the changed legal climate of the 1850s and 1860s. Far from being a sharp practitioner looking for any way to collect fees and costs, Roberts was very careful about warning the union that its chances were remote. He informed the union that 11 & 12 Victoria, c.44 (1848), the Vexatious Actions Against Justices Act, made it very hard to proceed civilly against Lipscombe. Roberts warned that because it was doubtful whether the men's threat to leave work was sufficient as a full day's notice, Lipscombe could argue that he was right on the merits of the case, which under that act was an adequate answer to any civil suit faced by a magistrate.

Roberts raised the possibility of a criminal information against Lipscombe. He cautioned that even though the hearing of this case was a 'mockery of a trial', Roberts knew from first-hand experience that it would be difficult to meet the high standards that the Court of Queen's Bench had set for proving malice or corruption. He added that if the criminal information did not work, he could initiate a writ of certiorari to attempt to quash the conviction, which, if successful, would at least permit Biggins and the others to recover their unpaid wages. Roberts was not optimistic on this front either, but wrote that the surprise arrest, transportation and isolation of the prisoners, the denial of an adjournment so counsel could be procured and the lumping of all the cases into one hearing were abuses that he was anxious to expose politically and legally. Offended by the rough treatment of the prisoners, and particularly their being shackled, Roberts also raised the possibility of a civil suit against the police. Despite Roberts' caution, the Central Committee of the Operative Stone Mason's Society was so 'exasperated with such a flagrant tyranny' that it authorized him to pursue legally the magistrate by any means.[7]

Roberts gave Lipscombe notice of his intent to seek a criminal information against him on behalf of Thomas Biggins for maliciously refusing to permit the stonemason to obtain legal counsel and hear his full defense and answer to the charge. Late in 1861, barrister Sergeant Wheeler applied to the Court of Queen's Bench for a rule nisi, which would have forced Lipscombe to respond with his own affidavits. The Judges at Queen's Bench conceded that Lipscombe had acted wrongly in not adjourning the case, but denied the rule nisi on the grounds that

---

[6]   Ibid.
[7]   Warwick University Modern Records Centre: MSS.78.OS.4.1.20.

Wheeler could not prove any corrupt motive or intemperate behavior by the magistrate.[8]

Roberts and Wheeler decided next to apply for a writ of certiorari to bring the records of this conviction before Queen's Bench, relying upon one well-used argument, and three innovative ones. Wheeler's application was heard by the full Court of Queen's Bench on 16 January 1862. Wheeler's first argument was a familiar one, the conviction failed to state the occupation of the defendants, which was necessary for establishing the jurisdiction of the magistrate under 4 George IV, c.34 (1823). Wheeler cited *R. v. Lewis and three others* (1844) and In Re: *Copestick* (1844), precedents created by Roberts' legal work. Mr Justice Crompton warned Wheeler that while the argument was sufficient to obtain a rule nisi to bring up the conviction, it might not prove satisfactory as a remedy. This was because 12 & 13 Victoria, c.45, s.7 (1849) gave magistrates the authority to amend legally flawed convictions that were called up to the superior courts by a writ of certiorari as long as the new documents remained consistent with the facts. Wheeler could make Lipscombe go to the trouble and expense of fixing this error on the conviction and providing affidavits showing that the occupation of the defendants was actually raised at the hearing, but getting it quashed was unlikely.

Wheeler's second argument was based upon The Summary Jurisdiction Act (1848) and The Prisoners' Counsel Act (1836). Both of these acts stipulated that prisoners in cases of summary jurisdiction had the right to have witnesses cross-examined, and to make their full defense and answer to the charge, by an attorney. Wheeler then presented affidavits describing the circumstances of the men's arrest, transportation, isolation and the refusal of Lipscombe to adjourn the hearing. Wheeler argued that because the men were prevented from speaking to anyone, and had no opportunity to obtain counsel, Lipscombe's ruling was a de facto denial of the rights granted by these statutes. He argued that the adjudication was therefore insufficient, and 'under those circumstances the magistrate had no jurisdiction'.[9] Wheeler went further still, suggesting that denying an adjournment to allow the prisoner to find an attorney was for practical purposes the same as hearing a case without having the defendant present.

Mr Justice Blackburn was skeptical of these arguments, which were very much at odds with prevailing attitudes of the Bar about advocacy.[10] He conceded that while the adjournment was 'a reasonable request, and that consequently the magistrate was wrong in refusing it', and 'it would have been much more proper to have granted an adjournment', he felt that it did not deprive the magistrate

---

[8] Warwick University Modern Records Centre: MSS.78.OS.4.1.20, MSS.78.OS.4.1.22; NA: KB 1/264/37.

[9] 11 & 12 Victoria, c.43, s.12 (1848); 6 & 7 William IV, c.114, s.2 (1836); Warwick University Modern Records Centre: MSS.78.OS.4.1.20, MSS.78.OS.4.1.22; NA: KB 1/264/37.

[10] Allyson May, *The Bar and the Old Bailey, 1750–1850* (Chapel Hill, 2003).

of his jurisdiction. Justices Crompton and Cockburn both emphasized that the acts gave attorneys who were *actually present in the courtroom* the right to be heard on behalf of the defendant, but an adjournment of the case to allow the defendant to find an attorney remained at the discretion of the magistrate. Neither of these acts said that a trial could not commence until the defendant had legal representation. Lord Chief Justice Cockburn agreed with Blackburn, stating 'my own opinion ... is that the magistrate ought to have adjourned the case; but the question is, whether the power of adjournment, being a discretionary power to be exercised by the magistrate', is one with which 'this court can interfere'.[11] He did not think it was.

This book has demonstrated what an important issue this was for workers in summary hearings. The unrelenting efforts of Roberts and other solicitors at Petty Sessions and the higher courts had done a great deal to undermine regimes of procuring, maintaining and disciplining workers at affordable rates that relied upon coercive statues enforced by local institutions of justice controlled by employers. In many places Roberts helped to make master and servant law bothersome for employers and dangerous for magistrates. Magistrates behaved far more carefully when he was present. Arguments that were dismissed out of hand when made by workers, were suddenly worthy of consideration when presented by Roberts.[12] His presence changed 10-minute hearings to three and four-hour-long trials. In order to prosecute workers under these acts, employers had to engage their own attorneys, and be prepared to endure these long hearings while listening to Roberts' fiery speeches about injustice and oppression. There were cases in which employers dropped master and servant charges against workers when they heard that Roberts had been contacted.

The publicity given to Roberts' cases was essential to mobilizing opposition to master and servant law and its administration by magistrates. The well-attended parades, public meetings and dinners celebrating the release of individuals who had been convicted under these acts drew public attention to the fundamental unfairness of these statutes and their enforcement. An employer who prosecuted workers under master and servant law risked having Roberts portray him as a tyrant in the courtroom and in the labor press, or worse, suffering from the attorney raising legal doubts about the validity of his contracts, rules or policies. If the employer lost, the resolve of workers who were opposing him would be strengthened from having their cause legitimated by 'constitutional law', and if he won, the perceived injustice would be increased and publicized further, alienating the same employees. A significant part of Roberts' strategy for fighting against master and servant law was simply to make it counter-productive for employers

---

[11]   Warwick University Modern Records Centre: MSS.78.OS.4.1.20, MSS.78. OS.4.1.22; NA: KB 1/264/37.

[12]   Challinor, *Radical Lawyer*, p. 79; see Chapter 4, the defenses offered by Wyke and Gerrard. See Chapter 7 and the behavior of T. B. Rose when Roberts was present in the Greaves case.

to use and magistrates to enforce. Indeed, Robert Steinfeld has found that many masters in different regions of England turned to minute contracts as a result of these difficulties and uncertainties of the law in the 1840s. He argues that the existence of these work arrangements helped to undermine master and servant law by demonstrating that employment relationships not enforced with penal sanctions were perfectly workable.[13]

Wheeler then argued to the court that the magistrate had no jurisdiction to try the seven cases in a single hearing. He pointed out that trying them as a group in practice prevented any of the persons charged from acting as witnesses for the other defendants, observing 'the effect of taking seven cases as one was to shut out evidence'. None of the judges went along with this argument, Blackburn saying that he did not 'see that it was any gross irregularity' because the facts were the same in all of the cases.[14] This was a dubious declaration, because there had been no opportunity at the hearing to challenge the facts of any of the cases.

Finally, Wheeler argued that 4 George IV, c.34 (1823) gave magistrates the right to abate wages coming due, not wages already earned. The four Justices dismissed this argument out of hand. They granted the rule nisi on the first ground, but rejected the other three. Cockburn re-emphasized that 'the magistrate ought to have adjourned the case, with a view to enable him to obtain legal assistance; but I do not think that this statute touches that part of the discretion of the magistrates in that respect'. Crompton made a statement that underscored the changed attitude of that Court toward magistrates' summary hearings. In his ruling he claimed 'our practice in cases of this kind, is that we do not interfere for every irregularity, or for every thing that we may think has not been wisely done in the course of a proceeding'. Prior to the mid-1850s, Queen's Bench appeared to have been prepared to interfere for *any irregularity* in magistrates' forms or proceedings. Crompton stated that the particular Jervis Act relating to summary hearings, which asserted the defendant's right to have his or her case presented by an attorney, came about because 'grave complaints were formerly made with regard to the administration of the law by justices', which had since been answered. The act settled forms and procedures that magistrates were to follow, but preserved their discretion in respect to many matters, including adjournment. Crompton added, however, that he felt that in this particular case Lipscombe had 'exercised his discretion improperly'.[15]

All Lipscombe had to do was correct the flawed conviction, and provide affidavits stating that Weaver or Simpson had testified at the hearing that Biggins and the others were stonemasons and contracted servants, which brought them within the act. Roberts and the masons' union waited in suspense for nearly seven months, as the magistrate's clerk refused to show the affidavits to Roberts. He

---

[13] Steinfeld, *Coercion*, Chapter 5.

[14] Ibid.

[15] Ibid.

answered Roberts' requests to see them before the hearing with a letter stating 'after the vindictive attack lately made upon Mr. Lipscombe in the Court of Queen's Bench in this matter, I conceive I should not … furnish you with anything but what you are strictly entitled'.[16]

On 2 July 1862 the Court of Queen's Bench reviewed the amended conviction and affidavits from Lipscombe, Weaver and Simpson. Simpson swore that at the hearing he informed the magistrate of the men's occupation as stonemasons, and the terms of the contract, and therefore Lipscombe had acted within his jurisdiction. Mr Holl, counsel for the masons, asked the court to exercise its discretion not to accept the amended conviction, taking the full circumstances into consideration. In another statement demonstrating how dramatically different the attitude of the judges of Queen's Bench had become toward summary proceedings, Crompton replied 'we certainly ought not to let a mere technical slip … decide such a case'. Wightman followed by asking Holl if 'there is anything on the merits of the case you can show us?'. The magistrates who had agitated during the 1840s for such distinctions to be made by the common-law courts would have been pleased. While the judges upheld the conviction, they by no means approved of the manner in which Lipscombe had exercised his discretion. They therefore granted no costs to the magistrate. Just as with Rose, the high-court judges used their discretion of granting, denying or imposing costs as a means of sanction. Roberts wrote to the Central Committee of the Stone Masons, stating that although he was disappointed with the loss, 'Lipscombe, will have the pleasure of paying all his own expenses – a result which is certainly a considerable punishment to him, at least £150'. He added that this expense, no small one for a clergyman to endure, 'will have the effect of curbing, in the future, the evil passions of tyrannical masters and corrupt magistrates'.[17] It was this type of rhetoric that the leaders of new model unions hoped to avoid.

The similarity between the issues at stake in this case, and the one that took place 16 years earlier in Longton, Staffordshire, is striking. The injustices of surprise arrests followed by isolation and rushed trials, as well as the refusal to adjourn the hearing so that the defendants could find an attorney, is sadly familiar. Also consistent was the practice of trying defendants in a lump trial, preventing them from testifying for one another. In both hearings the accused neither cross-examined prosecution witnesses, nor presented a defense of any kind. Contracts of employment remained far more binding upon workers than on their masters, whose right to dismiss summarily contracted employees continued to expand after 1850.[18] Just like John Williams and three others (1845), Biggins and the six masons experienced 'Justices' Justice', but, unlike the four Longton colliers, in this case 'Constitutional Law' was nowhere to be found. Parliament and the courts now gave far less rigorous scrutiny to warrants of commitment and convictions,

---

[16]   Ibid.
[17]   Ibid.
[18]   *Harmer v. Cornelius* (1858), 28 L. J. C. P. 85.

and provided magistrates with opportunities to correct the technical errors that had once given labor a remedy for the worst abuses in summary hearings.

By 1862, new legislation and changing priorities in the Court of Queen's Bench made it much more difficult for labor's legal representatives to challenge master and servant rulings. This book has shown that in the 1840s, the high-court judges appeared enthusiastic about using their power to raise the standards of legal professionalism followed by magistrates, who had previously operated with relatively little supervision. Before the Jervis Acts, high-court judges and barristers often justified the strict legal formalism with which they scrutinized magistrates' forms by pointing out that summary hearings deprived defendants of 'that palladium of English liberty', the jury trial. Roberts, as well as unionists in Sheffield, Warrington and elsewhere, also took advantage of controversial efforts in Parliament to expand magistrates' role in the judicial system. It is significant that consideration of bills to give magistrates the authority to hear particular offenses summarily were often accompanied by protests and petitions against the behavior of individual magistrates. These well-publicized protests challenged those arguing for the expansion of magistrates' summary powers.

Organized labor did more that simply exploit the controversy over the summary jurisdiction of magistrates, it made contributions to, and ultimately changed, the debate. Indeed, it might be said that trade unions played a leading role in challenging the wisdom of entrusting magistrates with greater judicial powers. Roberts' work drew trade unions into the controversy over the lay magistracy's summary powers. In the courtroom, speeches, journals, petitions and protests, labor's representatives complained about lay magistrates' imperfect knowledge of the law and the obvious conflict of interest that existed when industrialists and mine-owners adjudicated master and servant cases.

It seems highly probable that the Jervis Acts were introduced as part of an effort to answer the controversy that unionized workers, radical solicitors and Chartists had been instrumental in stirring up. These acts would enhance the legitimacy of 'Justices' Justice' with workers, and influential opponents of summary proceedings who sat in the courts and Parliament, and pave the way for a further expansion of summary jurisdiction. The Jervis Acts consolidated the laws much more than they actually changed them. The reforms that these acts brought about, however, can be seen as a direct Parliamentary response to the success that trade unions had in challenging magistrates' rulings at Queen's Bench. As this case demonstrates, 'faceless' warrants of commitment and conviction for practical purposes nullified certiorari as a remedy for labor, as did subsequent legislation permitting magistrates to amend legal errors in their forms. The Vexatious Actions Against Justices Act (1848) offered all but the very worst magistrates complete protection from civil suits for errors done in the execution of their office. The crucial role of trade union litigation in these important reforms, and indeed, in the history of the development of summary jurisdiction, has not previously been acknowledged by historians. It is often argued that in the second half of the nineteenth century trade unions looked to Parliament to reverse the setbacks handed to them by the high courts. During the 1840s, it was magistrates and employers who had looked to Parliament to reverse the gains won by trade unions from the Court of Queen's Bench.

At a deeper level, however, by capitalizing upon legal errors and omissions in magistrates' forms, Roberts was confronting the high-court justices (and members of Parliament) with their own ideology of impartial justice and rhetoric about the rule of law. He did this at a political moment when it was very important for those in power to preserve the belief that the formal rules and process of law was above all citizens, neutral, applying to all individuals equally. For the majority of citizens, who had no direct role in creating the law, the legitimacy of the legal system, and of the state generally, was heavily dependent upon the viability of this ideology. Roberts forced the justices of the higher courts to live up to their rhetoric about the rule of law during one of the more politically dangerous periods in English history. I am not saying that the strict legal formalism of the judges of Queen's Bench was simply a response to the Chartist movement, for it was far too deeply ingrained in legal thought and tradition for that to have been the case. Many historians of Chartism, however, have argued that the movement was undermined by economic recovery and timely concessions on the part of Parliament that showed that the existing system could work in the workers' interest even though they lacked the vote. The caution with which the government and judges avoided making martyrs in Chartist political trials has been often acknowledged.[19] It is entirely possible that high-court judges, who were politicians themselves, had a heightened sensitivity to the wider consequences of their rulings such cases. Throwing out the convictions of three or four dozen miners spread over five years was a small price to pay for preserving workers' faith in the legal system, showing them that the neutral formal processes of the courts could work for anyone, regardless of class interests. The reporting of the *Northern Star* from the 1840s suggests that the judges of the Court of Queen's Bench were very successful in enhancing Chartists' reverence and belief in 'Constitutional Law'.

By the 1860s, however, the political environment was considerably different. The disfranchised had become less threatening to those in power, and at the same time Parliament and the English legal system had come to depend heavily upon magistrates acting summarily. Although complaints about the actions of individual lay magistrates remained common, there was no longer resistance from the high courts or Parliament to their jurisdiction. Policy makers wanted to encourage, rather than discourage, magistrates to administer the fast, affordable and efficient justice that an over-burdened legal system increasingly required. For these reasons, errors on the face of warrants of commitment no longer provided a remedy for the injustices that occurred in summary hearings.

---

[19]   Dorothy Thompson, *The Chartists: Popular Politics and the Industrial Revolution* (New York, 1993); Jacqueline Fellague Ariouat, 'Rethinking Partisanship in the Conduct of Chartist Trials, 1839–1848', *Albion* 29/4 (Winter 1998): 596–621.

The best workers could hope to do in situations where they were unhappy with magistrates' rulings was to have issues of law brought before the high courts by having a case stated under the 1857 Summary Jurisdiction Act, 20 & 21 Victoria, c.43. This was very difficult to do if an attorney was not present at the original hearing. By 1862, it was nearly impossible to pursue a magistrate in civil court for errors made during his summary hearings, or to prosecute him for a criminal information, so long as he did not display truly extraordinary malice or corruption.

As was the case in *R. v. Bailey* and *R. v. Collier* (1854), Biggins and his co-workers were denied a fair hearing by a magistrate and redress from the high courts. Yet the news was not entirely bad for organized labor, and employees could still cling to some benefits from their engagement with the law. Queen's Bench used the mechanism of costs to sanction a magistrate who used his power and discretion unwisely. Weaver managed to save £3 10s in wages owed to the stonemasons, but he and Lipscombe paid more dearly as a result. The publicity that Roberts was able to bring to this case, both in trade and law journals, poisoned Weaver's relationship with a very high proportion of the stone masons who belonged to the national union, and impeded his ability to attract workers and meet a contract. That made this clearly an example of a counter-productive use of the coercive laws available to an employer. Of course, for larger new model unions hoping to present a less threatening image to employers and the state, the publicity surrounding this case was not helpful.

Still, the defendants did not recover their lost wages, and the high courts had rejected arguments on all of the important issues that Roberts and his barrister raised. In the 1840s the cases that Roberts won set precedents that could be used to help other workers win their freedom in the future, but during the 1860s the precedents of defeat could place new burdens upon laborers confronting the legal system. One is left to wonder: if the gains of trade unions in the 1840s were so fleeting, so easily taken away, how is the long-term significance of the early legal and political campaign against the penal sanctions of employment law to be judged?

The efforts of the 1840s had a lasting impact on trade union protest against master and servant law, and prepared the way for the movement's successes of the 1860s and 1870s. It made the composition of the magistracy, their conflicts of interest and imperfect knowledge of the law, subjects of trade union protest, drawing labor into debates about reform of the English legal system. Some might argue that the high court victories of trade unions distracted workers from the real problem, which was the law itself, rather than its enforcement. Such critics must keep in mind that campaigns to bring about the repeal the penal sanctions, and opportunistic efforts to mitigate or obstruct their use, were not in a dichotomous relationship. Union-funded litigation, in addition to using the most available means to impede efforts to coerce workers, also brought publicity to numerous injustices perpetrated upon workers under master and servant law that might have otherwise gone largely unnoticed. It underscored the ways in which employers used these laws to skew labor markets in their favor and prevent workers in many trades from improving their conditions. It highlighted and publicized the increasingly glaring inconsistency between the enforcement of employment contracts with penal sanctions and the compulsion of specific performance, and the remedies available for the breach of any other type of contract.

Roberts' work strengthened and focused labor's opposition to master and servant statutes, giving them a legal language for expressing their objections. For example, Roberts' work inside and outside of the courtroom helped to pull together the largest and most widespread expression of discontent with these coercive laws to that point, the defeat of the 1844 Master and Servant Bill. In those decades before the political support was available to repeal of the penal sanctions in master and servant law, Roberts and others were at least able to challenge the use of these statutes. Employers might have attempted to use the criminal and statute law and local legal institutions to control and direct workers in the mid nineteenth century, but rather than meekly submitting, workers looked to radical solicitors and the high courts for protection, contesting a legal system that many historians have assumed was simply a weapon for the masters' exclusive use and that labor sought to avoid. Chartists and trade unionists believed that the institutions of 'real law' and 'constitutional justice' belonged as much to them as to any other group in Victorian society, and were prepared to fight on this terrain.

In spite of his tireless efforts on behalf of labor for nearly three decades, William Roberts did not live to see the day when workers could no longer be imprisoned for breach of contract. Nonetheless, the victory that was the repeal of most penal sanctions of master and servant law, in 1875, belonged as much to him as it did to anyone in the Glasgow Trades Council or the Trade Union Congress. In his two appearances, he was by far the most knowledgeable and informed witness before Lord Elcho's 1866 Select Committee on the Law of Master and Servant, and he was also the most uncompromising in demanding the repeal of penal sanctions for workers' breach of contract. Roberts also forcefully argued against the jurisdiction of magistrates in master and servant cases, drawing upon his considerable experience to show the committee how they undermined the legitimacy of the law. Other witnesses echoed Roberts' arguments about the double standard inherent in the law, the injustice of compelling specific performance of the contract and the legal ignorance and bias of the magistrates who enforced it – the most common objections to master and servant law. These arguments later had an important effect on the shape of 38 & 39 Victoria, c.90 (1875), the Employers and Workmen Act.[20]

---

[20]   'Report from the Select Committee on Master and Servant; Together With the Proceedings of the Committee and Minutes of Evidence, Appendix, and Index', *Parliamentary Papers*, pp. 8, 70–81, 101–5. For arguments about the jurisdiction of magistrates, see testimony of Alexander Campbell (17 May 1866), pp. 13–23; Alexander MacDonald (29 May 1866), p. 28; C. Steele (29 May 1866), p. 32; W. Dronfield (29 May

This book has described the tactics, arguments and rhetoric utilized during a sustained legal and political campaign by trade unions and radical solicitors against the penal sanctions of master and servant law. Aggressive, inventive and resourceful solicitors like William Roberts used every legal and political tool at their disposal to obstruct and impede employers' attempts to imprison workers for breach of contract. Many of the arguments and legal issues raised by Roberts inside and outside of the courtroom became central to subsequent lobbying efforts for the repeal of imprisonment for breach of contract by workers. Roberts and other solicitors achieved a high level of success during the 1840s, which had a profound effect upon how workers understood the law and their place before it. These solicitors were successful because they shrewdly framed their issues to reflect the deep concern that many high court judges and members of Parliament had about the ability or desire of lay magistrates from an industrial social background to enforce the law in a manner that preserved its legitimacy. In raising these issues in the law courts and the court of public opinion, trade unions became an essential factor in the development of the laws that governed magistrates' summary hearings. The framing of these laws ultimately worked to the detriment of workers. This book has demonstrated that trade union resistance to the penal characteristics of employment law has a much longer history than is often acknowledged. It has described and examined one distinct period of this resistance, a decade in which workers engaged radical solicitors and turned to the high courts for protection, and did not look in vain.

1866), p. 36; J. Normansell (1 June 1866), p. 44; C. Williams (1 June 1866), pp. 50–51; G. Odger (15 June 1866), p. 90; W. Burns (19 June 1866), p. 108.

Appendix
Glossary of Key Terms

Barristers made up the branch of the English legal profession that had the exclusive right of audience before the Superior Courts, the Assizes and the Quarter Sessions. During the period covered by this book, barristers were not allowed to have direct contact with clients, but were instead instructed by solicitors who made up the junior branch of the legal profession in nineteenth-century England and met with clients. Barristers were men who had been 'called to the bar' after serving time at one of the four Inns of the Court.

Conviction was the written declaration stating that the magistrate had heard evidence and found the prisoners guilty of an offence within his jurisdiction and sentenced them accordingly. In master and servant cases it was common for the conviction and the warrant of commitment to be combined in the same form. In the second quarter of the nineteenth century, the high courts held these documents to an elevated standard of legal formalism, especially in cases determined summarily by magistrates. The judges of the high courts insisted that they provide all the necessary information to fully demonstrate that the offence was within the jurisdiction of the adjudicating magistrate.

Information in a summary hearing was the formal complaint, the statement under oath informing the magistrate of an offence within his jurisdiction. It was usually in written form and it contained the charge that the defendant was to answer. Sections 1 and 3 of 4 George IV, c.34 (1823) explicitly required that the information be made under oath by the complainant before the same magistrate who ultimately determined the case.

Petty Sessions were the periodic meeting of two or more magistrates for dispensing summary justice and handling other local judicial and administrative business. Many statutes conferring summary jurisdiction required two magistrates to hear the case. Master and servant proceedings were often heard at Petty Sessions, although they were also often determined by single justices acting alone in their own parlors.

Quarter Sessions were meetings held four times each year in each county and borough that were presided over by the justices of the peace and magistrates for the county or borough. These magistrates and justices of the peace sat with a jury and heard some indictable offences, although not ones that were capital offences. They also heard appeals of magistrates' rulings in Petty Sessions under statutes that permitted an appeal to Quarter Sessions (see Chapter 5). Some administrative business for the counties or boroughs was also handled at these meetings.

Solicitors made up the junior branch of the legal profession in England. They had the sole right to have direct contact with clients but were not permitted to plead in the Superior Courts, the Assizes, or the Quarter Sessions. They prepared the case and instructed Barristers who enjoyed the rights of audience before these courts. Solicitors were permitted to present cases before magistrates, at Petty Sessions and before the County Courts as well as provide other legal services (conveyancing, wills, etc.).

Summary Jurisdiction means the power granted by many statutes to justices of the peace and magistrates to convict and punish offenders themselves rather than committing them for a jury trial. During the eighteenth and nineteenth centuries, Parliament greatly expanded the legislation giving summary jurisdiction to Justices of the Peace and magistrates over a wide variety of offences, offering cheaper and speedier justice, but also fewer protections for the accused. This expansion continued accelerated further after 1847. When English men and women in the nineteenth century experienced the legal system, they were most likely to experience it before magistrates through summary hearings.

Warrant of Commitment was an order to the keeper of the house of correction commanding him to detain a prisoner for a specified period of time. In master and servant cases it was common for the conviction and the warrant of commitment to be combined in the same form. In the second quarter of the nineteenth century, the high courts held these documents to an elevated standard of legal formalism, especially in cases determined summarily by magistrates. The judges of the high courts insisted that they provide all the necessary information to fully demonstrate that the offence was within the jurisdiction of the adjudicating magistrate.

Writ of Certiorari was a writ that required the magistrates and their clerks to certify and return records of a judgment made by them, so the Judges of Queen's Bench could inquire into their jurisdiction, and quash convictions in which an error of law appeared on the face of the record.

Writ of Habeas Corpus was an order to the keeper of the house of correction to produce the prisoners at Westminster Hall and demonstrate the lawful authority justifying their imprisonment. In master and servant cases, this authority was often found on the warrant of commitment, which when brought up with the prisoners gave the Judges of Queen's Bench the opportunity to scrutinize it for omissions which failed to establish the magistrates' authority to sentence them.

Bibliography

Primary Sources Arranged by Archive

British Newspaper Library, Collindale

The Beehive
The Birmingham Journal
The Birmingham Mercury
The Cardiff and Methyr Guardian
The Colliery Guardian
The Durham Advertiser
The Durham Chronicle
The Gateshead Observer
The Glamorgan, Monmouth and Brecon Gazette and Merthyr Guardian
The Justice of the Peace
The Law Times
The Leeds Intelligencer
The Leeds Mercury
The Leicestershire Mercury
The Legal Observer
The Liverpool Albion
The Liverpool Chronicle
The Liverpool Daily Post
The Liverpool Journal
The Liverpool Mercury
The Manchester Chronicle and Lancashire General Advertiser
The Manchester Guardian
The Manchester Examiner
The Manchester and Salford Advertiser and Chronicle
The Manchester Times and Gazette
The Manchester Weekly Advertiser
The Merthyr Express
The Miners' Advocate
The Miner and Workman's Advocate
The Miners' Journal
The Morning Chronicle
Monmouthshire Merlin
The Newcastle Chronicle
The Northern Star

The Nonconformist
Pontypool Free Press
The Potters' Examiner and Workman's Advocate
The Salford Weekly News
The Sheffield and Rotherham Independent
The Sheffield Times
The Staffordshire Advertiser
The Times
The Walsall Advertiser
The Walsall Free Press and General Advertiser

Lancashire Record Office, Preston

Amalgamated Spinners, Self Acting Minders, and Twiners of Lancashire Correspondence Book, 1867–1871.
Leyland Sessions Minutes, 1851–59.
Operative Joiners and Carpenters of Burnley, Minute Book, 1850–1861.
Preston Warpers and Weavers' Correspondence Book, 1860–1868.
Rochdale Borough Magistrates' Court, 1844.
William Prowting Roberts Appeal To Quarter Sessions, 1853.

Local Studies Unit, Manchester Public Library, Manchester

Coroner's Depositions, 1851–1852.
Smith v. The Queen, Copy of Assignment of Errors (1853).
William and Joseph Stubs Papers.

National Archives, Kew, London

> Home Office Papers, Series 18, 43, 44, 45, 46.
> King's Bench Records, Series 1, 6, 21, 39.

Staffordshire Record Office

Convictions for Leaving Service, 1852.
Lord Hatherton Correspondence regarding Truck Wages, 1821. Journals 1817–1872.
Master and Servant Bill: Amendments to be Moved in Committee By Earl of Lichfield (1867).
Meeting of Deputations from Different Districts of the Potteries Held at The Wheat Sheaf Inn at Stoke-Upon-Trent Monday 3 September 1838.
The Trial of Thomas Cooper, 1843.
Truck Wages Newspaper Clippings.

Walsall Archives Service

W. H. Duignan travel diaries and correspondence.

Wigan Public Library

The Pitman's Strike Collection.

The Working Class Movement Library, Salford

An Address of the Executive Council to Their Several Constituencies (6 March 1844).
Amalgamated Society of Engineers Monthly Reports, 1850–1866.
Davis, James Edward. *The Master and Servant Act, 1867, With an Introduction, Notes and Forms and Tables of Offences* (London, 1868).
Full and Authentic Particulars of the Dreadful Explosion at Haswell Colliery on Saturday, September 28th, 1844, By Which Ninety-Five Lives Were Lost (Sunderland: R. Vint and Carr, 1844).
The Haswell Catastrophe! An Address From the Executive Council to the Miners of Northumberland and Durham (1844).
The Haswell Explosion (1844).
MacDonald, Alexander. *Handbook of the Law Relating to Masters, Workmen, Servants, and Apprentices in All Trades and Occupations, With Notes of Cases in England, Scotland, and Ireland* (1868).
Mather, James. *A New Edition: The Haswell Explosion and the Ventilation of Mines in A Letter to the Rt. Hon. Sir Robert Peel, Bart., M. P.* (1845).
Reports of the Colliery Case: *Williamson v. Taylor and Others* Tried at the Northumberland Assizes 4 August 1843.
Roberts, William P. *The Haswell Colliery Explosion, 28 September 1844, Narrative, Report of the Proceedings at the Coroner's Inquest, and Plan of that Part of the Colliery in Which The Accident Occurred* (Newcastle: M. Benson, 1845).
The Tailor and Cutter: A Trade Journal and Index of Fashion, 1867–1868.
To the Miners of Northumberland and Durham and to Those Parties who Illegally and Basely Promoted the Circulation of the Handbill Signed "An Unsophisticated Unionist and Hater of Humbug" (1844).
Trade Reports of the Boiler Makers and Shipbuilders' Society, 1859–1868.
The Trial of Dr Peter Murray McDouall, Surgeon of Lancashire (1848).
Viewers' Versus the Pitmen! Or Falsehood Versus The Truth. To the Deceived and Deluded Workmen (1844).
The Wingate Wire Rope Case: *Barkhouse v. Cargill and Others*, 2 August 1844.

The University of Warwick Modern Records Centre

Balance Sheet of the Receipts and Expenditure of the Public Subscriptions, Etc., for the Twenty-One Masons Who Were Indicted For Conspiracy From 17 October 1848 To 28 February 1849.
Fortnightly Reports of the United Society of Operative Stone Masons, 1856–1868.
The Minute Books and Monthly Reports of the Amalgamated Engineers Union, 1852–1857.
Operative Bricklayers' Society Trade Circular and General Reporter, 1861–1864, 1869.
Rules to be Observed By the Friendly Society of United Operative Tin Plate Workers of Wolverhampton (Wolverhampton, 1834).

Parliamentary Papers

'A Bill for Enlarging the Powers of Justices in Determining Complaints between Masters Servants and Artificers and for the More Effectual Recovery of Wages before Justices', *Parliamentary Papers* (1844), Vol. III (58), p. 223.
'A Bill [as amended by the committee] for Enlarging the Powers of Justices in Determining Complaints between Masters Servants and Artificers and for the More Effectual Recovery of Wages before Justices', *Parliamentary Papers* (1844), Vol. III (111), p. 229.
'A Bill [as amended by the Select Committee] to Facilitate the Performance of Duties of Justices of the Peace out of Sessions Within England and Wales, with Respect to Summary Convictions and Orders', *Parliamentary Papers* (1847–1848), Vol. I (375), p. 137.
'A Bill for the More Speedy Trial and Punishment of Juvenile Offenders', *Parliamentary Papers* (1847), Vol. II (136), p. 97.
'A Bill [as amended by the Select Committee] for the More Speedy Trial and Punishment of Juvenile Offenders', *Parliamentary Papers* (1847), Vol. II (435), p. 105.
'A Bill [as amended by the Select Committee] for the More Speedy Trial and Punishment of Juvenile Offenders', *Parliamentary Papers* (1847), Vol. II (464), p. 115.
'A Bill to Protect Justices of the Peace from Vexatious Actions for Acts Done in the Execution of their Office,' *Parliamentary Papers* (1847–1848), Vol. V (59), p. 181.
'Copies of the Several Affidavits Filed in the Court of Queen's Bench, on the Application Made in Michealmas Term Last, at the Instance of Arthur George O'Neill, for a Criminal Information Against Thomas Badger, Esq. And the Reverend W. H. Cartwright, Magistrates for the County of Stafford'. *Parliamentary Papers* (1843), Vol. XLIV (96), p. 195.

'A Copy of the Informations and Evidence Given Before the Magistrates Assembled in Petty Sessions at Warrington, On Monday 25th Day of January Last, On Which James Gerrard, Thomas Wyke, James Ireland, and John Dobson Were Sentenced to Three Month's Imprisonment With Hard Labour for Leaving the Service of Joseph Baxter Edelsten, File Manufacturer; Together With Copies of the Conviction and Warrants of Commitment, and of the Contracts Entered into by the Said Prisoners With the Said Joseph Baxter Edelsten', *Parliamentary Papers* (1847), Vol. XLVI (78), p. 487.

'Eleventh and final report of the Royal Commissioners Appointed to Inquire into the Organization and Rules of Trades Unions and Other Associations; Together with an Appendix Containing a Digest of the Evidence, Correspondence with Her Majesty's Missions Abroad Regarding Industrial Questions and Trades Unions, and Other Papers', *Parliamentary Papers* (1868–1869), Vol. XXXI (4123), p. 237.

'The First and Second Reports From the Select Committee of the House of Lords Appointed to Inquire Into the Execution of the Criminal Law, Especially Respecting Juvenile Offenders and Transportation: Together With the Minutes of Evidence Taken Before the Said Committee, and an Appendix', *Parliamentary Papers* (1847), Vol. VII (447), p. 1.

'First report of the Commissioners Appointed to Inquire into the Organization and Rules of Trades Unions and other Associations. Together with Minutes of Evidence', *Parliamentary Papers* (1867–68), Vol. XXXII (3873), p. 1, Vol. XXXIX (3890), p. 1.

'Report From the Select Committee on Master and Servant; Together With the Proceedings of Committee and Minutes of Evidence, Appendix, and Index', *Parliamentary Papers* (1865), Vol. VIII (370), p. 1.

'Report From the Select Committee on Master and Servant; Together With the Proceedings of Committee and Minutes of Evidence, Appendix, and Index', *Parliamentary Papers* (1866), Vol. XIII (449), p. 1.

'Report from the Select Committee on Masters and Operatives; Together With the Proceedings of the Committee, Minutes of Evidence, Appendix and Index', *Parliamentary Papers* (1860), Vol. XXII (307), p. 443.

'Report from the Select Committee on the Payment of Wages', *Parliamentary Papers* (1842), Vol. IX (471), p. 125.

'Report of the Commissioner Appointed Under the Provisions of the Act 5 & 6 Victoria, c. 99 to The Operation of That Act, and Into the State of Population of the Mining Districts', *Parliamentary Papers* (1844–1859), Vol. XVI (592), p. 1, Vol. XXVII (670), p. 197, Vol. XXIV (737), p. 383, Vol. XVI (844), p. 401, Vol. XXVI (993), p. 233, Vol. XXII (1109), p. 395, Vol. XXIII (1248), p. 571, Vol. XXIII (1406), p. 447, Vol. XXI (1525), p. 425, Vol. XL (1679), p. 759, Vol. XIX (1838), p. 517, Vol. XV (1993), p. 559, Vol. XVIII (2125), p. 549, Vol. XVI (2275), p. 497.

'Return of All Applications in the Court of Queen's Bench For Criminal Informations Against Justices of the Peace in Which a Rule Nisi was Granted,

January 1820- December 1830', *Parliamentary Papers* (1831), Vol. XV (99), p. 87.

'Return of All Applications in the Court of Queen's Bench For Criminal Informations Against Justices of the Peace in Which a Rule Nisi was Granted, January 1831–December 1833', *Parliamentary Papers* (1834), Vol. XLVIII (116), p. 249.

'Return of All Applications in the Court of Queen's Bench For Criminal Informations Against Justices of the Peace in Which a Rule Nisi was Granted, January 1834- December 1838', *Parliamentary Papers* (1839), Vol. LXIII (481), p. 431.

'A Return of the Date and Number of Convictions Under the Combination Act that Have Taken Place at Sheffield Petty Sessions from the 1st Day of January 1842 to the Present Time; Specifying Those Quashed on Appeal; Showing the Sentence Passed in Each Case, with the Name of the Magistrate or Magistrates by Whom Such Sentences were Passed', *Parliamentary Papers* (1847), Vol. XLVI (634), p. 541.

'A Return of the Number of Convictions each Year Since 1867 under the Fourteenth Section of "The Master and Servants Act, 1867", Distinguishing Convictions of Employers from Employed and Stating the Longest and Shortest Terms of Imprisonment, the Number of Appeals to Quarter Sessions and the Number of Cases in Which the Sentence was Reversed or Varied', *Parliamentary Papers* (1873), Vol. LIV (386), p. 229.

'A Return of the Number of Convictions each Year Since 1867 under the Fourteenth Section of "The Master and Servants Act, 1867", Distinguishing Convictions of Employers from Employed and Stating the Longest and Shortest Terms of Imprisonment, the Number of Appeals to Quarter Sessions and the Number of Cases in Which the Sentence was Reversed or Varied', *Parliamentary Papers* (1874), Vol. LIV (360), p. 395.

'Select Committee on the Payment of Wages Bill and the Payment of Wages (Hosiery) Bill: Reports, Proceedings, Minutes of Evidence, Index', *Parliamentary Papers* (1854),Vol. XVI (382), p. 1.

Printed Primary Sources

Address of the Select Committee of the Coal Trade To the Coal Owners of the Counties of Northumberland and Durham on the Subject of the Pitmen's Strike (Newcastle: William Heaton, 19 June 1884).

Carpenter, Kenneth (ed.), *Labour Disputes in the Mines: Eight Pamphlets, 1831–1844* (New York: Arno Press, 1972).

Cases of Distress and Oppression in the Staffordshire Potteries By Labourers Wages Being Paid in Truck (Burslem, 1831). Goldsmith-Kress Library of Economic Literature, Reel #26355.

Cooper, Thomas, *The Life of Thomas Cooper*, John Saville (ed.) (New York: Humanities Press, 1971, originally, 1872).

Dunn, Matthias, *A Historical, Geological, and Descriptive View of the Coal Trade of the North of England Comprehending Its Rise, Progress, Present State, and Future Progress to Which are Appended A Concise Notice of the Peculiarities of Certain Coal Fields in Great Britain and Ireland and Also a General Description of the Coal Mines of Belgium Drawn Up From the Actual Inspection* (Newcastle: Pattison and Ross, 1844).

Edgar, Arthur, 'On the Jurisdiction of Justices of the Peace in Disputes Between Employers and Employed Arising from Breach of Contract', in George W. Hastings (ed.), *The Transactions of the National Association for the Promotion of Social Science, 1859* (London: John Parker and Sons, 1860).

Ginswick, J. (ed.), *Labour and the Poor in England and Wales, 1849–1851: The Letters to the Morning Chronicle from the Correspondents in the Manufacturing and Mining Districts, the Towns of Liverpool and Birmingham, and the Rural Districts, Vol. 2 Northumberland, Durham, Staffordshire and the Midlands* (3 vols., London: Frank Cass and Co., 1983).

Ginswick, J. (ed.), *Labour and the Poor in England and Wales, 1849–1851: The Letters to the Morning Chronicle from the Correspondents in the Manufacturing and Mining Districts, the Towns of Liverpool and Birmingham, and the Rural Districts, Vol. 3 South Wales and North Wales* (3 vols., London: Frank Cass and Co., 1983).

Hansard's Parliamentary Debates, Third Series, Commencing With the Accession of William IV, Volumes 73–96 (London: Thomas Curson Hansard, 1843–8).

Harrison, Frederic, 'Imprisonment for Breach of Contract or the Master and Servant Act', in Edmund Frow and Michael Katanka (eds), *1868: Year of the Unions: A Documentary Survey* (London: Michael Katanka Books, Ltd., 1968, originally, 1868).

Hill, Frank, 'An Account of Trade Combinations in Sheffield', *Trades Societies and Strikes: A Report of the Committee on Trades Societies, Appointed by the National Association for the Promotion of Social Science* (London: John Parker and Son, 1860).

Jones, John, *Selsby and Others on the Prosecution of Jones and Potts, Narrative, Introduction, etc* (London, 1847). Goldsmith-Kress Library of Economic Literature, Reel 35390.

Mitchell, William, *The Question Answered: What do the Pitmen Want?* (Bishopwearmouth: James Williams, 1844).

Observations by the Committee of the Coal Trade on the Discussion Respecting the Demands of Their Late Workmen, Introduced During the Debate on the Motion to Repeal the Export Duty on Coals (Newcastle: William Heaton, 1844).

Pollard, Sidney (ed.), *The Sheffield Outrages: Report Presented to the Trades Union Commissioners in 1867 With an Introduction by Sidney Pollard* (New York: Augustus M. Kelley, 1971 (originally, London, 1867)).

Proceedings at the Gateshead Police Court, Saturday 23, 1847, In the Case of John Coulson, Glassmaker, Charged With Unlawfully Leaving His Masters' Service (Newcastle upon Tyne: Reported and Printed By John Selkirk, No. 74, Grey Street, 1847).

Reflections on the Injustice of the Truck System By a Staffordshire Morelander (London, 1830). Goldsmith-Kress Library of Economic Literature, Reel #26435.

Shaw, Charles, *When I Was A Child* (London: Caliban Books, 1903).

Smith, Charles Manley, *A Treatise on the Law of Master and Servant, Including Therein Masters and Workmen in Every Description of Trade and Occupation: With an Appendix of Statutes* (London: S. Sweet, Chancery Lane, Fleet Street, 1852).

A Voice From the Coal Mines: Or A Plain Statement of the Various Grievances of the Pitmen of the Tyne and Wear: Addressed to the Coal Owners, Their Head Agents, and a Sympathizing Public by the Colliers of the United Association of Durham and Northumberland (South Shields: J. Clark, 1825).

Williams, Montagu, *Later Leaves: Being the Further Reminiscences of Montagu Williams, Q. C.* (Boston and New York, 1891).

Secondary Sources

Abrahams, Gerald, *Trade Unions and the Law* (London: Cassell and Co., 1968).

Alexander, Sally, 'Women's Work in Nineteenth Century London: A Study of the Years 1820–1850', in J. Mitchell and Ann Oakley (eds), *The Rights and Wrongs of Women* (London: Penguin, 1976).

Allen, Joan and Owen Ashton (eds), *Papers for the People: A Study of the Chartist Press* (London: Merlin Press, 2005).

Allen, V. C., *Trade Unions and the Government* (London: Longmans, 1960).

Anderson, Alan, 'The Political Symbolism of the Labour Laws', *Bulletin of the Society for the Study of Labour History* 23 (1971): 13–15.

Archer, John, *By a Flash and a Scare: Incendiarism, Animal Maiming, and Poaching in East Anglia, 1815–1860* (Oxford: Oxford University Press, 1990).

Ariouat, J. F., 'Rethinking Partisanship in the Conduct of the Chartist Trials, 1839–1848', *Albion* 29/4 (1998): 596–621.

Arthurs, Harry, 'Special Courts, Special Law: Legal Pluralism in Nineteenth Century England', in David Sugarman and G. R. Rubin (eds.), *Law, Economy, and Society, 1750–1914: Essays in the History of English Law* (London: Professional Books, Ltd., 1984).

Arthurs, Harry, *Without the Law: Administrative Justice and Legal Pluralism in Nineteenth Century England* (Toronto: University of Toronto Press, 1985).

Arthurs, Harry, 'Without the Law: Courts of Local and Special Jurisdiction in Nineteenth Century England', in Kiralfy, Slatter and Virgoe (eds), *Custom,*

Courts and Counsel: Selected Papers of the 6ᵗʰ British Legal History Conference, Norwich, 1983 (London: Frank Cass and Co., 1985).

Ashton, Owen and Robert Fyson and Stephen Roberts (eds), *The Chartist Legacy* (Merlin Press, 1999).

Ashton, T. S., *An Eighteenth Century Industrialist: Peter Stubs of Warrington, 1756–1806* (New York: Augustus M. Kelley, 1970).

Atiyah, Patrick, *The Rise and Fall of Freedom to Contract* (Oxford: Oxford University Press, 1979).

Barker, C. B., *The Pilkington Brothers and the Glass Industry* (London: George Allen and Unwin, 1960).

Barker, C. B., *Pilkington: The Rise of an International Company, 1826–1976* (London: Weidenfeld and Nicolson, 1977).

Barker, C. B. and J. R. Harris, *A Merseyside Town in the Industrial Revolution, St. Helens, 1750–1950* (London: Frank Cass and Co., 1953).

Barker, T. C., *The Glassmakers* (London: Weidenfeld and Nicolson, 1977).

Barnsby, George, *The Social Conditions in the Black Country, 1800–1900* (London: Integrated Publishing Services, 1987).

Bartrip, P. W. J. and S. B. Burman, *The Wounded Soldiers of Industry: Industrial Compensation Policy, 1833–1897* (Oxford: Clarendon Press, 1983).

Barton, L. L., 'Contract and *Quantum Meruit*: The Antecedents of Cutter v. Powell',' *The Journal of Legal History* 8/1 (May 1987): 48–63.

Batt, John, '"United to Support but Not Injure": Public Order, Trade Unions and the Repeal of the Combination Acts of 1799–1800', *International Review of Social History* 31 (1986): 187.

Beattie, John, *Crime and the Courts in England, 1660–1800* (Princeton: Princeton University Press, 1986).

Beattie, John, 'The Scales of Justice: Defense Counsel and the English Criminal Trial in the Eighteenth and Nineteenth Centuries', *Law and History Review* 9/2 (1991): 221–267.

Behagg, Clive, *Politics and Production in the Early Nineteenth Century* (London, 1990).

Belcham, John, *Industrialization and the Experience of the Working Class: The English Experience, 1750–1900* (New York: Routledge, 1990).

Belcham, John, 'Radical Language, Meaning and Identity in the Age of Chartists', *Journal of Victorian Culture* 10/1 (Spring 2005): 1–11.

Belcham, John and James Epstein, 'The Nineteenth Century Gentleman Leader Revisited', *Social History* 22/2 (1997): 174–93.

Bentley, David, *English Criminal Justice in the Nineteenth Century* (London: The Hambledon Press, 1998).

Benyon, Huw and Terry Austin, *Masters and Servants: Class Patronage in the Making of the Labour Organization: The Durham Miners and the English Political Tradition* (London: Rivers Oram Press, 1994).

Biagini, Eugeneo and Alastair Reid (eds), *Currents of Radicalism: Popular Radicalism, Organized Labour and Party Politics in Britain, 1850–1914* (Cambridge: Cambridge University Press, 1991).

Blackshield, A. R., 'The Legitimacy and Authority of Judges', *University of New South Wales Law Journal* 10 (1987): 164–7.

Boase, Frederick, *Modern English Biography Containing Many Thousand Concise Memoirs of Persons Who Have Died Between the Years 1851–1900. With an Index of the Most Interesting Matter* (London: F. Cass, 1965).

Brass, Tom and Marcel Van Der Linden (eds), *Free and Unfree Labour: The Debate Continues* (New York, 1997)

Bronstein, Jamie, *Caught in the Machinery: Workplace Accidents and Injured Workers in Nineteenth Century Britain* (Stanford: Stanford University Press, 2008).

Brown, Kenneth, 'Trade Unions and the Law', in Chris Wrigley (ed.), *History of British Industrial Relations, 1875–1914* (Amherst: University of Massachusetts Press, 1982).

Brown, R., *Chartism* (Cambridge: Cambridge University Press, 1998).

Burgess, Keith, *The Origins of British Industrial Relations: The Nineteenth Century Experience* (London: Croom Helm, 1975).

Cairns, David, *Advocacy and the Making of the Adversarial Trial, 1800–1865* (Oxford: Clarendon Press, 1998).

Campbell, Alan B., *The Lanarkshire Miners: A Social History of their Trade Unions, 1775–1974* (Edinburgh: J. Donald, 1979).

Challinor, Raymond, *Radical Lawyer in Victorian England: W. P. Roberts and the Struggle for Workers' Rights* (London: I. B. Taurus, 1990).

Challinor, Raymond and Brian Ripley, *The Miners' Association: A Trade Union in the Age of Chartists* (London: Lawrence and Wishart, 1968).

Chase, Malcolm, *Chartism: A New History* (Manchester: Manchester University Press, 2007).

Chase, Malcolm, *Early Trade Unionism: Fraternity, Skill and the Politics of Labour* (Ashgate, 2000).

Clark, Anna, *The Struggle for the Breeches: Gender and the Making of the English Working Class* (Berkeley: University of California Press, 1995).

Cockburn, J. S. and Thomas Green (eds), *Twelve Good Men and True: The Criminal Jury Trial in England, 1200–1800* (Princeton: Princeton University Press, 1988).

Cole, G. D. H., *A Short History of the British Working Class Movement, 1789–1947* (London: George Allen and Unwin, 1948).

Cole, G. D. H. and A. W. Filson (eds), *British Working Class Movements: Select Documents* (New York: Macmillan, 1965).

Coleman, D. C., 'Combinations of Capital and Labour in the Paper Industry, 1790–1825', *Economica* 21/1 (February 1954): 32–54.

Colls, Robert, *The Pitmen of the Northern Coalfield: Work, Culture, and Protest, 1790–1850* (Manchester: Manchester University Press, 1987).

Cornish, W. R. and G. de N. Clark, *Law and Society in England 1750–1950* (London: Sweet and Maxwell, 1989).

Craven, Paul, 'Canada 1670–1935: Symbolic and Instrumental Enforcement in Loyalist North America', in Douglas Hay and Paul Craven (eds), *Masters, Servants, and Magistrates in Britain and the Empire, 1562–1955* (Chapel Hill: University of North Carolina Press, 2004).

Craven, Paul, 'The Law of Master and Servant in Mid-Nineteenth Century Ontario', in David Flaherty (ed.), *Essays in the History of Canadian Law* (Toronto: University of Toronto Press, 1981).

Crosby, T. L., *Sir Robert Peel's Administration, 1841–1846* (London: David and Charles, 1976).

Crowley, F. K., 'Master and Servant in Southern Australia', *Historical Society of Southern Australia* (1982): 32–43.

Cunliffe, Marcus, *Chattel Slavery and Wage Slavery: The Anglo-American Context, 1830–1860* (Athens: University of Georgia Press, 1979).

Curthoys, Mark. *Governments, Labour and the Law in Mid-Victorian Britain: The Trade Union Legislation of the 1870s* (Oxford: Oxford University Press, 2004).

Daintree, Daniel, 'The Legal Periodical: A Study in the Communication of Information' (PhD dissertation, University of Sheffield, 1975).

Dane, E. Surrey, *Peter Stubs and the Lancashire Hand Tool Industry* (New York: John Sherratt and Son, Ltd., 1973).

Darbyshire, Penny, 'The Lamp That Shows that Freedom Lives – Is it Worth the Candle?' *Criminal Law Review* (1991): 740–752.

Deakin, Simon, 'The Contract of Employment, A Study in Legal Evolution', *Historical Studies in Industrial Relations* 11 (Spring 2001): 1–36.

Deakin, Simon, 'Contract, Labour Law and the Developing Employment Relationship' (PhD dissertation, Cambridge University, 1989).

Derry, T. K., 'The Repeal of the Apprenticeship Clauses of the Statute of Apprentices', *The Economic History Review* 3 (1931–2): 67.

Dobson, C. R., *Masters and Journeymen: A Prehistory of Industrial Relations, 1717–1800* (London: Croom Helm, 1980).

Dockray, Martin, 'Cutter v. Powell: A Trip Outside the Text', *The Law Quarterly Review* 117 (October 2001): 664–82.

Drescher, Seymour, *Capitalism and Anti-Slavery: British Mobilization in Comparative Perspective* (Oxford: Oxford University Press, 1986).

Dunman, D., *The English and Colonial Bar in the Nineteenth Century* (London: Croom Helm, 1983).

Edwards, N., *The History of the South Wales Miners* (Liverpool: C. Tirling and Co., 1926).

Engels, Friedrich, *The Condition of the Working Class in England* (London, 1845).

Epstein, James, 'The Constitutional Idiom: Radical Reasoning, Rhetoric and Action in Early-Nineteenth Century England', *Journal of Social History* 23/3 (1990): 553–74.

Epstein, James, 'Feargus O' Connor and the Northern Star', *International Review of Social History* 21 (1976): 97.

Epstein, James, *In Practice: Studies in the Language and Culture of Popular Politics in Modern Britain* (Stanford: Stanford University Press, 2003).

Epstein, James, *The Lion of Freedom: Feargus O'Connor and the Chartist Movement, 1832–1842* (London: Croom Helm, 1982).

Epstein, James, 'The Populist Turn', *Journal of British Studies* 32/2 (1993): 177–89.

Epstein, James, 'Re-Thinking the Categories of Class', *Labour/ Le Travail* 18 (1986): 195–208.

Epstein, James, 'Some Organizational and Cultural Aspects of the Chartist Movement in Nottingham', in Dorothy Thompson and James Epstein (eds.), *The Chartist Experience: Studies in Working Class Radicalism and Culture, 1830–1860* (London: Macmillan, 1982).

Epstein, James, 'Understanding the Cap of Liberty: Symbolic Practice and Social Conflict in Early Nineteenth Century England', *Past and Present* 122 (1989): 75–118.

Epstein, James and Dorothy Thompson (eds), *The Chartist Experience: Studies in Working Class Radicalism and Culture, 1830–1860* (London: Macmillan, 1982).

Evans, E. W., *The Miners of South Wales* (Cardiff: University of Wales Press, 1961).

Evans, Jim, 'Change in the Doctrine of Precedent During the Nineteenth Century', in Lawrence Goldstein (ed.), *Precedent in Law* (Oxford: Oxford University Press, 1987).

Ewing, K. D., 'The State and Industrial Relations: "Collective Laissez Faire" Revisited', *Historical Studies in Industrial Relations* 5 (1998): 1–31.

Fairfield, Charles, *George William Wilshere Baron Bramwell of Hever and his Opinions* (London: Macmillan, 1898).

Fellague Ariouat, Jacqueline, 'Rethinking Partisanship in the Conduct of Chartist Trials, 1839–1848', *Albion* 29/4 (Winter 1998): 596–621.

Foster, David, 'Class and County Government in Early Nineteenth Century Lancashire', *Northern History* 9 (1974): 48–61.

Foster, David, 'The Social and Political Composition of the Lancashire Magistracy, 1821–1851' (PhD dissertation, University of Lancaster, 1972).

Foster, John, *Class Struggle and the Industrial Revolution: Early Industrial Capitalism in Three English Towns* (London: Weidenfeld and Nicolson, 1975).

Frank, Christopher, 'Britain: Defeat of the 1844 Master and Servant Bill', in Douglas Hay and Paul Craven (eds), *Masters, Servants, and Magistrates in*

Britain and the Empire, 1562–1955 (Chapel Hill: University of North Carolina Press, 2004).

Frank, Christopher, '"He might almost as well be without trial": Trade Unions and the 1823 Master and Servant Act – The Warrington Cases, 1846–1847', *Historical Studies in Industrial Relations* 14 (2002): 3–44.

Frank, Christopher, '"Let but one of them come before me and I'll commit him: Trade Unions, Magistrates and the Law in Mid-Nineteenth Century Staffordshire', *Journal of British Studies* 44/1 (2005): 64–91.

Fraser, W. Hamish, *A History of British Trade Unionism, 1700–1998* (Hampshire: Macmillan Press, 1999).

Fraser, W. Hamish, *Trade Unions and Society: The Struggle for Acceptance, 1800–1850* (London: George Allen and Unwin, 1974).

Freestone, David and J. C. Richardson, 'The Making of the English Criminal Law: Sir John Jervis and His Acts', *The Criminal Law Review* (1980): 5–16.

Furness, Joseph M., *Municipal Affairs in Sheffield* (Sheffield: William Townsend and Son, 1893).

Fynes, Richard, *The Miners of Northumberland and Durham: A History of their Social and Political Progress* (Wakefield: S. R. Publishers, 1873).

Fyson, Richard, 'The Crisis of 1842: Chartism, The Colliers' Strike, and the Outbreak in the Potteries', in Dorothy Thompson and James Epstein (eds), *The Chartist Experience: Studies in Working Class Radicalism and Culture, 1830–1860* (London: Macmillan, 1982).

Gash, Norman, *Sir Robert Peel: The Life of Sir Robert Peel After 1830* (New York: Longman, 1972).

George, Dorothy, 'The Combination Laws', *Economic History Review* 6/2 (April 1936): 172–8.

Godfrey, Barry, 'Judicial Impartiality and the Use of the Criminal Law Against Labour: The Sentencing of Workplace Appropriators in Northern England, 1840–1880', *Crime, History, and Societies* 3/2 (1999): 57–72.

Gray, Robert, *The Factory Question and Industrial England, 1830–1860* (Cambridge: Cambridge University Press, 1996).

Gray, Robert, 'Factory Legislation and the Gendering of Jobs in the North of England, 1830–1860', *Gender and History* 5 (1993).

Gray, Robert, 'Languages of Factory Reform in Britain, c.1830–1860', in Patrick Joyce, (ed.), *The Historical Meanings of Work* (London: Cambridge University Press, 1987).

Gritt, J. A., 'The Survival of "Service" in the English Agricultural Labour Force: Lessons from Lancashire, c.1650–1851', *Agricultural History Review* 25 (2002).

Haines, Brian, 'English Labour Law and the Separation from Contract', *The Journal of Labour History* 1/3 (December 1980): 277–81.

Hall, R. G., *Voices of the People: Democracy and Chartist Political Identity, 1830–1870* (London: Merlin Press, 2007).

Hammond, J. L. and Barbara Hammond, *The Skilled Labourer* (London: Longmans, Green & Company, 1919).

Harding, Alan, 'The Revolt Against the Justices', in R. H. Hinton and T. H. Ashton (eds), *The English Rising of 1381* (Cambridge: Cambridge University Press, 1984).

Harrison, Royden, *Before the Socialists: Studies in Labour and Politics, 1861–1881* (London: Routledge and Kegan Paul, 1965).

Harrison, Royden (ed.), *The Independent Collier: The Coal Miner as Archetypical Proletarian Reconsidered* (New York: St. Martin's Press, 1979).

Hay, Douglas, 'Dread of the Crown Office: The Magistracy and the King's Bench, 1740–1800', in N. Landau (ed.), *Law, Crime, and English Society, 1660–1830* (Cambridge: Cambridge University Press, 2002).

Hay, Douglas, 'England 1562–1875: The Law and its Uses', in Douglas Hay and Paul Craven (eds), *Masters, Servants, and Magistrates in Britain and the Empire, 1562–1955* (Chapel Hill: University of North Carolina Press, 2004).

Hay, Douglas, 'Judges and Magistrates: High Law and Low Law in England and Empire', in David Lemmings (ed.), *The British and their Laws in the Eighteenth Century* (London: Boydell Press, 2005).

Hay, Douglas, 'Master and Servant in England: Using the Law in the Eighteenth and Nineteenth Centuries', in Willibald Steinmetz (ed.), *Private Law and Social Inequality in the Industrial Age: Comparing the Legal Cultures of Britain, France, Germany, and the United States* (London: Oxford University Press, 2000).

Hay, Douglas, 'Patronage, Paternalism, and Welfare: Masters, Workers and Magistrates in Eighteenth Century England', *International Labour and Working Class History* 53 (Spring 1998): 36–9.

Hay, Douglas, 'Property, Authority, and the Criminal Law', in Douglas Hay, John Rule, Peter Linebaugh, Edward Thompson and Cal Winslow (eds), *Albion's Fatal Tree: Crime and Society in Eighteenth-Century England* (New York: Pantheon Books, 1976).

Hay, Douglas and Paul Craven, 'The Criminalization of Free Labour: Master and Servant In Comparative Perspective', in Nicholas Rogers and Paul Lovejoy (eds), *Slavery and Abolition* 15/2 (August 1994): 71–101.

Hay, Douglas and Paul Craven (eds), *Masters, Servants, and Magistrates in Britain and the Empire, 1562–1955* (Chapel Hill: University of North Carolina Press, 2004).

Hay, Douglas and Paul Craven, 'Master and Servant In England and Empire: A Comparative Study', *Labour/ Le Travail* 31 (Spring 1993): 175–84.

Hay, Douglas and Nicholas Rogers, *Shuttles and Swords: Eighteenth Century Society* (Oxford: Oxford University Press, 1997).

Hay, Douglas and F. Snyder (eds), *Policing and Prosecution in Britain, 1750–1850* (London: Clarendon Press, 1989).

Haynes, Michael, 'Employers and Trade Unions, 1824–1850', in John Rule (ed.), *British Trade Unionism, 1750–1850: The Formative Years* (London: Longman, 1988).

Hedges, R. Y. and Allen Winterbottom, *The Legal History of Trade Unionism* (London: Longmans Green and Co., 1930).

Heesom, A. J., 'The Northern Coal Owners and the Opposition to the Coal Mines Act of 1842', *International Review of Social History* 25 (1980): 270.

Highfield, William, 'Great Tin-Plate Workers' Strike', *The Blackcountryman* 5 (April 1972): 49–57.

Hinton, George W., *The Truck System: Including a History of the British Truck Acts, 1465–1960* (Cambridge: W. Heffer & Sons, 1960).

Holdsworth, W. S., *A History of English Law* (17 vols., London: Sweet and Maxwell, 1903–1972).

Hoppen, K. T., *The Mid-Victorian Generation, 1846–1886* (Oxford: Oxford University Press, 1998).

Huberman, Michael, *Escape From the Market: Negotiating Work in Lancashire* (Cambridge: Cambridge University Press, 1996).

Innes, Joana, 'Statute Law and Summary Justice in Early Modern England', *Bulletin of the Society for the Study of Labour History* 52/1 (1987): 34–5.

Jaffe, James, 'Competition and the Size of Firms in the North-East Coal Trade, 1800–1850', *Northern History* 25 (1989): 235–55.

Jaffe, James, 'Industrial Arbitration, Equity, and Authority in England, 1800–1850', *Law and History Review* 18/3 (Fall 2000): 543–9.

Jaffe, James, 'The State, Capital, and Workers' Control During the Industrial Revolution: The Rise and Fall of the North-East Pitmen's Union 1831–1832', *The Journal of Social History* 21, No. 4 (1988): 722.

Jaffe, James, *Striking a Bargain: Work and Industrial Relations in England 1815–1865* (Manchester: Manchester University Press, 2000).

Johnson, David, 'Trial By Jury in Ireland, 1860–1914', *Legal History* 17/3 (1996): 270–293.

Jones, A., 'Workingmen's Advocates: Ideology and Class in a Mid-Victorian Labour Newspaper System', in Shattock and M. Wolff (eds), *The Victorian Periodical Press: Samplings and Surroundings* (Leicester, 1982).

Jones, David, 'Thomas Campbell Foster and the Rural Labourer: Incendiarism in East Anglia in the 1840s', *Social History* 1 (1976): 5–43.

Joyce, Patrick (ed.), *The Historical Meanings of Work* (Cambridge: Cambridge University Press, 1987).

Joyce, Patrick, *Visions of the People: Industrial England and the Question of Class, 1840–1914* (Cambridge: Cambridge University Press, 1991).

Kahn-Freund, Otto, 'Blackstone's Neglected Child: The Contract of Employment', *The Law Quarterly Review* 93 (October 1977): 508–28.

Kahn-Freund, Otto, *Selected Writings* (London: Stevens and Sons, 1978).

Karsten, Peter, '"Bottomed Out on Justice": A Reappraisal of Critical Legal Studies Scholarship Concerning Breaches of Labour Contracts By Quitting or Firing in Britain and the U. S., 1660–1880', *American Journal of Legal History* (1990): 213–61.

King, Peter, *Crime, Justice and Discretion in England, 1740–1820* (Oxford: Oxford University Press, 2000).

King, Peter, *Crime and Law in England, 1750–1840: Remaking Justice from the Margins* (Cambridge: Cambridge University Press, 2006).

King, Peter, 'Decision Makers and Decision Making in the English Criminal Law, 1750–1800', *Historical Journal* 27 (1984): 25–8.

King, Peter, 'The Rise of Juvenile Delinquency in England, 1780–1840: Changing Patterns of Perception and Prosecution', *Past and Present* 160 (1998): 116–66.

King, Peter, 'Summary Courts and Social Relations in Eighteenth Century England', *Past and Present* 183 (May 2004): 125–72.

Kingsford, P. W., 'Radical Dandy: Thomas Slingsby Duncombe 1796–1861', *History Today* 14/6 (1964): 399–407.

Kirk, Neville, *Change, Continuity and Class: Labour in British Society, 1850–1920* (Manchester: Manchester University Press, 1998).

Klarmen, M. J. 'The Judges versus the Unions: The Development of British Labor Law, 1867–1913', *Virginia Law Review* 75/8 (1989).

Knipe, John, 'The Justice of the Peace in Yorkshire, 1820–1914: A Social Study' (PhD dissertation, University of Southern California, 1970).

Kostal, R. W., *The Law and English Railway Capitalism, 1825–1875* (Oxford: Clarendon Press, 1994).

Kostal, R. W., 'Legal Justice, Social Justice: An Incursion into the Social History of Work-Related Accident Law in Ontario, 1860–86', *Law and History Review* 6/1 (Spring 1988): 1–24.

Kussmaul, Ann, *Servants in Husbandry in Early Modern England* (Cambridge: Cambridge University Press, 1981).

Landau, Norma, *The Justices of the Peace, 1679–1760* (Berkeley: Univesity of California Press, 1984).

Landau, Norma, 'The Trading Justices' Trade', in N. Landau (ed.), *Law, Crime, and English Society, 1660–1830* (Cambridge: Cambridge University Press, 2002).

Lane, Joan, *Apprenticeship in England, 1600–1914* (Boulder: Westview Press, 1996).

Langbein, John, 'The Prosecutorial Origins of Defense Counsel in the Eighteenth Century: The Appearance of Solicitors', *Cambridge Law Journal* 58/2 (1999): 314–465.

Laybourne, Keith, *A History of British Trade Unionism* (London: Sutton Publishers, 1997).

Leader, John Daniel, *Sheffield General Infirmary* (Sheffield: The Infirmary Board, 1897).

Leader, R. E., *History of the Company of Cutlers in Hallamshire* (Sheffield: Pawson and Brailsford, 1905).

Linder, Marc, *The Employment Relationship in Anglo-American Law: A Historical Perspective* (New York: Greenwood Press, 1989).

Linebaugh, Peter, 'The Tyburn Riot Against the Surgeons', in Hay, Thompson, Linebaugh, Rule and Winslow (eds), *Albion's Fatal Tree: Crime and Society in Eighteenth Century England* (London: Pantheon Books, 1975).

Lloyd, Godfrey Isaac Howard, *The Cutlery Trades: A Historical Essay in the Economics of Small Scale Production* (London: Longmans, Green and Co., 1913).

Lobban, M., 'Strikers and the Law, 1825–51', in P. Birks (ed.), *The Life of the Law: Proceedings of the Tenth British Legal History Conference Oxford* (London: Continum International Publishing Group, 1993).

Lubenow, W. C., 'Social Recruitment and Social Attitudes: The Buckinghamshire Magistrates, 1868–1888', *The Huntington Library Quarterly* 40/3 (1977): 247–68.

Machin, Frank, *The Yorkshire Miners: A History* (Huddersfield: The National Union of Mineworkers, 1958).

MacRaid, Donald M. and David Martin, *Labour in British Society, 1830–1914* (London: Macmillan, 2000).

Manchester, A. H., *A Modern Legal History of England and Wales, 1750–1950* (London: Butterworths, 1980).

Martin, Ross, *TUC: The Growth of a Pressure Group* (Oxford: Clarendon Press, 1980).

Mather, F. C., 'The General Strike of 1842: A Study in the Leadership, Organization and the Threat of Revolution During the Plug Plot Disturbances', in R. Quinault and J. Stevenson (eds), *Popular Protest and Public Order: Six Studies in British History, 1790–1920* (New York: St. Martin's Press, 1974).

Mather, F. C., 'The Government and the Chartists', in Asa Briggs (ed.), *Chartist Studies* (London: Macmillan, 1959).

Mather, F. C., *Public Order in the Age of Chartists* (Manchester: Manchester University Press, 1959).

May, Allyson, *The Bar and the Old Bailey, 1750–1850* (Chapel Hill: University of North Carolina Press, 2003).

May, Allyson, 'Reluctant Advocates: The Legal Profession and the Prisoners' Counsel Act of 1836', in Allison May, Greg Smith and Simon Deavereaux (eds), *Criminal Justice in the Old and New World: Essays in Honour of J. M. Beattie* (Toronto: University of Toronto Press, 1998).

McCready, H. W., 'British Labour Lobby, 1867–1875', *Canadian Journal of Economics and Political Science* 22/2 (May 1956): 160.

McIlroy, J., 'Financial Malpractice in British Trade Unions, 1800–1930: The Background to, and Consquences of, Hornby v. Close', *Historical Studies in Industrial Relations* 6 (Autumn 1998): 1–64.

McKendrick, Neil, 'Josiah Wedgwood and Factory Discipline', *The Historical Journal* 3/1 (1960): 32–50.

McQueen, Robert, 'Master and Servants Legislation in the Nineteenth Century Australian Colonies', *Law and History in Australia* 4 (1987): 78–110.

McQueen, Robert, 'Master and Servant Legislation and Social Control: Rule of Law in Labour Relations on the Darling Downs, 1860–1870', *Law in Context* 10 (1992): 123–9.

McWilliam, Rohan, *Popular Politics in Nineteenth Century England* (New York: Routledge, 1998).

Moher, J., 'From Suppression to Containment: The Roots of Trade Union Law to 1825', in John Rule (ed.), *British Trade Unionism, 1750–1850: The Formative Years* (London: Longmans, 1988).

Moir, Esther, *The Justice of the Peace* (London: Penguin Books, 1969).

Morgan, Carol, *Women Workers and Gender Indentities, 1835–1913: The Cotton and Metal Industries in England* (London: Routledge, 2001).

Morris, J. H. and L. J. Williams, *The South Wales Coal Industry, 1841–1875* (Cardiff: University of Wales Press, 1958).

Morton, A. L. and George Tate, *The British Labour Movement, 1770–1920: A Political History* (New York: International Publishers, 1957).

Munn, Christopher, '"Scratching With a Rattan": William Caine and the Hong Kong Magistracy, 1841–44', *Labour History* 30 (1989): 193–227.

Musson, A. E., *British Trade Unionism, 1800–1875* (London: Macmillan, 1972).

Napier, Brian, 'The Contract of Service: The Concept and Its Application' (D.Phil thesis, Cambridge University, 1975).

Nossiter, T. J., *Influence, Opinion, and Political Idioms in Reformed England: Case Studies From the Northeast, 1832–1874* (London: Harvester Press, 1975).

Orth, John, *Combination and Conspiracy: A Legal History of Trade Unionism, 1721–1906* (Oxford: Clarendon Press, 1991).

Orth, John, 'Contract and the Common Law', in N. Scheiber (ed.), *State and the Freedom to Contract* (Stanford: Stanford University Press, 1998).

Orth, John, 'English Law and Striking Workmen: The Molestation of Workmen Act, 1859', *The Journal of Legal History* 2 (1981): 238–57.

Orth, John, 'The Law of Strikes 1847–1871', in Guy and Beale (eds), *Law and Social Change in British History: Papers Presented to the Bristol Legal History Conference (14–17 July 1981)* (London: Royal Historical Society, 1984).

Osborne, Bertram, *The Justice of the Peace, 1361–1848: A History of the Justices of the Peace for the Counties of England* (Dorset: Seghill Press, 1960).

Palmer, Robert, *English Law in the Age of the Black Death, 1348–1381* (Chapel Hill: University of North Carolina Press, 1993).

Palmer, Stanley, *Police and Protest in England and Ireland, 1780–1850* (Cambridge: Cambridge University Press, 1988).

Pelling, Henry, *A History of British Trade Unionism* (London: Macmillan, 1963).

Pelling, Henry, *Popular Politics in Late Victorian Britain* (London: Macmillan, 1968).

Philips, David, 'The Black Country Magistracy, 1835–1860: A Changing Elite and the Exercise of its Power', *Midlands History* 3 (1976): 161–90.

Philips, David, *Crime and Authority in Victorian England: The Black Country, 1835–1860* (London: Croom Helm, 1978).

Pickering, Paul, *Chartism and Chartists in Manchester and Salford* (Basingstoke: Macmillan, 1995).

Pickering, Paul, 'Class Without Words: Symbolic Communication in the Chartist Movement', *Past and Present* 112 (1987): 144–62.

Pickering, Paul, '"And Your Petitioners & c.": Chartist Petitioning in Popular Politics 1838–1848', *English Historical Review* 116/466 (2001): 368–88.

Pollard, Sidney, 'The Ethics of the Sheffield Outrages', *Transactions of the Hunter Archaeological Society* 7 (1957).

Pollard, Sidney, *A History of Labour in Sheffield* (Liverpool: Liverpool University Press, 1959).

Pollard, Sidney, J. Mendelson, W. Owen and V. M. Thornes, *The Sheffield Trades and Labour Council, 1858–1958* (Sheffield: Sheffield Trades and Labour Council, 1958).

Porter, J. H., 'Wage Bargaining Under Conciliation Agreements, 1860–1914', *Economic History Review* 23 (1970): 460–474.

Price, Richard, *British Society 1680–1880: Dynamism, Containment and Change* (Cambridge: Cambridge University Press, 1999).

Price, Richard, *Labour in British Society: An Interpretive History* (London: Croom Helm, 1986).

Price, Richard, *Masters, Unions, and Men: Work Control in Building and the Rise of Labour 1830–1914* (Cambridge: Cambridge University Press, 1980).

Pritt, D. N. and Richard Freeman, *The Law Versus the Trade Unions* (London: Lawrence and Wishart, 1958).

Prothero, Iorowerth, *Artisans and Politics in Early Nineteenth Century London: John Gast and His Times* (Kent: William Dawson and Son, 1979).

Pue, Wes, 'The Criminal Twilight Zone: Pre-Trial Procedure in the 1840s', *The Alberta Law Review* 21/2 (1983): 335–63.

Putnam, B. W., *The Enforcement of the Statute of Labourers During the First Decade After the Black Death, 1349–1359* (London: Macmillan, 1908).

Rendall, Jane, *Women in Industrializing Society: England, 1750–1880* (Oxford: Oxford University Press, 1990).

Rose, Sonja, *Limited Livelihoods: Gender and Class in Nineteenth Century England* (Los Angeles: University of California Press, 1992).

Rowley, Arthur S., 'Professions, Class, and Society: Solicitors in Nineteenth Century Birmingham', (PhD dissertation, University of Aston in Birmingham, 1988).

Rule, John, 'Employment and Authority, Masters and Men in 18th Century Manufacture', in Paul Griffiths, Adam Fox and Steve Hindle (eds), *The Experience of Authority in Early Modern England* (New York: St. Martins, 1996).

Rule, John, 'The Formative Years of British Trade Unionism', in John Rule
    (ed.), *British Trade Unionism, 1750–1850: The Formative Years* (London:
    Longmans, 1988).
Rule, John, *The Labouring Classes in Early Industrial England, 1750–1850*
    (London: Longman, 1986).
Salt, John, 'Isaac Ironside, 1808–1870: The Motivation of a Radical Educationalist',
    The British Journal of Education Studies 19/2 (June 1971): 183–201.
Saunders, Robert, 'Chartism from Above: British Elites and the Interpretation of
    Chartism', *Historical Research* 81/213 (2008): 463–84.
Saville, John, *The Consolidation of the Capitalist State* (London: Pluto Press,
    1994).
Sayer, K., 'Field-Faring Women: The Resistance of Women Who Worked in the
    Fields of Nineteenth Century England', *Women's History Review* 2/2 (1993):
    185–98.
Schwarzkopf, Judith, *Women and the Chartist Movement* (New York: St. Martins
    Press, 1991).
Shoemaker, Robert, *Gender in English Society, 1650–1850: The Emergence of
    Separate Spheres?* (London: Longman, 1998).
Shoemaker, Robert, *Prosecution and Punishment: Petty Crime and the Law in
    London and Rural Middlesex, c.1660–1725* (Cambridge: Cambridge University
    Press, 1991).
Simon, Daphne 'Master and Servant', in J. Saville (ed.), *Democracy and the
    Labour Movement: Essays in Honour of Donna Torr* (London: Lawrence and
    Wishart, 1954).
Simpson, A. B. W., *Leading Cases in the Common Law* (Oxford: Oxford University
    Press, 1995).
Skyrme, Sir Thomas, *History of the Justice of the Peace* (3 vols., Chichester:
    Barry Rose, 1991).
Smith, Bruce P., 'Circumventing the Jury: Petty Crime and Summary Justice in
    London and New York City, 1790–1855' (PhD dissertation, Yale University,
    1996).
Smith, Bruce P., 'The Presumption of Guilt and the English Law of Theft, 1750–
    1850', *Law and History Review* 23/1 (Spring 2005): 133–71.
Smith, Dennis, *Conflict and Compromise: Class Formation in English Society,
    1830–1914: A Comparative Study of Birmingham and Sheffield* (London:
    Routledge and Kegan, 1982).
Smith Porter, W., *The Medical School in Sheffield, 1828–1928* (Sheffield: J. W.
    Northend, Ltd., 1928).
Snell, K. D. M. *Annals of the Labouring Poor: Social Change and Agrarian
    England*, 1600–1860 (Cambridge: Cambridge University Press, 1985).
Soderlund, Richard, '"Intended as a Terror to the Idle and Profligate": Embezzlement
    and the Origins of Policing in the Yorkshire Worsted Industry, c.1750–1777',
    Journal of Social History 31/3 (1998): 647–70.

Spring, David, 'The Earls of Durham and the Great Northern Coal Field, 1830–1880', *Canadian Historical Review* 33/3 (1952).

Spring, David, 'The English Landed Estate in the Age of Coal and Iron, 1830–1880', *The Journal of Economic History* 11 (1951): 3–24.

Stainton, J. H., *The Making of Sheffield, 1865–1914* (Sheffield: E. Weston and Sons, 1924).

Stedman Jones, Gareth, *The Languages of Class: Studies in Working Class History, 1832–1982* (London: Cambridge University Press, 1983).

Steinberg, Marc, 'Capitalist Development, Labour Process and the Law', *American Journal of Sociology* 109/2 (2003): 445–95.

Steinberg, Marc, 'Unfree Labour, Apprenticeship and the Rise of the Victorian Hull Fishing Industry: An Example of the Importance of the Law and the Local State in British Economic Exchange', *International Review of Social History* 51/2 (2006): 243–76.

Steinfeld, Robert, *Coercion, Contract and Free Labour in the Nineteenth Century* (Cambridge: Cambridge University Press, 2001).

Steinfeld, Robert, *The Invention of Free Labour: The Employment Relationship in English and American Law and Culture, 1350–1870* (Chapel Hill: University of North Carolina Press, 1991).

Steinmetz, Willibald, 'Was There a De-Juridification of Employment Relations in Britain?', in Willibald Steinmetz (ed.), *Private Law and Social Inequality in the Industrial Age: Comparing the Legal Cultures of in Britain, France, Germany, and the United States* (London: Oxford University Press, 2000).

Stewart, M. and L. Hunter, *The Needle is Threaded* (London, 1964).

Sweeney, Thomas, 'The Extension and Practice of Summary Jurisdiction in England, c.1790–1860', (PhD dissertation, Cambridge University, 1985).

Swift, Roger, 'The English Urban Magistracy and the Administration of Justice During the Early Nineteenth Century: Wolverhampton, 1815–1860', *Midlands History* 17 (1992): 75–92.

Taylor, A. J. 'Combination in the Mid-Nineteenth Century Coal Industry', *Transactions of the Royal Historical Society, Fifth Series* 3 (1953): 23–39.

Taylor, A. J., 'Entrepreneurial Paternalism: The Third Marquis of Londonderry and the Coal Trade', *Durham University Journal* 33 (1973–4).

Taylor, A. J., 'The National Miners' Association of Great Britain and Ireland, 1842–1848: A Study in the Problem of Integration', *Economica* 22/85 (1955): 52.

Taylor, A. J., 'The Third Marquis of Londonderry and the Northeastern Coal Trade', *Durham University Journal* 48/1 (December 1955): 21.

Taylor, M., *The Decline of British Radicalism, 1847–1860* (Oxford: Clarendon Press, 1995).

Tholfsen, Trygrave, *Working Class Radicalism in Mid Victorian England* (London: Croom Helm, 1976).

Thomas, John, *The Rise of the Staffordshire Potteries* (New York: Augustus M. Kelley, 1971).

Thompson, Dorothy, *The Chartists: Popular Politics and the Industrial Revolution* (New York: Verso, 1993).

Thompson, Dorothy (ed.), *The Early Chartists* (Columbia, South Carolina: University of South Carolina Press, 1971).

Thompson, Dorothy, *Outsiders: Class, Gender and Nation* (London: Verso, 1993).

Thompson, Dorothy, 'Women and Nineteenth Century Radical Politics', in J. Mitchell and A. Oakley (eds), *The Rights and Wrongs of Women* (London: Penguin, 1976).

Thompson, Edward P., *The Making of the English Working Class* (London: Penguin, 1963).

Tomlins, Christopher, 'The Ties that Bind: Master and Servant in Massachusetts, 1800–1850', *Labor History* 30 (1989): 193–227.

Torrens, McCullaugh Torrens, *The Life and Times of the Rt. Hon Sir James Graham, Bart., G. C. B., M. P.* (2 vols, London: Saunders, Otley, and Co, 1958).

Trainor, Richard, *Black Country Elites: The Exercise of Authority in an Industrialized Area, 1830–1900* (Oxford: Clarendon Press, 1993).

Turner, J. W., 'Newcastle Miners and the Master and Servant Act, 1830–1862', *Labour History* 30 (1969).

Walton, John, *Chartism* (London: Routledge, 1999).

Walton, John, *Lancashire: A Social History, 1558–1939* (Manchester: Manchester University Press, 1987).

Warburton, William H., *The History of Trade Union Organization in the North Staffordshire Potteries* (London: George Allen and Unwin, Ltd., 1931).

Ward, J. T., *Sir James Graham* (London: Macmillan, 1967).

Webb, Sidney, *The Story of the Durham Miners (1622–1910)* (London: Fabian Press, 1921).

Webb, Sidney and Beatrice Webb, *The History of Trade Unionism* (London: Longmans, Green, and Co., 1902).

Wedderburn, K. W., *Labour, Law and Freedom: Further Essays in Labour Law* (London: Lawrence and Wishart, 1994).

Wedgwood, Josiah, *The Staffordshire Pottery and Its History* (London: Sampson, Low, Marston & Co., 1913).

Weiner, Martin, *Reconstructing the Criminal: Culture, Law, and Policy in England, 1830–1914* (Cambridge: Cambridge University Press, 1990).

Welbourne, Edward, *The Miners' Unions of Northumberland and Durham* (Cambridge: Cambridge University Press, 1923).

Williams, D., *John Frost: A Study in Chartism* (New York: Augustus M. Kelley, 1969).

Williams, J. E., *The Derbyshire Miners, A Study in Industrial and Social History* (London: George Allen and Unwin, 1962).

Woods, D. C., 'The Borough Magistracy and the Authority Structure of Black Country Towns, 1860–1900', *West Midlands Studies* 12 (1979).

Woods, D. C., 'The Operation of the Master and Servants Act in the Black Country, 1858–1875', *Midlands History* 7 (1982): 93–115.

Woodward, D., 'The Background to the Statute of Artificers: The Genesis of Labour Policy 1558–63', *Economic History Review* 33, Second Series (1980): 32–44.

Yelland, Cris, 'Speech and Writing in the *Northern Star*', *Labour History Review* 65/1 (2000): 22–40. .

Zangrel, Carl, 'The Social Composition of the County Magistracy in England and Wales' *The Journal of British Studies* 11 (1971): 113–25.

Index